I0100319

MASONIC ORTHODOXY
J.-M. Ragon

MASONIC ORTHODOXY
followed by
Occult Masonry
and
Hermetic Initiation

by

Jean-Marie Ragon

Author of the Interpretive Course on Initiations
Ancient & Modern, etc.

Let us uncover all that is false, to
reveal what is true.

(1853)

Translated and Introduced

by

Sâr Phosphoros

TriadPress
Fox Lake, IL

Masonic Orthodoxy: Followed by Occult Masonry and Hermetic Initiation
by Jean-Marie Ragon
Translated and introduced by Sâr Phosphoros

Published 2023

ISBN: 978-1-946814-05-0

Triad Press, LLC
123 S. US Highway 12 #33
Fox Lake, IL 60020

Translator's Introduction

Every serious student of Masonic history knows of this classic work; few have actually read it. For whatever reason, this classic tome has remained unavailable to the English-speaking world - except in its original French - since its initial publication in 1853. This has made its accessibility extremely limited. We are therefore very pleased that all English-speaking Masonic enthusiasts may now read and evaluate this work for themselves. This work, like those of Thory decades earlier, is not a perfect work. There are a number of technical and historical errors of which I am aware, and surely a number of which I am not. But that does not mean that the work is without immense value. To paraphrase A.E. Waite, when writing of Thory in his *New Encyclopedia of Freemasonry*, we may criticize it, but we may not dispense with it.

So, having just declared this work indispensable, let us proceed with a few criticisms. The intention is certainly not to dissuade the reader from this important work, but rather to point out a few areas where the reader should exercise caution.
Let us first address his peculiar notions on the word Freemasonry and the French equivalents. In English, the only real distinction made between designating the modern order of speculative Freemasonry from the older operative masons, is in the use of capitalization. Thus, a freemason may refer to a member of an operative guild, whereas a Freemason is a member of the order of Free and Accepted Masons. In French, however, the operative freemasons are referred to as maçons-libres; literally, "free masons." When speculative Freemasonry was imported into France from England, a new word was used to describe it: Franc-maçonnerie or franc-maçonnerie (the capitalization is irrelevant here).

Now, the above-mentioned fact would not even be worth pointing out if not for Ragon's utter disdain for the operative masons. He seems to find particularly appalling the notion of the philosophical fraternity of Freemasons being known under the same name as the operative guilds, claiming, in essence, that they have absolutely nothing in common. He therefore sees the question of ancient minutes, lost or otherwise, to be an entirely moot topic. He criticizes the English – and the Americans too for that matter - of confusing "francmaçonnerie" with the "maçons-libres." Though, no such distinction has ever existed until the French felt it necessary to invent a new term; a term entirely unneeded, except to placate the noble sensibilities of the French mindset.

Ragon, indeed, is disdainful of a great many things in the Masonic world; none so much as high grade Masonry. Within the maze of rites and systems known collectively as "écossisme" (from "écossais" meaning Scottish), Ragon sees everywhere the hand of the Jesuits who, he is sure, have inserted Templarism into Freemasonry as a way to subvert the aims of the Masonic Order, and bend them towards the will of the Catholic Church. In his obsession to find a Jesuit origin to the high grades, he does not seem to realize how improbable it is that a Catholic institution would seek to utilize Freemasonry to further its aims - and Templar Masonry at that! This fanatical obsession - which has been largely discredited - makes it impossible to determine what, if any, influence the Jesuits may have ever had on the institution. This sort of conspiratorial fanaticism always does a great disservice to seeking the truth; for once the slightest grain of evidence is discovered, the mind of the conspiracist tends to see it everywhere, thereby discrediting even what little evidence there may have originally been.

If Ragon's anti-Catholic sentiment is blatantly overt, there is perhaps also the sense of a passive anti-semitism perceived in his extreme dislike for biblical narratives within Freemasonry, preferring the Egyptian motifs and the traditional Indo-Iranian religions of the Vedas and Zoroaster. He seems to only barely tolerate the Biblical facade of the Blue Lodge degrees. He is repeatedly very insistent that "true Masonry" has nothing to do with Biblical subjects. Now, one could perhaps argue that the essence of Freemasonry transcends the Biblical motifs - which it does; and that modifications or rectifications may be made to present these essential qualities outside any Biblical narrative; but to insist that Masonry has nothing to do with Biblical topics seems frankly unbelievable. But he seems not to have been alone in this sentiment, seeing what his beloved Grand Orient has excised from Freemasonry - down to the Grand Architect himself in some cases. It is a very peculiar thing that the land that has produced some of the most profoundly mystical and spiritual rites, would also be the one to convert to a dogmatic atheism what was in fact founded upon the very opposite. That is not to say that Ragon is advocating any sort of atheism, but his attitude has certainly contributed to the humanist philosophy that would win the day in mainstream French Masonry.

Ragon, like many scholars, reveled in nothing so much as the opportunity to debunk fraud and falsehood. But his seeming desire to see fraud and deceit everywhere has caused him to dismiss a great number of things without actually supplying the scholarly research to back up his claims. When he does cite evidence, it is usually in the form of another author who shares his views - but again, without any actual evidence of the claims.

There is no question that Ragon was a great amasser of information, but his actual scholarship, that is to say his ability to verify the accuracy of the information and to critically and impartially analyze the information, leaves something to be desired, at least by modern academic standards. He too often allows his personal biases and preferences for what he feels *should be the case*, to cloud his ability to clearly examine and articulate what actually *is the case*. Ragon can often be bitingly sarcastic; but given his often lacking knowledge on a particular subject, it is sometimes difficult to determine whether his comments and questions merely feign an ignorance in order to be snarky, or if they reflect a true ignorance in the matter. For example, in his discussion on the Philosophical Scottish Rite, he feigns not to comprehend how the three symbolic grades make up the basis of the system while remaining outside the system. It is certainly clear that the three Blue Lodge degrees are a prerequisite to admission. But Ragon goes on about "how may symbolism be outside of a system?" and claiming it to be a contradiction, and so forth. These sorts of comments are troublesome; for if, on the one hand, this concept is truly foreign to him, then he is not the expert in Masonry that he claims to be. On the other hand, if he is merely being sarcastic, then that is most unfraternal, in which case he is not the Mason he claims to be.

It may seem that I have been unduly harsh in my criticism of Ragon, and perhaps I have. But after reading this work you may feel that I have not gone far enough. Although I have been involved with various forms of French Masonry and continental Masonry in general, in one form or another, for over twenty years, I came up through American Freemasonry; specifically, the Free and Accepted Masons of Wisconsin and its affiliated rites. So, when I read Ragon's comments, criticisms and dismissals of the various rites that are important to me, such as some of the "écossais" rites, the rites of Misraim and Memphis, the Elus Cohen and Martinism, etc., it irks me a little bit. But when I read what he has to say on the so-called errs of English/British/American Freemasonry, his harsh criticism has an even greater sting; especially since he dares to attack the very system that gave rise to all other forms of Freemasonry

- even if indirectly at times.

Now, this is not to say that all of Ragon's criticisms are unfounded, quite the opposite. He points out many blatant absurdities in the French Masonic world from the time of Freemasonry's introduction thereto up to Ragon's day. But the fact that he has several valid criticisms makes it all the more frustrating when poor scholarship enters into the matter. It is sometimes difficult to distinguish Ragon's personal biases, dislikes, and delusions from some of the frankly unpleasant facts about the Masonic institution. Sometimes even basic scholarship is lacking, such as in the misspelling of names that are sufficiently well known to the Masonic annals. For example, when speaking of Jean-Baptiste Willermoz, he calls him *Willermez*; and we know this not to be a mere typographical error, as it is repeated throughout. And there are a number of errors of this sort, as well as of certain dates. And Ragon's frequent use of clever tricks of semantics do not always hold up to critical analysis.

This book, as the title suggest, is in fact three works: The first, Masonic Orthodoxy, being the principal and longest work, followed by two shorter works on Occult Masonry and Hermetic Initiation. In my opinion, Ragon is at his best in the latter portions of this work concerning the occult and Hermetic philosophy, where his true insight into the symbolism of the Blue Lodge shines forth. But while his cutting cynicism ebbs, his scholarship is often arbitrary or incomplete; and his knowledge of etymology leaves something to be desired.

Finally, a few words should be said on certain terminology used throughout the work. First, as mentioned previously, the term "écossais" means "Scottish"; and the multitude of (falsely called) "Scottish" grades and systems are known collectively under the French term "écossisme." There is really no good way to translate this word in a way that is grammatically and substantially meaningful. It has therefore been left in its original form. The term "écossais" has often been translated as "Scottish," but occasionally has been left in the original French when it becomes grammatically problematic. The 2nd degree of the Blue Lodge or Symbolic Masonry, is called in the English systems "Fellowcraft"; but in the French system is called "Companion." I have left it as "Companion" in nearly every instance herein, in order to reflect the difference between the two systems, except when referring specifically to English Masonry, in which case I have rendered it as "Fellowcraft." In France, a lodge is sometimes referred to as a "workshop." Know, then, when this term appears within the text, that it merely means "lodge"; there is no special distinction to be made. Note also that I have rendered the French word "culte" simply as "cult." This word means: religion, rite, or form of worship, etc., and should be taken in this sense. It does not hold the negative connotations commonly associated with the word in English, as that of being dangerous or manipulative - at least not any more than would be applied to the word "religion." The abbreviation S.A.S. is used occasionally to address certain royal personages. It may be read as His Most Serene Highness. Likewise, the abbreviation S.M.S., appearing less frequently, indicates His Most Serene Majesty. Finally, in the Third Part of this work, the title of which I have translated as "Philosophical Masonry or Hermetic Initiation," the French title actually reads "Maçonnerie *Philosophale*" not "Maçonnerie *Philosophique*." This word, *philosophale* or *philosophal* is typically only seen in the term *pierre philosophale*, the philosopher's stone. But the word for "philosopher" in French is "philosophe." So, the proper way to say, "philosopher's stone" would be "pierre de philosophe." But instead, there is a special term: philosophale. Ragon's use of it here is intended to mean an *alchemical* Masonry. It seemed, though, that to translated it as "Alchemical Masonry" would stray a bit too far from the original wording.

In the end, for all of the problems found in this work, many of which have been rectified by later scholars, this is truly a classic work of Masonic history. For all of the errors, biases, and conspiracy theories, there are even more examples of useful historical data and wise insights from a man who unquestionably loved and dedicated his life in service of the Craft. For the true Masonic enthusiast, this work will inform, entertain, and sometimes infuriate. Translating this work has been sometimes challenging but always rewarding. I only hope that the modern readers of this volume will receive as much joy as it has brought to me.

Sâr Phosphoros
Sovereign Grand Commander
Christian Knights of Saint-Martin
21 December 2017

ANALYTICAL TABLE OF CONTENTS

Foreword

FIRST PART

CHAPTER 1

CHAPTER II – MASONIC ORDER

CHAPTER III – INSTITUTION OF MASONRY IN FRANCE

CHAPTER IV – GRAND LODGE OF FRANCE

CHAPTER V – SUSPENSION OF THE WORKS OF THE GRAND LODGE

CHAPTER VI – GRAND ORIENT OF FRANCE

CHAPTER VII – FREEMASONRY IN ENGLAND

CHAPTER VIII – FREEMASONRY IN SCOTLAND

CHAPTER IX – FREEMASONRY OR MODERN INITIATION

CHAPTER X – SUPERMASONIC INSTITUTIONS OR THE HIGH GRADES BY CHRONOLOGICAL ORDER

CHAPTER XI – COUNCIL OF THE EMPERORS OF THE EAST AND WEST

CHAPTER XII – PHILOSOPHICAL MASONRY

CHAPTER XIII – RITES INTRODUCED IN FRANCE SINCE 1800

CAHPTER XIV – YORK RITE OR MASONRY OF THE ROYAL ARCH

CHAPTER XV – VARIOUS REGIMES CREATED IN GERMANY

CHATER XVI

CHAPTER XVII – ORDER OF AFRICAN ARCHITECTS

CHAPTER XVIII – SWEDENBORG

CHAPTER XIX – ECOSSISME

CHAPTER XX – FOUNDATION OF A SUPREME COUNCIL 33RD DEGREE, AT PARIS

CHAPTER XXI – ON THE BROTHER PYRON

CHAPTER XXII – VARIOUS OPINIONS ON THE SCOTTISH RITE AND ON THE HIGH GRADES

CHAPTER XXIII – UNIVERSALITY AND UNITY OF FREEMASONRY

CHAPTER XXIV – ON THE REFORM OF THE SYMBOLISM

CHAPTER XXV

SECOND PART
Occult Masonry or Treatise on the Occult Sciences

CHAPTER XXVI

CHAPTER XXVII

CHAPTER XXVIII

CHAPTER XXIX

CHAPTER XXX

CHAPTER XXXI

CHAPTER XXXII

CHAPTER XXXIII

CHAPTER XXXIV

CHAPTER XXXV

CHAPTER XXXVI

CHAPTER XXXVII

CHAPTER XXXVIII

CHAPTER XXXIX

THIRD PART
Philosophical Masonry or Hermetic Initiation

CHAPTER XL

CHAPTER XLI

CHAPTER XLII

CHAPTER XLIII

CHAPTER XLIV

SUMMARY

CHAPTER XLV

Foreword

"The one who establishes principles less
makes a book than gives a book to make."
(Baron Massias, *Principes de littérature.*)

During our Masonic career which, already, dates back a half-century, we have had, in our excursions to the United States, in England, in Holland, in Belgium, in a part of Germany, in Switzerland, and in France, in our principal cities so richly populated by educated men, many occasions to fraternize and converse with Masons of consideration, whose dignities and grades were eminent, and, nearly always, the profane erudition was found quite superior to the Masonic instruction. There was not, save on rare exceptions, any unity of thought, any fixity of views, any well stated opinion on the origin of the order, on its secret aim, on the conjectures that we draw from the *initiatic outlines* consigned in the three symbolic grades: did they refute the judgment which has just been brought forth? The reply was: *You may well have reason.* But all considered the Lodges as excellent schools of morals, where they learn to practice virtue; to honor God with a pure heart, through good actions, without occupying themselves with anything of other cults that they render elsewhere; to obey the laws, without getting mixed up, as Masons, with the political cogs which produce them[1]; to love humanity and to relieve one's brothers. Without doubt, there are few associations which may be honored to have such principles so completely, to observe them with as much impartiality, and to traverse the ages on such bases. According to this picture, Freemasonry[2] ought to produce only loyal, honest, and philanthropic citizens; and though its works are kept within the bounds of secrecy, we have known for a long time now that its secrets consist in no more than the means of recognition which are composed of a tongue spoken universally, and of a language mute for the ear, but very significant for the eye and the touch; but these means themselves are no longer secret: time and printing have unveiled them. Then, to what good is the terrible oath imposed upon the initiate? Certainly, if it were modern, it would be of an entirely other style; but it is ancient; it is the one that the Egyptian initiate uttered. It has been reproduced to show that the institution is a renovation, a continuation of the mysteries of Asia, of Egypt, which were also schools, but where they taught all the sciences and all the arts. However, these studies, this knowledge, however *profound* or *elevated* that they were, did not exact such an oath, and since it had existed, there was a mysterious sanctuary where the goddess *Isis was without veil.* They received there the *grand initiation* with the knowledge of the sacred doctrine, that it would be proper to reintroduce, if they would have the present oath cease to be a nonsense.

We have also remarked that, in general, the Masons scarcely know the Masonry of their lands, how they have instituted it there, nor the history of the authority which directs it; these are things, however, that it is important to know. Although Masonry is the same over the whole globe (we do not speak of the high grades, none of which are Masonic), the spirit that each nation attaches to it is not generally uniform; it is philosophical in France, congregational and biblical in England and the United States, Catholic in Prussia, etc.

When Thory made his *Acta Latamorum*, informs *Capharnaum*, where are found pell-mell, each day, the Masonries of several nations, he had not included that the order, alone, classifies and may instruct; it is therefore a collection of documents to remake on another plan; it is, despite its numerous errors, still consulted, because there is no other, and we will add that the systematic partiality of the author towards the Grand Orient of France has been harmful to the value of the historian.

They have said with reason that ignorance begat error, and this latter, all the evils; Masonry, which is a light opposed to the darkness of ignorance in order to stop the deadly effects thereof, if it had been more studied, would have, constantly and without impediment, let its adepts enjoy the blessings that it sheds. But the ignorance of its principal chiefs has caused all the tribulations which overwhelm it still. Masonry is ONE, its point of departure is ONE. All the rays emanated from the primitive hearth were pure and regular; all that these new centers of light have constituted and constitute in their turn is good and regular; but all that does not arise therefrom ought to be mercilessly rejected into the nothingness.

We demonstrate that after the destruction, in the Gauls, of the druidic colleges by Julius Caesar, the ancient initiations expired. There was an age long sleep. Philosophical Masonry, which existed neither in fact nor in name, was conceived and consigned in three rituals, in 1646, by *Ashmole*, who rediscovered the ancient initiation, as *Mesmer* rediscovered magnetism; and on June 24, 1717, moral Masonry took a public and regular existence in the Grand Lodge of England. It is from this primitive hearth that the Masonic world has drawn the light that enlightens its works. It neither knew nor practiced but three symbolic grades which contain the true Masonry, and it is to this number that was limited the right that it granted to confer grades.

What they call *écossisme* did not exist. *Ramsay*, fugitive in Masonry as in religion, invented some Templar grades. This sectarian was born in Scotland, his grades were called Scottish [écossais], and all the grades invented since were also named Scottish, although unknown in Scotland. Thus, *Scottish grades* do not signify *grades from Scotland*; there is no *écossisme* in true Masonry: Read us and you will be convinced. The G.L. of England has never recognized écossisme.

These principles are quite simple. Why have the chiefs of French Masonry nearly always neglected the application thereof? The primary fault belongs to the *Grand Lodge* which had the weakness to tolerate the establishment, in the kingdom, of all these hearths of discord which, under the names of *Chapter of Clermont*, *Council of Emperors of the East and West* (Sovereign Prince Masons!), *Sovereign Council of the Knights of the East*, etc., etc., have come to sow error, to spread disunion by destroying the Masonic unity, and to undermine, in its foundations, the authority of the Grand Lodge which it would ere long escape.

But the chiefs of the authority who have succeeded these latter have profited in nothing from the past, and have not been better inspired than their predecessors, when, in 1804, some adventurers are come from America to establish themselves shamelessly at Paris in order to sell their rites there with the help of fraud and falsehood. If the officers of the Grand Orient of that time had known the orthodox principles of the institution, if they had examined the legality of their origin emanating originally from one UNIQUE CENTER, and if they had not lost sight that they possessed legitimately the rites in question (equivocal rites, without known origin), would they have given the example, painful still, of Masons who are going to receive, *under oath and with recognition*, grades which they possessed more legitimately than those granted to them? This is a most injurious trick that their ignorance has played on them; for, more educated, they would have overturned the false altar, and annihilated these nascent schemes, the shame of the Order.

Could one not say, with some reason, that ignorance is, for many adepts, the veil which covers Freemasonry? The fault must fall again on the administrators of the Order, who, to avoid the evil that it produced and the wrong that it causes the institution, would have had, for a long time, to establish *courses of instruction*, where the laureates would have been, with the old educated members, the *only ones fit* to fulfill the five primary offices of the Lodge (*we give the plan thereof* in chapter XXIII).

We have said that Masonry is the science of *physical*, *moral*, and *spiritual* life, indicated gradually in the symbolism. The elementary study of a Freemason ought to be that of the grades, yet he ought not limit it, if he wishes to educate himself, to the degrees which compose the rite that his lodge works; but he ought to seek to know the grades of all the systems or of the principal systems, from where flow a multitude of detached grades of which one may not give any account, for want of a preliminary and general instruction. How few Masons do we encounter who understand the spirit of the grades that they possess, or the aim of the rite that they profess, and of which the study has often been limited to spelling the same words without having understood the other side of the page!

Indeed, one may read with benefit certain Masonic works, by beginning with those where are found explored the field of interpretations and origins; if they do not enlighten the reader completely, they only give him the key to attain to the knowledge of the mysteries, that is to say of the *things veiled*, attractive study, where a first discovery leads to all the others, or at least to those which are important to make. But, in general, the books on Masonry are to be read with prudence, we have nearly said with defiance, because of the systematic spirit of the authors.

The one takes, and with reason, initiation at its origin; he has it descend, from age to age, among various nations that it enlightens and civilizes; it assists with its transformations in the philosophical schools of Greece, of Italy, and in the ancient colleges of Priests that it *debarbarizes*, until it finally takes the *veiling* name of Freemasonry, without is adepts having dreamt of constructing the least wall. These continuations of the ancient wisdom have become Masons in the manner of Apollo, of *Amphion*; do we not know that the ancient poets, initiates, speaking of the foundation of a city, meant the establishment of a doctrine (see pp.18-19).

Other authors have Masonry descend from the *foundation* of the Temple of Solomon. To conceive of such an origin is to be unacquainted with any initiatic inspiration. It has given rise to the *Levitical*, *Biblical*, *Solomonian* grades, to the York Rite or Masonry of the Royal Arch, etc. (see the *Thuileur général*). This temple has served later as re-veiling, under political and religious pretexts (see pp. 14), when the ancient doctrine had to take the name of *Freemasonry*.

Others have it re-emerge only at the *Crusades*, with the *Knights of Palestine*. This category is different. Let us re-read the old Templar grades, composed since Ramsay, we will find there this admission, that the Templars take Masonry as a veil in order to shelter their system, and by this propagative means, to spread their doctrine (see chapter XXV). Masonry existed, therefore, since they borrowed from it the veil and the form.

Others attribute Masonry to the Jesuits. The Jesuits have found Masonry in three grades *ready-made*; they have considered it as an excellent means to arrive at their aim, *universal domination*. They have borrowed from the Templar system. They have invented the majority of the *Scottish* grades. They have modified the work of Ashmole, favorite of Charles I, devoted, like them, to the Stuarts. From there, the imperfection of the grade of Master (see pp. 14). Wishing, like Ramsay, to enslave Masonry to Catholicism, they have indeed taken care to say, in the first grade of écossisme, that Masonry is a cult, that the true initiation would have taken good care to observe. The grades with daggers and their nocturnal works have been fabricated by them. We also owe to them that grade with *genuflections*, the *Rose-Croix*, which may certainly not figure in the ancient initiatic ladder, where despite this, it forms today the fourth rung (since it is given after the mastership), which is a displaced superfluity, a monstrous pleonasm of ancient symbolism, and, consequently, an error; for the son of Mary ought not be the understudy of Hiram. They have made of an alchemical grade a Christian grade! The true Masonry does not put religious beliefs into grades, it respects them as it respects the doctrines thereof, with which it has in common the purity of morals, the spirit of beneficence, the well-being and independence of humanity.

Finally, other authors, blindly breaking the chain of transmission, renounce a noble origin in order to date Freemasonry back, this science of sciences, only to the colleges and schools of architect-builders. These writers are only the historians of the *trade-guild*, which has no relation with Masonry but as a secret association, and all the rest differs therefrom. The operative companions, whose admission to their mysteries do not make apprentices, but *initiates*, have, in part, the myth of *Hiram* (*see who is Hiram*, chapter IX); but they have never taken but to the letter. It is to the point that one branch of the trade-guild accuses another of being the descendants of the assassins of Hiram, and from there, reproaches, insults, bloody fights, in the case of an encounter. If the *initiates* in construction had consorted with the Freemasons, they would have been enlightened and disabused on the *Hiramic* fiction; they would have learned that Hiram, who has never been an architect, but a founder, has never run into the slightest danger in the temple of Jerusalem. The mysterious ceremonies of the companions are based on the mysteries of Christianity, the putting into practice of which, in their reception, has exposéd them formerly to serious pursuits of the authorities, who regard these ceremonies as sacrilegious and punishable profanations.

Having subjected themselves to Catholicism, because of the privileges granted by the popes, as much to them as to corporations of Italian architect monks, for the construction of religious edifices, they have persisted therein: their annual feasts are celebrated by a solemn mass, the offering a bread to *bless*, and a banquet.
Freemasonry is a stranger to these customs: it is the religion of the soul, and it does not impose any religious yoke upon its initiates; it leaves to each brother his form of worship. It does not pretend to be one, because a Mason cannot have two cults: it leaves that subtlety of conscience to the Scottish systems.

This digression which, perhaps, is not misplaced here, has taken us away from our point of departure. Let us return there to explain the aim of our research.

The number of Masonries surpasses sixty. We conceive that these productions have only the form as Masonic: all different and often with grades belonging to other systems. This mass of rites is due only to the speculative fabrication of the high grades, from where there results as many schisms as rites. The true Masonry, composed of three degrees, does not give rise to schism.

In this quantity, there are found some bizarre rites and grades. They have their partisans, who believe themselves as good and true Masons as the true initiate. What to do? Instruct them, by furnishing them the means to compare the various regimes, to trace back, as far as it is possible, the origins, and to seek to penetrate the aim of each sect; several contradict themselves, the reader will profit therefrom to educate himself and judge. We have collected all that appears to us to be of interest. We relate nearly in their entirety some of the most instructive histories.

We also give all the relates to the *Knights of Palestine*, the *Knights of the Temple*, the *Unknown Philosopher Judges*, their successors, the *Knights of Christ*, and their continuers in Portugal.

Our documents on *Jesuitic Masonry*, on *Écossisme*, on the *Strict Observance*, on the *Scottish Directories*, on the *Knights Beneficent of the Holy City*, and above all on the *founders* of the various systems, in Germany and in Sweden, initiate the reader completely who, if he is unaware of these things, knows nothing in Masonry.

It is in these struggles raised between all these enlighteners of humanity that the light, that is to say the truth, springs forth, on the side of which they operate only too often.

Nothing of all this is, at its basis, *true* Masonry; but, as they still practice several rites thereof, though erroneous, and as so great a number of Masons of our day appear proud to wear some insignia thereof, it is therefore necessary to make known all these conceptions, so that those who are unaware of them may enlighten themselves and gain a taste for these useful explorations.

It is therefore to realize the thought of offering a GENERAL MASONIC INSTRUCTION that, for a long time, we have occupied ourselves with collecting and coordinating numerous materials proper to the attaining of this aim. Encouraged by the desire to be useful, we have not recoiled before this immense work. It shall form seven volumes; each of them may be detached from the others. Its title shall be FASTES INITIATIQUES [INITIATIC ANNALS].

Here is, in summary, the composition of each volume (large in-8vo):

First Volume. It treats:

1. On ancient philosophy and initiations or mysteries, from *Zoroaster* until our era, when the science of the sages[3] disappeared and existed only among some scattered adepts, escaped from the swords of *Caesar's* soldiers.
2. On the origin of the schools or colleges of *architect-builders*, extinguished in the 4th century; replaced by Italian architect monks, and guilds (*operative*) under the title of free-masons. We give the history of these material builders only to respond to the writers who have the origin of Freemasonry descend from these associations. (See chapter VII.)
3. History of the institution of PHILOSOPHICAL MASONRY in the Grand Lodge of England, on June 24, 1717; *idem* in Ireland, in 1722, and in Scotland, November 30, 1736, up to this day, with the list of the Grand Masters, the first of which was ANTHONY SAYER, at London.

Second Volume. It contains:

1. The general and chronological history of the Masonic Order *in France.*
2. The history of the works of the *Grand Lodge of France*, from 1756 to 1799;
3. The history of the works of the *Grand Orient of France*, from 1773 to 1854;
4. The history of the works of the Mother-Lodge of the *Philosophical Scottish Rite*, from 1770 to 1814, with the table of the seventy-four lodges constituted by it;
5. The history of the works of the *Supreme Council of the 33rd Degree*, from 1804 to 1854;
6. Historical notices on the Rite of *Ramsay*, 1728 (Templar system);

The Sovereign Council, Sublime Mother-Lodge of the *Excellents of the French Grand Globe*, 1750;

The *Chapter of Clermont* (Templar system), 1754;

The *Scottish Directories* of the Dresden Reform, Templar system, 1755, with the historical report in three eras;

The Council of *Emperors of the East and West*, Sovereign Prince Masons, 1758, with the nomenclature of the rite called *Heredom* or *Perfection*, in 25 degrees, and a copy of the powers given, on August 27, 1761, to the Jew *Stephen Morin*, in order to propagate this rite in America (extinguished in 1781);

The Sovereign Council of the *Knights of the East*, 1762 (extinguished in 1781);

The *Grand Chapter General of France*, 1782, united with the Grand Orient of France on February 17, 1786;

The Sacred Order of the Sophisians, 1801;

The Scottish Grand Lodge General of France, 1803;

The *Supreme Council of America* at Paris, 1812;

The Masonry of *Misraim*, autocratic regime, 90 degrees, 1814, with the characteristics of the 67th to the 90th degree;

The Rite of *Memphis*, called *Oriental*, in 92 degrees, 1839;

The *National Grand Lodge of France* professing only the symbolism, 1848-1851, and other régimes.

The Masonry of *Adoption*, in 5 grades and 8 grades detached.

Notices on twenty-four *androgynous* Masonries;

Finally, the *General Table* of around 1,600 lodges constituted or reconstituted by the Grand Orient of France.

Third Volume containing:

1. The Mosaic Masonry called *English* or Masonry of the *Royal Arch* or *York Rite*, in 4 and 5 degrees, 1777;
2. *Templar Masonry*, grades and rituals, *Knights of Palestine*, list of Grand Masters, etc.;
3. *Jesuitic Masonry*, grades, rituals, etc.;
4. The *Masonry of Germany*, Swedish (Templar) system in 12 grades, 1736;

Evangelical Masonry of the *United Brethren* of the order of the religious Freemasons, or order of the *Mustard Seed*, 1739;

Christian Masonry of *Saint Joachim*, 1760;

Strict, Late, High, and *Narrow Observance* (Templ. syst.), status, histories, etc., and Knights Beneficent of the Holy City, 1762, etc.

System of *Swedenborg*, in 8 grades, divided into 2 temples;

System of *Schroeder*, in 7 grades, 1766;

Order of African Architects, that is to say continuators of the Egyptian mysteries, 1767;

System of Schroepffer, 1768; Masonry of the 72;

System of *Zinnendorf* (modified Swedish régime), 1770;

Order of the *Initiated Knights* and *Brethren of Asia in Europe*, in 5 degrees, 1780;

Eclectic Masonry (the first three grades), manifesto to of the Grand Lodges of Frankfort and Wetzlar, 1783;

The *German Union* or the XXII, by *Bahrdt*, in 6 grades., 1787.

System of *Fessler*, in 9 grades (1796); Masonic reform; and various *rectified* and *reformed* régimes.

Fourth Volume, where is found:

1. The chronological history of the institution in the *European States* hereafter:

Austria	1725	Naples	1735

Baden (duchy of)	1737	Piemont	1739
Bavaria	1737	Poland	1738
Belgium	1740	Portugal	1727
Bohemia	1744	Prussia	1737
Brunswick	1744	Russia	1731
German Confederate	1738	Sardinia	1737
Denmark	1742	Savoy	1739
Spain	1726	Saxony	1737
Hanover	1732	Sweden	1730
Hesse	1780	Switzerland	1736
Holland	1730	Turkey	1738
Hungary	1744	Wurtemburg	1780
Italy	1733	Westphalia	1811

2. In the *extra-European States*, namely:

Africa	1735	Algeria	1832

North America, historical brief on each of its thirty-three states:

Canada	1721

South America:

Brazil	1823	Mexico	1820
Columbia	1838		

The West Indies:

Haiti	1749	Malta	1730
Cuba	1793	Ionian Isles (Corfou)	1811
Guadalupe	1770	Ile de France	1778
Martinique	1783	Ile Bourbon	1821
Jamaica	1743	Marquise Isles	1843

India:

Bengal	1728	Bombay	1820
Madras	1779	Pondichery	1820

Egypt (Alexandria)	1810	Oceania (Sidney)	1800
China (Canton)	1810	Australia (Adelaide)	1843
Persia (Ispahan)	1842		

Fifth Volume. It contains:

1. *Forestry* Masonry in five Orders;
2. Notices relating to the *Illuminati* of Stockholm, of Bavaria, of Italy, and other non-Masonic *secret societies*;
3. Some curious statutes, several rare *rituals*, whose tenor develops and explains the secret aim of the rites to which belong the grades that they treat;
4. *Pieces in support* of advances made; *sentences, proclamations, decrees,* and *bulls* emanating from the civil and religious authorities of several lands, against the Masonic Order and its members, and other instructive *documents.*

Sixth Volume. It is dedicated to *Hermeticism* and to the *occult sciences.* One finds there:

1. Forty-five *initiatic* grades, both detached and belonging to several Hermetic rites; with the alphabets, tableaux, signs, and hieroglyphic figures;
2. *Mesmerian Masonry*, rite of *Universal Harmony*, with the characters employed in Mesmer's theory of the world;
3. Notices on various *magnetisms*, *on somnambulism*, and on *magism*;
4. Notices on *psychology, physiology, physiognomy, chiromancy*, and *phrenolgy,* etc.;
5. *Iatric* (medical) Masonry, with the hieroglyphs and the *Hermetic Star*;
6. Notices on *thaumaturgy*, *astrology*, *cabala, divination*, etc.;
7. Relations of each *planet* to *the principles* of the Hermetic philosophers, where we find the key of the mythological interpretations of the ancients;
8. Exposé of the *principles* or *opinions* of the principal philosophers, ancient and modern;
9. Finally, the SACERDOTAL ART or HERMETIC SCIENCE, with the explanation of the fables and of the symbols under which was veiled the work of transmutation.

Seventh and final Volume, is the TUILEUR GÉNÉRAL [General Tyler]. Around four hundred grades, belonging to RITES known and *detached*, will each have here its TYLER, with interpretive notes. All will be followed by a NOMENCLATURE of more than nine hundred grades.

In this immense work, that the desire to instruct, alone, makes one to undertake, are a multitude of things that we cannot enumerate without doubling, in the table, the detail of each volume, which would have been wearisome for the reader: those that we indicate suffice to make known the existence of that which is to be found therein, without it being necessary to state them.

Do we deceive ourselves to think that a studious Mason, who will have the one part of this work and having perused the other, may, without presumption, hope to be, from that moment, in a position to know, to judge, and to appreciate the merit of the institution to which he belongs? For he will know how to distinguish the true from the false, that is to say to separate truth from error; the impostors will no longer have a grip on him. Such is the aim that we have proposed to achieve.

Without doubt, our work, fruit of long research, is imperfect, that is to say incomplete, especially in the hundred histories of the lands where Masonry is or was instituted; but what we have gathered thereof gives generally a sufficient idea of its local physiognomy. Moreover, we have opened the way, it is vast, for others, more able, to traverse more successfully.

Nevertheless, such as it is, this work appears to us to be able to be, by itself, a sort of Masonic library, a storehouse of documents, a code of practical and intellectual instructions, where are grouped all the facts, all the attempts of the past, which teach how to steer into the future, in order, by means of the concourse of educated brethren of good will, to come to give to our noble, institution all the perfection that it expects of the light of its adepts.

In order to render, from here to the printing, if it is to take place, our Fastes Initiatique worthy of all, we invite all our brethren, French and foreigners, to address at

Dentu, bookstore-publisher, at Paris (Palais-Royal, galerie d'Orléans, 18), or at the offices of the journal "le Francmaçon," edited by the brother Ducheuaux-Dumesnil, quai des orfèvres, 58, with documents that they believe would render more complete the category of the materials classified in each volume. We will reproduce, while indicating the name of the senders, those of the pieces that we do not possess and which would appear of a general interest, just as we will act thereby with regard to the brothers who have already bestowed such on us.

They will send it to press when we will have gathered three hundred subscribers. The volumes will be in-8vo, beautiful paper, of around 500 pages. One may subscribe per volume.

The price of the first volume alone will be 10 fr.

That of the second, third, fourth, and fifth volumes, 8 fr. each.

The sixth and seventh will cost 10 fr. each, because of the small text and the numerous hieroglyphs and drawings.

The price of the seven volumes will be 50 fr. for the first three hundred subscribers.

Masonic Orthodoxy

As to the book that we have the privilege to submit, under the title of Masonic Orthodoxy, to the judgment of our brethren, we limit ourselves here to pray them to read our *epigraph* and to peruse the *table of contents*; it is the sole magnet which may attract their attention, if they love *orthodoxy* and the *truth*; with contrary dispositions they must reject the work; we have written it in the aim of enlightening and contributing to the projected reforms. The greatest difficulty has not been putting the abundance and variety into this work but putting unity into this variety.

FIRST PART
MASONIC ORTHODOXY

FIRST CHAPTER

Let us unveil all that is false,
to get back to what is true.

Before entering into the material, let us recall quickly, in order to facilitate the intelligence of the subject, which is going to occupy us, what we say, in the *Fastes Initiatique*, on the very modern origin of *Freemasonry*, in Europe.

We have established, in the 1st volume, the annihilation, in the world, of the ancient initiatic mysteries with the ruin of *Alésia*[4] or *Alise*, great city of Celtic Gaul, capital of the Mandubians, in the first Lyonnaise, the Thebes of the Celts, ancient metropolis and tomb of the initiation, of the druidic cult, and of Gallic liberty.

We know that Vercingetorias, from the land of the Arvernes, incited to rebellion, 53 years before our era, against the Roman yoke, all of central Gaul submitted to *Caesar*. They named him chief of the confederation. Despite marvels of intrepidity, this celebrated leader was vanquished; then, besieged the following year in Alesia, he underwent there a heroic struggle and was forced to surrender. After having adorned the bloody triumph of the conqueror, he was strangled, in 47 years before the present era. Caesar, in his barbarous rage, had seen to slaughter the garrison, massacre the inhabitants and the priests of the college, pillage and raze this rich and scholarly city.

Not far from here flourished *Bibracte*, the mother of the sciences, the soul of the primitive nations, city equally famous for its sacred colleges of the Druids, as its civilization, its schools where they taught 40,000 students: philosophy, literature, grammar, jurisprudence, medicine, astrology, occult sciences, architecture, etc. Rival of Thebes, Memphis, Athens, and Rome, it possessed an amphitheater, surrounded by colossal statues, for the gladiators, and containing 100,000 spectators, a capitol, temples of Janus, Pluto, Prosperine, Jupiter, Apollo, Minerva, Cybel, Venus, Anubis, and in the middle of these sumptuous edifices, the naumachy with its vast basin, unbelievable construction, gigantic monument where floated the barks and galleys destined to nautical jousts; then a large parade-ground, an aqueduct, fountains, public baths; finally, great walls, the foundations of which go back to heroic times.

But *Sacrovir*, leader of the Gauls who revolted against the Roman despotism, under Tiberius, was defeated in the year 21 by *Silius*, near that great city and was given death with his conspirators, upon a pyre, before the eyes of the besiegers, before the sack of the city.

The courtesans of the era (Gaul has never lacked them) have changed the celebrated name of Bibracte into that of *Augustodunum* which, by contraction and in order to veil, while perpetuating it, the shame of the flatterers, has become *Antun*.[5]

Arles, founded 2,000 BC, was sacked in 270. This metropolis of the Gauls, restored forty years later by *Constantine*, still preserves some remains of its ancient splendor: amphitheater, capitol, granite obelisk 17 meters high, triumphal arch, catacombs, etc.

Thus ended the Celtic and Gallic civilization; already Caesar, in a barbary worthy of Rome, had accomplished the destruction of the ancient mysteries by the sack of the temples and of the initiatic colleges, and by the massacre of the initiates and the druids.

Rome remained; but it never possessed but the lesser mysteries, that shadow of the secret science; the greater initiation was extinguished.

Historians (of *operative masonry*) speak of the guilds of builders that the senate sent into the Gauls, behind Roman armies, in order to rebuild the eight hundred cities that, by the report of *Pliny*, Caesar had destroyed with all the Celtic and Druidic monuments. These builders were indeed able to restore some enclosures and to reconstruct some edifices; but they were not able to found any *initiatic colleges*. Savants in civil and sacred architecture, they were strangers to the mysteries of the secret doctrine, which had to undergo a sleep of more than fifteen centuries before being re-awakened.

Indeed, these associations of builders and of various professions had nothing which resembled the ancient philosophical doctrine, which they had no mission to spread, nor that of present Freemasonry, which did not exist; but, they say, in this confraternity of workers, they were given the title of *brothers*; this proves nothing: an inquisitor, who spoke to his audience, made use of this expression; but those of his *brothers* who did not think as him were soon condemned and burned alive. Moreover, there existed at Rome a college of *Arval Brethren*, composed of twelve principal citizens for the sacrifices of the *Ambarvals* (the Roman Rogation Days), who, certainly, did not claim to be initiated into the Egyptian mysteries. The operative builders had not, and could not have, this pretention. It is the non-initiated writers who, since the rebirth of initiation, at the end of the 17th century, have given to these confraternities of *operative masons* an importance unknown to their profession. These blundering authors have had their successors who, disdainful of the luminaries of the time, *who walk* and *unveil*, have, still in our day, imitated the same follies, that is to say walked, in spite of the light, in the same darkness, and they continue to take works on masonry for *Masonic works*.

All the statutes which grant privileges to these useful confraternities confirm what we say: let us consult the constitution of 926, submitted to the *King Edwin* and approved by the representatives of the workers' guilds of the kingdom, which founded at York the headquarters of the confraternity of operative masons (*freemasons*). We find nothing there pertaining to regulations for a philosophical society: Freemasonry has, therefore, nothing to do with this pact of builder masons, which could not have been edited to *regulate* later the *Freemasonic institution*. We regret to be, on this subject, in opposition with our excellent brethren of the United States, who believe themselves the successors of the builders of whom it is a question at York. Their prolonged error is too great for them and their brethren who write not to disabuse them sooner or later. *The Masonry of York* was no more Freemasonry then than it is since the *York Rite*.

Whatever may be true, or nearly so, in the histories that they have made on the confraternity of *Heredom* (of Kilwinning) in favor of operative masons who, they say, took part in the army of the King *Robert Bruce*, at the battle of Bannockburn, in 1314, cannot have any relation with the Freemasonic institution, whose doctrine and mission were not yet known.

The raising of the tower of Kilwinning, in 1151, is cited as being the first construction made in Scotland, by a guild of foreign workers. Jongleurs, come later, have the origin of *Scottish Masonry* go back to this fact. This is nothing but absurd; that a capable architect had illustrated this construction by a new order under the title of *Scottish architecture* is understandable; but it would not be called *Scottish Masonry*, for they do not say *Corinthian Masonry, Doric Masonry*.

The society of the *Saint Mary's Chapel*, founded at Edinburgh in 1298; the *jurisdiction* established, in 1424, by *James I* on behalf of the confraternity of operative masons in the Kingdom of Scotland; the *hereditary patronage* granted, they say, in 1487, by James II, seventy years old, to William *Saint-Clair*, for the prosperity of the confraternity; the letter of *James VI*, protector of these masons, addressed September 25, 1590, to Patrick *Copeland*, with this title: *Warden* in the art and *craft* of masonry in the district of Aberdeen, Bamff, and Kincardine, do not concern in the least the world of Freemasonry.

In 1425, the English parliament suppresses, in the whole kingdom, the assemblies of freemasons, because *they disrupt the good order, and the labor of the workmen is publicly interrupted.* Could they have said as much, later, of the peaceful feasts of the Freemasons at the solstices? Have they ever interrupted the erection of public edifices? This act took place under the nonage of *Henry VI*, who, upon attaining the throne, revoked, they say, these prohibitions. The novelist-masons attribute this determination to the illuminations that he received from a freemason on the doctrine of its incorporation. From here, that fabulous *examination*, commented, they say, by Locke in 1696, that this monarch would have to submit to an *initiate* before entering the *Order.* The brotherhood of builders was never an Order, and the conversation with the King by an initiate (*in the secret sciences*) would have remained unknown. Thus, this piece passes for one of the fables by which the so- called Masonic histories multiply.

Let them cast a glance upon the *statutes and regulations* of the *confraternity of the stone-cutters of Strasbourg*, dating from April 25, 1459, which are reproduced, rather poorly, incidentally, in some Masonic collections. They are based on the *statutes of the free-masons of Germany*. They will not find, in the one or the other, but some rules for the workers; yet some authors, we refrain from qualifying their erudition, see therein the origin of Freemasonry, whereas the contexture of these regulations indicates only a monarchal origin, that of the monk-builders, quite confirmed in their ceremonial, the observance of which still exists in our day at the celebration of the annual feasts of the confraternities of the trades, where a solemn mass and the blessed bread are obligatory.

In 1681, William *Penn*, a great number of the English, and among them, many members of the confraternity of the free-masons, passed into America, from where originated *Pennsylvania* (*Penn's forest*, which was given to this Quaker by *Charles II*). The colony built upon the Delaware, in 1683, the beautiful city of *Philadelphia*, or *City of Brethren*, read *City of Quakers* (theists, philanthropists, and republicans, who are recognized by their "theeing and thouing"). Until 1800, the Congress of the United States was held in this city; it was then transported to Washington.

A rather evident and most conclusive proof that these numerous members, *accepted* into the English brotherhood of operative builders, were not and did not believe themselves Freemasons, is that no Freemasonic workshop, that powerful means of union and civilization, nearly indispensible in a nascent colony (see *only Algeria*), has been founded by them in their capital, for the reason that there was not yet any Freemasonry upon the globe. It is their successors who, fifty-one years after the foundation of Philadelphia, saw among them, on June 24, 1734, several Freemasons who had addressed themselves to the Grand Lodge of Boston, (constituted on April 30, 1733, by the Grand Lodge of England), to obtain constitutions to open a lodge in their city. Benjamin *Franklin*, so celebrated since, was its first Worshipful Master.

But in 1646, the celebrated antiquarian Elias Ashmole, great alchemist, founder of the Oxford Museum[6], had been admitted, with colonel *Mainwarring* into the brotherhood of operative masons at Warrington, into which they began to admit individuals ostensibly foreign to the art of building.

This same year, a Rose-Croix society, formed according to the ideas of the *New Atlantis of Bacon*, assembled in the meeting room of the freemasons at London. Ashmole and the other brothers of the Rose-Croix, having recognized that the number of craftsmen was surpassed by that of the workers of intelligence, because the first were each day growing weaker, whereas the latter increased continually, thought that the moment had come to renounce the formula of reception of the workers, which consisted only in some ceremonies slightly similar to those utilized among all the tradesmen, which had, up until then, served to shelter the *initiates* in order to join with the adepts. They substituted them by means of the oral traditions that they used for their aspirants to the occult sciences, a written mode of initiation calculated on the ancient mysteries and on those of Egypt and Greece; and the first initiatic grade was written such, nearly, as we know it. The first degree having received the approbation of the initiates, the grade of Companion [Fellowcraft] was drawn up in 1648; and that of Master a little while after; but the decapitation of Charles I in 1649 and the side that Ashmole took in favor of the Stuarts, brought great modifications to this third and final grade become biblical, all while leaving as its basis that great hieroglyph of nature symbolized towards the end of December. This same era soon saw the birth of the grades of *Secret Master*, *Perfect Master*, *Elect*, and *Irish Master*, of which Charles I is the hero, under the name of *Hiram*; but these grades of political coteries were professed nowhere; nevertheless, later on they would make the ornament of écossisme.

1650. But the non-worker members, *accepted* into the guild, made it take, especially in Scotland, a political tendency: the heads (*protectors*) of the Scottish workers, partisans of the *Stuarts*, worked in the shadows towards the re-establishment of the throne destroyed by *Cromwell*. They made use of the isolation which safeguarded the gatherings of the *freemasons*, in order to hold, in their locale, secret meetings where plans were conceived in security. The decapitation of *Charles I* had to be avenged. In order to achieve this and collect themselves, his partisans proposed a *Templar* grade, where the violent death of the innocent J.B. Molay calls for *vengeance*. Ashmole, who shared the same political sentiment, then modified his grade of Master and substituted for the Egyptian doctrine, which made it uniform with the first two degrees, a biblical veil, incomplete and incongruous, just as the Jesuit system demanded, and of which the initials of the sacred words of these three degrees reproduced those of the name of the Grand Master of the Templars. This is why, since that era, the initiates have always regarded the *grade of Master*, sole complement of Freemasonry, as a *grade to remake*. It is, without doubt, according to this reform that the two columns and the words of the first two grades have also received biblical names.

1703. *Important decision of the freemasons* who admitted *openly*, into their association at London, persons foreign to the art of building[7]. The philosopher Masons, called accepted, for a long time with the operative builders, were going to be found powerful enough to operate *publicly* the transformation so desired.

1714. *George I* began his reign. The Masonic authors regard this era as the end *of the dark times of the Masonic Order*. They deceive themselves, there did not yet exist any Masonic order: this era is only the end of the guilds of operative builders whose existence had become precarious, since their secrets in architecture had fallen into the public domain[8].

CHAPTER II
Masonic Order

1717. *Only* from this era dates the Masonic Order: the association of builders were but one or several guilds and was never an order. As to the word Masonic, this qualificative was never created for them; heedlessness or ignorance could alone endow them thereof; for, we repeat, a work of masonry is not a Masonic work.

This year, the corporation counted no more, at London, than four societies, called *Lodges*, possessing the rolls and ancient titles of the confraternity and operating under the *head of the order of York*. They gathered in February; they adopted the three rituals drawn up by Ashmole. They shook off the yoke of York and declared themselves *independent*, and *government of the confraternity*, under the title of Grand Lodge of London.

It is from this central and *unique* hearth that FREEMASONRY, that is to say the ostensible renovation of the secret philosophy of the ancient mysteries, set forth, in all directions, in order to establish itself among all the peoples of the world.

The first Grand Master elected was Ant. *Sayer*, esquire. (See our *Précis hist. d'Angleterre*[9].) The other so-called previous Grand Masters were only patrons, as have all the guilds. - It is therefore evident that Freemasonry was professed at London before being known at York, which made quite useless representations and protestations on this subject, and it had to be: the composition of the members and the aim of the two institutions differed too much for it to be otherwise. Philosophical Masonry, or the science of civilization had, sooner or later, to prevail over the masonry of tools or the art of building. This creation, which was the signal of a struggle which was prolonged between the Freemasons and the operative masons, shared between the two order heads of London and York, brought the new body to trace the limits of the respective jurisdiction.

In order to declare its supremacy, the brotherhood at York gave itself the qualification of *Grand Lodge of all England*; vain effort! Its influence diminished while the rival body made rapid progress. Then it believed it prudent to temporize, and relations, amicable in appearance, were established between the two groups.

1720. They have lamented, and some lament still, the burning that took place this year at London, of the archives of these workers. Why these regrets? What was burned? Estimates, plans, construction prices, memoranda of masonry, contracts, wage regulations, etc. Did the initiates, which there were doubtless among them, write them? Certainly not. If material architecture has lost there some documents of comparison with the means of present construction, moral and philosophical architecture has not a page to lament. It is thus that, without reflection, they give importance to that which cannot have any, and that they compare the burning of this unhandy or needlessly cumbersome rubbish to the fire of the library of Alexandria; it is the same metaphor which still sees to compare operative masons to the Freemasons.

A proof that the Grand Lodge of London did not believe to base its return to the ancient philosophy upon the operative guild of York, is that it dated its first acts by the year 5717. Which has made ignorant writers and fabricators of rites believe that, since Freemasonry dated from the birth of the world (according to the Jews), it is that Adam had been the *Venerable* of the first lodge: Masonic *Unity* was then an incontestable thing.

1725. To count from this era, Freemasonry was spread into the various states of Europe; it made its debut in France, beginning in 1721, by the institution, on October

13th, of the lodge *l'Amitié et Fraternité*, at Dunkerque; at Paris, in 1725; at Bordeaux, in 1732 (the lodge *l'Anglaise*, no. 204), and at Valenciennes, on January 1, 1733, *la Parfaite-Union*. It penetrates into Ireland in 1729; in Holland in 1730; the same year, a lodge was established at *Savannah*, State of Georgia (America); then at Boston in 1733. It appeared in Germany in 1736; the Grand Lodge of Hamburg is instituted on December 9, 1737; as eventually into the other States of Europe and extra-European lands, always under the active and intelligent direction of the Grand Lodge of England[10].

In 1736, Scotland saw arrive the moment when the *operative* masons were nearly entirely expelled by the workers of intelligence; the veil remains, but the aim changes. The Church understood this change, and the prelates did not accept the high dignitaries of the new Order. Since 1695, all the guilds of freemasons were asleep in Scotland.

On November 30, day of Saint Andrew, 32 guilds, duly convoked by a circular of July 11, gathered, at Edinburgh, in the locale of Saint Mary's Chapel, to the effect of *organizing* the association *on new bases*, and constituting themselves into the Grand Lodge of Saint John of Edinburgh. They gave there the reading of an act, dated from November 24, by which, yielding to the force of things, William *de St.-Clair* renounced, for himself and his, the charge of *hereditary chief and governor of the freemasons in Scotland*, and granted them liberty of suffrage. He is, by unanimity, elected Grand Master by those assembled, who installed him immediately.

On June 24, 1737, the Grand Lodge decided that all the lodges of Scotland, who would recognize his jurisdiction, will be held to having their constitutional titles corroborate and agree. The greater number of the lodges submitted to this decision. There was only scarcely the so-called Mother Lodge of the little borough of Kilwinning which resisted it, wishing to preserve its independence and *its supremacy*, as if it were a question of continuing the manner of the operative guilds. The new mode of philosophical initiation that it did not have the right to exercise without becoming *schismatic*, rendered, from this very day, its existence null with regard to Freemasonry, and the Grand Lodge of Edinburgh has failed in its duty by not signaling this bastard association as not belonging, in any manner, it and its adherents, to the nascent family of Freemasons. For a long time yet it delivered lodge constitutions. This rivalry of power, which drew its strength only form the ignorance of the dupes that it made, gave place to lively disputes, which often troubled, in the most grave manner, the peace of the confraternity and ceased only in 1807, era in which this supposed Grand Lodge finally consented to recognize the authority of the Grand Lodge of Scotland, and placed itself under its banner with all the lodges which arose from it. It was placed, without number, at the head of the list of the lodges of Scotland. Its works were regularized, and its president was instituted Provincial Grand Master of Ayrshire.

The Grand Lodge made, the same day, another decision which abolished the custom of holding the grand assembly on the day of Saint John of winter, and fixed the period thereof to November 30, day of Saint Andrew, patron of Scotland. This decision did not do honor to the initiatic knowledge of the Grand Lodge Saint John of Edinburgh. It is even a derogation of its title. The operative masons, with whom it has, perhaps, not wished to assemble, were more in the right in this regard[11].

Perhaps too it has wished to dedicate, by this period, the anniversary of its foundation. Let us leave Scotland momentarily.

CHAPTER III
Institution of Freemasonry in France

The first lodge founded outside the Kingdom of England was that of the *Amitié et Fraternité* at Dunkerque, on October 13, 1721, by *Jean*, Duc de *Montaigu*, Grand Master of the Grand Lodge of England.

English Masonry Frenchified at Paris

In the year 1725, English Masonry made its debut at Paris with the costumes, the ceremonial, and the rituals fixed at London in these later times. It is there introduced by English Masons of distinction. They established the first lodge, whose name has remained unknown, with *Hure*, English restaurant-keeper, at the rue des Boucheries, in imitation of the lodges of England, which held their assemblies in taverns. The English who were found at Paris and many French were admitted to these new mysteries, which received, for the first time, the name of Franche-Maçonnerie. The number of brethren increased, and they founded the lodge of *Gouftand*, English lapidary.

On May 7, 1729, a brother named *Le Bréton* established, at rue des Boucheries, the lodge of Saint Thomas at the *Louis-d'Argent*, in an inn having for its sign the Silver Louis. Although third in date, it is the first regular lodge of Paris and the second of France, because it received from the Grand Lodge of England, whose regime it followed, *the only one which then existed*, a *constitution* that the previous had not. Thus, does it figure at no. 90, among the first one hundred twenty-nine lodges, in the table prepared in 1735 at London[12]. The chronicles make mention of two other lodges under the titles of *Saint-Martin* and *Saint-Pierre*, which would have been constituted in this same year.

In 1732, a new lodge was formed in the house of *Landelle*, restaurant-keeper, rue de *Bussy*, whose name it bore, which it changed into that of *Loge d'Aumont*, because the duke of this name had received initiation there up to the grade of Master.

On December 24, 1736, the four lodges assembled and elected for their Grand Master the *Comte d'Harnouester*, in absence of *Lord Derwentwater*, who is reputed to have fulfilled this dignity as founder of the first lodge at Paris. At this gathering of election, the Scot Ramsay, of baneful memory, fulfilled the functions of Orator[13].

It is regrettable that, too submissive to the prohibition against writing anything, these lodges have not left any proper documents to throw some light on the first works of the Freemasons at Paris.

In this period, other lodges had been established in the provinces: some of them, attributing to themselves the powers of the Grand Lodges, delivered constitutions, and founded workshops[14]. These abuses, which appear strange to us, were frequent because, in this era, the constitutions were personal to the brethren who obtained them, and because the functions of the Venerable were for life. Every brother of a free condition, provided with the grade of Master, and having been Surveillant of a lodge, was apt to be constituted *irremovable venerable*. The patents were in his name, he was the proprietor thereof, and he had the right to name his two Surveillants. He depended only upon himself alone, and governed the brethren in an absolute manner; thus, each of them could say: *The lodge is where I am*, or rather, like Louis XIV, *I am the lodge*. These anomalies did not delay to produce *disorder* and *scandals*, which were quelled later.

1738. Lord d'Harnouester, first Grand Master regularly elected, before returning to England, had manifested the desire to see himself replaced by a French Grand Master. The Masters of the lodges of Paris having assembled, fixed their choice on the *Duc d'Antin*, one of the lords of the court who had shown the most zeal for the prosperity of the institution.

Louis XV, deceived by little unenlightened courtiers or by fanatics, had, without success in truth, prohibited from the court the lords who had themselves received as Freemasons, but being informed of this project, he declared that whoever will have presided over the Freemasons in the quality of Grand Master will be at that instant put in the Bastille.

On June 24, this nomination is accepted by the new Grand Master who is solemnly installed. The monarch did not give effect to his declaration, but the Châtelet [Parisian law court], less generous, continued, according to its decision of September 14, 1737, to exercise its prescriptions against the members of the Order who cannot oppose it but by the influence of their names or their employ.

On December 11, 1743, the lodges of Paris name for perpetual Grand Master the Comte *de Clermont*, prince of the blood, who succeeded the *Duc d'Antin*, deceased.

December 27. Solemn installation of the new Grand Master, whose election had been confirmed by the lodges of the provinces. Those of Paris established a Grand Lodge composed of persons of distinction. In order to recognize the benefit of England, which has endowed France of the Masonic Institution, the Parisian lodges convinced the Grand Lodge to take the title of English Grand Lodge of France, title that it preserved until 1756.

English Grand Lodge of France

Despite this title, the Masonry was no less an entirely French Masonry, distinct, in spirit, from the Grand Lodge of London, from which it drew its origin, and superior to those of Scotland, America, Germany, etc., that is to say that free- masonry (*material masonry*), although transformed among these nations, had preserved there with the name (that it would have been necessary to modify) an original stain from which their perspicacity could not preserve them, stain that time has not yet erased. The blessed name "franc-maçon" which is not the translation of "freemason," produced upon the Parisian spirit the useful effect which would result from this new institution. Free-masonry would not have taken in France[15], does one believe that the French had consented to bear the vulgar title of free- mason [maçon -libre]? Certainly not; but that of franc-maçon has so greatly conveyed the sense of the high importance of the civilizing mission imposed by the new institution, that the French lodges rejected that ridiculous vanity of public processions, abandoned the corporations of artisans, and did not solicit their admission or participation in the laying of the first stones of the public monuments, ceremonies altogether foreign to those of its rituals and its aims, unless it be a question of raising an edifice at the expense of the Order, for its use or in order to be consecrated by it with its blessing. The French knew well that it was not a question of building the least wall, by adopting the title of Freemason [Francmaçon], but it understood that initiated into mysteries veiled under the name of *Freemasonry*, and which could only be the continuation or renovation of the ancient mysteries, they became *Masons* in the manner of *Apollo*, of *Amphion*: do we not know that the ancient poets, initiates, speaking of the foundation of a city, meant the establishment of a doctrine. It is thus that Neptune, god of reasoning, and Apollo, god of hidden things, presented themselves in the quality of *masons* to Laomedon, father of Priam, in order to aid in the construction of the City of Troy, that is to say to establish the *Trojan religion*. It is thus that Amphion, by another allegory, raised the walls of Thebes by the sounds of his lyre.

They have made, and with reason, to the *English G.L. of France*, a grave reproach, for the inconveniences which resulted therefrom; it was to have granted personal constitutions to the lodge Masters, by virtue of *irremovable Masters* for Paris only: "There resulted therefrom two great inconveniences; the one, that the Venerables were occupied only with their personal workshops; the other, that the distinguished brothers who directed the G.L., finding in their works ennui, dryness, and monotony, neglected them. They fell into decadence, and the Masonry of Paris into scorn, whereas it was followed in the provinces, with activity, zeal, and *delights*," (*Etat du G.O.*, v. I, p. 13).

1744, June 5. The chamber of police of the Châtelet renews its prohibitions made against the Freemasons from assembling in lodges and forbade the houses and tavern-keepers from receiving them, under pain of three thousand francs penalty.

The Prince *de Clermont*, circumvented by secret enemies of the Order, no longer appeared at the works; at his example, the lords who supported him ceased, as *faithful courtiers*, to appear in their workshops, which were then found abandoned to themselves. In truth, he found a substitute in the financier *Baure*, whose incapacity or negligence rendered him unworthy of the honor that they granted him. He broke up the assembly of the G.L. and let disorder invade the administration; the election of the Venerables was neglected. To strengthen the administration, they believed it good to institute for Paris *irremovable* heads of lodges. This means led to anarchy; for these irremovables, for the most part, adjudicated the presidency in perpetuity and even the ownership of the lodge: they saw simple Masters create other Masters and deliver lodge constitutions, fabricate titles, antedate charters, etc.

They made a lively display to the G.M., who was disposed to give the unfit financier a more worthy successor, when an obliging agent of the *secret affairs* of the prince, the dance instructor *Lacorne*, succeeding in snatching from the heedless head a title which, under the denomination of *Particular Substitute of the G.M.*, rendered this schemer absolute master of the whole Masonic administration. This derisory nomination excites as much indignation as sorrow. The dealer in whip-cracking, defying all the murmurs, seized the reins of the administration, populated the G.L. with his creatures, and, with their support, this unworthy head of the association became powerful. All the men of good company, of honest morals, gave their demission or ceased to take part in the works.

If we add to these shameful disturbances those that gave rise to the people from the retinue of the English *pretender*, delivering to the first come, for a feeble sum, powers to hold lodge, and constituting by their authority *Mother Lodges* and *Chapters*, without having been authorized by any legal authority, one may get an idea of the state of Masonry in France in this era, and of which the present era still feels the pernicious influence that it has produced. We will speak on this again more amply while treating the high grades. Our aim, before that, is to initiate the reader into the facts, more or less Masonic, which have occurred in England, Scotland, and France, up to the establishment of the G.O., so that he may better understand the origin of the high grades and appreciate their value.

CHAPTER IV
Grand Lodge of France

1756. Masonry, beyond its deplorable dissensions, continues to show strong blows of destruction: it is invaded by strange and unworthy systems of rites and grades, the basis of which was falsehood or vengeance, and of unknown origin for the most part. The French infatuation for the novelty sometimes placed these charlatanesque productions in vogue, which had of Masonry only the form. In the hope of stopping this pernicious influence, the G.L., despite the state of stupor into which the administration of *Lacorne* had thrown it, solemnly abandoned of the title of *English G.L. of France*, in order to take and bear solely that of Grand Lodge of France.

This change of title added nothing to the power of the G.L., nor did it bring any amelioration to the critical situation of Masonry. The independence and schemings of the turbulent Masons (*Lacorne coterie and others*) continue. They create lodge Masters at Paris and in the provinces; they founded *Chapters*, *Councils*, and *Tribunals*, which, for their part, also established lodges and chapters, diverse and confused creations, the history of which it is impossible to trace, nor even to give the nomenclature, since no regular register was yet kept in these various associations, and since the G.L. itself did not draft precise minutes of its assemblies.

1758. There was established, at Paris, a *Council of Emperors of the East and West, Sovereign Prince Masons, substitutes General of the Royal Art, Grand Surveillants and Officers of the Grand and Sovereign Lodge of Saint-John of Jerusalem* (at what Orient?). This comical introduction which, under a usurped veil, destroyed Masonic equality, one of the bases of the institution, would have had to be scoffed at and rejected with scorn. Vanity and the love of decorations judged it otherwise: there were multitudes to obtain the twenty-five *grades* of which was composed the pretended instruction of the new régime.

Up to here, Masonry, *and that is the true one*, was modestly and logically composed of three grades: *Apprentice, Companion, and Master*. But all that the passions have of the deadliest for humanity: ambition, pride, false knowledge, have introduced into its midst a Masonry of which the pompous names of its degrees do not succeed in disguising its falsity.

It is from Ramsay that originates the first *supermasonic* system, which mercilessly broke the unity of doctrine, falsified the Masonic dogma, and perverted the simplicity of the order. The poison inoculated itself among credulous and avid men; and, the impulse given, Masons of Lyon arrange the *Templar system*, natural product of the *Knight of the Temple* of Ramsay; *Stuart* instituted at Arras a *primordial* chapter; the Chevalier *de Bonneville* believed to diminish the evil by founding a chapter of high grades for the distinguished Masons; then comes the Council of Emperors of the East and West, Sovereign Prince Masons, with its twenty-five degrees, for which were infatuated Masons who had attained to the grade of Master, and who were blind enough to abase themselves in recognition of twenty-two classes of *superiors* who knew no more than they. The century will have scarcely passed away that there will appear empirics who, being aware that the Masonic breed, just as the other part of the human race in general, is incapable of profiting from the lessons of the past, imagine themselves, with the help of a great falsehood, adding to these twenty-five degrees new elements of discord *classified in eight grades*, in order to bring the nomenclature thereof to thirty-three.

Ten years later, foreign speculators will arrive with a vast rack whose compartments, for the most part, are void, but whose labeling is raised to the round number of 90 - Will this be all? No:

A fool always finds one more fool who imitates him.

Indeed, *fecund inventors* will find it very opportune, in an age when the man who thinks has not a minute to lose, when electricity, in enjambments of a hundred leagues per second, is become the messenger of ideas, the swiftness of the steam being found much too slow, to imagine, for the instruction of their adepts, a *scientific* ladder of ninety-two, then ninety-three rungs, and which will stop without doubt at the ninety-ninth. - But let us not anticipate, these supposed Masonic creations will reproduce in their place. We make, at this moment, only a reflection: If these strange aberrations had existed in the time of Erasmus, we doubt that he would have dared to make the *Eulogy of Folly*.

1760. A lodge founded by the Comte *de Beurnonville*, and which was composed of the most notable persons of the capital and the premier lords of the court, was preserved from the mania of the new grades. Its sessions took place at the Nouvelle-France, in the north of Paris.

1761. This year, Masonic disorder is at its peak at Paris and in the provinces, where patents and charters are delivered by three constituting powers, seated in the capital, namely: the G.L., the Lacorne faction, and the Council of Emperors.

1762. The G.M., satisfying the complaints brought against the Lacorne administration, discharges him of his functions as *Particular Substitute* and names to replace him, in the quality of Substitute General, the brother *Chaillou de Joinville*. This choice is generally approved; the parties which formed the two G.L.'s are brought together, a reconciliation is operated. The G.L. of France announces, by a circular, this happy event to all the lodges of the capital and the provinces. The two bodies assemble on June 24 to no longer form but one sole Grand Lodge. The reorganization of the works gives place to new regulations, and constitutions are delivered, under its authority, for the union and regularity of the works.

Humiliated, but ever audacious, *Lacorne* revived the zeal of his partisans. Their turbulence is such that the G.L. is forced to banish them from its midst.

The G.L. of France pursued with much calm and dignity its honorable career; but the Lacorne faction did not remain idle. A lively and daily struggle is established and lasts years.

1763. The G.L. is troubled in its works by the Chapter of *Clermont* and by the chapters and councils which, in spite of its authority and its rights, continue to deliver constitutions at Paris in the provinces. This. rivalry harmed the institution and favored the introduction, into the lodges, of all sorts of rites, grades, and systems contrary to the original aim of the order.

1765, June 2. The members of the old G.L., who had been forced to admit those of the Lacorne faction, saw them with pain sitting among them, as much with regard to their civil state, in general not very honorable, as with regard to their ignorance in the administration of the lodges: they had resolved to expel them. The period of the election occurred on this day, none of them were elected; they are incensed at this proceeding, which was a mistake, for some of them were worthy, and *they would be avenged thereof*; from this, the end of the G.L. could be predicted.

June 24. Celebration of the feast of the Order and installation of the officers. No members of the Lacorne faction assisted there: all withdrew from the G.L., against which they had printed and distributed injurious libels, while protesting strongly against the recent elections.

1766, April 5. The G.L., without examining whether the wrongs are not on its part, *banished* from its works and from the Masonic association the authors and distributors of the libels directed against it and in which they protested-against the elections of 1765. The following May 14, it formulated a new decree against the *banished* brethren.

August 14. Offended, on all sides, by the administrative and constitutive operations of the chapters, councils, and colleges of the high grades, the G.L. issues a decree which *suppresses* all their constitutions, forbids the lodges from paying regard thereto and from recognizing them, under pain of being declared irregular and stricken from the rolls. - How could they expect the high-grade brothers, who without doubt directed their workshops, to consent to *degrade themselves*? It takes very little to know Masonic pride, that is to say the incorrigible human pride. It is necessary, from the outset, to oppose the establishment of these false Masonries, or, later, to force them to enter into the common center in order to direct and administer them. We see that the G.L. hastened to its ruin.

This decree, which suppressed likewise the provincial G.L.'s, excites new divisions in the French lodges. The councils of the high grades persist and continue to constitute and to address circulars and disturbing instructions.

These high workshops had all the more success, as their members had succeeded in establishing as a rule that the privilege of the capitularies or constitutions in the superior degrees belonged to them to the exclusion of the G.L. Despite the evidence of this abusive act of usurpation of power, a number of Masons submitted to this tacit convention and rendered the G.L. impotent in its action, by reducing it to a secondary existence, presage of its end.

1766, October 2. They challenge, in the G.L., the productiveness of the decree of August 14 against the chapters and councils of the high grades, and, demonstrating the necessity of the reunion of these bodies into the center of French Masonry, they propose to divide the G.L. into three chambers, one of which would have to do with the symbolic degrees; the second, the high grades up to écossisme, and the third, other superior grades.

The request is unfortunately rejected: the G.L. refuses to admit the chapters of the high grades to sit within its midst; this capital mistake will be fatal for it, for the union will take place with the dissidents. Indeed, this rejection, joined with the decree of August 14, did not suit the vanity of a multitude of Masons who then, as yet today, saw Masonry in the titles, in the ornaments, and in the pompous ceremonies, rather than seeing it in the principles and in its dogma. These recalcitrants would no longer stop their useless protestations, they would soon break the stubbornness which was an obstacle, by throwing disorder and impotence into the heart of the G.L.

1766, February 4. The G.L. continues to undergo tribulations: assembled to celebrate the feast of the Order, the *banished* brothers presented themselves in great number and threw trouble into the session, where they penetrate despite the guardians. They demand imperiously to take part in the solemnity. Upon a positive refusal, they gave themselves over to violence; the paths indeed are soon reciprocal; the scandal is complete.

The next day, the civil authority gives orders to the G.L., who obey, to cease its assemblies, which were not resumed until 1771. The legal exercise of the Masonic authority is thus found long suspended (*four years*).

CHAPTER V
Suspension of the works of the Grand Lodge

The *banished* brethren, unknown to the authority, although provocateurs and responsible for the scandal, are not included, or do not regard themselves as such, in the measure, and assemble clandestinely in a locale, in the outskirts of Saint-Antoine, in order to abuse a usurped power.

1770, February 28. The *banished* brothers continuing actively their clandestine works, the members of the G.L. are disturbed thereby. They made a useless proceeding with the lieutenant of police, to obtain the authorization to resume their assemblies, suspended since 1767. However, a general session is convoked for this day, but the pusillanimity of the majority of the members prevent it from taking place; some old brothers went there, but finding only a small number, they retired. The sleep of the G.L. was prolonged to the profit of its adversaries, for which all the means of success were good.

1771, June 15. Death of the G.M., the Prince *de Clermont*[16]. This event is going to put an end to the apathy of the G.L. It gathered. But its assemblies were passed in projects of reorganization and useless discussions. It saw only itself, and, by a culpable inertia, when it was necessary to act in the general interest of the Order, it left to the dissidents, better inspired, the care of rendering real services to the common cause.

June 16. From the day after this demise, the banished brothers, to whom had been, little by little, gathered, in great enough number, distinguished Masons, tired of the inaction of the G.L., and with the cooperation of the chapter and council heads who, having to avenge themselves of the decrees issued against them, aimed to be recognized and to be an integral part of a constituting body. After reconciling, they find access to the Duc *de Luxembourg*, a Mason full of urbanity, and solicit his support, in order to obtain from the Duc *de Chartres* his acceptance for the nomination that they desired to make of S.A.S. to the Grand Mastership of the Order in France. The request is received. In this interview, the banished brothers rendered themselves powerful with the Duc de Luxembourg. They adroitly demonstrated to him that it was in the interest of the Order that the Duc de Chartres reunite the two masterships, in order to concentrate all the Masonic operations under one sole authority. The Duc yielded to these reasons: the acceptance was drawn up in this sense.

June 21. The banished brothers, bearers of the promise of acceptance of the Grand Mastership by the Duc de Chartres, presented themselves to the G.L., gathered in general assembly, and set as condition of the renewal of this acceptance the repeal of the decrees of April 5, and May 14, 1776, which have them stricken from banishment, and the revision of all the operations made during their absence. These conditions are accepted.

June 24. The G.L., gathered in general assembly, proceeds with the election of the G.M., and the Duc de Chartres is named, unanimously, *G.M. of French Masonry and Sovereign Grand Master of all Scottish Councils, Chapters, and Lodges in France*. This prince thus succeeds his uncle, and the union of the two Grand Masterships operated without need of sanction the reunion of the two bodies.

July 26 and August 9. The brethren *pardoned by amnesty* having signaled abuses, thefts, and extortions committed in the administration of the G.L., request the nomination of a commission of inquiry, charged with presenting a plan, in order to remedy the disorders which, afflict French Masonry. The G.L. names eight commissioners to whom it gives full power on this subject, and charges them to make a report.

August 14. For the regularity of the works of the lodges, regulations are published under this title: *Statutes and regulations of the very respect. G.L. of France, as much for its government as for that of the regular lodges concerning their relations with it, decreed by deliberation of the said G.L., on August 14, 1771, to be executed and observed starting from the said day* (in-8vo of 55 pages).

September 10. For a long time, constitutions had been delivered by Masons of all parties to a multitude of lodges in France; others had been drawn up by the banished brothers; and others by Chaillou de Joinville, from la Chaussée (see his *justificative memoire*), etc. in the name of the G.L., during the suspension of its works. It passes a decree bearing that all the lodges of France will be held to having their constitutions renewed, and that to this end, all those existing will have its secretariate examined by six commissioners, in order to endorse them and set the precedence of the lodges.

October 17. Circular of the G.L., announcing the election of the Duc *Chartres* to the dignity of G.M. and his acceptance. Not foreseeing the events, it notified the lodges that the installation of the G.M. was to take place at the end of the following November (1771) (it did not take place until November 28, 1773, *but by another body*), and it invited them to assist, by deputies, in this solemnity. It gave notice at the same time of the project that it was to write, the *General History of the Masonic order in France*, and requested information from their administrators. (*This work has not been made.*)

December 17. Creation of the twenty-two *Provincial Grand Inspectors*, charged with visiting all the lodges of the kingdom, to maintain there the execution of the regulations, to verify the rolls, with the charge of keeping written records of their operations, in order to give an account to the G.L. in the assemblies of quarterly communication. The duration of these functions is set at 3 years.

1772. This year will be memorable in the Masonic annals of France.

The state of inertia in which the G.L. of France, whether by timidity, or by lack of agreement and uniformity among the members become less numerous, had let the Masonic works languish for too long, and ended by discontenting, discouraging, and disquieting the sane and numerous parts of the French Masons, who aspired to a better state of things, capable of delivering the institution from an ever-growing anarchy. Already, it became evident that this apathy of the G.L. and the vexations which rend it are soon going to give birth to a new important era in Freemasonry.

January. The eight commissioners name on July 26, with powers to review the operations of the G.L., held conferences connected with a numerous party that openly protected the Grand Administrator General, the Duc de Luxembourg; it is a question less of satisfying the vow of the rather extensive mandate of the G.L., than of secretly advising on the means of annihilating its power. The conspiracy begins.

June 18. The Administrator General makes, in the session of this day, presided by him, the deposit of two important pieces; the one, from April 5, is the acceptance of the Grand Mastership by the Duc de Chartres; the other, from May 1, is relative to the powers with which the Duc de Luxembourg was invested by the last G.M., deceased, and by virtue of which he confers the initiation to the new G.M.

Word for word copy of the acceptance: "The year of the great light 1772, 3rd day of the moon of Jiar, 5th day of the 2nd month of the Masonic year 5772, and of the birth of the Messiah, 5th day of April 1772, by virtue of the proclamation made in Grand Lodge, assemble on the 24th day of the 4th month of the Masonic year 5771, of the very high, very puissant, and very excellent prince, S.A.S. *Louis-Philippe-Joseph d'Orleans*, Duc *de Chartres*, prince of the blood, for GRAND MASTER of all regular lodges of France and that of the Sovereign Council of Emperors of the East and West, sublime Scottish Mother Lodge on the 26th of the moon of Elul, 1771, for Sovereign G.M. of all the Scottish Councils, Chapters, and Lodges of the Grand Globe of France, offices that the said A.S. has been willing to accept for the love of the Royal Art, and finally to concentrate all the Masonic operations under one sole authority. In testimony whereof, the said A.S. has signed the official proclamation of acceptance. *Signed*: Louis-Philippe-Joseph d'Orleans."

Word for word copy of the no less curious official proclamation of the Duc de Luxembourg:

"We, Anne-Charles-Sigismond *de Montmorency-Luxembourg*, Duc *de Luxembourg* and Châtillon-sur-Loire, peer and first Christian Baron of France, brigadier of the armies of the King, etc.

"Vested by the late S.A.S. the very respected and very illustrious brother Comte *de Clermont*, G.M. of all the regular lodges of France, with the entire fullness of his power; not only to rule and administer the Order, but for the most brilliant function, that of initiating into our mysteries the very respectable and very illustrious brother *Louis-Phillippe d'Orleans*, Duc *de Chartres*, called then by the desires of the whole of Masonry to the supreme government.

"We certify to have received, in our quality of Administrator General, the acceptance by writing of the prince; thus, we mandate to the G.L. of France to notify all the regular lodges thereof, in order to participate in this grand event, and to unite with us in what will be for the glory and good of the Order.

"Given at our Orient, the year of the moon 1772 and of the common era May 1, 1772, affixed with the seal of our arms and countersigned by one of our secretaries.

"*Signed*: Montmorency-Luxembourg. - By my Lord, *signed*: d'Olessen."

The conspiracy continues: the amnestied brothers, driven either by vengeance or by a spirit of dissidence which is often perpetuated within the fractions of a numerous body, whose composition ceases to be homogenous, followed carefully the progress of the revolutions begun, which they encouraged with all their efforts. On their side, the eight commissioners to whom were joined Lodge Masters, deputies, the Council of Emperors of the East and West, as well as the Council of the Knights of the East, continue their secret conventicles. The sessions are held at the Hôtel de Chaulnes sur les Boulevarts. *Lalande* says that they were *quite numerous and well composed*, (*Memoire historique sur la Maçonnerie*). In these conferences, they lose sight, from the outset, of the special objective of the gatherings and the limits of the mandate issued by the G.L.: the idea of a general reorganization, openly propagated by the Duc de Luxembourg, seduced all the minds; a radical and imminent change appeared inevitable.

The G.L. still has a great deal of respect, as a Masonic body, for the antiquity of its origin; but its power diminishing each day in equal proportion to the abuses that it allows to be introduced or that it no longer prevents, makes a new name and a new organ indispensably necessary for controlling the *chaos*. One will not, therefore, be astonished to see this body, before its complete failure, be eclipsed, then extinguished before a new, young, vigorous authority, which will draw its origin and its strength from the very midst of the G.L., whose efforts to return to life will be useless.

Among the Lodge Masters and deputies, there are found, in the final conferences, those who object in favor of the established principles. These honorable brothers do not adopt the projects which would over-throw the power of the G.L.; they are expelled. Soon the agitation becomes extreme; grave accusations of extortion, embezzlement, theft, and abuse of power, were brought against the most influential members of the old G.L. and its dignitary officers; and under the pretext, and perhaps with good intention, of extirpating from the abuses and regenerating the administration of the Order, they truly conspired the ruin of the oldest French Masonic body. "They prepared," says *Lalande*, "new statutes; they remedied the abuses by rendering above all the Lodges Masters removable, and electable by the majority of votes." - This was an immense good: the perpetual Mastership of the lodges was an imminent danger for the Order, and the cause of a multitude of abuses.

It was born from the strange defection of the Comte de Clermont, G.M. (see 1744). It was necessary to have it cease; but this useful change could have been introduced without concussion. Reason alone would have carried it out little by little; *but the stubborn resistance to all change does not permit such action.*

If the eight commissioners, who took part in all these operations, had faithfully fulfilled the duties that their mandate dictated, they would have informed the G.L. and would have called on it to cooperate, as administrative body, with the ameliorations that it had no interest to repel. They had no failure to fear, having the support of an immense majority, at the head of which figured the Administrator General. But these simple representatives of the first Masonic body believed themselves omnipotent. The G.L. did not recall any acting agents who, *with its very knowledge*, exceeded its orders, and it was soon punished thereby. In administration as in politics, steadfastness is necessary; the power which binds is not long to fall. Truly, the G.L., we have demonstrated, was not in possession of the fullness of action, for want of agreement among its members, the greater part of which labored and applauded at the fall of its power, preliminaries accustomed to every change of government. The position was critical, the consequences were inevitable.

1772, December 24. The eight commissioners, who, without knowing it, were the agents of more enlightened Masons, act, without convoking, and with cause, those whose powers they hold, to submit to them the results of their work; and this *octovirate*[17], reunited with the numerous brothers from the various parties who assisted in the conventicles, after a preparatory exposé and being supported by the general suffrage, DECLARE solemnly, that the *old G.L. of France has ceased to exist*, that it is replaced by a new *National Grand Lodge*, which will make an integral part of a new body which will administer the Order, under the title of the GRAND ORIENT OF FRANCE.

Thus was carried out, without blow, but not without regrets and protestations, that revolution in which had been implicated, in very great part, the G.L.'s own members, to whom those who did not approve this change had remained perhaps too indifferent. But they were, in general, so fatigued by the dissensions and abuses which had stigmatized the final years of this Masonic era, that the lodges of the correspondence, in the hope, certainly without doubt, of a better future, applauded, nearly unanimously, the new order of things.

1773, May 24. The brother *Chaillou de Joinville*, old Substitute General of the G.M. the Comte de Clermont, abandons the party of the G.L., and requests of the G.O. letters of *Honorary Substitute*; after having made known, through the brother *Savalette de Langes*, that he approved of all that had been done. This event adds further to the embarrassment of the G.L., who names, in place of this turncoat, the Prince *de Rohan*.

August 30. The G.L. fights and resists, but too late, without energy and without uniformity. The alliance reduced and ever disunited is already more than half broken. The sole act of strength to which it is determined, and which was sterile, is to assemble and declare, on this day, the new body which has been formed near it, at Paris, under the title of National G.L., illegal, surreptitious, and irregular. (see *its circular.*) It strikes with disqualification all the Lodge Masters who assist or would assist in its works, unless they retract, within a week, the errors into which they have fallen, at the instigation of some *disturbed and turbulent spirits*. - Vain attempt by an expiring power. The G.L. was no more successful in its subsequent efforts to re-establish its Sovereignty. (see *its historical notice.*) A power which proclaims its impotence becomes ridiculous and falls.

CHAPTER VI
Grand Orient of France

Regeneration and Reorganization of Masonry in France

We have seen, in the summary of the works of the G.L. of France, how they have arrived at having to seek a means of saving Freemasonry, compromised by the inertia of that assembly. Its influence diminished each year, due to its mistake of having overseen the ostensible introduction, in its jurisdiction, of monstrous systems, whose pompous balderdash awed the ambitious spirit of the numerous and less enlightened Masons, which invaded, little by little, its poorly ruled and poorly defended domain, and ended up driving out the directing power.

If the eight commissioners who, in appearance, seem to have failed in their duty, for not having informed the G.L. of the *transformation* considered, have no longer cooperated or at least assisted in the gatherings, it is without doubt that, in agreement with the Administrator General, and knowing the systematic resistance of the stubborn leaders of this debilitated body, they foresaw the uselessness and danger of their course, the result of which could have been a scandal, or a delay fatal to the general interests: it was a question of saving the institution and not of humoring the self-love of headstrong incapables. They have had reason, therefore, to act in this way, and the success obtained so peacefully absolves them.

Finally, on December 24, 1772, is solemnly proclaimed the erection of the GRAND ORIENT OF FRANCE, a new power entirely unconnected with the mistakes of the past; a strong power of a near unanimity, or rather of the unanimity of all the Masons who, fatigued by continual decapitations, aspire to a better future; legitimate power as much as all those which have, with good reason, ruled over the men, since the general assent which has saluted its ingenious and true title, that other foreign Masonic powers have imitated since, joined by the support of the Grand Administrator General of the Order, and later that of the G.M.[18].

What more beautiful justification of its origin than the adoption of the eminently Masonic principles proclaimed, for the first time, by this body in the Masonic universe!

The G.O., composed of Grand Officers, of elected Venerables of all the lodges or their deputies, is a sort of *National Diet*, where all the interests may have themselves heard, and all the reeds obtain satisfaction. It leaves the choice of officers to the *annual* election of the brethren, and allows the lodges of the provinces, like those of Paris, to cooperate with the administration and general legislation of the association; that is to say that renouncing the *oligarchy* of the Grand Lodge, and basing the government of the Order upon the *representative system*, so as to serve as model to the political governments, it confides this government to the *representatives* of the workshops. Its constitution, entirely liberal, suppresses the irrevocability of the Venerables who, henceforth, cannot fulfill the same functions for more than three consecutive years. It thus annihilated any usurpations which were decorated by the title of *acquired rights*. The G.O. was not unaware that by attacking, in their pride and perhaps in their means of existence, irremovable Venerables, a good number of whom trafficked in Masonry and considered the lodges of which they were the heads as their property, they would revolted against the new statutes, which indeed occurred. It preferred to sacrifice to justice its nascent influence, which it could, by a good administration, recover later; we are grateful for it.

1773, March 5. First assembly of the G.O. in its *National G.L.* The gatherings succeeded one another nearly without interruption until June 24[19]. They adopt the new constitution of the Order, under the title of *Statutes of the Royal Order of Freemasonry in France.* The composition of the G.O. is brought to 77 members, *namely*:

3 honorary Grand Officers,
15 honorary Officers,
45 active Officers,
7 Venerables acting in the lodges of Paris,
7 Deputies from the provincial lodges.

This body is divided into three chambers: a chamber *of administration*, a chamber *of Paris*, and a chamber *of the provinces*. With them is a *lodge of counsel* to deal with the appeals of the decisions of these three chambers.

March 8. The nomination, made by the old G.L., of the Duc *de Chartres* for G.M., is confirmed, as well as that of the Duc de Luxembourg for Administrator General. They continue to occupy themselves, along with the Masters of the lodges of Paris and those of the provinces who are found there, with the general good of the institutions. The decisions, made in the assembly which had proclaimed the G.O., are sanctioned. The choice of the fifteen honorary Officers and the nomination of the ordinary Officers are deferred to the Duc de Luxembourg, who designates, for the honorific posts, brothers invested with grand names and eminent places, in order to gain the benevolence of the government and to more solidly establish the operations of the G.O.

March 9. They proclaim the *National Grand Lodge of France* as the sole and unique tribunal uniting the fullness of the powers of the Order.

June 24. The organization of the G.O. having concluded and its statutes decreed, the Duc de Luxembourg assembles the members thereof, in the number of 81, and gives them a brilliant feast, at the Vauxhall de Torré, rue de Rondy; this was the first feast of the Order, celebrated by the G.O.

June 26. The code of new Masonic laws is definitively decreed by the G.O., which ordered the printing thereof and sent it to the lodges with a circular of this day.

These statutes, printed in-4to (35 pages), are the first that the G.O. had decreed. They comprise four chapters, the latter three of which are of little importance: they treat on the formalities to follow for the elections of officers, prerogatives of the G.M., assemblies of the G.O. and its chambers, and the organization of the bureaus, of the correspondence, and of the administration. As to the first chapter, it presents more of interest, for it contains the entire new constitution, under the title of *Statutes of the Royal order of Freemasonry in France*. It says there:

"The body of the Royal Order of Freemasonry, under the distinctive title of *Masonic Body of France*, shall be composed of the *regular Masons* alone recognized as such by the G.O.[20], which shall recognize, henceforth, as *regular Masons*, only the members of regular lodges alone, and as *regular lodges*, only those which will be provided with constitutions granted or renewed by it, and it alone will have the right to deliver them[21].

It shall recognize henceforth, as *Lodge Venerable*, only the Master raised to this dignity by the free choice of the members of his lodge. The Masonic body in France shall be represented at the G.O. by all the active Venerables or deputies of the lodges. The G.O. shall be composed of the *National Grand Lodge* and all the active Venerables or deputies of the lodges of both Paris and the provinces, which would be able to assist in its assemblies. Its seat is invariably fixed at the Orient of Paris. It alone has the right of legislation in the Order."

Followed by the composition of the National G.L., the lodge of counsel, and that of the three chambers by which the Order is governed, as well as their prerogatives, etc., etc.

Except for general facts or those relating to the subject that we are treating, we shall speak no further of the operations of the old G.L., whose existence was extinguished with this century, nor of those of the G.O. They are found detailed in the notices from where this summary is extracted, and which concerns these two bodies, whose active rivalry, which will last twenty-seven years, was ended in 1799 by an honorable fusion into the G.O. of France (see the *Fastes initiatiques*).

Before coming to the institution of the associations and of the *supermasonic* systems and grades, let us briefly cast a retrospective eye on Masonry (*Freemasonry*) in England and Scotland.

CHAPTER VII
Freemasonry in England

From the year 1728, the Scot *Ramsay* had sought to have adopted, at London, his new Masonry, composed thus of three grades: *Écossais, Novice*, and *Knight of the Temple*. He made it Jesuitically descend from the crusades; attributed its invention to Godefroy de Bouillon, and claimed that the Lodge of *Saint Andrew*, at Edinburgh, was the headquarters of the true Order of Freemasons, whom he claimed were descendants of the knights of the crusades. His request and his doctrine were rejected. But this trickery was exploited in France and Germany, where it gave birth to that mass of misshapen and often monstrous conceptions, decorated by the name of *Scottish grades*, of which *écossisme* is found partly composed. How Masonic is this origin! Well, it is because Ramsay was born in Scotland, that nearly all the false grades invented since take the name of *Scottish*, and that is why they have remained unknown in Scotland.

1732. The Confraternity of York, which begins to be purified, makes to its regulations, drawn up by *operative masons*, some changes analogous to the new aims of Freemasonry.

1734. The G.L. of London constitutes lodges in Lancashire, at Durham, and in Northumberland. These three workshops were found in the district of the Confraternity of York. This latter, wounded by this proceeding, separates its interests from those of the G.L. of London which, strong by its authority and its supremacy in the new philosophical direction given to the institution, then has inserted into the book of constitutions of Anderson (then at *press*) this paragraph:

"The foreign lodges, under the patronage of the G.L. of England, such as those of the city of York, of Scotland, Ireland, France, and Italy, affect a blameworthy independence and refuse to recognize the jurisdiction of the G.M. of England. Yet, all hold their constitutions, laws, and regulations, from the brethren of Great Britain, who have deemed to reward their zeal by confiding in them the secret of the Confraternity. These ingrates forget that the splendor of which they enjoy come to them only from England, etc."

1738, April 27. The G.L. names provincial deputies with power to establish workshops in cities of the jurisdiction of York. This encroachment renews the divisions between the lodges of the south and the north of England. All correspondence is interrupted. The York Lodge, still ruled by builder-masons, does not see that, in this new regime, it is only what the G.L. of London wills it to be; and that before all, it ought to be submissive and has no right to constitute. It still believes itself Metropolitan G.L. Yes, of the *brotherhood of operative masons*, but not of the institution of the Freemasons; from here comes its error and the mistake of its adherents.

A certain number of them, joined with the discontented brothers (*there will always be those*), separate themselves from the regular workshops and form, in London, assemblies contrary to the laws of the G.L. In order to withdraw from its authority, they claim to fall in under the banner of the G.L. of York; that is to say that they remain or become again members of the brotherhood of *builder masons*, entirely foreign to the Freemasons.

This discord could only harm the Masonic progress, because the dissidents, in the blindness of passion, will join with the *narrow* and routine brothers who reproached the G.L. of England for having introduced *innovations* (improvements), for having *altered* (modified) the rituals, and for having *suppressed* antiquated ceremonies, as if the practice of building had an identical relation with that of morals and philosophy. However, the brother I. Ward, since Earl of Udley, succeeded in reconciling, at least momentarily, the two parties.

1739. The reconciliation, carried out the previous year, is broken, the disputes emerge again, the peaceful brothers withdraw, threats of scission manifest themselves, it becomes urgent to put an end to these debates: the question is sent before the general assembly.

They establish there, in principle, that the G.L., *alone*, has the right to constitute Masonic societies[22] in England, to govern them, and that its G.M. is to be considered as the universal G.M. of all the lodges of Europe. A circular is addressed, in this sense, to all the regular lodges, in order to invite them to cease all correspondence with the dissidents and their lodges.

The seceders, wishing to flee an authority that decided to maintain its decision with steadfastness, and recognizing that any protestation would be useless, attempted a subterfuge whose success shows that the philosophical progress that the G.L. had caused Masonry to make had not educated anyone; such power has routine, even over the spirit of Masons!

The recalcitrants, restoring the *alterations* of the old rituals and the substitution of new customs for the old by the G.L. of England, publish against it a writing in which, after having complained about the vexations that had been exercised against the *brethren* (operative builders), whose sole aim was to uphold the laws and customs of *free-masonry*, in the purity of the ancient (*operative*) guild, they declare that they are separate from those *modern Masons* (workers of intelligence), in order to form a new guild of *ancient Masons* (material workers) under the constitution of York, established, as we have seen for the *operative builders*.

A part of the regular lodges of London, seduced by this circular, separate themselves from the G.L., join themselves to the malcontents, and they found in the capital a *second rival G.L.*, whose existence, *intramural*, remained in a sort of obscurity, until December 27, 1813, period of its fusion into the first G.L. - However, the G.L. of Scotland and that of Ireland, the majority of whose members do not understand the transformation, declare themselves for the dissident G.L. and do not resume their correspondence with the first, after a treaty of union, the G.L. of Scotland in 1806, and that of Ireland in 1808.

These unfortunate divisions, instigated by a guild antipathetic then to the true Masonry, did not stop the progressive march of the G.L. of England, unique head, *then*, of the Masonic Order in the world. It constituted lodges in India, in America, and in the various States of Europe[23].

A member of the operative guild who, in 1748, was admitted, by curiosity, *he says*, to the works of the G.L., where he appears to have learned nothing, has published, in 1778, a pamphlet against it, having as its title: *Epistle addressed to the members of the fraternity* (its ancient *brethren*) on the difference which exists between the ancient and modern Masonry in England.

But this difference may only be established by comparing the two associations, which have no relation but in name, borrowed to serve as a veil for the new institution, or rather *renewed* from antiquity. That is why, in his writing, the author *Laurence Dermotte*, whose intelligence could not be elevated to comprehend the symbolism of the steps of the three grades that he ridicules, has been able to say nothing good nor true. He addresses nine question which he resolves in blindness; here are two of them:

4th question: May a modern Mason communicate, with all confidence, all his secrets to an ancient (*operative*) Mason? He answers: *Yes*.

5th question: May an ancient Mason, with the same confidence and without any other formality, communicate all his secrets to a modern Mason? He answers: *No*; "for," he says, "although science be ever necessary to comprehend what concerns an art, an art may thus sometimes be exercised without any idea of the science."

We see that it is a question here only of the material art of building, whose secrets, long since become common knowledge, are quite useless to the *Freemason* for whom the art of building is not a profession[24].

He adds that the ancient Masons (*free-workers*) understand each other everywhere and will be misunderstood by modern Masons: this is quite possible and quite immaterial to the latter who also have their universal language, but who do not have and cannot have any relation with them. On the other hand, do the operative Masons comprehend the language of the philosopher Masons treating on the high sciences or on the ancient mysteries whence they derive? We leave these workers to geometrize and to improve themselves in their honorable guilds, whose aim is to furnish habitations to the rich, who can remunerate them; and we leave the Freemasons to labor with zeal and free of charge, in the lodges, at the perfecting and the happiness of humanity, by enlightening and improving men, rich or poor, weak or powerful. The one is a material and *compulsory* profession, since every man must have a profession in order to live. The other is the effect of an often-onerous devotion and a voluntary abnegation. Both are honorable, but not comparable: who would seriously dare to put into comparison the plan where would be found traced the magnificent Church of Saint Paul and the plan where would be found described the immortal work of Milton, two masterpieces, without doubt, but which it would be folly to compare?

What prevented the G.L. of England from establishing, little by little, this line of demarcation? It was its duty. By failing therein, it has thrown upon Freemasonry, for ages, a confusion which divides it still, and which was elucidated only in France: it should, from the outset, have abjured the trivial denomination (a *falsehood* for its members) of *freemason* and adopted (if national pride had permitted it) the French name of *franc-maçon*, which has nothing in common with the other but the ending. Then, the division would become clear and all quarrels cease.

Do they believe, we repeat, that Freemasonry [Francmaçonnerie] would have succeeded in Paris and taken root in France, if the French had had to take the vulgar title of maçon-libre, which was carried, from the time of Charlemagne and Louis-le-Débonnaire, by the operative builders, before those of Great Britain? For *freemasonry* [maçonnerie-libre] is passed from France to England, and Francmaçonnerie is passed from England into France; but the title of Francmaçon was adopted, because it indicated an immense difference between the works of these two associations and their material. Indeed:

"The operative masons have been able to imagine a *Tower of Babel*, that an ambitious madman wished to raise unto the heavens, in order to take refuge against a new flood, but whose material impotence threw *confusion* and *dispersion* among the workers. - The wise creators of our institution have raised an edifice of a *higher* conception, since it attaches man to Divinity by the purity of his morals, the wisdom of his dogmas, and his love of humanity, to turn back that deluge of evils which threaten it. And, to the inverse of the confusion in language, it presents a universal language, which re-connects all men, and makes of them but one sole union, even when they are *dispersed*. - Whence comes this difference?

It is that the builder-masons make use of perishable materials, which the Freemasons do not use, whose materials are these:

"The first triangular stone of their symbolic monument is *God, Virtue, Charity*. These workers of intelligence, animated by the spirit of *zeal, constancy*, and *regularity*, labor under three masters: *Fraternity, Tolerance, Equality*; they have for guides, *reason, truth, steadfastness*, and for doctrine that of Zoroaster, their founder, and that of Confucius.

"The *Companions* draw their triangular stones from the catacombs of *Memphis, Eleusis*, and *Athens*, and render homage to the benefactors of humanity, to Triptoleme teaching agriculture, and to *Thales* and *Pythagoras*, teaching wisdom. - Foreign companions have, later, extracted their stones from the caves of *Upsala, Heredom*, and *Kilwinning*.

"The *Masters* sum up the works of nature, classified in the three kingdoms: *mineral, vegetable, animal*, represented by the triangle, image of God, of which the three kingdoms are the manifestation. They know that time has for its measure the *past, present*, and *future*, and they preoccupy themselves thereof; that everything has a *beginning* (*birth*), a middle (*existence*), and an end (*death*); that man shows *soul, spirit*, and *body*, and who is endowed with three intellectual powers, *memory, understanding*, and *will*. All these ternary materials contribute to the erection of the great social edifice, which counts as many divisions as there are branches of instruction. *Physics* distinguishes bodies by *shape, density*, and *color*; with the prism, it splits up the light and finds the three primary colors, *yellow, red*, and *blue*; it admits three elements, *earth, fire*, and *air*; water being considered a condensed air. *Chemistry* analyzes the bodies, that it divides into three tangible principles: *earth, water*, and *salt*. Alchemy believes the universe to be animated by three chemical principles: *salt, sulphur, mercury*. *Medicine* observes in man the structure of the *solids*, the movement of the *fluids*, the *play* of the *passions*. The thinker has examined the three spiritual edifices, the *Veda*, the *Gospel*, the *Qur'an* which help him to compare religions with Masonry.

"It is thus that the *Master* philosopher, who has studied morals, the exact and secret sciences, religions, politics, the harmony of sounds and of the universe, raises his edifice unto the Empyrean, where, with the assistance of astronomy, he may travel like the geographer over the globe."

CHAPTER VIII
Freemasonry in Scotland

In Scotland, the lodge of *Kilwinning* complains, in 1744, that in the lists prepared by the G.L. of Edinburgh, it is shown only under the no. 2, whereas in the quality of most ancient and *Mother Lodge of Scotland*, it had, *it said*, rights to the first place. The G.L. concluded that *seeing as the lodge of Kilwinning has not produced any documentation which establishes its right of seniority, while on the contrary the Lodge of Saint Mary's Chapel has produced one which goes back to 1598, the latter has the right to be inscribed as the first.*

The Kilwinning Lodge was very offended by this decision. It had lost its documents, or rather it never had them; but they were not unaware that it was the oldest guild of Scotland. Then they had to inscribe it first, considering the public notoriety, or to refrain from including it in the list of the lodges, since, contrary to the later ones, it could not justify its origin through authentic documents. This circumstance, which could have led to troubles, did not, however, produce this effect.

We see clearly that the G.L. did not include its position nor its rights. Its composition, without doubt, did not allow it: it occupied the supreme power in the new institution. Now, what were the supposed lodges of the borough of Kilwinning, of Saint Mary's Chapel, and others which had been asleep (see *above*) in 1695, societies of *operative freemasons*, and re-awakened, with the same titles, several years after 1736, date of the introduction of Freemasonry into Scotland, under the authority of the G.L. of Edinburgh? It is evident that they had remained *foreign societies*, without any relation to Freemasonry. There was not, therefore, any other rank to observe, for their inscription upon the rolls, than that of the date of their admission into the new mysteries: the antiquity of an annulled body, because of its heterogeneity, could not carry any weight.

Let us continue the curious examination of the legend that has been made of the Kilwinning Lodge.

A long while after, this *Mother Lodge*, as it titles itself, transported its seat to Edinburgh, where it established itself under the denomination of ROYAL GRAND LODGE and of GRAND CHAPTER OF THE ORDER OF HEREDOM OF KILWINNING, abandoning the administration and the idea of the *three symbolic degrees* to the GRAND LODGE OF SAINT JOHN, also seated at Edinburgh, and reserving the *right* to confer the high grades and to constitute chapters[25].

This G.L. took the title of *Royal* or of the *Royal Order*, because formerly the kings of Scotland had, *it said*, presided over the guild of *operative masons*, from which the Scottish Masons believe to have descended; and because the King *Robert Bruce*, founder of the Order of the Garter, has protected this guild, of which he would have, *it says again*, taken, for himself and his successors, the title of *Patron* or G.M.

Since the reunion of Scotland, the kings of England are by right, *because of this*, G.M. of the Royal Order of Heredom (*on legend*).

The works of this G.L. are presided over by a deputy G.M., who takes the title of *governor*, under the characteristic name of *Wisdom*; manner of *incognito* introduced, in Scotland, by the Jesuits.

LET US CLARIFY AND SUMMARIZE. - Foreign builder-masons, who were refugees in Scotland, were employed to build, in 1150, the tower at the Abbey of Kilwinning, in the hamlet of this name. The memoires from this period say that their language was unknown to the inhabitants. This small guild constituted itself by itself. Others rose up who took their titles from a recognized general guild; that of Kilwinning, as being the first node, which had been formed, was given, by its own authority, the quality of MOTHER-LODGE, and delivered constitutions to operative societies. And because the kings of Scotland had protected this profession (*as all the others*) it added, *because of this*, to its title the denomination of ROYAL, which could, perhaps, be accorded to every Scottish guild, but not uniquely to one portion. The habit of usurping had become for it a right of possession. We know that its modern partisans write that *in 1314 this lodge was elevated to the rank of ROYAL GRAND LODGE OF HEREDOM or HERODOM* (they are not in agreement) *by Robert Bruce, King of Scotland, who founded on this occasion the order of this name* (Heredom or Herodom), *on behalf of the Freemasons* (they did not exist, *read* operative masons) *who had fought for him.* - The Lodge of Kilwinning has never been able to furnish authentic proof of this Scottish fable. The writers, so-called Freemasons, have for a long time made of Scotland a fertile *Gascony*, whose flag, stamped on the famous tower, fluttered over the mount *Heredom* or *Herodom*, invisible in Scotland.

What brought this lodge into the *new institution*, when after a forty-one-year sleep (since 1695) [26], it was convoked on November 30, 1736, at the general meeting at Edinburgh, to the end of organizing FREEMASONRY there, already active in England, France, and Ireland? Thirty-two guilds or lodges, answering this call, constituted the *G.L. Saint John of Edinburgh*, to which the Kilwinning Lodge refused, the following year, to submit to the required verification, so indispensable in such a case, its authentic documentation certifying the legal and regular existence of its claims. It did not possess any documentation: all was usurpation. Thus, did it base its refusal upon its intention to preserve its *supremacy* and its *independence.* Its supremacy? - Over what? since the operative guilds no longer existed. - Its independence? - Free to remain a guild of *operative masons*, but a *bastard* guild, that is to say without constitutive letters patent. In such a way that this supposed *Mother Lodge* brought, like the other societies, into the common nucleus, only the old documents relating to the art of building, and the formulary for the meetings and admissions. But it brought, less than the others, constitutions, proving thus that it had labored and was constituted illegally, irregularly, and that all its operations were to be regularized or nullified.

Then, much later, it came into the bosom of Freemasonry, regularly established everywhere and without it, to declare itself *Royal Grand Lodge* at Edinburgh, where it established itself and *Grand Chapter of the Order of H.-D.-M.* (with this orthography, there is no longer any ambiguity) of *Kilwinning*, others say *and of Kilwinning* (what has not been clear from the beginning remains ever cloudy). It abandons the *administration* and the *notion* of the three symbolic degrees to the G.L. of Saint John; but without these degrees, which are the whole of Masonry, of what is it G.L.? And in order to abandon them, it is necessary to have possessed them; from whom did it hold them? From its customary omnipotence, without any regular power having consecrated it.

But it has reserved the *right* to confer the high grades and to constitute chapters.

Here, the scene changes, but the tactic remains the same: it is no longer the small village of operative masons erecting itself into a *lodge*, then, by the same authority, declaring itself *Constituent Grand Lodge* and then *Royal* G.L.; but it arrives in the capital and constitutes itself there, ever by its own authority, *Metropolitan* and *Sovereign Power*, under the title of GRAND CHAPTER OF THE ORDER OF H.-R.-M. OF KILWINNING.

Ever curious, we will ask again from what regular chapter did it hold legal powers to erect itself into a Grand Chapter? We cast a glance upon all the supposed chapters which had then established themselves in the same manner, and we are persuaded that this was again of its own authority, but an authority which had grown and which, even in its eyes, has become very respectable. We will also ask, what were the grades that it professed, what was the aim of its doctrine? We have seen then, since 1649, they invented politico-*hiramite* grades, not professed in the lodges, but communicated secretly in the conventicles in favor of *Charles I*, decapitated. The rite of *Ramsay* in three degrees, rejected at London in 1728, was brought up to seven grades in 1736, era of the introduction of Freemasonry into Scotland. A multitude of supposed *high grades* had arisen nearly everywhere and principally in France. Did it make a choice among this *chaos*, the shame of their authors? Finally, its choice made, its nomenclature decreed, it intended to turn it to its advantage.

As regards its denomination of Royal Order of H.-R.-M., it attributes it to Robert Bruce, like, in our time, a famous rite, likewise *Scottish*, was attributed, in order to give currency to it, to *Frederick* the Great who, rightly, had the most profound disgust for the high grades.

We remark on the word *Heredom* that its use, almost political, could scarcely fit this chapter, for it appears certain, by the confidential letters of the period, that this word had been imagined only to serve as veil to the secret cabals established at the castle of Saint-Germain-en-Laye, by the partisans who had accompanied, at this residence, *Charles-Edward*. They corresponded mysteriously with their friends remaining in England, from 1740 to 1745 [27], on behalf of this pretender, who returned this last year into Scotland. Which would prove, indeed, that the word Heredom (signifying *hæredum*) served to designate the *castle of Saint-Germain*, where the prince lived.

Then, it is evident that Robert Bruce, King of Scotland, has not created, in 1314, the Royal Order of *Heredom* (or of the castle of Saint-Germain), since the name of Heredom was invented only in 1740 in order to veil the name of the place where the secret conventicles were held, under the *Masonic* forms and discretion. - We see here again, as elsewhere, that Scotland may often render points to the Garonne.

Let us continue the history of this Masonic body, never constituted, ever constituting.

It occupied the public Mason very little until 1785; however, on January 5, 1767, the G.L. of the Royal Order of Heredom of Kilwinning submitted its statutes to a revision, in order to place them in harmony with the spirit and progress of Masonry (*they were therefore not?*). On the following October 5, it decided that the number of its members, fixed at 112, would be increased indefinitely.

1785. The Royal G.L. emerged, little by little, from its long obscurity. Having renounced the symbolic works, that is to say the true Masonry, whose direction it had abandoned to the G.L. of Edinburgh, in order to stick to the collation of the *high grades*, that is to say to pretend Masonic fictions, it announces its sessions, which become more consistent. Human pride leads here, to receive these high grades, even unto members of the G.L. of Scotland, moreover (such empiricism has power!), unto Grand Masters, such as the Counts *de Leven* and *de Melville*, the Knight Adolphe *Oughton*, commander-in-chief of the army of Scotland; Lord *Westhalt* and the Knight William *Forbes*.

1786, May 1. This power established at Rovena a GRAND CHAPTER OF HEREDOM. The Br. Mathéus, merchant, is the provincial G.M. *for all of France*. - We have demonstrated how equivocal, illegal, the existence is of the Royal G.L., which holds its power only by its own will. How can it transmit what it lacks, the *authenticity*, the *regularity*, to the chapter that it founds at Rouen and that it arms with a fantastic power *over all of France*?

Guillaume *Masson* fulfilled then the functions of deputy G.M. governor, and *de Murdoch*, those of Grand Secretary.

They give this period as the date, *supposed*, of the foundational statutes of the Rite called *Ancient and Accepted Scottish*, designated under the pompous title of Grand Constitutions of 1786; it is still a fact to be clarified, so nebulous is all that appertains to the fictive word of *Heredom.*

On October 4 of this year, the Royal G.L. constituted, at Paris, a chapter of Heredom, in the name of Nicolas Chabouillé, counsel at parliament, on behalf of the members comprising the Chapter *du Choix*, established by him at Paris.

On the following December 11, it delivers an attestation declaring that the patent of a *Chapter of Rose-Croix*, brought to light by the doctor *Gerbier*, called *emanated from Edinburgh in 1721*, is a false title (this date proves it, see Grand Chapter General of France). It charged, previously, on October 14, its Secretary General, the Br. *Murdoch*, with enlightening on this subject the Br. *Matheus*; here is an extract from his letter:

"*The Royal G.L. of H.-D.-M. or of Saint Andrew, seated at Edinburgh in Scotland, is established there* FROM TIME IMMEMORIAL." (There are always, in the documents emanating from *Heredom*, some gasconades which make the reading amusing, instead of instructive: for example, this immemoriality which dates only from a certain number of years after 1736. *See above.*)

"*It has taken the title of* ROYAL LODGE, *because the Kings of Scotland have in former times presided over it in person, and because it has continued to consider as its G.M. the King of Scotland, now King of Great Britain.*" (The official minutes of these royal sessions would be as difficult to exhibit as the patents of the foundation of the Lodge. Moreover, the wording of the Grand Secretary here is defective, for the Royal G.L. could not take the title of *Royal Lodge* since it already had it, says the Grand Secretary, and the Kings of Scotland, by having explained to them by the architect-builders the estimates of the construction projects which interested them, scarcely suspected that these conversations, quite ordinary in such cases, would pass later, under amplifying pens, for *presiding over the Royal G.L.*) Let us continue, this is amusing.

"*Well before 1720 and 1721, some unfortunate circumstances have forced Masonry to dwell in obscurity, and the Royal G.L. has long remained shrouded in a deep sleep.*" (But the history which precedes teaches us that it was only several years after 1736 that the lodge called *Kilwinning*, from the name of its village, came to Edinburgh with the usurped title of *Mother Lodge* and took there the denomination of Royal G.L., which will be coming into its dormancy, as well as its high grades, for its long sleep.) Stand by!

"*In the year 1736, the Br. SAINT-CLAIR of ROSLIN established at Edinburgh a* GRAND LODGE OF SAINT JOHN, *to which he transmitted the authority which had been given, formerly, to some members of his family, to fulfill the place of G.M. of the Order of Saint John.*" (Halt, monsieur Grand Secretary: it is all very well, when you travel in the clouds of écossisme, to have us see rainbows of all colors; but when you deign to set foot in history, it is no longer permitted to *fabulize*. Here is the truth: in 1736, the operative guilds with their protectorate, *Saint-Clair*, asleep since 1695, reawakened for only a moment in order to *transform themselves*, according to the desire of the era. William Saint-Clair, yielding to the force of circumstances, gave his demission on November 24, and six days later, on November 30, thirty-two lodges constituted the *G.L. of Saint John of Edinburgh*. It was not, therefore, by W. Saint-Clair that was established this G.L., which, the same day, chose with justice this Br. as its G.M.) Let us continue.

"*This G.L. took the simple title of* LODGE OF THE ORDER OF SAINT JOHN, *because being constituted by a simple Master, whose powers were limited to the third grade, it could occupy itself only with what concerned symbolic Masonry, and it has always continued the same.*" (You are therefore still on the side of the true, Br. Grand Secretary: if the G.L. took a simple Symbolic title, analogous to the régime that it professed, it is because in this era, as you would know, there was not yet any *supermasonic régime* nor any pertaining to *chapters* of note. The egg which contained the *Grand Chapter of Heredom*, which was probably incubated by your *Royal G.L.* during its long sleep, and even, according to its confession, several years still after 1736, had not yet produced its fruit.) What follows is going to confirm what we tell you:

"*It was only some years after 1736 that the Royal G.L. emerged from the cloud which held it, lone enveloped.*" (It had not entered into its cloud as G.L, how could it emerge therefrom forty-five years later ROYAL G.L.?) "*Its works then resumed 'vigor.'*" (Not *then*, you have said yourself several years later, which, in Scottish style, signifies a long repose.) "*And it no longer occupied itself but with what concerned high Masonry, leaving the notion of symbolic Masonry to the G.L. of Saint John, whose members then pass into the Royal G.L., in order to there be received into superior grades. - Thus, the G.L. of Saint John receives Masons into the first three grades, and the Royal G.L., which does not receive any member unless he is a Master, advances them in the high grades.*" It is not in this way, Br. Grand Secretary, that things ought to transpire in good and regular Masonry. The G.O. of France had, therefore, reason to request, before any discussion with your ROYAL G.L., that it justify its authority and its legal existence and whence comes its right to constitute chapters in lands under French domination, in defiance of the concordat made between the G.L. of France and those of England and Scotland, in 1767 (see Grand Chapter General of France). And when the illegality is so flagrant, what, then, may be, in the eyes of the true Mason, the value of the chapters that it constitutes, and of those established by these latter?[28]

OBSERVATION

We have thought it indispensible, in order to make our institution well understood, to enter into all the details which precede and which are extracted from the works (for what concerns the subject that we treat) of the three great Masonic powers: the G.L. OF ENGLAND, the G.O., as legal successor of the G.L. OF FRANCE, and the G.L. OF SAINT JOHN OF EDINBURGH, which, originally, have spread the TRUE MASONRY into the universe. Our aim is to separate the error from the truth, to enlighten our readers, and to put them in a position to *judge* the case that they ought to make of the *false Masonry* invented by sectarians or audacious speculators, whose successive encroachments into the credulity and vanity of the Masons have forced the G.L.'s which, from the beginning, have lacked skill and energy, to have to adopt into their midst, or suffer beside them, the monstrous exercise of these so-called HIGH GRADES.

In the following chapters, we shall pass in review of the various *supermasonic* establishments constituted by the caprice of their founders, like the Royal G.L. of Edinburgh, and of which some have survived.

CHAPTER IX
Freemasonry or Modern Initiation

Freemasonry rests upon three fundamental grades, summarizing or being obliged to summarize the triple study which ought to occupy the Mason: *Whence he comes* (the study of God); *who he is* (the study of oneself and his perfecting); and *whither he goes* (the study of his transformation into another future).

In 1646, we have seen that *Elias Ashmole*, aided by *initiates* who, in proportion as their number increased, had not ceased to observe the diminishing progress of the operative guilds which served to shelter them, and which, all extinguished, or nearly, were still deep-rooted in England, protected by their separation from the continent, Ashmole, *we say*, occupied himself with regenerating, under this architectural veil, the mysteries of the ancient Indian and Egyptian initiation, and with giving to the new association an aim of union, fraternity, perfecting, equality, and knowledge, by means of a *universal bond*, based upon the laws of nature and the love of humanity.

He created, according to the traditions and the ancient documents that he was able to collect, the first grade, which presents the greatest analogy with the ancient initiation: it teaches morals, explains some symbols, indicates the passage from barbary to civilization; it goes to the admiration and recognition of the G. Arch. of the Univ., makes known the fundamental principles of *philosophical Masonry*, its laws and its customs, and disposes the neophyte towards philanthropy and study. Its *works*, like those of the grades which follow, instead of opening in the morning and closing in the evening, recall and commemorate the conferences had mysteriously with his disciples or initiates by ZOROASTER, our founder, that is to say our point of departure (*which was not, without doubt, the first, which opened at noon and closed at midnight*[29], followed by a frugal meal.

The SECOND GRADE, composed in 1648, and submitted, like the first, to the approbation of the initiates, is a faithful and progressive continuation of the same analogy, harmonized with the doctrine of Thales and Pythagoras. This grade disposes the neophyte to the study of the natural sciences and of the globe, of astronomy and the philosophy of history; it leads him to research the courses and origin of things; to know *oneself* in order to become skillful in directing others, and to comprehend all that *human happiness* may draw from the *Masonic* association, by means of work, knowledge, and virtue.

THE THIRD GRADE, composed in 1649, completes the analogy of the modern mysteries with the ancient initiation. The knowledge of this grade teaches to lift the veil which covers its new mysteries; it admits, therefore, the most elevated philosophical and theosophical studies; it gives the key of the poetic and religious myths of ancient and modern times, and it completes perfectly the ancient initiation or *lesser mysteries*. We are going to have the proof thereof.

In Egypt, the third grade is called the *Door of Death*. The tomb of *Osiris* which, because of his assassination, *supposedly recent*, still bears traces of blood, was raised into the middle of the *hall of the dead*, where part of the reception was made. They asked the aspirant if he had taken part in the murder of Osiris. After other trials and despite his denials, he was stricken, or they feigned to strike him on the head with the blow of an axe[30]. He was knocked down and covered with little bands like the mummies; they lamented around him; lightning flashed; the *supposed* dead was surrounded with fire, then restored to life[31].

We find again, in the modern rite, the reproduction of this Egyptian fable, only instead of Osiris, inventor of the arts, or the sun, one takes the name of *Hiram*, which signifies *raised* (epithet which belongs to the sun) and who was skillful in the arts.

Let us examine the march of the sun from the summer solstice, and the allegory, in this decreasing period, of the last three months, represented as *companion assassins*.

The explanation of this astronomical fact and of the *instruments* of the pretended death is going to give us the interpretation of the grade:

The sun, at the summer solstice, provokes, among all that breathes, the songs of recognition; then, *Hiram*, who represents it, may give to whom has right to it, the *sacred word*, that is to say, life. When the sun descends into the inferior signs, the *mutism* of nature begins, Hiram can no longer, therefore, give the sacred word to the companions who represent the last three *inert* months of the year[32].

The first companion is reputed to strike Hiram weakly with a 24-*inch gauge*, image of the twenty-four hours that each diurnal revolution takes: first distribution of time which, after the exaltation of the great star, makes a weak attempt on its existence, by bearing upon it the first blow.

The second struck him with an iron *square*, symbol of the last season, figured in the intersection of the two straight lines which would divide, into four equal parts, the zodiacal circle, whose center symbolizes the heart of Hiram, where end the points of the four squares representing the four season: second distribution of time which, in this period, bears a greater blow upon the solar existence.

The third companion strikes him mortally upon the forehead with a *strong blow of the mallet*, whose cylindrical form symbolizes the year [année in Fr.] which means circle, ring [anneau in Fr.]: third distribution of time, whose fulfillment bears the final blow to the existence of the *expiring* sun[33].

From this interpretation, we have concluded that *Hiram*, founder of metals, become the hero of the new legend, with the title of architect, is *Osiris* (the sun) of modern initiation; that *Isis*, his widow, is the *Lodge*, emblem of the earth (in Sanskrit, *loga*, the world) and that *Horus*, son of Osiris (or of the light), and son of the widow, is the Freemason, that is to say the *initiate* who inhabits the terrestrial lodge (*child of the widow and of the light*)[34].

We have seen that after the decapitation of Charles I, in 1649, whose death they wished to avenge, they imagined, for the secret conventicles, a templar grade, where the violent death of the innocent *J.B. Molay* calls for vengeance.

Ashmole himself, who shared this political sentiment, modified, in this aim, his grade of Master and substituted for the Egyptian veil, which made it entirely uniform with the first two degrees, a supposedly *Biblical* veil, that is to say more *Talmudic* than Biblical[35], but disparate and incomplete. Although based on the ancient symbolism, it was retouched in such a way that the partisans of the Stuarts, of which Ashmole was a part, seemed to find dedicated therein their regrets and their hopes, as demanded the Jesuitic system of that time. It is because of this that the initials of the sacred words of the three grades (J.B.M.) reproduced those of the name of the G.M. of the Templars, and that the two columns also bore, as in the Bible, the initials J.B. - The mysterious temples of Egypt had these columns, but they were squared, oriented like the pyramids and signified *Orient* and *Occident*. The modern ones, which are the reproductions thereof, are round because of their relation to the solar system and signify *the two solstices*: all these temples, ancient and modern, have been and are but a symbol of the great temple of nature.

In Ireland, when they wished to persecute, in these times of trouble, the Freemasons of this kingdom, they never failed to find, in the fable of Hiram, an assured sign of their rebellion against the reform in favor of the Catholic religion. (See *l'Histoire de Charles Ier*, by Coming. London, 1727.)

We have just given a slight idea of the Masonry called very foolishly *symbolic*, as if the so-called high grades were without symbolism, or as if any mysteries could exist without symbols; and we think it necessary to warn the Master who comes to be admitted, it would be the same with all the grades above his own, that he ought not, any more than the Egyptian initiation, give himself the idea that his *initiation* taught and revealed to him the truth. This would be an error. The truth is not taught anymore in the new than in the old institution. But they *make thin its veil*, and the one who profits from the documents that he receives knows more and better than the one who comes out of a profane college of philosophy. The Egyptian priests never removed the veil which covered the statue of Isis (*nature*). They themselves have never seen it without this veil. Because nobody is worthy of the truth, unless he can, according to the obstacles that one averts and the course that one traces out for himself, succeed in discovering it for himself. That is why we recall to you that inscription on the temple of Delphi: *Know thyself*. If he does not find the truth in himself and by himself, it could be dangerous for him to know it, because, appreciating it poorly or incompletely, he could only make a poor use thereof.

Initiation means *death* and *rebirth into another life*: be occupied with instructing yourselves in the truth: it is enough that they have stripped you of the old man. Two serious reproaches, under the less polite name of *absurdities*, are made to the collation of this grade and with reason: 1st, a man still lives, although covered with dirt for twenty-four hours, and *in an advanced putrefaction*.

2nd, the *Venerable* takes here the role of the most evil Companion who *killed* Hiram, although he called scorn and hatred upon this assassin.

In order to obviate these monstrosities, it is necessary, *they have said*, to put into a narrative and not into action the fable, better conceived, of Hiram, or of any other personage borrowed from the temples of Egypt, whose archives are no longer here to flatly contradict the invention of the narrative.

But who knows if the modification carried out by *Ashmole*, celebrated antiquarian and great alchemist, has been preserved to us faithfully; which we doubt with reason. Thus, for a long time, the initiates regard the third grade to be re-made, and, above all, to complete; for, to ask a Mason his age is to ask him his grade. Now, the Master adds to his response the words *and more*, in order to express that he knows not only the mysteries of the *Mastership*, but also those that one may derive therefrom; indeed, they have become the type of a multitude of other degrees, which are only superfluities.

They have said on this grade: "Nothing is more ridiculous than the emblem of the temple of Solomon, as an imitation that ought to have in sight the *moral temple* that Masonry proposes.

"Solomon was, without doubt, full of wisdom and knowledge; but history presents men wiser and more scholarly than he. And where would be the necessity of forming a particular society, mysterious and inaccessible to the view of the world, in order to occupy oneself, *secretly*, with the architecture of a temple, with the wisdom of its author, with the knowledge of its workers, and with the catastrophe of one of its *architects*?

"Let us look at these things as a Judaic allegory, and not make thereof the point of origin of our institution, well anterior to Solomon, for that would be to take a relatively modern figure, for a reality which dates from the first of the three Zoroasters," (*Essai sur la Francmaçonnerie*, by Laurens).

We reply that it is precisely because this point of origin would be absurd and this institution ridiculous, that it is necessary to seek another motive in the emblem of this temple, which appeared only after *Memphis* and *the Pyramids*, and that re-veilers applied to the secret initiation, then to Freemasonry, and we find this motive in the high and secret mysteries of the Order, the result of which has produced the splendid temple and the magnificent palace of Solomon, who was initiated into the secrets of nature and employed, *wisely*, his knowledge to render his kingdom illustrious and to glorify God. Without doubt, before him, an emblem more fitting and with the same meaning existed; but, under this point of view, the Solomonian emblem suits the *true initiates*, although imperfectly represented for the simple Masons of the symbolism.

The spirit of *unity* ought to direct Freemasonry. Its aim, which is *universality*, is found only in the first three grades; only there is *Masonic unity* represented by a *sole décor*. The sects are born as soon as other *ribbons* come to corrupt the simplicity of the institution; which takes place.

Speculators, charlatans, sectarian schemers, have come to do to the true and unique Masonry what ambitious innovators have done to religion. The moral of the two institutions is made to unite all men; what divides them? In religion, the *schisms*; in Masonry, the *rites*. The schisms indicate the obscurity of a system which does not have truth as its basis: there is no schism in mathematics. The three symbolic grades, which have nature for their basis, have not produced and do not produce any schism.

The high grades (the Masonry called *superior*) are therefore false and dangerous, since they give place to schisms, to enmities, to lawsuits, to the excusable libels of Baruel and others, and to the persecutions of the authority; strange and unworthy productions which, instead of peace, union, and love, make an object of discord and hatred.

Let us reject, then, all the rites without exception. Let us add, if it is necessary, to the third rectified grade, a fourth *administrative* grade, in which the previous grades receive a final explanation, and where will be revealed, to the brethren who will be judged worthy, all the interpretations of the high grades of all the rites.

There are no Chapters, Councils, *Tribunals* (in Masonry, this last word is derisive and misplaced), or Consistories *without Lodges*. Let the lodges be purified, then, of this venom, which corrupts their stem, and which has caused Masonry so many tribulations, persecutions, and victims. The Masonic reason, stronger than the vanity of the Masons, will triumph and necessarily lead to this result, in the interest of the general unity.

Have we not before our eyes, as proof of this truth, the fine example that has been ceaselessly given to the wise Masons by the ancient and respectable Lodge of *Les Neuf-Sœurs* [The Nine Sisters - that is, The Muses] at Paris, the members of which, who have succeeded one another since 1769, have never worn, and do not wear still, but the simple ribbon of the Master, the only one which has decorated *Helvetius, Lalande, Court de Geblin, Benjamin Franklin, Voltaire*, and other illustrious brothers, who, under this modest decoration, were surely equal to the 33°, the 90° and the 93° of today.

CHAPTER X

Supermasonic Institutions
OR ON THE HIGH GRADES,
BY CHRONOLOGICAL ORDER

RITE OF RAMSAY
(1728)

Andrew Michael RAMSAY, man of letters, born at Ayr, in Scotland, in 1686, died at Saint-Germain-en-Laye in 1743, after having been a Quaker, Anabaptist, Anglican, Presbyterian, came to Cambrai, where Fénelon converted him to Christianity. Having become since the tutor of the son of a great lord (the Prince *de Turenne*), he believed himself made to instruct the universe, and to govern it; he gave, consequently, lessons to Cyrus (see *Voyage of Cyrus*), in order to become the best king of the universe and the most orthodox theologian, rare qualities which appear rather incompatible.

As vacillating in Masonry as in religion, he left the first, the path of truth, that is to say that he has disfigured the symbols thereof in order to apply them to matters which were foreign to it. He thus opened a deadly route, where intrigue and evil passions delayed not to invade; and all the genuine ancient truth of the *Masonic symbolism* was necessary in order not to succumb to the redoubtable blows of the forgers of all colors, whose race is not extinguished.

Ramsay served devotedly the cause of the *Stuarts* and influenced by the Jesuits, he attempted to attach himself to the re-establishment of Catholicism in England, by means of Freemasonry, under the Templar veil. In this aim, and outside of the true Masonry, he created, in 1728, his first system, composed of these three grades:

1. *Écossais*,
2. *Novice*,
3. *Knight of the Temple*[36].

They are grafted upon the three symbolic grades, in order to better deceive. This number was brought to seven in 1736, year of the institution of Freemasonry in Scotland.

Ramsay gave to his grades the name of his land, and, since then, nearly all the grades which were invented took the name of *Scottish*, although unknown in Scotland; from here also come the *Masonry* called *Scottish*, and the so-called *Scottish* Lodges, Mother Lodges, and Grand Lodges.

This system, composed under the Jesuitico-Templar inspiration, and which had some analogy with the situation of the Stuarts, was rejected by the Grand Lodge of England, in 1728, perhaps because its members were in a large part partisans of Charles I, but without doubt also because then the good Masonic sense refused to recognize as true, grades foreign to the original and general aim of the institution.

In France, where novelty carries it away too often over reason, these grades were received, as well as others that we see figure in various rites, and of which several have been attributed falsely to Ramsay, like, for example, the grade of *Kadosh*. He attributed the invention of his régime to *Godefroy de Bouillon*, and claimed, with as much truth, that the Lodge of Saint Andrew, at Edinburgh, was the headquarters of the true Order of *Freemasons*, whom he said to be the descendants of the knights of the crusades. - Of the *operative masons*, perhaps, but never have they formed an order. - Of the *Freemasons*? No. And behold, therefore, the creator of that famous *Grand Lodge of Saint Andrew of Scotland*, ever constituting, but which was never constituted! What an origin!

German lodges, imitating those of France, will also allow themselves to be carried away; but, later, the doctrine of Ramsay was modified there, and its grades were *reformed* or *rectified.*

PETIT-ELU
(1743)

This grade, created at Lyon in 1743, appears to have for its aim to avenge the death of Jacques *Mabiot* or *Mabiotte*, fanatic and impious confessor of William the Conqueror. See the *four-times respectable Scottish Master of Saint Andrew of Scotland*, Jesuitic grade (Fastes initiatique).

The author of the Avertissement, printed in 1781, concerning the grade of *Knight Kadosh*, which it calls *a fanatical and senseless web, that a multitude of so-called Masons regard as the ne plus ultra of Masonry*, says:

"If we are to believe the brother Baron de Tschoudy, in his *Écossais d'Écosse*, the first rung of the Kadosh has been imagined at Lyon in 1743, under the title of *Petit-Elu*, which breathes only vengeance. From the development of this Petit-Elu, they have formed therefrom the *Elect of the Nine* or *of Pérignan*, the *Elect of the Fifteen*, the *Illustrious Master*, the *Knight of the Anchor* or of *Hope*, and finally the *Grand Inspector Grand Elect* or *Knight Kadosh*."

The *Sov. Council, Subl. Scottish Mother Lodge of the French Grand Globe* has, by decree of March 9, 1780, proscribed this grade, which had been denounced by it as *dangerous* and *of a reprehensible moral.* (See, for the complement of this grade, our *Tuileur général.*)

REFORMED OR RECTIFIED REGIME OF DRESDEN

This régime was based on the Templar system of Ramsay. The ritual of initiation is divided into two parts: the OUTER ORDER, comprising the three symbolic degrees, and the INNER ORDER, composed of three grades, forming a religious system based on knighthood. These two orders are bound by an intermediary grade, the *Scottish Master of Saint Andrew*, in which they chose the candidates for the *Knights Beneficent of the Holy City*. Here is its nomenclature:

Outer Order	1. Apprentice, 2. Companion, 3. Master.
Intermediary grade.	4. Scottish Master of Saint Andrew.
Inner Order	5. Equestrian Chapter, 6. Novice, 7. Knight.

This régime produced several DIRECTORIES called *Scottish* which had a denomination and a particular magisterial seat, each exercising in its jurisdiction a supposed *Masonic* supremacy.

Bordeaux had the Directory of Occitania, 2nd province.

Lyon had the Directory of Auvergne, 3rd province.

Strasbourg had the Directory of Burgundy, 5th province.

These three distinct establishments, united by the same principles, the same doctrine, and the same Masonic forms, were called FRENCH LANGUAGE. They corresponded with Chambéry, which had the directory of *Italy* or of the *Austrian Lombardy*. Several French provinces, among others Alsace, Franche-Comté, Dauphiné, and Provence, counted several lodges constituted by these directories.

It is from the far reaches of Germany that arrived in France this cloud of symbolic grades, or supposed as such, fantastical beings emerged from the vapors of the mind of Ramsay. The *Masonic* doctrine of this scheming innovator, amalgamated into the three original grades, distinguished them, particularly from the new grades, that, in the Scottish Directories, the mania of distinctions had enhanced by the sharp title of *Rectified Regime*.

By a solemn act decreed and signed on April 13, 1776, the three directories made their union with the G.O. of France, reserving the right to constitute, but with the obligation to submit to the endorsement and confirmation by the G.O. of the constitutions which emanated from each of them.

On March 6, 1781, the Scottish Directory of *Septimanie*, sitting at Montpellier, asked for and obtained from the G.O. the same favor as the other directories.

Such ought not to have been the system of the G.O.; it ought to have enlightened the Masons, to whom it was easy to demonstrate, as yet today, that beyond the ancient hieroglyphic symbol of the Mastership, there is nothing more than superfluity, aberration, and charlatanism: "*Every rite*," says the author of the *Livre bleu*, "*which takes a 4th grade in order to attain to perfection, no longer belongs to the* true Masonry." And this is the case of the rite of the *Scottish Directories*, unknown in Scotland.

They have for their Grand Master the Duc *de Bouillon*, G.M. of the G.O. of Bouillon.

GRAND ORIENT OF BOUILLON

This Masonic body, which no longer existed in 1774, has founded several lodges in France. It had its seat at Bouillon, city of the Netherlands, and for Grand Master, the Duc *de Bouillon*, its founder, under the title of Protector. It counted among its members many persons of distinction: mentioned here are the Prince *de Rohan*, the Prince *de Guéménée*, the Duc *de Montbazon*, and others that the Duc de Bouillon had introduced there.

We read around the seal of this G.O.: *Godfredus, Dei gratia, dux Bulloniensis, protector.*

This ephemeral power delivered its constitutions and its capitularies in the name of the metropolis of Edinburgh *(Royal Grand Lodge)*, which makes the presumption that its doctrine and its grades had some analogy with those of the régime, called Scottish, of that time.

SCOTTISH MOTHER LODGE OF MARSEILLE
(1750)

We give the following nomenclature, which exists in several collections, and, in some of them, under the title of:

Scottish Rite, called *Philosophical*, of the *Scottish Mother Lodge*.

We point out that the title of *Mother Lodge* is, according to us, very misplaced in Masonry, where all the lodges are *sisters*. We approve of the title of *Grand Lodge*, given to representative bodies charged with administering the Masonic Order, but to whom it is forbidden to practice the grades.

This rite contains eighteen grades:

1. Apprentice,
2. Companion,
3. Master,
4. Perfect Master,
5. Grand-Écossais
6. Knight of the Black Eagle,
7. Commander of the Black Eagle,
8. Rose-Croix,
9. True Mason
10. Knight of the Argonauts,
11. Knight of the Golden Fleece,
12. Apprentice Philosopher,
13. Knight Adept of the Eagle and the Sun,
14. Sublime Philosopher,
15. Knight of the Phoenix,
16. Adept of the Mother Lodge,
17. Knight of the Iris [rainbow],
18. Knight of the Sun.

We believe it necessary to attribute this rite to the establishment founded at Marseille before 1750.

A travelling Mason, whose name and titles have remained unknown, instituted, they say, at Marseille, at this time, a Mother Lodge, under the title of *Saint-Jean d'Écosse*. We have proofs that it flourished in 1751. From 1762, its denomination *was Scottish Mother Lodge of France*. But we ought not confuse it with the lodge of *Saint-Alexandre d'Écosse et du contract social réunis*, which has taken, during the very existence of the Scottish Mother Lodge of France, at Marseille, the parallel title of *Scottish Mother Lodge of France*, and which, in its nomenclature, comprised of twelve grades, has borrowed eight of them from the one we have just given, without its obliging historian, the brother *Thory*, having taken the trouble to justify these two not very Masonic matters.

The Scottish Mother Loge of Marseille, or Scottish Mother Lodge of France, constituted lodges in the Levant, in the colonies, in Provence, at Lyon, and at Paris itself. Its locale at Marseille was one of the most beautiful which existed in Europe.

This *Scottish Mother Lodge of France* which, in imitation of the *Royal Grand Lodge of Edinburgh*, is answerable only to itself, having constituted itself, that is to say not having been originally so, resisted for a long time the attempts made and repeated for its union with the G.O., keeping its independence and above all its title which, according to it, authorized it to constitute lodges and chapters.

In 1812, it was presided over by the Venerable Master *Rigordy*, president of the customs tribunal.

JACOBITE PRIMORDIAL CHAPTER OF ROSE-CROIX OF ARRAS
(1747)

Charles Edward Stuart, called the Pretender, staying at Arras and wishing to recognize the *beneficence* of the Masons and their care for his person, delivers to them a bull of institution of a *Primordial Chapter*, under the title of *Écosse Jacobite*, and gives its administration to several notables of the city, among others to the advocates *de Lagneau and de Robespierre* (the father of the National Convention). Here is the tenor of that bull:

"We, Charles Edward Stuart, King of England, France, Scotland, and Ireland, and, in this quality, substitute G.M. of the Chapter of H., known under the title of *Knight of the Eagle* and *the Pelican*, and, since our adversity and misfortune, under that of *Rose-Croix*; wishing to testify to the Masons of Artois how grateful we are towards them for the proofs of beneficence that they have lavished on us with the officers of the garrison of the city of Arras, and of their attachment to our person, during the stay of six months that we have made in this city,

"We have, on their behalf, created and erected, let us create and erect, by the present bull, in the said city of Arras, a *Holy Primordial Chapter of Rose-Croix*, under the distinctive title of *Écosse Jacobite*, which shall be ruled and governed by the Chevaliers *Lagneau* and *de Robespierre*, both advocates; *Hazard* and his two sons, all three physicians; J.-B. *Lucet*, our upholsterer, and Jérôme *Cellier*, our clock-maker, to whom we permit and give power to make, as much by them as by their successors, power to create two chapters in one same city, however populated it may be.

"And so that faith be added to our present bull, we have signed it by our hand and to this had affixed the secret seal of our commandments, and had it countersigned by the secretary of our cabinet, on Thursday, 15th day of the 2nd month, the year of the incarnation 1747.

"Signed Charles Edward Stuart.

"In the King's name, *signed*: Lord of Berkley, secretary."

This chapter erected some others, but in small number. In 1780, it instituted at Paris, a Chapter of Rose-Croix, under the title of *Chapter of Arras, of the Valley of Paris*. This chapter was united with the G.O. on September 27, 1801. It had been declared first suffragan of the *Chapter of Écosse Jacobite*, with the right to constitute.

RITE OF THE VIEILLE-BRU, OR OF THE SCOTTISH FAITHFUL
(1748)

In 1748, one year after the creation of the *Jacobite Chapter of Arras*, by Charles Edward *Stuart*, the rite of the *Vieille-Bru* or of the *Scottish Faithful* was established at Toulouse, in testimony of recognition towards the Masons of this Orient, who, *says the Chronicle*, had favorably received Sir Samuel *Lockhard*, aide-de-camp of the Pretender[37] during his stay in this city.

This rite, composed of nine degrees, was divided into three chapters, which took the name of *Consistories*.

The first chapter comprises	Apprentice, Companion, Master, Secret Master.

The second contains four degrees, designated under the title of Elect. Its system is Templar.

The third chapter was formed of the initiates of the secrets of scientific Masonry. This régime was administered by a *Council*, whose members had the name *Menatzchim*, or supreme chiefs of the rite.

The G.O., not recognizing in it an aim moral or scientific enough, refused, in 1804, to admit this rite, that the title did not favor. They have also claimed that the charter from the King of England was far from offering the characters of authenticity. It continued, they say, to be practiced in the south of France until 1812, which was, without doubt, its fatal year, for on February 8, the directory of the rites rejected anew the request upon review of this régime formed by the lodge *Napoléomagne*, at Toulouse, and this refusal is based on the same causes.

SOVEREIGN COUNCIL, SUBLIME MOTHER LODGE OF THE EXCELLENTS OF THE GRAND GLOBE OF FRANCE

(1752)

One power of the high grades was formed around the year 1752, under the ostentatious title of *Sovereign Council, Sublime Scottish Mother Lodge of the French Grand Globe*; then it was called *Sovereign Council, Sublime Mother Lodge of the Excellents of the French Grand Globe*[38]. We are missing the nomenclature of its grades.

This body has published several fulminating decrees against new grades introduced furtively into the Masonic ladder called *Scottish*.

The Sovereign Council expresses itself thus in a decree of March 9, 1780, the text of which is curious to preserve:

"Having taken into consideration the denunciation made of several dangerous, factitious, and illusory grades, which have been introduced into Masonry, whether through ambition, ignorance, or cupidity, and having recognized that the *Petit-Elu, the Elect of the Nine or of Pérignan, the Elect of the Fifteen, the Illustrious Master, the Knight of the Anchor or of Hope*, are only rungs of a reprehensible moral which leads to the dreadful grade of *Grand Inspector General*, or *Knight Kadosh*, or *Knight Elect*, or *Knight of the Black Eagle*, surmounted by illusory and extraneous *Commandries*, as much in the *Sovereign Commander of the Temple* as in that of the *Écossais of Saint Andrew of Scotland*, imagined and brought to Paris by the late Baron de Tschoudy, which is reproduced today in the Scottish Directories of Dresden, adopted at Lyon, Strasbourg, and Bordeaux, which is but a modification of the Grand Inspector Knight Kadosh, etc. the aim and rewards being the same, with the cord and the vengeance taken, that this one justly blames; that the grade Écossais of Saint Andrew of Scotland, no less dangerous by its projected emigrations, by its artfully presented sophisms, would tend towards the subversion of the true Masonry; that the so-called grade of *Rose-Croix* and its adherents present absurdities which could be otherwise qualified; that that of *Knight of the East*, surmounted by the *Commanders of the East*, foolish and bastard production, presents only a false development of the Masonic letter, without being able to adapt itself to its spirit, etc., etc., DECREES that the said grades be suppressed and proscribed from all the lodges, where the true light is esteemed, etc."

"By another decrees of November 27, same year, this Sovereign Council suppresses the titles of *Scottish, English, Irish, Scottish Saxon, Africans of Berlin, Reformed Masons of Brunswick*, etc., and re-establishes the old title of excellent, because, says the decree: *By preserving longer a foreign denomination, source of an infinity of abuses, detrimental to the good order, peace, and union, which ought to reign in all the lodges of France, it would be exposéd to the just reproaches of the wise and legitimate Masons.*" (Extract from a printed document, Atlantic format, signed: *Labady*, by mandate of the *Sovereign Council, Sublime Mother Lodge*, etc.)

This Sovereign council has claimed to have the rights of the G.L. in France, in which it has perhaps been confused or that it will be received into its midst, while losing its title. Indeed, we read, in the notification which precedes the grade of *Grand Inspector, Grand Elect,* or *Knight Kadosh*, printed at Paris in 1781, this note, p. 18: *In 1766, the Sovereign Council, sublime Mother Lodge of the Excellents, had printed the discourse of its Orator, so that all the Lodge Masters, to whom it was addressed, may note on the day indicated on the proposed union, with full and entire knowledge of cause.* In 1772, the union of the Sovereign Council and the G.L. was decreed in assembly. - This G.L. was, without any doubt, the dissident and restless fraction, which then received the proposition made on October 2, 1766, by the brother Gouillard[39] to the G.L. which rejected it; for a note from the same notification, p. 9, says on this subject: "*Many Masons are unaware that in October, 1766, the Sovereign Council, Sublime Mother Lodge, called of the Excellents, proposed to unite itself with the very respectable G.L.; that the suspension of its works prevented the execution of this proposition which was definitively decreed in 1772* (with the banished Br.); *reason for which the acceptance by writing of His Most Serene Highness to the Supreme Grand Mastership of April 5, 1772, was conceived in the name of the Sovereign Council, sublime Mother Lodge, called of the Excellents of the French Grand Globe, and of the very respectable G.L. of France.*" Thus is found explained this historical point.

RITE OF THE CHAPTER DE CLERMONT
(1754)

In 1754, the unfortunate state in which the institution was found by the admission into the different grades of a multitude of individuals without merit, convinced the Chevalier *de Bonneville*, aided by elite Masons, to found, in the name of the Grand Master and under his auspices, a chapter of *high grades*, under the title of *Chapter de Clermont.*

He installed it, on November 24, in a very beautiful locale constructed expressly at *la Nouvelle-France*, near Paris.

Fatigued by the dissentions which dishonored the Parisian lodges, in consequence of the irremovability of their chiefs, the more distinguished Masons of the court and of the city soon yielded to this particular union which became numerous, but whose existence was scarcely four years.

The Templar system, created at Lyon in 1743, according to the reform of Ramsay, becomes the régime of the new Chapter, which, in the beginning, counted only these three grades:

1. Knight of the Eagle or Master Elect;
2. Illustrious Knight, or Templar;

3. Sublime Illustrious Knight.

But these grades soon become more numerous.

The Baron von Hund took, in this Chapter, the high grades, and with them, the idea of the régime of the *Strict Observance*, which he established in Germany, his homeland, a short time later; but his production, born from error, could not maintain itself there. We shall soon speak thereof.

The Chevalier de Bonneville had believed to diminish the evil by founding this Chapter; he only increased it; for form its debris there was formed in 1758, a new Chapter which was entitled *Council of Emperors of the East and West*, which long played a role in the Masonic order, and which, for this reason, has the sad advantage of being the point of origin of the supermasonic establishments.

CHAPTER XI
COUNCIL OF EMPERORS OF THE EAST AND WEST

In 1758, there was formed, at Paris, a Chapter of high grades, called *Council of Emperors of the East and West.* Its members were entitled *Sovereign Prince Masons, Substitutes General of the Royal Art, Grand Surveillants and Officers of the Grand and Sovereign Lodge of Saint John of Jerusalem.* They constituted Lodges, Chapters, and Colleges[40]. Their degrees of instruction were composed of twenty-five grades, under the title of *Heredom,* divided into seven classes, the doctrine of which had as its basis the *Templar system.* This Council was divided into Colleges, in which these classes were conferred. Here is the list of the grades, with the distances of obtainment.

NOMENCLATURE OF THE RITE OF HEREDOM OR PERFECTION

Classes	Grade	Months	Distances
1st	1. Apprentice.	3	15
	2. Companion	5	
	3. Master	7	
2nd	4. Secret Master	3	21
	5. Perfect Master	3	
	6. Intimate Secretary	3	
	7. Intendant of the Buildings	5	
	8. Provost and Judge	7	
3rd	9. Master Elect of the Nine	3	7
	10. Master Elect of the Fifteen	3	
	11. Illustrious Elect, Chief of the Twelve Tribes	1	
4th	12. Grand Master Architect	1	5
	13. Knight Royal Arch	3	
	14. Grand Elect, ancient Perfect Master	1	
5th	15. Knight of the Sword or the East	1	9
	16. Prince of Jerusalem	1	
	17. Knight of the East and West	3	
	18. Knight Rose-Croix	1	
	19. Grand Pontiff or Master ad Vitam	3	
6th	20. Grand Patriarch Noachite	3	9
	21. G.M. of the Key of Masonry	3	
	22. Prince of Lebanon, Kn. Royal Axe	3	
7th	23. Knight of the Sun, Prince Adept, Chief of the Consistory	5	15
	24. Illustrious Kn., Grand Commander of the White and Black Eagle, Gr. Elect K.-H.	5	
	25. Very Illustrious Sov. Prince of Masonry, Grand Kn., Sublime Commander of the Royal Secret	5	
			81

The mysterious number of months in which one must be initiated in order to arrive successfully at the final grade formed the number 81: 8 and 1 make 9, as 8 and 1 make 81, as 9 times 9 makes 81, all perfect numbers. A Mason who had fulfilled his time, received at last, they say, the *Rose-Mystique* (the Templar Secret).

In 1759, this Council constituted, at Bordeaux, a *Council of Princes of the Royal Secret,* which also constituted several workshops and delivered charters. Thus, the provinces, where the whirlwind of follies would be less dangerous for the good spirits, did not recoil before the dangerous innovations: we have already said that Lyon, Arras, Marseille, Toulouse, and Bordeaux, had taken the initiative over Paris.

On August 27, 1761, the Council of Emperors delivered a patent of Deputy Grand Inspector to the *Jew Stephen* MORIN, whom the affairs of commerce had called to San Domingo. The aim of the Council was to propagate overseas its Masonry called *of Heredom* or *Perfection.* There is not the slightest doubt that audacious tricksters, securing this rite in order to exploit it to their profit, modified it at Charleston (*United States*) and introduced it, 43 years later, at Paris, place of its creation, while overburdening it with eight degrees that they attributed to *Frederick* the Great, who held the higher grades in horror.

This act, singularly remarkable for the period, sent word that in matters of *vanity, Christians* and *Israelites* understood one another admirably. We reproduce it here, because being the principal cause of the misdeeds within Masonry, it is necessary that it be before the eyes of the reader[41].

This Council continued to constitute, at Paris and in France, workshops, concurrently with the G.L. of France and the *Lacorne* G.L., which supported it. What did those who were opposed to the unity of power think of this anarchy?

In 1762, on September 21, commissioners of the Council of Emperors and the Council of Princes of the Royal Secret, at Bordeaux, decree there, they say, the regulations on their Masonry of *Heredom* or *Perfection* in thirty-five articles and determine, in the high grades, the doctrine of the Council of Emperors. How did this body not have its statutes at that time?

This date, attributed to the regulations of the Rite of Perfection, called the *Grand Constitutions of 1762,* is not confirmed by any document. There no longer remains at Bordeaux any trace, any remembrance of the supposed *Consistory* which would have decreed them. We know that fraud willingly presided over the birth of these false Masonries; and, despite this, these constitutions, more than equivocal, still serve as rule for the lodges of the rite called *Ancient* and *Accepted.* What is more, the Supreme Council of the 33rd Degree invokes them in its decrees, considering them as the primitive charter of the organization of the *Ancient Rite,* upon which it has attributed a dogmatic power.

1762. This year, some malcontent brethren (as there will always be) separate themselves from this Council, and, in order to compete with it, they instituted, on their own authority, as it is custom, so it appears, in écossisme, a *new council* called KNIGHTS OF THE EAST.

1780. Around this era, the Council of Emperors and its fraction of the *Knights of the East* are reduced, in order to reciprocally strengthen themselves, to recruiting from men of low station, of whom, with money, they made *Prince Masons.*

The gathering of a determined number of *Princes of the Royal Secret* (25th and final degree, corresponding to the 32° of the rite called *Ancient* and *Accepted*) formed the SUPREME COUNCIL OF PRINCE MASONS, and the dignitaries of the Council took the title of GRAND INSPECTORS GENERAL.

On January 22, the Council of Emperors makes known, by a circular, that it takes (ever by its own authority) the title of SUBLIME SCOTTISH MOTHER LODGE OF THE FRENCH GRAND GLOBE, SOVEREIGN GRAND LODGE

OF FRANCE. They were not, however, unaware that this title already belonged to a Masonic power, of which we have spoken.

In this circular, the Council proposes to the Masons, by subscription, a work entitled: *Précis historique de la Franche-Maçonnerie française* [Historical Brief of French Freemasonry]. If the manuscript existed, the work has never appeared.

1781. Finally, this Council, which has wished to compete with the G.L. of France, the G.O. itself, and all the *sublime powers of the high grades*, is fallen into a complete disrepute. This body, at first commendable, gradually descended far enough to dare to propose, by subscription, in a circular, the Masonic grades of its archives, at the rate of *six francs* per installment. Thus, in order to revive interest, this sublime council published the grades of its archives against the will of its donors: vain efforts, useless and culpable imprudence, the public opinion, that is to say the opinion of all the Freemasons, men of sense, abandoned it, and these superb Masons disappeared forever from the Masonic scene. From their debris and that of the *Knights of the East*, cropped up another chapter of high grades, which, also of its own authority, constituted itself GRAND CHAPTER GENERAL OF FRANCE.

Thus, was extinguished this Rite of *Heredom*, unknown in Scotland and which ceased to be practiced in France because of the power which, by its authority, had been given the direction thereof.

But in 1803, there was reported by a certain brother *Haquet*, old notary at San Domingo, who practiced it, by his own authority, at the Lodge of the *Sept- Écossais*, at Paris, and dared to bring it to the G.O. He knew the terrain and knew that, entirely occupied with the present, the members of this body would have forgotten the past. The G.O., which was legal *possessor* of this rite through the mediation of the Grand Chapter General and the G.L. of France, of which it is the incontestable successor, believed it necessary to accept this gift, which it was not; and, to reward the brother *Haquet*, it named him *President of the Grand Consistory of Rites*.

SOVEREIGN COUNCIL OF THE KNIGHTS OF THE EAST

1762. Some malcontent brothers separated themselves from the Council of Emperors of the East and West, and reject its doctrine. In the aim of competing with it, they establish, at Paris, a new Council of *high grad*es. It is founded, on July 22, by Pirlet, clothing tailor, under the title of SOVERIEGN COUNCIL OF THE KNIGHTS OF THE EAST. The ritual was drafted by the Baron *de Tschoudy*, author of the *Étoile flamboyante* [Blazing Star]. We see him, with astonishment, figure among the members of that coterie, which delivers, on its own authority, constitutions and charters; but it propagated a sounder doctrine than that of the Council of Emperors; for it takes the Masonic initiation back to the Egyptians. Its rite was composed of only fifteen grades, since it stopped at the *Knight of the East* (or of the *sword*). (See the nomenclature of the Council of Emperors.)

In 1766, this Council published an address to the French Freemasons, in which it invited the lodges and the chapters to not recognize the filiation that was claimed to exist between the Freemasons and the *Templars*, and to proscribe every grade which would have a direct or indirect connection with this system, which was that of the *Council of Emperors* or the Rite of *Heredom*, today the *Ancient and Accepted Scottish Rite*.

The author of a notification which precedes the grade of G.I., G.E., *Knight* KADOSH, having to speak on these Masons, expresses himself thus, page 11: "...A Sovereign Council of the *Knights of the East,* whose dark and winding steps have been known only long after their fraudulent explosions. Let us admit, however, in their defense, that they were the first to hurl thunderbolts upon this grade of G.I., G.E. (*Grand Inspector, Grand Elect*) in 1766; but their insidious existence, their attempts against the *G.L. of France*, that they have succeeded in destroying in part, does not leave them enough consideration to win the respect for their decisions. What is more: they have brought complaints, denunciations of the reception of this grade, since the proscription pronounced by them, and we do not see any trace that they have set about to deal severely with that refractory to their decrees," (*booklet* in-12mo, of 84 pages; Paris, 1781).

1769, May 28. Death of the Baron de Tschoudy, 40 years of age. He bequeathed to the archives of the Council several manuscripts, and among others the work entitled *l'Ecossisme de saint-André*, with the condition that they do not have them printed; but the Council did not bear this in mind, it published them, it sold them, and it fell into disrepute.

1780. The Council of the Knights of the East and that of the *Emperors* are, for some years, reduced, in order to maintain themselves reciprocally, to recruiting people of low station and at any cost.

1781. These two bodies, stricken by disrepute, immediately fall into decadence and disappear from the Masonic scene, to return to the nothingness whence they had emerged. (See Council of Emperors.)

From their debris is going to crop up another Chapter of *high grades*, constituting itself, by its own authority, GRAND CHAPTER GENERAL OF FRANCE.

GRAND CHAPTER GENERAL OF FRANCE
(1782)

This chapter of *high grades*, or GRAND CHAPTER GENERAL OF FRANCE, composed from the debris of the old *Council of Emperors of the East and West, Sovereign Prince Masons*, and from the Council of the *Knights of the East*, to which had been joined brethren called *high grade*, was formed and constituted, at Paris, in 1782, of its own authority (like all the Masonic bodies called *Scottish*), in the aim of constituting others in France.

In 1785, it was, according to serious conferences which had taken place, on the point of carrying out its union with the G.O. But in one of its assemblies, the doctor *Gerbier* presented himself and maintained to the Grand Chapter General that its qualification was usurped (*he said rightly*), and that it belonged, by right of seniority, to the chapter that it presided over (*he lied*).

To play this role, Gerbier had a secret understanding with a merchant of Masonic decorations, dwelling place Dauphine, to fabricate, in Latin, the patent of his chapter. Here is the translation thereof:

"From the Orient of the world and from the Grand Lodge of Edinburgh, where reigns *Faith, Hope*, and *Charity*, in peace, unanimity, and equality, the 21st day of the 1st month of Hiram 5721 and according to the posthumous hieroglyph of the Savior, 1688.

"Salutations, salutations, salutations.

"We, the undersigned, disciples of the Savior, to all those who have or who could have interest therein, *let it be known*: That we have created, on behalf of the French, a *Grand Chapter of the Rose-Croix*, the supreme see of which, in the name and under the full power and authority of our brother *Duc d'Antin*, peer of France, of a reputation worthy of this rank, or of any of our brother knights, accomplished in every point, which is to be furnished by the Chapter or by the said Lodge with authentic letters, shall reside in perpetuity at Paris, to enjoy there the privilege of propagation and constitution in the interior of France alone. With these conditions, we declare, by these presents, united by our seal and our signature, that the said chapter follow freely its natural genius; consequently, may it be blessed, honored, and may faith be added to it.

"Given at the Orient of the Universe, the 23rd year of *our reign*. *Signed*: Bardoux, Barlay, Ardidenowitz, Rittary, Chulquet, Keyssovet, Fortoret, Bainet, Huiwin, Dreyts, Major Bakrmann, signor Cuttin, Hindrelaet, H.-S. Bonut, Burnet, *secretary*."

The parchment bore stains from spilt wine, through clumsiness, while affixing these false signatures in the tavern, near the grand Châtelet, where the two forgers had dined.

In order to give authenticity to a piece of which they must have heard spoken for the first time, it was necessary to prove that the *Grand Chapter of the Rose-Croix* had operated and constituted; consequently, Gerbier exhibits the *Brief of the Rose-Croix*, the tenor of which is this:

"In the name of the G. Arch. of the Univ., supreme remunerator of virtue, pure source of all perfections, truth, and justice, and under the auspices of the G.M., the brother *Duc d'Antin*;

"To all the Free-Masons spread over the surface of the earth and over the liquid plain of the seas, *salutations*, and *let it be known*, that WE, G.M. and officers of the *Lodge of Saint John*, founded and established at the Orient of Paris, under the august title of *la Parfait-Union*, have initiated into our works and mysteries of the Royal Art and received into the grade of *Doctor* and *Prince of Rose-Croix*, on April 21, 1721, our beloved brother de QUADT, lieutenant-general of the armies of the king, and, after having recognized in him the requisite qualities, have, today, elected him third venerable of the respectable lodge, in faith of which we have had sent to him the present certificate, at the bottom of which he has signed *ne varietur*, that we have had our secretary countersign, in order to authorize him to enjoy clearly everywhere, and in perpetuity, all the honors which are due to him in his said quality, in all the chapters and in all the *regular* lodges, and recognized as such; offering the reciprocal to all our brothers spread over the surface of the earth and over the liquid plain of the seas: for such is our power.

"GIVEN by US, master and officers of the lodge *Saint John*, founded and established at the Orient of Paris, under the august title of *la Parfait-Union*.

"At the Orient of Paris, under the mysterious seal of our arms, the year of light 5721, the 23rd day of the 4th month, and, according to the ordinary style, June 23, 1721.

"*Signed*: Carnuccinoli, Ven.; the Chev. de Beaupré, 1st Surv.; Haudet, 2nd Surv.; the Marq. de l'Aigle, *ex-Ven.*; the Marq. de Crécy, de Saint-Mazart, Bognet, P. de Lorrain, Le Rat, *Orat.*; Baron de Suiset. - Sealed and delivered on the said day, June 23, 1721, *signed*: Martois.

"By mandate of the lodge *la Parfait-Union*, *signed*: Muisieux, secret. gen."

The brazen audacity which gave birth to these productions may only be exceeded by the profound ignorance of their authors, and the strange blindness of those that they had intended to deceive.

First, the style of these pieces has never belonged to any chancellery, called *Masonic*, of any lands.

Then the date of 1721, which would be anterior by four years to the introduction of Freemasonry at Paris, and, consequently, by seventeen years to the nomination of the *Duc d'Antin* as G.M., would have necessarily had to enlighten any Mason even slightly educated.

Then, the putting forth of an imaginary lodge, *la Parfait-Union*, which would have likewise existed four years before the Parisian Masonry, without the latter suspecting it.

Finally, from 1695 to 1736, era of the transformation of the operative guilds of Scotland into *Freemasonic lodges*, there had been, in this kingdom, a complete suspension of meetings, and the total absence of constituting Masonic bodies.

Despite all these insupportable proofs stated by two obviously false materials, these pieces, of which the first presents fifteen false signatures and the second twelve, thrust upon several influential members, who believed or feigned to believe *Gerbier* at his word and led to the concordat of March 24, 1785, which unites the false *Chapter of Rose-Croix* to the *Grand Chapter General of France*, in order to form with it but one same body.

This Grand Chapter then carried out its union with the G.O. on February 17, 1786, and, relying upon the patent of 1721, that it had possessed for only six months, it had stipulated, in the concordat, the depository of this title into the archives of the G.O. This body, which had, without doubt, some interest in closing their eyes on these maneuvers, of which it was supposedly unaware, conferred upon it the qualification of METROPOLITAN CHAPTER, which, emboldened in a widening path, dared to date its works back to the impossible, March 21, 1721.

We think, indeed, that the lodge *l'Ardente-Amitié*, of Rouen, upon which has been founded the *Chapter of Heredom*, and that the Chapter de Choix, two fruits of the tree from Mount Heredom, cultivated by the *Royal* G.L. of Edinburgh, protested, but vainly, against these monstrosities. The Royal G.L. was even consulted, in September, on the authenticity of the parchment of *Gerbier*; it was not difficult, according to what we have just established, to prove the falsity of this claim: declaring to have, up to the present, delivered for France, constituting powers (see p. 47 *for their legitimacy*) only to the brothers *Mathéus* and *Chabouillé*. Its declaration is dated from December 11, 1786, day of the celebration of the feast of *Saint Andrew* and of his *Masonry*, 5786.

This piece arrived at Paris long after the union of the Grand Chapter General to the G.O. of France. Already, the brother *Murdoch*, Grand Secretary of the Royal G.L., had transmitted, on October 14, to the brother *Mathéus*, analogous documents (see p. 48). Moreover, would these documents have reached them before the union, they would not have prevented it: the secret aim of the G.O. was to incorporate into itself the Grand Chapter General of France, whose original regularity mattered little. It was without doubt as equivocal as that of the Royal G.L. of Edinburgh, but it wished to make use of it like a club, in order to annihilate écossisme in France, or, at least, to put an end to the intolerable encroachments and to the dominating ambitions of the establishments of all sorts, supposedly *Scottish*; for we repeat, since the reform of Ramsay, who, being Scottish, gave to his rite the name of his land, all that was then invented everywhere took the name of Scottish.

The G.O., which had had its motives for acting thus[42], refused, with reason, all discussion with the Royal G.L. or its *jurisdictions*, before it had justified *its authority* and its *legal existence*. It thus fell back, and with cause, upon the fact that this G.L. did not have the right to give such attestations in the lands of French domination, even less to constitute chapters there which would hinder its operations, in defiance of the concordat made between the G.L. of France and those of England and Scotland, in

1767, etc.

There was nothing to reply to; the Royal G.L. killed itself; things stop at that point.

ORDER OF THE BLAZING STAR
(1766)

The Baron *de Tschoudy*, spiritual and caustic writer, is the author of the *Étoile flamboyante*. He was born at Metz in 1730 and died at Paris in 1769. We have seen that he had composed some grades and rituals for the *Council of the Knights of the East*, of which we were astonished to see him as a member.

In 1766, he instituted, outside of this ephemeral Council, the *Order of the Blazing Star*, composed of chivalric grades, going back to the crusades, according to the Templar system of the Jesuits.

This production renewed with spirit, under new forms, the doctrine of Ramsay. Skillful partisan of the Jesuitic school, the author attributes the foundation of Freemasonry to *Peter the Hermit*[43], that famous provocateur of the *crusades*, and he determined its model, character, and origin on the religious and chivalric institutions, with which the crusades inundated Christianity.

"CRUSADES." The true cause of the crusades against the East, says *Laurens*, is still unknown. The conquest of the holy land is the apparent aim that the history does not characterize enough. The spirit of conquest is not the spirit of the Gospel. Politics, which judges only by the results, sees, in this gigantic conception, only the complement of all the madness and the source of an infinity of evils that time alone has enabled us to forget.

"Indeed, the delirium of the crusades, far from propagating the benefits of Christianity, served only to deprave its doctrine, to produce the dissolution of morals, by introducing, into the West, the vices of the East, by violently agitating the spirits, and by disposing them, in the midst of a war undertaken in the name of the divinity (DIEU LE VEUT!), towards the fury of religious wars, which gave the impulse to all the excesses, which, for a long time, have dried up the breast of Christianity, and singularly retarded the progress of reason," (*Essai sur la Francmaç.*, by Laurens, 2nd edit., p. 87; Paris, 1806).

"And this would be our origin! - What would be more than foreign and contrary to all the probabilities, would be to see an enlightened, philosophical, essentially tolerant society, rise up in the midst of an immense army, *in the middle of a heap of men and women lost in crimes, among which*, says the president HENAULT, *the true Christianity was as rare as virtue*," (Hist. Chronol. de France).

The secret aim of the crusades (*papal secret*) was to substitute, at Constantinople, the Western (*Roman*) Church for the Eastern (*Greek*) Church, and not, as some have believed, to rebuild the temple of Jerusalem. Christians re-erecting a Jewish temple! What an idea!

The Jesuitic order on the point of collapsing in Germany, the Jesuits published, among other works, of their partisans, the *Étoile flamboyante* where *Tschoudy* does not fail to announce the *Order of the Knights Beneficent of the Holy City*, last refuge of the Jesuits.

"The *Blazing*, or Pythagorean, *Star* is the *pentagonal star* of the seven sages of Greece, that the Jesuits, says *Bonneville*, who saw them everywhere, have soiled by their letter G (initial of general)."

The Baron de Tschoudy, brother full of zeal, spirit, and frankness, has, in his *Étoile flamboyante*, praised Masonry in men who love it with a passion; but he criticizes its abuses with ardor.

He calls the *high grades* an expensive occasion for the dupes, he gives the nomenclature thereof and it is written: From where comes to us this *merchandise*? And by what fatality has such an evil drug acquired so prodigious a market? All that is a degression, all that envelopes an object under *superfluous* accessories, more proper for debasing it than raising it, is a vice that must be destroyed:
it is the shame of reason, the detriment of the spirit, and the poison of the heart."

The Br. *Boileau*, enthusiastic Mason, expresses himself, on certain grades of the Scottish scale, and principally on the grades *with a dagger*, with a similar energy, in his scholarly memoires. (See *les Annales maçonniques* by Caillot, 1708 and 1709.)

ADONHIRAMITE MASONRY (by the same author)

It exists in the work of Baron *de Tschoudy*, having as title *Receuil précieux de la Maçonnerie adonhiramite* (1 vol. in-12mo., in 2 parts, the first is 144pp., the second is of 166 pp.; Paris, 1787).

It includes thirteen grades; the author has been able to enrich, by curious notes and scholarly observations, the first three degrees; this preference justifies the opinion common to educated Masons, that the true Masonry does not extend beyond the symbolic régime.

1. Apprentice,
2. Companion,
3. Master,
4. Ancient Master,
5. Elect of the Nine,
6. Elect of Pérignan,
7. Elect of the Fifteen,
8. Little Architect,
9. Grand Architect,
10. Scottish Master
11. Knight of the East,
12. Rose-Croix,
13. Noachite or Prussian Knight.

The Baron de Tschoudy has labored, in Masonry, only to propagate the Jesuitic system, thus has he dedicated this rite *To the Instructed Masons* (read to *the Jesuits*).

Tschoudy was not the only one who imagined mysterious systems and grades, under Masonic forms. We are going to cite some other principal authors, for the instruction of the brothers newly admitted into the institution.

CHAPTER XII
Philosophic Masonry

RITE OF THE ELUS COËNS OR PRIESTS
(1754)

This rite, called at first by the name of its author, *Rite of Martinez-Paschalis*, was composed, in 1754, by this chief of the sect of *Martinists*. Martinez is believed to be Portuguese and Jewish. He formed, according to Swedenborg, a school of Cabalists, called *Coëns* or *Cohens* (*priests*, in Hebrew), at Marseille, Toulouse, Bordeaux, etc., and at Paris, where he brought it in 1767; but he was only able to have it adopted there eight years later. He died at Port-au-Prince (*San Domingo*); his works are: the *Protée*, the *Axiômes*, the *Roue*, the *Monde*.

This régime forms a series of nine grades, divided into two classes, *to wit*:

1st CLASS:	1. Apprentice,	2nd CL.:	6. Companion Coën,
	2. Companion,		7. Master Coën,
	3. Master,		8. Grand Architect.
	4. Grand Elu,		9. Kn. Commander.
	5. Apprentice Coën,		

The aim of this régime is the regeneration of man and his reintegration into his primitive innocence and into the rights that he lost through the *original sin*; it is the system of *Swedenborg* and of all the great mystifiers of the period. Its partisans, chosen with a great circumspection, devoted themselves to supernatural knowledge and professed in general singular opinions on matters of *mystical religion*. This order was formerly widespread in Germany. We find, in the majority of the large cities, societies designated under the name of *lodges of Coëns*. (See *Swedenborg*, hereafter.)

RITE OF PERNETY, OR ILLUMINATI OF AVIGNON
(1766)

This rite, created by Pernety[44], around 1766, was practiced at Avignon in 1778, and transported, the following year, to Montpellier under the title of

Academy of True Masons[45].

This academy was composed of the partisans of the system of *Zinnendorf*, of the Society of the Two Eagles, and that of the *Apocalypse*, which shone brightly, for some time, in the south of Europe, of the *Illuminati of the Zodiac*, of the *Black Brothers*, and of the *Elus-Coëns* (Cabalistic society).

The Masonry of Pernety is *Hermetic*. He was aided in its foundation, at Avignon, by the Comte *de Grabianca*, who, in 1787, organized there a society called *Swedenborgian*. This new sect, contained at first in the secrecy of a lodge, soon showed itself publicly. Well before this era, they occupied themselves, in this city, with mystical doctrines, and the sectarians were known under the name of *Illuminati of Avignon*.

It is, they say, an old Venerable of the Mother Lodge of the county of Venaissin who instituted this academy at Montpellier. They practiced there the following six grades:

1. True Mason,
2. True Mason in the Right way,
3. Knight of the Gold Key,
4. Knight of the Iris,
5. Knight of the Argonauts,
6. Knight of the Golden Fleece.

A breaking up of this academy has without doubt given birth to:

Chapter of the Knights of the Golden Fleece

They professed therein only the last five degrees above.

This chapter, or Academy, has constituted, on March 5, 1785, at Saint-Pierre de la Martinique, an ACADEMY OF TRUE MASONS, which was, on the following June 18, installed by the brother *Goyer de Jumilly*. Here is a passage from his discourse, which is entirely in the style of the principles of this society: "To seize the burin of Hermes in order to engrave upon your columns the elements of the natural philosophy; to call to my aid Flamel, the Philalethete, the Cosmopolite, and our other masters, in order to reveal the mysterious principles of the occult sciences; such would seem to be, illustrious knights, wise academicians, the duties charged to me by the ceremony of your installation...The fountain of the Comte de Trévisan, the pontique water, the tail of the peacock, are phenomena which are familiar to you, etc."

The Academy has later taken the denomination of

Russo-Swedish Academy

Which leads one to supposed that it associated itself with alchemical chapters which existed then in some cities of these States.

There existed already, at Warsaw, a society called

Academy of the Ancients or of the Secrets

It was founded there by the colonel *Toux de Salverte*, on the principles of a society which was established at Rome under the same name, at the beginning of the 16th century, by J.B. *Porta*, celebrated natural philosopher, born at Naples around 1540, died in 1615.

This academy also occupied itself with occult sciences. It was dissolved during the troubles of Poland.

RITE OF BENEDICT CHASTANIER (the Illuminated Theosophists)
(1767)

Chastanier, French Mason, established, in 1767, at London, a purely *Christian theosophical* secret society, whose object was to propagate the system of Swedenborg. The sect soon became public.

He founded the ILLUMINATED THEOSOPHISTS, and modifying the rite of Pernety, he instituted, at the number of six, the grades entitled:

1. Apprentice Theosophist,
2. Companion Theosophist,
3. Master Theosophist,
4. Sublime Ecossais or the Celestial Jerusalem (Illuminated Theosophist),
5. Blue Brother,
6. Red Brother.

RITE OF PHILALETHES OR SEEKERS OF THE TRUTH
(1773)

The Rite of *Philaletes* or *Philalethes*[46] was founded at Paris, in 1773, in the lodge of Amis-Réunis (*formed expressly*), by the brothers *Savalette de Langes*, Guardian of the Royal Treasury, *Court de Gébelin, de Saint-James*, the Vicomte *de Tavannes*, the President *d'Hericourt*, the Prince *de Hesse*, etc.

The moral aim of the Philalethes was the perfecting of man and his union with the one from whom he emanated, according to the principles of *Martinez* or of *Martinism*; the regeneration of man and his reintegration into his primitive innocence, as well as into the rights that he lost through the *original sin*.

This rite was divided into twelve classes or *chambers of instruction*, portioned into two divisions, or six grades each, bearing the names of *Lesser* and *High Masonry*, to wit:

Lesser Masonry	1. Apprentice,	High Masonry	7. Rose-Croix,
	2. Companion,		8. Kn. Of the Temple,
	3. Master,		9. Unknown Philosopher,
	4. Elect,		10. Sublime Philosopher,
	5. Écossais,		11. Initiate,
	6. Kn. of the East,		12. Philalethe or M. of all Grades

This society possessed very fine archives, and everything precious that its library had in mystical works was found in a library in Paris in 1806 and purchased for the archives of the *Philosophical Scottish Rite*, as indicates its annual of 1809, p. 116.

These Masons have had their regulations printed, an instruction on the origin of the Philalethes, in-8vo, and several annuals, among others the one where twenty lodges, French and foreign, figure as following the doctrine and the régime of the Philalethes, that the Abbé *Baruel* calls *the abortions of Swedenborg*.

In 1783, at the death of the founder, the Philalethes cease to gather.

This philosophical Masonry submitted, at Narbonne, in 1779, at the lodge of the *Philadelphes*, whose name it has taken in some rituals, some notable modifications, which produced the PRIMITIVE RITE, that the authors, remaining unknown, claimed to hold from England, and to have translated it to Narbonne.

On February 15, 1785, the Philalethes convoked at Paris a FRATERNAL CONVENT, whose aim was to research, in the ten articles of the *Proponenda*, to wit:

Art. 1. What is the essential nature of the Masonic science, and what is its distinctive character?

Art. 2. What era and what origin may one reasonably attribute to it?

Art. 3. What societies, or what bodies or individuals may one believe to have anciently possessed it, and what are the bodies by which it has successively passed in order to perpetuate itself unto us?

Art. 4. What societies, what bodies or individuals may one believe to be, at this moment, its true depositaries?

Art. 5. Is the tradition which has preserved it oral or written?

Art. 6. Has the Masonic science any relation with the sciences known under the name of *occult* or *secret sciences*?

Art. 7. With which one or ones of these sciences has it the greatest connection, and what are these connections?

Art. 8. What nature of advantages ought one expect from the Masonic science?

Art. 9. Which of the present régimes would be best to follow, not as general coordination, but as the most proper to have zealous and laborious disciples make prompt and useful progress in the true Masonic science?

Art. 10. Why, by a general agreement, do all the Masons call their assemblies and the place in which they are held LODGES? What is the origin and true definition of the word *lodge*; of the word *temple*, another name given, by custom, to the place of assembly; of the phrase opening and closing the works; of the word *Écossais* or *d'Écosse*, for the high grades; of the word *Venerable*, given by the French to the master of the lodge, and of that of *Master in Chair*, given by the Germans?

This convent had been decided August 24, 1784, in a meeting of the members of the twelfth class. The first circular was signed and sent on September 24, announcing the opening of the convent for Tuesday, February 15, 1785.

On October 26, 1784, they passed a decree conveying that the G.L. will not be called to the meeting, although the request had been made in a previous session. On November 13, *Savalette de Langes* is named president of the convent; the Baron de Gleichen, commander of the order of Denmark, and the Marquis *de Chef de Bien* are named secretaries, the one for the German language and the latter for the French language. They sent the *Proponenda* and the second circular to two hundred twenty-eight brothers convoked, among whom figured, on the rolls, the brothers *Duchanteau* (Touzay), professor of theosophy, and *Eteilla*, professor of magic, at Paris.

On December 28, they read to the commissariat of the convent letters from the Prince *Ferdinand of Brunswick* and *Luneburg*, from the brothers *Mesmer*, professor of magnetism, at Paris, and *de Saint-Martin*, by which they refused to participate in the operations of the gathering.

In January 1785, the *Swiss Masons* deliberated in the city of Zurich on the responses to make to the *Proponenda* of the convent of Paris: they decreed that they would not take any part in the operations of this assembly.

On the 27th of this same month, the Marquis *La Rochefoucault* and the doctor *Lafisse*, having been invited as associate members of the *Mother Lodge of the Philosophical Scottish Rite*, this authority expressly forbade its members from assisting at this convent, seeing as it did not belong to brothers of its association to give separately any information on these dogmas; that these documents ought to emanate from the headquarters of the rite itself, if it judges it appropriate to give them.

We see that the system of landmarks existed already in Germany, Switzerland, and France.

This year became celebrated in the Masonic annals by the opening of this first philosophical convent. All the instructed Masons, to whatever rite they belonged, were called there: the convocation was general, for France and the foreigner.

The opening of the convent took place on February 15, by the brother *Savalette de Langes*, who held it in the form of a lodge, at the grade of Apprentice.

March 10. *Joseph Balsamo*, called Comte *de Cagliostro* was, as the other brothers and as being the creator of an *Egyptian Masonry*, invited to take part in the convent and to expound his doctrine there. Audacious or imprudent, *Cagliostro*, who also called himself Comte *de Felix*, responded that he accepts. He promises the truth, and *to make seen, by acts of visible effects, God and the intermediary spirits which exist between man and the Divinity*; but he demands, before everything, that the library and the manuscripts of the rich archives of the lodge of the *Philalethes* be delivered to the flames. Soon recognizing the danger of his imprudence and his position, he calls to his relief the influence attached to his name; but it is impotent to defend him against the investigation of the most loyal and most scholarly Masons. The convent, having received his promises, forces him to fulfill them. A correspondence was established on both sides (see its notice). Cagliostro multiplies the difficulties, seeks to escape through subterfuge, envelopes himself with mysticism and an artificial dignity. This sort of defense deceives nobody. Not being able to escape, he withdraws, leaving in the minds of the members of the convent the troublesome conviction that he has wished to deceive the elite of Masonry, with as little good faith as he had placed, in other matters, to abuse simple and credulous men.

On May 26, the convent is closed. The intermediary commission is persuaded that if the assembly has not been very numerous, it is probably that the place of the gathering (Paris) had not been agreeable to the majority of the persons invited. Consequently, it deputed the brother *Tassin de l'Etang*, to Lausanne, in order to engage the Masons of this city to give asylum to the *convent of the Philalethes*, at the time of its return; the Swiss having appeared in the greatest number, the place seemed most suitable.

On July 16, the Swiss directorial committee deliberated and decides that it cannot consent to this request. It persists in its first resolution, yet while leaving to its members the faculty to take part, *individually*, in the new operations of the convent, be it assembled in Prussia or in any other part of Germany.

The convent addresses three circulars to the Masons, to give an account of the operations of 1785, and to announce a prorogation of the assembly for July 15, 1786 (it did not take place until March 8, the following year). In this circular, the convokers expressed themselves thus (p. 20): "We believe it necessary to announce with frankness that the *aim*, the *desire*, and the *hope* of the convokers, of all the brethren present at the first works, and of a great number of those from whom we have received reports, is to profit from the reunion of the luminaries and from the zeal of the brethren, in order, according to *the characters of the science known to us* and nearly generally *acknowledged*, to attempt to create, in all of Europe, a *new Philalethe association*, by writing up what is known to us of Masonry, and especially by reforming and purifying it in a manner to form a *body of Masons*, or *men of desire*, capable of successfully seeking the truth, disposed towards sacrificing all to merit it, and to be worthy, as much as human weakness may permit, to *possess it*; and this desire of our hearts is all the more reasonable, as we believe, more than ever, certain that it exists, that the greater number of Masons of this century, are not *seeking* it, not *meriting* it, not *finding* it, and that, without doubt, it is the fault of the Masons and not of Masonry."

On March 8, 1787, takes place the opening of the second assembly of the *convent of Paris*, in the hotel of the brother *Savalette de Langes*, rue Saint-Honoré. After twenty-nine gatherings, several of which were notable by the courses given by the brother *Court de Gebelin* and Lenoir[47], the convent saw itself forced to suspend indefinitely the conferences which, while elevating the Masonic science to a height unknown until then, would have made the glory of the Order, if they had been able to vanquish the tepidity and habitual indifference of the Masons for serious instruction.

On March 15, *Eteilla* was called to the sessions on his reputation of education in the occult sciences; he gave, at Paris, public courses in magic, and he regularly exercised the profession of fortune-telling.

On April 3, the Prince *de Hesse-Darmstadt* sent a memorandum and a plan for the reform of Freemasonry.

On the 24th, we read a curious report on a *somnambulist* who, in his magnetic episodes, has given to *Lenormand* the most interesting developments on matters theosophical and metaphysical: to this account was joined the official report of all the speakings of this somnambulist.

This second convent was closed on May 26, 1787. Here is an extract from the letter written by *Savalette de Langes*, to determine the end of the assemblies:

"My Brothers, the little zeal of the very small number of those convoked who, more by consideration of politeness and friendship than by a true interest, come rarely, remaining a short time, to the assemblies of the CONVENT, show to me, to my great regret, that it is not only prudent, but even necessary, to give up. I propose therefore...to declare its closure, etc."

An intermediary commission was named for the rest of the operations; it assembled on the following June 8, and this was the sole and final gathering.

The approach of the French Revolution will further only too much these troublesome dispositions. They already were feeling that the general interest would outweigh the individual interest; and, in this great social movement, the Mason disappearing before the citizen.

NOTES ON SOME PRINCIPAL MASONIC CONVENTS

At the occasion of the convent of the Philalethes, whose intentions were excellent, we are going to cite several convents among which we will not always find the same purity of principle.

The first *philosophical* convent was instituted on November 26, 1777, by the Mother Lodge of the *Philosophical Scottish Rite*, at Paris. Its opening took place on the following December 26.

It had as its object to give courses on subjects relating to the history and dogmas of Freemasonry for the instruction of the members of the Order. Every Mason, to whatever rite he belonged, had the right to request his admission, even to bring his luminaries, while conforming to the regulations of the convent. *Court de Gébelin* was the first that they heard there: he gave, in seven sessions, a dissertation on the most likely allegories of the Masonic grades. Similar gatherings have taken place in Germany.

In 1778, on August 12, November 25, and December 27, the preparation, the opening, and the closing of the works of the *Convent of the Gauls* took place at Lyon, under the presidency of the brother de Willermez.

"The promoters of the convent of Lyon," says *Thory*, "may have had good intentions, but they are accused of lacking delicacy in the means that they employed in order to achieve a reform. They have discontented many people, fomenting divisions and misunderstandings. They have mixed themselves up with intrigues at the occasion of the Duc *Ferdinand Brunswick*, whom they wished to place at the head of the lodges of the Régime (*Reformed* or *Rectified*); finally, they have allowed themselves suppositions and have advanced counterfeited facts, which has done them great harm in the mind of the public. Their principal object was to reform the Masonic Order, with which they have not occupied themselves: they have used all their time to correct the rituals, and this was only an accessory motive of the gathering; still have they left therein many superfluities and puerilities. Their new instructions are fables, loose and too diffused; their fiscal system is unjust and badly ordered," (Acta Latom.).

Moreover, this convent gave the first abjuration of the Templar system. A German author has said on this subject:

"The abjuration of the convent of Lyon was made by injunction of the police, who had declared that they were opposed to the propagation of any system which would tend toward recalling the Templars and their customs; but this abandon was only simulated, and the brethren remained connected with the lodges of the *Strict Observance* of Germany, as province." (*Das Ganze aller Gewerbe*, p. 74.)

Members of the Scottish, Helvetic, *German*, and *Roman* directories, who had assisted at the convents of Germany, the previous year, took part in the one of Lyon and influenced it.

CONVENT OF WILHEMSBAD. On September 9, 1780, the first circular of the convocation of all the *Scottish Grand Lodges of Europe* at the *Convent of Wilhemsbad*, near Hanau, was sent; a second announced the opening for October 15, 1781; a third prolonged it to the time of Easter, 1782; and a fourth fixed the opening definitively at Tuesday, July 16, 1782. It effectively took place this day, under the presidency of the Duc *Ferdinand de Brunswick*.

In this convent, prepared by that *of the Gauls*, held at Lyon in 1778, and which had been assembled under the pretext of a general reform in the Masonic Order, TEN QUESTIONS were proposed: the principal ones tended towards knowing whether the Masonic Order must be considered as a purely conventional society, or if indeed one may deduce its origin from a more ancient order; and what was that order? Did the Order have *general superiors* existing then? Who were these superiors? How was one to define them? Did they have the faculty to command or to instruct? ...etc. None of these questions were put into motion: they limited themselves to declaring that *the Masons were not the successors of the Templars*. They instituted an order of Beneficence (*the Order of Knights Beneficent of the Holy City of Jerusalem*), and the Duc *Ferdinand de Brunswick* was placed at the head of the *reformed lodges*.

One remarkable thing, is that at the twenty-eighth session, the Scottish lodge of *Frédéric au Lion-d'Or* sent to the convent a memorandum accompanied by a letter from *Frédéric de Brunswrick*, in which he offered to communicate *new knowledge*, to indicate the *major unknown superiors*, to send, before long, the great ritual manuscript preserved by the *Clerici brethren* (the clerics), etc.; and the convent determined that the assembly had renounced *all unknown and hidden superiors*; that it had decreed new rituals; and finally, that the old ones were useless to the reform (*Actes du conv. de Wilhemsbad*, nos. 161, 162, 164).

It is certain that this convent had no other object than that of removing from Freemasonry the Templar system[48], and to place the Duc *Ferdinand de Brunswick* at the head of the reformed lodges: thus, did they take great care to remove therefrom all those who they knew to manifest a contrary opinion. They were refused entrance to the assembly, and particularly the deputies of the *chapter* and the *Mother Lodge of the Croissante-aux-Trois-Clefs*, of Ratisbonne, and the Marquis *de Chef de Bien* (*eques a capite galeato*), as representing the lodge *Amis-Réunis*, of Paris, (*De conventu generali Latamorum*, p. 138).

PRIMITIVE RITE OR OF THE PHILADELPHES OF NARBONNE

(1779)

This rite was imagined and founded at Narbonne on April 19, 1780, by the so- called *Major and Minor Superiors General of the Order of Free and Accepted Masons* (such are the terms of the constitutional patent of this rite). It was attached to the lodge of the Philadelphes[49], under the title of *Première lodge de Saint- Jean réunie au rite primitif, au pays de France*, and in which it had taken its Masonic rank on December 27, 1779, day of its request. The lodge of the Philadelphes had printed in 1790, following the table of the members of its composition, a curious fragment, entitled: *Notion général sur le charactère et l'objet du rite primitif*, (booklet in-8vo of 51 pages), where we find precise and detailed information on the system of this régime.

It is formed by THREE CLASSES of Masons who receive *ten degrees* of instruction. These classes or degrees are not the designation of such or such grades, but of the denomination of collections that it suffices to display, as far as they are capable thereof, in order to have flow therefrom a nearly infinite number of grades. Thus, the first six degrees designate the knowledge of the grades analogous to those which they include, to wit:

1st Class	1. Apprentice 2. Companion 3. Master	in all the rites,
2nd Class	4. Under the titles of	Perfect Master, Elect.
	5. Under the titles of	Architect. Sublime Écossais.
	6. Under the titles of	Knight of the Sword. Knight of the East. Prince of Jerusalem.
3rd Class	1st	Chapter of ROSE-CROIX. It posses the ideas which, in some régimes fixes the Masonic cult and the veneration of a multitude of respectable brothers.
	2nd	Chapter of ROSE-CROIX. It is depositary of historical documents very curious by their type, their comparison, their variety.
	3rd	Chapter of ROSE-CROIX. It is occupied with all Masonic Class knowledge, physical and philosophical, the products of which may influence the happiness and the material and moral well-being of *temporal man.*
	4th	And last chapter called of the BRETHREN ROSE-CROIX OF THE GRAND ROSARY. It makes its assiduous study of particular knowledge on ontology, pneumatology, in a word, on all parts of the sciences that they call *occult* or *secret.* Their special object being the reintegration of the intellectual man into his primitive rights.

The Primitive Rite has been united into the G.O. by the lodge of the

Philadelphes, on the favorable report of the directory of Rites, in 1806. It is no longer practiced today in France, and it differs from the one which, they assure us, is professed in Belgium.

The lodge *la Bonne-Amitié*, at Namur, constituted on February 9, 1770, by the *Primitive Scottish Rite*, at Edinburgh (where no rite bears this name), and reconstituted by the G.O. of France, June 24, 1808, professes this rite, and has never ceased, *it says*, to correspond directly with *the chief body of the metropolitan and constituting order*. It must not be confused, this rite informs, which has thirty-three degrees, with the philosophical rite conceived at Narbonne.

We add that in 1818, circulars announced the organization of a *Primitive Scottish Rite*, which would have been introduced at Namur in 1770, by the *Metropolitan Grand Lodge of Edinburgh*, Masonic authority often invoked by the charlatans, although not existing, at least legally.

This rite of modern creation is composed of thirty-three degrees, taken, for the most part, from the Scottish series called *Heredom*. It had for its principal author the brother *Marchot*, advocate, at Nivelles.

Its jurisdiction seems not to have exceeded the precincts of Namur, where it was practiced, as it would seem, by the lodge *la Bonne-Amitié*. That of the Vrais-Amis de l'Union, at Brussels, possessed an areopagus of the 19th degree of this rite.

Here is the nomenclature of this bastard régime, where dominates, under the Templar veil, the Jesuitic grades:

1. Apprentice,
2. Companion,
3. Master,
4. Perfect Master,
5. Irish Master,
6. Elect of the Nine,
7. Elect of the Unknown,
8. Elect of the Fifteen,
9. Illustrious Master,
10. Perfect Elect,
11. Little Architect,
12. Grand Architect,
13. Sublime Architect,
14. M. in the Perfect Architect,
15. Royal Arch,
16. Prussian Knight (Noachite),
17. Knight of the East,
18. Prince of Jerusalem,
19. Venerable of Lodges,
20. Knight of the West,
21. Knight of Palestine,
22. Sovereign Prince Rose-Croix
23. Sublime Écossais,
24. Knight of the Sun,
25. Grand Écossais of St. Andrew,
26. Mason of the Secret,
27. Knight of the Black Eagle,
28. Knight Kadosh,
29. Grand Elect of the Truth,
30. Novice of the Interior,
31. Knight of the Interior,
32. Prefect of the Interior,
33. Commander of the Interior.

RITE OF MARTINISM

Louis-Claude, Marquis de *Saint-Martin*, officer of the Regiment of Foix, celebrated theosophist, called the *Unknown Philosopher*, was born at Amboise in 1748. Nourished on the systems of *Paschalis* and *Swedenborg*, he composed a particular philosophy therefrom, all of pure spiritualism, which connects everything to God, and preached it with success at Paris. We have from him: *Des Erreurs et de la Vérité* (mystical work); *Rapports entre Dieu, l'homme et l'univers; l'Homme de désir; le Ministère de l'homme esprit;*

Translations of some works of Boehme.

In this rite, which bears his name, he modified the doctrines of his master *Martinez-Paschalis*. (See the rite of Élus-Coëns.) We find in the grades of Saint-Martin, as in all his works, ridiculous superstitions and absurd beliefs.

We call *Martinist Lodges* those which profess the rite of *Martinez-Paschalis* or that of *Saint-Martin*.

This latter was originally composed of ten grades divided into two temples, the first of which contains seven grades, and the second three. Here are their names:

1st Temple:
1. Apprentice
2. Companion,
3. Master,
4. Ancient Master,
5. Elect,
6. Grand Architect,
7. Mason of the Secret,

2nd Temple:
8. Prince of Jerusalem,
9. Knight of Palestine,
10. Kadosh or holy man.

This rite was reduced to seven grades in the régime having for its name: *Reformed Écossisme of Saint-Martin*, widespread in Germany and Prussia, to wit:

1. Apprentice,
2. Companion,
3. Master,
4. Perfect Master,
5. Elect,
6. Écossais,
7. Sage.

PHILOSOPHICAL SCOTTISH RITE

This rite is attached to universal Masonry, by means of the three symbolic grades of the Ancient and Accepted Scottish Rite, *which form its base, although remaining outside of the system*, says the ritual. It is therefore two rites in one. Understand who may this contradiction, and how the symbolism may be outside of a system, if it really forms its base.

This rite, which is nearly the same as the Hermetic Rite of Montpellier, was modified by the brother *Boileau*, physician at Paris, one of the most distinguished adepts of *dom Pernety*, and recognized in France as the *Grand Master of Hermetic Masonry*. He instituted, in 1776, in the lodge *Contrat-Social*, formerly *Saint-Lazare*, at Paris, aided by commissioners of the *Grand Lodge of the County of Venaissin*. (See *Mother Lodge of the Philosophical Scottish Rite*.)

Its nomenclature is thus composed:

1.
2. Knight of the Black Eagle or Rose-Croix of Heredom of the Tower
3. (divided into three parts).
4. Knight of the Phoenix, with two boards,
5. Knight of the Sun,
6. Knight of the Iris,
7. True Mason,
8. Knight of the Argonauts,
9. Knight of the Golden Fleece,
10. Grand Inspector, Perfect Initiate,
11. Grand Inspector, Grand Écossais,
12. Sublime Master of the Luminous Ring.

We see that with the three symbolic degrees, the number of grades of this rite would be raised to fifteen. (See our *Tuileur général* in the *Fastes initiatiques*.)

On October 17, 1783, a bull from the Grand Master of the United Lodges in Basse-Saxe, Livonie, and Courlande, dated July 11, 1776, had instituted the brother BOILEAU as NATIONAL GRAND SUPERIOR of the lodges and chapters of the *Philosophical Scottish Régime* in France, with power to create, in opportune time, a *tribunal head of the order* and suffragant tribunals, the members of which, under the title of *Grand Inspector Commanders*, would be charged with the maintenance of the dogma and with the high administration of the body, etc. - From what authority did these united lodges hold their constitutions and their rite? We are unaware.

Whatever it may be, the brother BOILEAU founded this day, October 17, at Paris, the TRIBUNAL HEAD OF THE ORDER, and transported to himself all its *rights*, conforming to his instructions.

He transmits his title of National Grand Superior to the Baron *de Bromer*, who was then chosen as *President*, as well as to all his *legitimately* elected successors.

SUFFRAGANT TRIBUNALS OF THE TRIBUNAL HEAD OF THE ORDER OF THE PHILOSOPHICAL SCOTTISH REGIME

There existed in France only five *regular* tribunals of the constitution of the tribunal head of the order, established near the Mother Lodge of this rite, to wit:

The tribunal of *Douai*, attached to the lodge *la Parfait-Union*,

The tribunal of *Puylaurens*, attached to the lodge *la Parfait-Amitié*,

The tribunal of *Toulouse*, attached to the lodge *la Sagesse* and to that of *l/Union*,

The tribunal of *Angers*, attached to the lodge *le Père-de-Famille*,

The tribunal of *Dunkerque*, attached to the lodge *l'Amitié-et-Fraternité*.

Two others, likewise, established for France, are found in foreign lands since 1814, these are:

The tribunal of *Anvers*, attached to the lodge *les Elèves de Minerve*, and the tribunal of *Brussels*, attached to the lodge *la Paix*.

These tribunals ought not be confused with the chapters or tribunals of the 31st degree of the *Ancient* and *Accepted Scottish Rite*. The rites, ceremonies, attributions, and decorations of the members of these chapters have no relation with those of the tribunals of the *Philosophical Rite*.

ACADEMY OF THE SUBLIME MASTERS OF THE LUMINOUS RING
(1780)

"Without wealth, without power, Masonry has seen emerge from its midst a thousand innovators, whose excesses it has not been able to quell. From here, the creation of a multitude of grades, and even rites resembling it more or less." (*Dictionn. maçon.*, p. 2.)

The Academy of the Sublime Masters of the Luminous Ring was founded in France in 1780, by the brother *Grant*, Baron Blaerfindy, Scottish colonel, according to the

Pythagorean doctrine. It is, without doubt, one of those numerous daughters of the ancient Masonry. In 1784, it was attached to the lodge *la Parfait-Union* at Douai.

It is divided into three grades: the first two are dedicated to the study of the historical part, where they indicate Pythagoras as the founder of Masonry and where they have his school revived. (Pythagoras did not suspect Freemasonry: he professed the secret doctrine, and initiated his elite disciples into the *occult sciences*, practiced in the *greater Egyptian mysteries.*) The third grade is dedicated to the study of dogma[50].

MOTHER LODGE OF THE PHILOSOPHICAL SCOTTISH RITE

This association has always taken care to hide its origin. It has called a *rite* its collection of Hermetic grades, which have nothing *Scottish*, nor *Philosophical*, for they say *philosopher's stone* [pierre philosophale] and not *philosophical stone* [pierre philosophique]; its definitive title ought, therefore, to be *Mère-Loge du rite philosophale*.

It was founded at Paris on April 2, 1776, under the title of *Contrat-social.* Its installment took place on the following Mar 5, by the commissioners of the County of Venaissin. This lodge had been constituted in 1766 under the name of *Saint-Lazare*, by the dissident G.L. (*Lacorne*), composed of brothers excluded from the G.L. of France. Then, having placed itself on the side of the G.O., at the time of the Masonic revolution of 1772, it had itself constituted anew by this authority, under the title of *Saint-Jean d'Écosse du Contrat-Social*; and then it took, "by means of *derisive* and *illusory* titles, the quality of *Scottish Mother Lodge*, without knowing what a *Scot* is, the reason for which they speak of Scottish, nor what it substitutes, says a writer of the period, author of G.-J. G.E." (*Avertissement*, p. 12.)

This supposed Mother Lodge has shown, by the pen of brother *Thory*, that in Masonry, as in the profane world, arrogance is often the lot of the upstarts.

On May 21, the G.O. refuses to inscribe upon its rolls the title of *Mother Lodge*. The order to renounce this title is issued on December 9, under pain of being stricken from the list of regular lodges.

August 18. Act of incorporation of the M.L. of the County of Venaissin into the M.L. of the Philosophical Scottish Rite in France.

On February 20, 1777, the Grand Assembly for Chapters is issued a decree which forbade the lodges and chapters of the régime from practicing or recognizing the grade of *Knight of the Temple* and all others having a connection to the system of the *Templars*, whether of the Strict Observance, or of Dresden.

May 18. After a year of discussion and resistance, the G.O. strikes this association from the general rolls of the Order, by reason of its title of *Scottish Mother Lodge of France.*

On October 4, 1780, it gave to the brother *de Montausier* powers of deputy in order to establish at San Domingo and in the French isles, the *Philosophical Masonry*. (To be understood, say therefore *philosophale* or *Hermetic Masonry*.)

On November 5, 1781, all contestations between the G.O. and this Mother Lodge are reconciled by a concordat passed between the commissioners of the two bodies: the Mother Lodge surrenders all claims to this title with regards to the G.O., and consents to preserve it, in its correspondence, only with regard to the lodges of the *Philosophical Rite. The right to constitute lodges in foreign lands is reserved to it*; but yet it consents to employ the expression *agréger* [to admit into a society, to incorporate] instead of *constituer* [to constitute], in the establishments that it may form in the interior of France.

1782. *Écossisme* reappears down to the symbolic grades, but ever in order to dominate: they found, on its behalf, at Paris, on July 7, the lodge of *Saint-Alexandre d'Écosse*; it served as refuge, in 1804, to the lodge of the *Contrat-Social*; it thus took the title of Scottish M.L. of France, under the name of *Saint-Alexandre d'Écosse et du Contrat-Social réunis.*

On July 27, the Mother Lodge decreed that it would not recognize the Egyptian Rite of Cagliostro and that it will be addressed in a circular to the lodges and chapters of the Philosophical régime, in order to invite them "to steer clear of innovators in Masonry, which are all the more dangerous since they remove the true Masons from the aim to which the brothers of the Order ought to tend; and seeing as the brother *Devisme*, one of its members, has been signaled as being part of the lodge *la Sagesse-Triomphante*, working at Lyon, under the Egyptian régime, the M.L. decides that he will return to Paris, *in order to give an account of his conduct*."

On March 10, 1788, C.-A. *Thory* is named *conservator for life* of the books, manuscripts, and monuments comprising the general archives of the Philosophical Order (*we are unaware of what has become of them*).

On May 7, the M.L. names a commission to examine the work of Nicolas *Bonnewille*, entitled: *Les jesuites chasses de la Maconnerie et leur poignard brise par les maçons* [The Jesuits Driven Out of Masonry and Their Dagger Broken by the Masons], etc.
The commissioners, on May 21, made their report, where they presented this writing *as a childish production by a perverse mind, and a poison prepared to become a destructive scourge on Masonry*, etc. (where they have not included, or submitted to without knowing, the Jesuitic influence). On June 28, on the conclusion of the Grand Orator, the M.L. decrees that the book *shall be burned* in the outer hall.

On October 22, the Scottish M.L. lent its temple and gave its support to the lodges of the new Scottish Rite called *Ancient* and *Accepted,* assembled in order to organize a G.L. of this régime and to rival the power of the G.O. (This operation is perhaps *Scottish*, but it is not *Philosophical*.)

Here is what this M.L. has done most importantly: it initiated on November 24, 1808, *Askeri-Khan*, ambassador of Persia at the court of France. After his reception, the neophyte gives to the M.L. the Damascus blade with which he is armed and says:

"Sirs, I promise you amity, fidelity, and esteem. They have told me, and I cannot doubt it, that the Freemasons were good, charitable, full of love and attachment for their Sovereigns; suffice that I give you a present worthy of true Frenchmen. Receive this sabre which has served me in 27 battles; may this homage convince you of the sentiments that you have inspired in me, and of the pleasure that I have to belong to your order!"

On November 23, 1809, the general archives of the Order are enriched by the curious collection of *Indian idols* from the celebrated cabinet of the Baron *de Horn*. On the following December 14, his nephew made a gift to the archives of an *Indian mythological manuscript*, written on thirty sheets of white wood, with a seal containing three lines in Sanskrit characters. (*Al. Lenoir* has described these idols in his book entitled: *La Franche-Maçonnerie rendue à sa véritable origine*.) (See for more details on this association our *Précis historique*.)

OPINION of the brother Bezuchet on the M.L. of the Philosophical Scottish Rite:

"M. *Thory*, one of its members, has endeavored to give a great importance to this workshop (see *Acta Latamorum*, etc.). He signals its works at every occasion, in the smallest details. He puts it constantly in line with the G.L. and the G.O., and sometimes above. Time, that eternal judge, and the good sense of the Masons in general, have refuted the vanities of the historian and of his work itself: the lodge, stricken with a mortal languor, has ceased entirely to exist.

"The Scottish Mother Lodge had beautiful archives, a nice deposit of books and manuscripts, and a rare collection of medals, all objects of a rather great value, and acquired by the revenues of the lodge. The brother *Thory* was the conservator thereof; the lodge having been extinguished; he has preserved these objects. He himself has since died. They say that his widow has become their conservator in her turn; but when this lady dies, will her heirs, who have no legitimate right, since so many precious acquisitions have been made by the revenues of the members of the lodge, also be the conservators, or, better to say, the owners? This question could concern the Masonic authority in France, or better yet the tribunals, if the interested parties were advised one day to reclaim their rights." (*Précis historique de l 'Ordre de la Francmaçonnerie*, 1829, p. 71.)

The list of workshops constituted by the *Scottish Mother Lodge of the Philosophical Scottish Rite*, at Paris, puts the number thereof at seventy-four. (See the *Fastes initiatiques*.)

In the review that we have just made, one has had to remark that the *Hermetic grades* occupy a rather large place in the majority of the rites, because indeed, there is no complete initiation without the study of the *occult sciences*. We treat, in the second part of this work on *Occult Masonry*, and, in the third, on *Hermetic Masonry*, so worthy of the attention of the educated Mason.

Before passing to some rites which have appeared in France since 1800, we are going to cast a glance on the *Masonry* (which it is not) *of the so-called brother Enoch*.

RITE OR MASONRY OF THE BROTHER HENOCH
(1773)

This unusual rite was composed of four grades, to *wit*:

1.	Laborer,	aim:	friendship, beneficence,
2.	Workman,	aim:	fidelity owed to the Sovereign,
3.	Master,	aim:	submission to the Supreme Being,
4.	Architect,	aim:	the perfection of all the virtues.

The brother Enoch, who has made himself, in 1773, historian of this rite of his invention, tried to accredit it and spread it by means of the fiction that we are going to read:

"It assures, very seriously, that *Louis-le-Débonnaire*, Emperor of Germany and King of France, accepted its Grand Mastership in 814, at the feast of Saint John of winter.

"Pleased," *he says*, "with the fidelity to the Sovereign that the (*operative*) masons professed, he wished to recognize this attachment by a particular favor. He ordered that in all the lodges of these States, at the reception of workmen, the second master would decorate the candidate with a *sword* that he would wear *in lodge* in order to be of service in the defense of his prince and the homeland. He wielded the trowel, received the four grades (*which were only invented* in 1773, that is to say 959 *years after* 814) and was elected grand master." Enoch added:

"The other Sovereigns (*of what lands?*) continued to honor the Order with the same privilege, so that all the masters are decorated with the sword."

The brother Enoch thus defines *his Masonry*:

"A holy and pious society, of kind men, who have *as their foundation* discretion; *as their aim*, service to God, fidelity to his prince, and charity towards his neighbor[51], and *as its lesson* to erect an allegorical building to the virtues that it teaches, with certain signs to recognize one another," (Chap. 3)[52].

To define Freemasonry so inexactly, the brother Enoch had without doubt some *metaphorical* reason, as when he had preside, in the time of Adam, over the first lodge, the archangel *Saint Michael*, with the dignity of Grand Master of the Order, probably because Saint Michael, crushing the demon, is the symbol of the genius of the good (*the light*) vanquisher of the genius of the evil (*darkness* or *ignorance*).

When the conservators of the ancient doctrines believed it necessary to take the symbolic veil of a guild of *freemasons*, in order to throw off course the espionage which could have been introduced furtively or at the indiscretion of bad intentioned brethren, the brother *Enoch* has supposed that then, in some manner, they *Masoned*, and here is how he indicates these works, which are also of his invention:

There were large and small triangular stones (some old manuscripts have taught him that they were formed from boards or cardboard); each of them bore a letter. These stones, united, formed words such as *charity*, *beneficence*. They thus erected a *speaking wall*. The Laborers (*Apprentices*) would choose the stones and carry them. The Workmen (*Companions*) would arrange them in order, in a manner to regularly make the walls or pillars. The *Masters* would examine, order, and correct the works. The *Architects* would give the orders to the Masters and decide the difficulty. The Grand Master (*Venerable*), the First and Second Master (*1st and 2nd Surveillants*) labored to bind the walls at the corners. The *Master of Ceremonies* saw to the good order everywhere. The Masons of each grade would ask those of inferior grade the explanation of the works and the *instruction* they gave. - The artlessness of this account exempts the reader from feeling the desire to know any more thereof.

CHAPTER XIII
Orders and Rites Introduced Into France Since 1800

SACRED ORDER OF THE SOPHISIANS
(1808)

Quies, justitia, sane ambo in sede.

This régime, founded in 1801, at Paris, in the lodge of the *Freres-Artistes* by the brother *Cuvelier de Trie*, Venerable, had the pretention of deriving directly from the Egyptian mysteries, under the title of *Sacred Order of the Sophisians*, established in the pyramids of the French republic.

This order owes its origin to some French generals, taking part in the expedition of Egypt. It was then brought to the lodge of the *Artistes*.

The Order is placed under the auspices of H. (Horus). It is divided into three classes:

1st, the *Aspirants* (they are mute, and respond only by yes or no),

2nd, the *Initiates*, and

3rd, the *members of the Greater Mysteries*.

The rule of themaspirants is in eighteen articles and bears this motto: "Study is the sister of Horus."

The last article is conceived thus:

"The philanthropy which characterizes the Freemasons being the first virtue required in a Sophisian, nobody, in the pyramids of the French republic, is received as an *Aspirant*, unless he knows the *acacia*, and unless he has labored in the *Middle Chamber*."

"Done in the great pyramid, the year 15,509 of the era of the Sophisians, and of the republican era the 1st of vendémiaire, year IX" (September 23, 1801)[53].

Composition of the Order:

The GRAND ISIARCH, organ of the supreme tribunal; he alone bears the word.
On his jewel is a sun with the motto: *Non lucet omnibus.*
He has the augural baton.

4 ISIARCHS or PHILISIARCHS, *perpetual officers* bearing the augural baton.

6 inferior officers: 1 HARPOCRATES, bearing the urn, prince of the subaltern officers.
2 HORUPHILES, carrying the sword raised, adjuncts of Harpocrates.
1 HERMORUS, carrying the bare sword, commands the exterior.
1 TROPHADOR, charged with housekeeping expenses.

1 NOMARCH, bearing the banner of the tribunal.

7 superior officers: 1 AGATHOS, carrying an open purse.
6 SOSIS, conservators of the Order.

10 subaltern officers: 2 CERICES or *Mercuries*, bearing the caduceus; they are under the orders of the Hermorus.
2 DIACTORUS, bearing a mace, King at Arms.
4 PASTOPHORES, charged with carrying the ark; they are the guardians thereof.

HONORS due to the officers of the different classes:

1st ORDER: the Sacred Ark, the tribunal of Isiarchs, the Grand Isiarch, alone: The sword in the right hand, the point lowered and touching the ground; the left hand covering the eyes, the thumbs stretched out over the left Temple, the right foot back.

2nd ORDER: the Isiarch alone; the Agathos and the Sosis all together: The sword in the right hand, the point lowered and touching the ground. The left hand at order over the heart.

3rd ORDER: one Sosis alone, the Harpocrates at the head of the subaltern officers and the Nomarch: The left hand at order over the heart, the right hand on the hilt of the sword.

ANNOUNCEMENTS. All the announcements are made, and all the orders are given by whistles, the number of which is ruled. To this end, the Hermorus wears, around his neck, an *ebony whistle*, which he uses only to signal what happens at the exterior. The Harpocrates wears a *silver whistle* in order to repeat to the Grand Isiarch the signals from the exterior, or to transmit to the Hermorus the orders of the tribunal. The Grand Isiarch has a gold whistle to command.

CLOSING. The Grand Isiarch announces that the ark is deposited and covered with the religious veil; then he gives the signal by *seven whistles* and the session is ended.

Here is the mysterious ladder of this ephemeral Order:

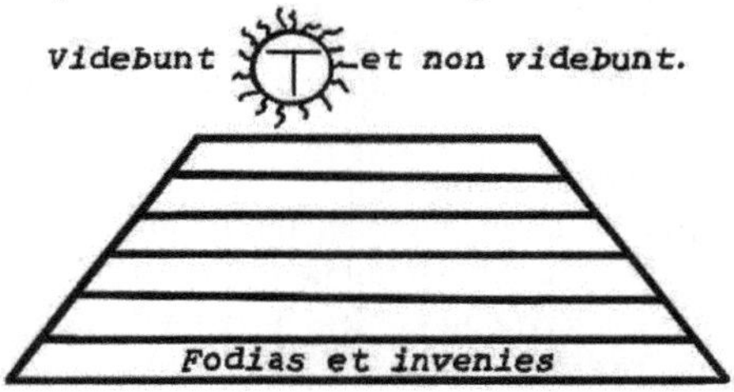

RITE OF MISRAIM CALLED EGYPTIAN RITE, OR BETTER, JUDAIC RITE (1805 and 1814)

This rite represents autocracy. One alone, under the title of *Sovereign Grand Master Absolute*, governs the workshops of the rite; it is irresponsible. This profane anomaly recalls the *divine right.* This régime, which has from Masonry only its borrowings from rites already known, is not even *Masonic* in its forms.

At a period when it was a question of reducing the recent number of the thirty-three degrees of écossisme, reduced in fact to five in practice (the three *symbolic grades*, the *Rose-Croix*, and the *Kadosh*), is presented Misraimism, with its ninety degrees, divided into four series, subdivided into seventeen classes, to wit:

The 1st series called *Symbolic* comprises the grades from 1 to 33, divided into 6 classes.

The 2nd series called *Philosophical* comprises the grades from 34 to 66, divided into 4 classes.

The 3rd series called *Mystical* comprises the grades from 67 to 77, divided into 4 classes.

The 4th series called *Cabalistic* comprises the grades from 78 to 90, divided into 3 classes.

The Sovereign Grand Masters Absolute, *supreme power of the Order*, 90th degree, arrogate to themselves the right to rule ALL THE RITES, which are, *they say*, only *detached branches of the Misraimite tree*. We must congratulate them on the immense extent of their knowledge, as well as their great *constituting* ministers, on the extraordinary talents with which they must be furnished in order to govern *all the rites existing upon the globe*.

This monstrous rite, for which its authors have drawn from Écossisme, Martinism, Hermeticism, and from the Masonic reformations, the majority of its degrees of instruction, was brought from Italy into France, in 1814. Here is what is said of it by the author of the *Histoire pittoresque de la Francmaçonnerie*, who has practiced this regime: "It is in 1805 that several brothers, of discredited morals, not having been able to be admitted into the composition of the *Scottish Supreme Council*, which had been founded in this year at Milan, imagined the *Misraimite* régime. A brother *Lechangeur* was charged with collecting the elements thereof, classifying them, coordinating them, and drafting a project of *general statutes*. In these beginnings, the postulant could only attain to the 87th degree. The three others, which completed the system, were reserved to the *unknown superiors*; and the very names of these degrees were hidden from the brethren of the inferior grades. It is with this organization that the Rite of Misraim was spread into the kingdoms of Italy and Naples. It was adopted notably by a Rose-Croix chapter, called *la Concorde*, which had its seat in the Abruzzi. At the bottom of a brief or diploma, delivered in 1811, by this chapter, to the brother *B. Clavel*, war commissioner, figures the signature of one of the current chiefs of the rite, the brother *Marc Bédarride*, who then only had the 77th degree. The brothers *Lechangeur*, *Joly*, and *Bédarride* brought *Misraimism* into France in 1814."

Paris then intends, in 1814, to speak, for the first time, on the *Rite of Misraim*.

In 1816, eleven brothers belonging to the rite, displeased, and scandalized by the traffic that *imposters* dared to make of this Masonry, and in the laudable and impartial aim to put an end to it, resolved to purify the ark and to create a new Supreme Council of the rite: they formed a *Supreme Council, 90th degree*.

The members charged to fill the officers were the brothers *Ragon*, bureau chief, venerable founder of the chartered lodge of the *Trinosophes*; *Gaborria*, Sov. G.M. Absolu., at the 90th and last degree, Valley of Naples; *Décollet*, Chief of the administration of monies and medals, and *Méallet*, Secretary of the Academic Society of the Sciences, under the presidency of brother *Joly*, authorized to *create*, *establish*, and *constitute* in France the Rite of *Misraim* in the four series and in all the degrees which comprise them, by virtue of the *powers* which had been delegated to it at Naples, in 1813, by the power established in this capital.

They declared, in their statutes, to not recognize in France any other Masonic and legal authority than the G.O., and, on October 8, they delivered the rite to it, which was accepted. Commissioners were named on both sides; the discussion was drawn out at great length. The officers of the G.O., consulted in particular, had promised their adhesion. The brother *Langlacé*, Orator, announced it formally in the discourse that he pronounced on June 24, 1817, day of the solstitial feast; but the leaders of the G.O. would judge otherwise, and the rite was rejected on the following December 27. The *presenters*, who wished to arm the G.O. with this rite, so that no one could continue to abuse it, renounced it forever, and declared their *Supreme Council* of the *90th degree dissolved*.

We do not relate here the summary of the last four degrees (87 to 90) which was given to each of the five members of the *examination committee* having as title: *Arcana Arcanorum*; it is found in the *Cours interprétatif des initiations*, p. 344 and following.

This rite (that of the *Bédarride brothers*) is, from the 1st to the 66th degree inclusive, only a pillage made of the crude rite called *Ancient* and *Accepted* of thirty-three degrees, and from various collections of grades invented in France since 1730. This rite does not really begin, then, until the 67th degree, and goes along only upon *Biblical* subjects, with which true Masonry has nothing to do, and on subjects relating to *Israelism*, which has no connection to Egypt, which is well anterior to all that. That is why we call it the *Judaic Rite*. We give, in the General Tiler, the tiler of each of the ninety degrees.

The grades of the rite, that is to say from the 67th degree to the 90th, each have their characteristic, that we reproduce here.

The solemn feasts of this rite are fixed at the very days of the equinoxes; the one of spring is celebrated under the name of *Awakening of nature*, and that of the autumn under the name of *Repose of nature*.

RITE OF MEMPHIS CALLED ORIENTAL
(1839)

The *Egyptian* Rite of *Misraim*, bizarre collection of various rites and grades, none of which is Egyptian, seems to have inspired the brothers *Marconis* and *Mouttet*, who have attempted to institute, in 1839, at Paris, then at Marseille and Brussels, a new rite called MEMPHIS, composed of ninety-one degrees, whose nomenclature and statutes are found in a booklet in-12mo of 240 pages, that the brothers have published the same year, under the title of *l'Hierophante*. In this booklet, it is said on p. 6 that *the Rite of Memphis recognizes as its immediate founders the Knights of Palestine or Rose-Croix Brethren of the Orient*.

Be that as it may, the authors, in a new book having for its title *le Sanctuaire*, printed since, have added to this rite, already monstrous, a 92nd degree, transmitted, no doubt, by some successors of the Knights of Palestine, and they have modified their first nomenclature. We reproduce, in the *Tuileur général*, the new list, for the curious Masons that these sorts of things interest.

The régime is divided into three series, which are subdivided into seven classes, *to wit*:

1st SERIES. It contains 3 classes from the 1st to the 35th degree. "It teaches morals, gives the explanation of the symbols, disposes the adepts towards philanthropy, and makes known to them the first historical part of the Order."

With some very slight variations in the titles, these degrees are those of the Scottish régime. They have added to the vestments a sky-blue tunic. We will ask the authors why, when they pillaged a rite or borrow from a known grade, do they alter its means of recognition, as if the memory did not already have enough to retain?

2nd SERIES. It comprises 2 and a half classes from the 36th to the 68th degree. "It teaches the natural sciences, the philosophy of history, and it explains the poetic myth of antiquity. Its aim is to elicit the research of causes and origins, and to develop the humanitarian and sympathetic sense."

We find in this series some well-known grades, but which are not at all oriental.

3rd SERIES. It comprises half of the 6th class and the 7th, from the 69th to the 92nd and final degree. "It makes known the complement of the historical part of the Order; it occupies itself with high Philosophy, study of the religious myth of the different ages of humanity and admits the most daring philosophical studies." The order does not have one pay until the last seven degrees. (See the Scottish Rite.) The others, up to the 92nd, are granted by merit and are given *gratis*.

It gathers to their corresponding grades the Masons of all the rites.

This rite, as that of Écossisme, is wrong to consider Freemasonry as a cult. This may suit the Jesuitico-Templar Masonry, which has never been the true one.

The Memphisians celebrate a feast of the order each year, at the spring equinox, under the name of *Awakening of nature* like the Misraimites.

The banquet is obligatory; it is held at the first grade (*that of Scottish Apprentice*). There are *seven* obligatory toasts. The symbolic names of the table utensils are as in the Scottish and French Rites.

DECORATIONS

The order of Memphis has *three* great legionary decorations and one symbolic.

1. The Grand Star of Sirius.
2. The decoration of the legion of the Knights of Eleusis;
3. The decoration of the legion of the Redoubtable Sadah.

Symbolic decoration: that of the Golden Fleece.

GOVERNMENT OF THE ORDER

It is ruled by five supreme councils:

1. THE SANCTUARY, where is found the venerated Ark of the traditions (*as among the Sophisians*);
2. THE MYSTICAL TEMPLE, Grand Empire of the Sovereign Princes of Memphis;
3. THE LITURGICAL COLLEGE;
4. THE SOVEREIGN GRAND CONSISTORY GENERAL of the Sublime Princes of Masonry;
5. AND THE SUPREME GRAND TRIBUNAL of the Grand Defenders of the Order.

We invite the reader to see p. 21, on this rite, and that of *Misraim*, p. 20, the reflections that they have suggested to us; and we think that the title of *rite* ought not be given but to single systems, unique and not *multiple*, and whose doctrine and dogma are developed, without interruption or mixture, in a very limited series of well-coordinated grades, and that it is an extraordinary abuse of this title to give it to a monstrious collection of grades of *every nature*, invented outside of the true Masonry, such as are presented to us by the thirty-three degrees of Écossisme, the ninetieth of *Misraim*, and the ninety-two of *Memphis*, which, certainly, are not and cannot be rites, or indeed we would find ourselves authorized to name GENERAL RITE our collection of around 400 titles, collection which, although more numerous, would not be more deformed or less ridiculous, as *a rite*, than the three collections that we have just cited.

We add here *a model of a diploma* whose tenor can be but a pleasant distraction for the serious reader.

MODEL OF DIPLOMA

A divine ray teaches a Mason that to pierce the night of time, it is necessary to open the book of the revelations.

It says that in creating man, God gave him the light and imposed duties on him.

A LA GLOIRE

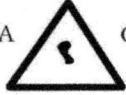

DU SUBLIME ARCHITECTE DES MONDES

The human eye, aided by the light and by virtue, penetrates the depths of the high mysteries.

Pity of the misfortunate.

Honor to courage.

IN THE NAME OF THE GRAND HIEROPHANT

TO ALL THE MASONS SPREAD IN THE TWO HEMISPHERES

Salutations, Friendship, Fraternity

TO ALL THE LODGES, CHAPTERS, AREOPAGOI, SENATES, COUNCILS WORKING OUR ANCIENT AND PRIMITIVE RITE

Union, Prosperity, Courage, Strenght, Tolerance

We, Grand Hierophant, Sovereign Pontiff, G.M. of the Light, and member composing the Grand Empire of the Masonic Order of Memphis, MAKE KNOWN that the T.·. C.·. F.·. possesses from the to the degree, and that in this quality he is part of .
CONSEQUENTLY we invite and pray, by virtue of the supreme powers in which we are vested in our above said qualities, all the Lodges, Chapters, Senates, and Councils to recognize, in his quality, our beloved brother , to receive him fraternally and to give him aid and protection in need, desiring that he enjoy the rights and prerogatives which are granted to him by the general statutes of the Order.
Open in his presence, porticos of our Temples! Venerated Orient, cast your most brilliant splendors! May the stars of the firmament, in sacred number and in mysterious order, come to meet him! And may our brother harmony celebrate his coming! May the standard unfurl before him its glorious folds! And may our brother penetrate into the temple, surrounded by the supreme honors due to his eminent dignity!
Given in the sanctuary where reposes the venerated ark of the traditions, place enlightened by a divine ray, where reigns peace, virture, knowledge, and the fullness of all goods.

Valley of Paris, the day of the month of 5, 8..

(How can one find, in the middle of the 19th century, hands... couragous enough to seriously sign such things?)

ORDER OF FRENCH NOACHITES
(1816)

Napoleonian Masonry

The terror of 1815 yet reigned, when this Order, which had many partisans, was founded at Paris in 1816. Its conception is owed to faithful friends of the Emperor NAPOLEON I, who had brought to mind all the circumstances of his death; to those old companions of his glory, who had fought with him on the Rhine and the Danube, to the Ocean and the Mediterranean; surmounted, in his steps, the Alps and the Pyrenees, and for whom the isles of Elba and Saint Helena are what Mecca is for the Osmanli.

This order was divided into three degrees:

1. *Knight*,
2. *Commander*,
3. *Grand Elect* in three points
    1. *Secret Judge,*
    2. *Perfect Initiate,*
    3. *Knight of the Oak Crown.*

We find, in each degree, allusions easy to comprehend; let us cite:

1st DEGREE Acclamation:

Glory to the Architect (*Napoleon*)!

INSTRUCTION

Question. - Under what master have you labored?

Answer. - Under the architect Phaleg.

Q. - *Who was Phaleg?*

A. - A skillful worker whose Masonic knowledge will elevate to the direction of the works of the tower of *Babel.* He labored fourteen years as App., Comp., and Master (from 1790 to 1804) and ten years as *architect.*

Q. - *What is this tower?*

A. - A vast edifice which was to shelter men from a new flood.

Q. - *Where was it situated?*

A. - On a plain between two mountains and two lakes.

Q. - *How many levels did it have?*

A. - Eight.

Q. - *What were their names?*

A. - Adam, Eve, Noah, Lamech, Naamah, Phaleg, Oubal, Orient, (the eight initials comprising the word Napoleon).

Q. - *How old are you?*

A. - I have lived ten years (from 1804 to 1814).

CLOSING

Q. - *What time is it?*

A. - The hour when the workers of the tower were dispersed.

ANNOUNCEMENT

Let us keep it in our hearts! The lodge is dark. Glory to the architect!

2nd DEGREE

The aspirant carries an urn covered with a veil.
Q. - *What is your name?*
A. - Fidelis.
Q. - *Whence come you?*
A. - Insulæ (from an isle).
Q. - *What have you seen?*
A. - Salixium (a willow).
Q. *What did you bring back?*
A. Urna (an urn).
Q. *What does it contain?*
A. Cineres Phalegi (the ashes of Phaleg).

CLOSING

Q. - *What time is it?*
A. - Five-fifty. - *Consummatum est!* etc.

The Grand Master of this order was the general *Bertrand*, then at Saint Helena, and who did not suspect this honor. In his absence, the Order was directed by a *Supreme Commander* and two lieutenants. This order is Masonic only in form. It existed with much discretion for several years; then it was extinguished. (See the *Tuileur général.*)

PHILOSOPHICAL PERSIAN RITE

We read in a note from the authors of the rite:

"Under a magnificent sky, and in a land so fertile, so delicious, that they place there the cradle of the human race and the terrestrial paradise, at the sources of the Euphrates and the Tigris, which recalls at once such grandeurs and such ruin, rises the rich and strong city of *Erzeroum*, emporium of the commerce of the Indies, and filled with merchants from all the nations of Europe and Asia. This continual passage of educated and independent foreigners, the vicinity of Persia, the remembrances ceaselessly renewed, by the travelers, of the doctrine of *Zoroaster*, of the *Brahmins*, of *Confucius*, the modern theories mixed with the principles of ancient philosophy, all his contributed to fixing, among some sages of Erzeroum, ideas which have given birth to a beautiful Masonic system."

This system is composed of seven grades:

1. Attending Apprentice,
2. Adept Companion, Squire of Beneficence,
3. Master, Knight of the Sun (*taken from the 29th degree of Écossisme*),
4. Omnirite Architect, Knight of the Philosophy of the Heart (*enthusiasm*),
5. Knight of Eclecticism and of the Truth,

6. Master Good Shepherd (*this grade is the complement of the first five*),
7. Venerable Grand Elect (*this is less a grade than an eminent dignity*).

The first three grades form the *Symbolic Order*, the following two, the *Capitulary Order*, and the last two the *Areopagite Order*. One cannot pass from one grade to another, without possessing the historical, philosophical, and Masonic knowledge, which makes the object of the grade which precedes it.

The author of the Dictionnaire Maçonnique says, on this subject:

"European Masons and some Asiatics that they have received have founded and held in the greatest secrecy a *Mother Lodge* of a particular rite, under the title of:

"Children of the Primitive Light,
"to the glory of the Sublime Ordainer of the Worlds,
"and for the moral perfection of families."

"These Masons, who hold in the greatest secrecy a new rite, have committed the fault of communicating with too much eagerness their mysteries to those indiscreet. They have therefore attempted to establish at Paris this new Masonry; but it does not appear that they have succeeded therein."

This is the latest innovation that they have undertaken to enter upon the three original grades. The name of these grades is modern and indicates an origin entirely Parisian and not Persian.

One may, without doubt, bring Masonry back to its source with its European costume; but if, per chance, which is not in the nature of things, Egypt or any other classical land of the primitive initiation, produced, today, a Masonic rite, it would not be and could not be but the reproduction of the ancient rituals; and the types, based on nature, are invariable; *Hiram* would disappear to give place to *Osiris*, or indeed to an even more ancient Persian or Indian type; and this *renewed* Masonry, more rational than the existing one, because of the changes that the force of circumstances has, without doubt, obliged it to submit in order to perpetuate its principles under a new veil, this renewed Masonry, say we, and which would preserved all its primitive perfume and its secular forms, would certainly take at Paris and everywhere. But in order to produce such grades, a vast initiatic instruction is necessary, stripped of prejudices or habits that we possess, more or less, without knowing it, and, above all, to leave entirely the modern disguise to don again the ancient costume. When will come this chef-d'œuvre?

The unfruitful attempts made, in these latter times, by the heads of experimental lodges, demonstrates the difficulty of the undertaking, as the same time that they show THEIR PAPERS, which they believe *complete*, are far from equaling the beautiful simplicity of our rituals, true canvas, but very ingenious canvas, which, in the hands of an able Venerable, receives, according to the person being initiated, a varied embroidery, seductive and ever new, which interests, pleases, and instructs.

CHAPTER XIV
English Masonry

YORK RITE OR MASONRY OF THE ROYAL ARCH

The ever so wise lodges of England did not know how, any more than those of other nations, to guard themselves against the invasion of the high grades. There came to be established at London, in 1777, a new initiation called the *Masonry of the Royal Arch*. This insignificant and entirely Biblical system is composed of four grades:

1. Mark Master[54],
2. Past Master or Excellent Mason,
3. Super-excellent Master or Mason,
4. Holy Royal Arch.

The 1st degree rests upon a rather unintelligible allegory relating to a keystone which is reputed to have belonged to the principal arch of Solomon's temple, and to the discovery of the *hidden treasure* containing the emblems of the old law. We find again the same subject at Upsala, in *Swedish Masonry*.

The 2nd degree gives instructions for the constitution and installation of lodges, for the receptions, for the laying of the first stone of the public edifices, for the dedication of Masonic temples, and for the funerals of brothers. This grade prepares the Mason to fulfill, with regularity, the functions of a lodge president.

The 3rd degree is drawn from this passage of *Chronicles*, chapter VII:

"Solomon having finished his prayer, fire descended from heaven, consumed the offerings and the victims, and the majesty of God filled the house... All the children of Israel... prostrated themselves face to ground, and worshipped the Lord, because he is good, and his mercy is eternal."

Finally, in the 4th degree, they commemorate the misfortunes of the Jewish people during their captivity under Nebuchanezzar, their reintegration by Cyrus into the Holy Land, and the construction of the second temple by the cares of Zerubbabel[55].

We believe that this Masonry was invented in Scotland by the Jesuits, who brought it into England, where it received the name of *York Rite*, whose last grade, *Holy Royal Arch*, symbolizes the *Christian Church*. It is by fraud that they have called it the *York Rite* or *Rite of the Ancient Freemasons* (operative masons). These workers had only one initiation, their mastership, quite different from that of Freemasonry. It is therefore a mockery to attribute this connection to the ancient guilds of operative masons, notwithstanding the regulations of the Grand Chapter of the Royal Arch, *revised* in 1807, and the concordat of 1813, which recognizes the four grades that we have just indicated, although it regards the 4th grade as a dependency of the Symbolic Master, though it has assemblies called *chapters* and its officers apart.

The constitutions of the York Rite date from the very origin of the world. *Adam* is the first Mason[56], etc.

This rite is the continuation of the Mosaic law, an anti-Masonic law, which renders it foreign to the true Masonry.

It appears to have been invented in order to establish a sort of transition between the true Masonry and the Masonry called *Scottish*, and to thus fill a lacuna.

In reality:

The primitive or *Symbolic Masonry*, the only pure one, the only true one, is the doctrine of the natural religion and the divine moral preceding therefrom.

The Masonry called *York Rite* professes the Judaic philosophy, which is an alteration of the primitive religion, despite its democratic principles.

The Masonry called *Scottish* is, with a deformed mixture of Mosaism, but the Christian doctrine Masonified, put into grades by ambitious Masons.

American Masonry comprises the York Rite or Royal Arch in five grades, whereas only four are present here; but what does the number matter, when the grades have so puerile a basis in the eyes of the true Masons.

The American Masons say that the Evangelical doctrine adds to the teachings of the natural law that the patriarchal régime bequeathed to them, of the rational philosophy that the Hebrews brought from Egypt, and of the preparatory law that Moses promulgated, in view of the Sovereign *Regenerator* of the human race.

These Masons submit to their view the Mosaic doctrine of the great legislator, in the same manner as they modified the primitive doctrine.

Thus, the York Rite, essentially Mosaic, is to Écossisme, which is essentially Christian, what Symbolic Masonry, or natural law, is to the York Rite, and, according to them, the grades of the three rites are bound to one another in the same sense as Christianity is bound to the Mosaic law, and by this to the natural law.

The true Masonry has but three grades. Anterior to the known religions, it continues its pacific and incessant march, because its unalterable aim is the amelioration of men without distinction of class, climate, philosophical, political, or religious opinions. The high grades of the other rites, similar to religions, divide men, because if they make disappear from their doctrines all that is not in the truth, to what would be reduced the rest? But every man who profess the high grades would be an intolerant sectarian, like the religion he represents, unless he had been regenerated, previously, by the symbolic doctrine common to all the rites, which professes the beneficent and sublime dogma of universal tolerance, and embraces, into its bosom, the universality of Masons.

The authority which, in 1717, has separated itself from the *operative masons*, which has changed their customs, introduced with a new dogma, a new ceremonial, had every right, then, to *make redundant* the work of Ashmole, but on the condition to do it well: with *Ashmole* it was *Zoroaster* and the *Pyramids*, that is to say the ancient initiation; with the *Royal Arch*, it is the *Temple of Solomon*. Solomon and his temple are not initiators, but products of initiation: Solomon as an initiate of Egypt, and his temple, as an imitation of that of Memphis. It is therefore to err extraordinarily to make of these results a primitive point of departure.

The York Rite, presented to the gathering of rites, in 1804, was rejected by the G.O., *without doubt*, says Thory, *by motives which do not hold to Freemasonry*. Perhaps it is because of its presenter, the brother *Hacquet*, who professed it, at Paris, to the lodge of *Sept-Écossais*[57].

There exist other supposed Masonic régimes; they will find their place in the *Fastes initiatiques* with the documents which concern them.

We are going to give an historical summary of the principal regimes, called, also, Masonic, which have been practiced in Germany.

CHAPTER XV
Various Régimes Created in Germany

Freemasonry debuted in Germany through *Hamburg*. The first lodge dates from December 6, 1737[58]. - We will not speak here on the regular workshops, the works of which are generally conducted with wisdom and dignity; but we are going to give a brief summary of the *extra-Masonic* establishments or régimes.

CONFRATERNITY OF THE UNITED BRETHREN OF THE RELIGIOUS ORDER OF FREEMASONS, OR THE ORDER OF THE MUSTARD SEED
Evangelical Masonry, Silesia, 1739

The first innovations which were introduced among the German Masons, enthusiasts of the marvelous, date from 1739. It is to this period that we fix the ostensible establishment of the CONFRATERNITY OF THE UNITED BRETHREN, whose mysteries rested upon the passage from the Gospel of Saint Mark (chap. 4, verses 30-32), in which Jesus compares the Kingdom of God to a *mustard seed*, which, although the smallest of all seeds, pushes forth, nevertheless, such great branches, that the *birds of the sky may rest under their shade.*

The aim of the association was the *propagation of the Gospel*, under the Masonic veil.

The brethren wore as a *jewel* a gold ring, and, crosswise, a *green ribbon*, from which was suspended a second *jewel*, having a plant or a seed upon a gold cross, with these words: *Quod fuit ante? - Nihil* (What was before? - Nothing).

Device of the Order: *Keiner unser lebt ihm selber* (none of us lives for himself). This motto was engraved on the ring.

According to the statutes, the brethren had, each year, to hold a great assembly in the chapel of the castle of *Guadenstadt*, in Silesia, and to celebrate, furthermore, two annual feasts on March 15 and April 16.

This confraternity existed in Germany before the introduction of the Templar grades of Ramsay. N.L., Count *Zinzerdof* (that some authors have confused with Zinnendorf), born at Dresden in 1700, died in 1760, having adopted the principles of the *United Brethren*, created, in concert with some others among them, in 1721, a sort of monastery at Herrnhut; from here arises the sect of the *Herrnhuters*.

Here is another order of the same type.

ORDER OF SAINT JOACHIM
Christian Masonry, Bohemia, 1756

This order was, they say, established in Bohemia around 1756.

The candidates swore to *believe in the Holy Trinity* and to never *waltz*. They only admitted nobles.

We read in note 15 from the *Essai sur la secte des Illuminés*, attributed to Luchet (p. 219, Paris, 1789), that Jean-Henri, Baron *Ecker von Eckosen*, private counselor of *Hohenlohe-Welburg*, and his brother Jean-Charles, Baron *Ecker von Eckosen*, intimate counselor of legation, were "*Grand Cross of the Temporal Order of the Foundation of the Most*

High or Divine Providence..."

"This order was called, for some years (at least since 1786) the Order of SAINT JOACHIM... extracts from its statutes are recorded in the *Journal éclectique* (Lubek, gr. 3), 2nd book, 1785, p. 1. According to these notices, the Order had been established at *Leutmeris*, in Bohemia, in 1756. We find here the ceremonies of reception. The procession goes to the chapel of the Order, the candidate remains at the sacristy; the knights enter into the chapel where the ecclesiastic gives a discourse. After this, they introduce the candidate and ask him if it is still his free will, and if he wishes seriously to enter the Order. After having affirmed this, they exhort him to give it careful consideration, and they lead him back. Brought back then, questioned again and received after, he gives an oath and receives the habit of the Order; at the end they chant the *Te Deum*, etc."

One sect, important by the role that it has played, is that of the...

FREEMASON CLERICS OF THE STRICT OBSERVANCE

This was a corporation of *Cabalists*, *Alchemists*, and *Necromancers*.

This extraordinary title (*Freemason Clerics*, etc.), which presents a multitude of incoherent ideas, aroused attention towards the middle of the 18th century. It was formed, in Germany, as a society of *reformed Masons*, that is to say more connected to the true spirit of the institution than the ordinary Freemasons. The study of *Cabala*, of the *Philosopher's Stone*, and of *necromancy* or *the invocation of the spirits*, occupies them principally, because, according to them, the knowledge of all these things formed the system and the aim of the ancient mysteries, of which Freemasonry is the continuation. (See hereafter *Occult Masonry*.)

"It is in one of these *acromatic* societies that was initiated, at Vienna, with the greatest pomp, the Marshal *de Richelieu*, ambassador from France, under the reign of Charles VI. The reception took place in a nocturnal assembly, and the mysteries of the mystagogy were celebrated with the greatest solemnity. The things were pushed so far that the affair burst into the world. Public mockery and even Louis XV did not spare the Marshal of France. The court of Vienna published an edict against *magic*," (*Les Jesuites chasses de la Francmaç.*, p. 76).

Latin is the language of their chapter. They recognize the Catholic, Apostolic, and Roman religion as the sole and unique one. The heads of lodges wear, in their functions, the dress of Catholic bishops. The brethren have *long white frocks with a red cross on the left side and a red hat in the shape of a hexagon.*

To be received, it was necessary to have all the chivalric grades of the Strict Observance, that is to say to be a *Templar.*

Their object was to summon and command the *spirits*, to seek the *Philosopher's Stone*, and to establish the *thousand-year empire.*

They assert that the Baron *von Hund* embraced the Catholic religion in order to be admitted.

The known superiors were, in 1788, the Baron *von Raven*, at Rumfeld, in Mecklenburg; the private counselor *Duffel*, at Zell, and the preacher *Starck*, at Koenigsberg, become first preacher at the court of Darmstadt.

This charlatanism won Paris; but *Cagliostro* appeared in order to make a diversion there and to make them forget the *Freemason Clerics of the Strict Observance.*

The Clerics had their ceremonies, their signs, and their particular figures. They formed among them a body and wished to direct the Strict

Observance. They had some influence over the other Masonic sects; but their pretensions have lost them.

The professor *Woigt*, from Leipsig, revealed their magical and Cabalistic mysteries in the *Historical Acts*, a work which appeared then at Weimar, as well as in the *Journal of the Freemasons*.

CHAPTER XVI

Before broaching the matter of the *Strict Observance* and analyzing the rites of the various German reformers, we believe that it is useful to enlighten those of our readers who would not be initiated into the facts relative to these reformative endeavors, by submitting to them, as first light, the remarkable opinion of a disciple of *Zinnendorf,* it is known under this title:

CONFESSIONS ON THE DIFFERENT MASONIC SYSTEMS IN GERMANY

"I defy and resist whomever it may be to combat my assertion, that no one may give any ideas on the Masonic Order, its history, or its aim, nor on the explanation of its hieroglyphs and secrets, without leaving the spirit in some uncertainty. Each presumptuously assumes the right to explain, in his manner, the symbols and doctrine of this society, and it is from here that derives these different systems which have divided the Order.

"When, at the beginning of the last century, Masonry passed from England into France and into Germany, they knew only the first three grades. They were content to follow the ceremonial thereof with a silent veneration; to leave *unexplained* the hieroglyphs; to recognize the Grand Lodge of London as the head of the order of all the Masons, and to regard the Masonic institution as a gathering of men called to noble and charitable actions. However, shortly after, the din began to be spread that there existed yet other grades, above all a grade of *Knight of Saint Andrew of Scotland.* It even arrived then from the travelers from England and Scotland who claimed to have received it there, and who effectively communicated the *written fragments* thereof, by means of which they counterfeited a *Scottish grade* of the same name, that they have conferred in some lodges, which drew attention to the development of the Masonic hieroglyphs. Adventurers made the most of this curiosity and made use of the most respectable Order to attain to their particular views.

"The Jesuits had already misused Freemasonry in England and especially in Scotland and had formed a faction there. The principal chiefs of this coterie lived and schemed at the court of the *Pretender,* whom they made to believe that all these machinations had only taken place in the aim of restoring him to the throne of England; but they hid their designs: they spread into England and France the idea that Freemasonry was but a continuation of the *Order of the Templars*, of which the *Freemason Clerics* possessed the high sciences, and whose treasures, still hidden, would soon appear, so that the Order, which would have *the Pretender* as Grand Master, would be powerful enough to be able to defend these clerics. However, as the Jesuits could not draw anything from such an invention, in Germany, they had recourse to another superfluity, and they spread there, by their emissaries, this fable, that the *true superiors* of the Freemasons were to be sought only in an ancient fraternity yet existing: *the so-called Rose-Croix.* It is thus that began to be spread, among the Freemasons, this taste for the marvelous, this thirst for the high grades, and this belief in the *unknown superiors*, and that the ancient brethren, who possessed the true knowledge, withdrew themselves, abandoning a society which labored in a manner so little worthy of its institution.

"As the Jesuits did not appear openly, and as they had no other intention than to put disunion into Freemasonry, to then fish in troubled waters, and as they had spread the din of these innovations only in order to see how the public Freemason would receive them, it was introduced, on all sides, by swindlers and adventurers, who, upon all sorts of fables, founded from castles in Spain, proclaim new Masonic grades, and who, in the end, gave themselves as the *unknown superiors* that they seek.

"During the Seven Years War, there arrived, among others, in Germany, a French commissioner, who brought with him trunks full of decorations, and conferred, at a price, forty-five *grades fabricated in France*. Such was the state of anarchy in which Masonry was found, when another schism appeared.

"The Jesuits, believing the moment come to definitively get a hold of a society that they had so well confounded, have enter the scene a man of whom we could not say for certain whether he was *deceived* or *deceiver*, whether he knew for whom he worked, or whether he was only an instrument made use of by people that he did not know *himself*. This man was the Baron *von Hund*, who renewed this allegation, that *Masonry was but the continuation of the Order of the Templars*. He claimed to have been received Templar in France by an Englishman, in the presence of the secretary of the Pretender, who, himself, was the Grand Master of the Order. He added that he had been presented as such to the Pretender; that, since then, he had ceased to occupy himself with the Order and to correspond with his superiors (*the clerics*), until the moment when *M. de Marschall* provincial Grand Master of the 7th province, had transmitted to him this dignity upon his death bed; that he was therefore authorized to continue and to propagate this Order and Freemasonry.

"However, and despite all these assurances, he had, for all legitimation of these pretentions, only a diploma written in unknown characters. His cronies fabricated for him an uninterrupted list of supposed *Grand Masters*. (See that of the Strict Observance), and although they were not supported by any historical document, they applied all the Masonic hieroglyphs to their system, and here, where the tableaux and the ceremonies could not give them, they created them anew. But they continued to be unaware of where the priests of the Order had hidden themselves, them, their knowledge, and their treasure. The public did not ask any more of them, and willingly believed all that was related to them. They tried to lead the princes into this system, and each to race after this chimera, which opened to him a winning perspective; the princes sought here treasures and power; their subjects were promised their decorations and protections; the plebeians rejoiced in their new state of *knights*, and the visionaries already saw themselves, in perspective, associated with the celestial beings.

"They accused all the other systems of heresy and invalidity. They established lodges and chapters everywhere and, above all, they tried to receive therein, without the least regard for morality, people of standing and influence and priests, as much to be sure not to be banished a second time, as to acquire riches and to procure for themselves relief in the eyes of the public; AND THIS IS THE WHOLE ANTIMASONIC SYSTEM OF THE STRICT OBSERVANCE.

"The doctor of law *Zinnendorf* was also received a Templar; but seeing how little these people worked regularly, and not believing to be able to make good use of their poorly disposed plan, he separated himself from this system, and, claiming that he was in contact with the *true and wise clerics*, in Sweden, he founded a new system in nine grades: the first three are under the protection of the G.L. of London, which he recognized solely to have the right to install, at Berlin, a G.L. of Germany. As to the six other degrees, the last of which has remained unachieved, the innovator led his disciples here in the path of morals and knowledge, by exciting them to virtue, charity, and the culture of their faculties.

"Some lodges, remaining faithful to the old Observance, received, without difficulty, many individuals for their money, with which they performed ceremonies; played with the hieroglyphs, without understanding them; made good cheer, good digestion, and gave some alms: HERE ARE THE ANCIENT ENGLISH LODGES OR THE LATE OBSERVANCE...

"In France, they amuse themselves with some fifty grades, up to what some Hermetic enthusiasts had penetrated into some of the lodges.

"In Sweden, the king made known that he had resolved to publicly re-establish the *Templars*, and that he had obtained from *the true clerics the secret of the grand magical arts.* He probably hoped to engage, by this means, many German Templars to establish themselves in Sweden and to support with their money his poor kingdom; but he hoped in vain. They discovered, by providential chance, this deceit, and the *Illuminated Chapter* lost its renown of truth and virtue.

"During this time, different branches of the *Rose-Croix* were widespread; each of them tried to seize Masonry. We do not wish to anticipate the opinion that one is to form of this society. Those who desire to be further instructed may consult a German work entitled *The Compass of the Wise.* The one who, after having read it, feels inclined to have themselves received into this Order, will see what there is to learn at the end of six years.

"For the educated men, it is verifiably established that the true Rose-Croix has never existed and that this name has seen only to hide an allegory established by *Valentine Andrea* in his *Fama Fraternitatis* and in his *General Reformation of the Whole Wide World*, that visionaries and adventurers have appropriated to their views. The confused system of the *Hermetic Philosophy* is known by all those who have studied even a little the *Philosophical History*. But it becomes further evident, through the writings of the German Rose-Croix, that they had not even penetrated the sense and the spirit of this system, and it is beyond doubt that these societies, in which there were very respectable members, had been induced into error by ignorant adventurers, who could teach nothing; but who wished, on the contrary, to learn, to spy, and to render themselves masters of all the Masonic lodges.

"As, sooner or later, all trickery betrays itself, we can see all this from a very tranquil eye; but, unfortunately, the general penchant for the marvelous, and especially then, in Germany, the rage of alchemy, from which the Jesuits knew so well to draw their faction, sustained as they were by the German Rose-Croix, had so enrooted itself that a good number of persons had allowed themselves to be drawn to pursue speculative chimeras...

"Let us return to the *Strict Observance*, since it dominated for a certain time.

"The Jesuits and their emissaries hoped that it would no longer be a question of *secrets* or *treasures*, when they would have closed the mouths of the antagonists, by dispatching revenues to the principal members, by means of funds that they would draw from the enormous costs of the receptions (*Statutes of the Strict Observance*, art. 12); but they were deceived.

"The common stock of the Masons always asked, as much after as before the death of the Baron *von Hund*, that they come into connection with the *clerics*, which, effectively, had been promised to them.

"There remained, therefore, no other means than to have appear on the scene people who would play that role. Many gave themselves to this comedy, who, since then, have affected pretentions to wisdom, instruction, and impartiality, and who give the same airs thereof in their writings. They also had *clerics* appear who paraded only phrases instead of knowledge. There appeared, moreover, from time to time, some prophets, for example, at *Wiesbaden*.

"Yet, as they saw themselves deceived on all sides, and as the true aim of the Strict Observance became clearer than they had hoped, they finally opened their eyes, and they judged it fitting to send someone to Italy, in order to inquire at the court of the pretender whether what the Baron *von Hund* and the other authors had advanced was accurate. It would have been wiser to take this step twelve years sooner, before so many people had let themselves *be led by the nose*; but it seems that it was stipulated that all would be begun backwards.

"They learned at the court of the Pretender that the *whole history of the Templars* was but invention and falsehoods. It was impossible to keep secret for very long so sad a discovery; it did not delay, therefore, to be highly divulged through writing. The Jesuits would not be discouraged; they forged new plans which soon rand aground, because the Masonic world was no longer credulous. "In the midst of so great an embarrassment and in order to escape the insults and reproaches of the brethren, heads of the Strict Observance convoked, at Wilhelmsbad, a final convent, whose reasonable Masons knew well, besides, beforehand, what they had to expect therefrom.

"The two princes, who were its ardent promoters, had, without doubt, the purest and most impartial views for the Order; but as the game of the Templars would necessarily cease, and as it was upon this game that was founded the power of the *superiors*, very few Masons wished to consent to obey them.

"It was impossible for them to give any explanation of the *hieroglyphs*, since they did not possess it. As to the enormous sums which had been collected for twelve to fourteen years[59], they were unable to give a faithful account thereof, this money having been administered with much negligence, although with probity. On the other hand, the Masons no longer wished to content themselves with the ordinary pastime of the hieroglyphs, and they could expect nothing important or suitable from a mob of masons, the greater number of which had been received indifferently and had been placed at the head of the system only in political views. They hoped, therefore, to see arrive at this convent foreign Masons who would show off their treasures of knowledge; but those who possessed it did not want to deposit it in such hands, nor to subject themselves voluntarily to the yoke.

"There arose therein some mystical chimeras; but as this was only visions or fables without foundation, the plurality rejected them, and there no longer remained any other resort but to invent a new system. From here was born the system of the *Knights Beneficent of the Holy City of Jerusalem*.

"It would therefore be useless to seek to prove that this Masonry of the *Strict Observance* did not succeed, in whatever it be, in making men better, wiser, or happier; that it has occupied itself only with a game; that it has rendered itself laughable and contemptible in the eyes of the world, and it has become the theatre upon which have exercised idle actors and charlatans."

We have found this dissertation instructive enough to be inserted in its entirety.

STRICT OBSERVANCE

This was the third Masonic innovation of the Jesuits. It entertained among the adepts the dangerous hope of resuming possession of the riches of the ancient

Templars. The *Chronological History* of its Grand Masters is none other than the history of the generals of the Jesuits. The first idea of the uninterrupted continuation of the order of the Templars is due to the Marquis *de Lernay*, who first saw it admitted by a lodge of Berlin. The Prince de Clermont was its G.M., and, under this name, the Jesuits succeeded in introducing this new system. P.C. signified *patres claræ montani.*

They conferred, in this system, only six grades; the 7th was *clerical* and its existence was hidden. The cord around the neck of the candidate to the grade of Scottish Knight symbolized the protestants, that they regarded as criminals of high treason. A brother could not advance in grade until after a fixed period, unless he had obtained a dispensation from the Grand Chapter.

This *Observance* had been formed by a scission introduced into Freemasonry for insignificant motives, but to which they gave importance.

From this scission was born the STRICT OBSERVANCE (*observentia stricta*).

But a scission of the Strict Observance, occurring at Vienna in 1767, gave birth to the LATE OBSERVANCE (*observantia lata*).

They each had their symbolic grades and their particular high grades.

Frederick William II, King of Prussia, refused, in 1786, to continue his royal protection of Freemasonry in his States, unless these two systems were reunited; which they did, at least in appearance, for there never existed any act of reunion, and each kept its inner organization, and continued, as in the past, to caution its members against its rival.

The one who wished to join the *Strict Observance* was obliged to sign the *act of obedience* of the Baron *von Hund*, by which he promised willingly *et sine nulla reservatione*:

1st to give *absolute obedience* to the provincial G.M. of the 7th province (the Baron *von Hund*), and to all the superiors named or to be named by him.

2nd, to submit oneself entirely to the instructions of these *superiors*, notably with regard to the lodges of the *Late Observance*; to do or to permit to be done what they order, without ever pretending to fathom the intention or aim thereof.

3rd, to observe the greatest secrecy and not to make oneself known to anyone outside the circle of the Strict Observance, not to entertain any Masonic correspondence without permission of the *superiors*; to deliver to them any letters received, and to await their instructions on the responses to make.

4th, to submit oneself, of good will, to the penalties which could be imposed upon him by superiors.

He had to promise all this, under penalty of the loss of *honor* and the *vision* of God.

The cipher of the high grades is nearly indecipherable, because it could be changed in different manners in the middle of a phrase.

It was not permitted to the high grades to have oneself initiated into the high grades of another secret society without authorization of the superiors;
and it was forbidden to the high-grade knights to convene with brothers of inferior degrees who possessed grades above their own.

The *very bad* administrative organization was the work of *Schubarth and Kleefeld*. The *clerics* were introduced into the Order by the doctor *Starck*.

The public had knowledge of this system by the publication of a small German work, published under the title of *The Stumbling Block* and *The Rock of Scandal.* They believed that, in order to neutralize the harm that this work caused to the renown of the Order in the eyes of the Masonic people, there was nothing better than to assemble a general convent: such was the true and original motive of the Convent of Wilhemsbad.

SYSTEM OF THE STRICT OBSERVANCE

The Order of the Strict Observance was definitively founded in Germany by the brother Charles *Gathel*, Baron *von Hund*, Lord of Altengrotkau and Lipse, who was received a Mason at Francfort-sur-Mein in 1742, and initiated at Paris, in 1754, into the high grades of the Chapter of Clermont. This innovator, animated by the thought of Ramsay, that *every true Mason is a Knight Templar*, the order of which, according to him, has always existed, divided his new Masonry into different grades, and based his order in imitation of that of the Temple, over a vast territory, divided into nine provinces, which comprised all the countries of Europe.

The system of Ramsay being known in Germany before the foundation of the Chapter of Clermont, and, consequently, the admission of the Baron to the superior or Templar Order at Paris, he found there a predecessor in the person of the Baron *de Marschall*, to whom he addressed himself.

The Templar regime then comprised six grades, to wit:

1. Apprentice,	Symbolic.	
2. Companion,		
3. Master,		
4. Scottish Master,		
5. Novice,		
6. Templar, divided into 3 classes, under the name of	*Eques,* *Socius,* *Armiger*[60].	

Between 1763 and 1770, the Baron van Hund added a 7th degree under this name:

7. *Eques professus.*

Later still, he joined thereto a branch of *Freemason Clerics*, who cultivated natural and divine magic, chemistry, and alchemy.

The historical part of this system is limited to the secret continuation of the *Order of the Templars*; here is the *history* that it communicated:

"In the year 1303, two knights of the Order: *Noffodei* and *Sguin de Florian*, were punished for their crimes. The latter lost his commandery of Montfaucon. They asked the provincial G.M. for new commanderies, and as he refused them, they assassinated him at his country home, near Milan, and hid his body in the garden, under some brush. They took refuge at Paris and accused the Order of the most horrible crimes, which led to the ruin of the Order and the torture of the G.M. who was burned alive in 1314.

"The provincial G.M. of Auvergne, Pierre *d'Aumont*, fled with two commanders and five knights. In order not to be recognized, they disguised themselves as Masons, changed their names, and called themselves *Mabeignac* (it is from here that derives the Master's word Mac-Benac). They landed on the Scottish isle Mull, where they found the Grand Commander *Hamptoncourt*, George *Harris*, with several other brothers, and resolved to constitute the Order there.

"They held a chapter at Saint John in 1312. Aumont was named G.M. there. In order to withstand the persecutions, they adopted signs and words, in the manner of the Masons, and called themselves *Free and Accepted Masons*, to indicate, by this means, that they had set themselves free and had accepted other customs[61].

"In 1361, the residency of the G.M. was transported to Aberdeen, and it is in this manner that the Order has been successively preserved and spread into Italy, France, and Germany."

The Basse-Saxe was erected in the country by the G.M. *Charles Stuart* the pretender and proclaimed as such in 1745. As to the Chapter of Aberdeen, the Grand Priory was confided to *Kessler*, of Sprengeisen, in 1750.

The catechism of the 4th grade (*Grand Écossais*) contains among others these questions:

Q. - *How many symbols do they present to a Scottish Master?*

A. - Four: the *lion*, the *fox*, the *monkey*, and the *sparrow-hawk*.

Q. - *Explain them.*

A. - An Écossais ought to join to the qualities of a Master: the heart of a lion, the finesse of a fox, the spirit of a monkey, and the swiftness of a sparrow- hawk (bird of prey)[62].

The tableau is drawn in white upon a green background. At the corners are found the four beasts indicated. In the middle is represented a coffin surmounted by an eight-rayed star.

The system teaches that this grade signifies *the re-establishment of the Order of the Templars by Aumont*, on the Scottish isle of Mull; which is but an *allusion* to the re-establishment of the *Jesuit hierarchy*.

In the 5th grade or Novice, the Prior or Commander, who was at the same time chief of the diocese, made the reception in place of the provincial G.M.; he had the title of *Superior*; he occupied an arm-chaim surmounted by the arms of the G.M.

During the reception, they extinguished all the lights and lit one sole lamp while saying: *I do this in memory of those who have been and who are no more*. After the taking of the oath, they re-lit three flambeaux and said: *I do this in memory of those who have been, who were no more, and who are anew*.

The neophyte was obliged, after the reception which was made in the name of the G.M., to kiss the pommel of the sword of the superior who told him *that he had only just entered into a noviciate* of three years, during which he had to render himself worthy of advancement by a *blind obedience* to his superiors.

There was no longer any tableau, and they declared openly to the newly received that it was no longer a question of Masonry, but of the *Order of the Templars*, of which he had begun the *noviciate*.

The 6th grade or *Knight Templar* was divided into *Eques*, *Socius*, and *Armiger*.

They held chapter; the aspirant removed the apron lined in green, and the *commisssarius ordinis*, performing the function of prior, had him give the oath in the Latin language. The installation of the newly received was done likewise in Latin; they told him, among other things, while giving him the helmet: *Ordo te clibano contra hostes olim fidei, nunc ordinis ut eo magis intercepias per duellum.*

The new knight then deposited upon a table a free gift for the præses, then he kneeled before him in order to receive by his hands the *red cross* of the Order and *a gold ring* that he had to wear on the little finger of the right hand. He received arms of the Order and a characteristic or *motto relating to it* (relating to these same arms. The members of the Strict Observance lost their family name and signed with this characteristic; system adopted by the *Scots of Kilwinning*.)

The reception of an *Armiger* was little different; at that of *Eques*, they were only called *Frater*.

A third reception was that of the *Sociorum et Amicorum Ordinis*. It was not without importance. If the candidate was a person of distinction, they regulated his introduction, be it by squires, knights, or commanders. Instead of swearing an absolute obedience, he promised by oath *perfect esteem and devotion to those who received him among them.* After the reception, they led him to his place, while saying: *Take possession of the place that the superior Order grants you by preference, in order to assist it, in case of need, by your good counsel and your name.*

This last institution made known enough the origin of this Order, for the true Order of the Templars did not have these *amici socii*[63], they are none other than what formed the second class of the Jesuits. This class was composed of priests and laity, who lived in the world and served the Jesuits, especially at courts; called themselves *jesuitæ in voto*, because they had made the vow to take the habit of the Order as soon as it pleased the *pater generalis*.

Then came the reception of the *fratres servientes*, the *socii*, and the *amici ordinis*.

The Baron *von Prinzen* was the first who founded a chapter of this system, at Berlin; it did not delay in spreading.

In 1763, the Baron *von Hund* came to Neuvierden, in Pusac, and declared himself G.M. of the 7th province; for Germany was divided into provinces of the Order.

A certain *Johnson*, who claimed to possess much more extensive instructions than those of the Baron *von Hund*, announced himself a little later at Jene, as Grand Prior of the Order.

During his stay at Altemburg, he wore out, day and night, the brother knights and nobles who inhabited the neighboring lands, and who were members of the Order. They were obliged to mount a horse at the first order that he gave them, even were it during the night, under penalty of seeing themselves shut up in dark chambers, if they were slow to the convent of the Templars, at Altemburg. The Baron von Hund recognized Johnson as Grand Prior of the Order and obeyed him.

But all this was only dupery; for von Hund himself had accredited this adventurer, who was a Jew named *Leicht* or *Leucht*, in order to grow his system, to give him more authenticity, and to draw the most profit possible. But soon, whether he found that Johnson could become dangerous to him, or that he feared him betraying his secret, von Hund himself declared that this man was only an adventurer. A short time later, he was arrested on the order of the intimate adviser *von Fritsch*, fervent partisan of the baron, member of the Strict Observance; and tutor then of the minor prince *von Weimar*. Johnson was transported to Warburg (old, fortified castle near Eisenach); he was kept at the expense of the Strict Observance; he died suddenly, apparently because, *they say*, the moment approached of the majority of the young Duke von Weimar.

Following this affair, von Fritsch reclaimed at the convent of Brunswick the reimbursement of 3,000 rix-dollars (12,000 fr.), as alimentary expense for Johnson.

The enthusiasm for this Order began to cool. They sought, in order to raise it, to make thereof a sort of *tontine*; they taxed the high grades from 300 to 1,000 rix-dollars (1,200 to 4,000 fr.), but this plan was not successful. They added to it a *clerical branch*.

The Jesuits had recourse to this new invention to divert the attention of the lovers of secrets. *Starck*, professor at Rostock, and since preacher at the court of Kœnigsberg, then at Darmstadt, was the head of this branch, the most active members of which were the Baron *von Raven*, at Ranefeld, in Mecklenburg, and the counsellor of the court of appeals of Veffel, at Zell.

The *clerics* were part of the 7th province (following the composition of their general chapter, useless here). (See the *Fastes initiat.*)

Although they had seduced a great number of the curious who desired to profit from the *clerical* knowledge, the convent held at Kohlo, in 1772, in order to unite the clerics to the Strict Observance, did not have entirely the result that they hoped. Another convent was held; there appeared a new imposter named *Gugomos* (like

Schropfer, sometime later), who brought new charlatanries, but who took flight soon after.

The Duke von Brunswick convoked, towards the end of 1782, a new convent at Wilhemsbad, *to research the true aim of Masonry*. Its result was that *all the knights recognized that they were not true Knights Templar*. They agreed that in the future, they could only give, in their final *Masonic* grade, an historical instruction on the Templar Order.

To that end, they also composed new manuscripts. All remained more or less as before: one of the branches of the Strict Observance continued to create Templars; another performed alchemy, a third waited patiently for what the superiors would do.

Yet the Baron *von Hund* died a good Catholic, having abjured his religion for Roman Catholicism, and having continually near him a capuchin friar. Then there occurred ridiculous circumstances with regard to the *Chevalier Stuart*, pretender of England.

This knight, having come into Germany to seek his bride, the Princess of Stolberg, was secretly received Templar by von Hund and recognized by himself as G.M. of the Order. In reward, he gave to von Hund a patent of provincial G.M. for Germany and antedated it. This patent was the only one that von Hund could exhibit at the convent of Kohlo in order to establish his legitimacy. The poor knight Stuart, overcome with joy, nearly lost the reason thereof, because they assured him that the Order would not take any rest until it had put him in possession of some important lands, even if it were only in America; and they persuaded him that it formed a powerful faction, which counted among them a great number of Sovereigns. Thus, when he returned to Rome, he made a solemn entrance and had himself preceded by heralds, who proclaimed him King, reclaiming, for him, the honors due to the kings; but the Pope, wiser than he, was opposed thereto. All of Europe laughed at this affair, that all the gazettes published, without, however, knowing the true motives.

The Templar system had also spread into Alsace and Lorraine, under the auspices of the Duc *de Chartres*; but for fear of some contention with the police, its members, united at the convent of Lyon, changed their name to that of *Knights Beneficent of the Holy City*. Saint-Martin, called the *Unknown Philosopher*, and *Willermez*, of Lyon, were the principal movers of this change, which no longer had anything Masonic. They composed several mystical grades, the spirit of which has been divulged by the writings of this school, such as *les archives mytho-hermétiques, des erreurs et de la vérité*, etc., etc.

Here is the distribution of the provinces of the Order, before the Convent of Wilhemsbad:

1. Province of *Aragon*,
2. —— of *Auvergne*,
3. —— of the *Occident*, or of *Languedoc*,
4. —— of *Lyon*,
5. —— of *Burgandy*,
6. —— of *Great Britain*,
7. Province of the *Basse-Saxe, Elba, Prussian Poland, Livonia,* and *Courlande.*
8. —— of *Upper Germany, Po, Tiere, Italy,* and *Sicily.*
9. —— of *Greece* and the *Archipelago.*

DISTRIBUTION OF THE PROVINCES, AFTER THIS CONVENT

1. Prov. of *Lower Germany, Poland,* and *Prussia*
4. Prov. of *Italy* and *Greece.*
5. —— of *Burgandy* and *Switzerland,*

(they have given it this rank because it was put first into activity),
2. —— of *Auvergne,*
3. —— of the *Occident,*
6. —— of *Upper Germany,*
7. —— of *Austria* and *Lombardy,*
8. —— of *Russia,*
9. —— of *Sweden.*

They struck from the rolls the provinces of *Aragon* and *Lyon*, because they were not active, and that of *Great Britain*, because there was no cause to hope for its return[64].

Each province was subdivided into *Priories*, *Prefectures*, *Commanderies*, *Scottish* (Jesuitical) Lodges, and *Symbolic* Lodges, where Masonry is a cult.

All the provinces, after the death of the Baron von Hund, were subordinated to the general G.M., the Duke *Ferdinand of Brunswick*; but each province had its provincial G.M.; the 7th had the Baron von Hund.

The statutes are in 16 articles and have as title: *Statutes of the Illustrious Order of the Strict Observance.* They confirm the idea that one is to acquaint oneself, by what precedes, on the nature and aim of the Order. Let us cite some articles:

"Art. 1. Although the rules prescribed by the Order, in the first time of its existence, are still obligatory for each of our brothers, then especially as they have submitted themselves thereto, by oath, at the time of their reception, it is also certain that these obligations undergo some *restrictions*, and that they are applicable only in the cases where they may be suitably observed, according to the differences of religion, morals, and political government of the various lands in which we live. It is therefore in this respect that the brethren of the Order are to consider these rules, which will ever be for them a respectable monument of antiquity, and it is, *after these restrictions*, that they have to observe and to execute the obligations that they have contracted."

Thus, it is not a question of an absurd attachment to these rules, nor to the *ancient possessions.* For the first were *specific*, whereas the others were only casual; moreover, the chiefs of the Order have never had ideas romantic enough to hope one day to reclaim the property of the ancient brethren.

"Art. 6. As the Order has generally recognized the good of being hid *under the cloak of Freemasonry*, under which we have found ourselves in security for so many years, prudence counsels us not to lift this veil; at least we ought not do it in our day, PERHAPS EVER; in any case, not before we find that this veil is insufficient or *useless* to protect us from curiosity. We ought, on the contrary, to continue to build our entire system upon Freemasonry, *as upon its foundation stone.* It is *that* which is to furnish us the men that we can employ to put into practice our good intentions."

Let the dupes of Écossisme who can *read* understand!

Ramsay, the Baron von Hund, and their partisans lied therefore when they advanced that every true Mason is a Templar, since on the contrary they knew that every Templar, in order to exist, had to be a Mason. Can a true Mason, who has knowledge of this article, the meaning of which is revealed, moreover, at each step in this work of darkness, remain in such an order, *no matter the title under which it is hidden*, without being at the same time a *perjured Mason* and a *false brother*?

"Art. 13. Our efforts to consolidate our well-being and that of the Order ought to accord us the benevolence of the princes who have at heart the prosperity of their States. When we will have gathered funds through our activity and through the indicated means, we ought necessarily occupy ourselves (after having payed the various advances of the brethren who will have contributed to the good of the Order, and the orders and prebends to the dignitaries, according to their seniority) with using all excess money to acquiring *real property*, and to *found establishments* which contribute, at the same time, to the particular good of the Order and to that of the States. The establishment of factories and charitable institutions, the encouragement of certain branches of commerce and of indigenous and other manufacturing, are things which may assure us the benevolence of the princes and the approbation of the public, and never will they envy the benefits that the Order and its members draw therefrom, when it is demonstrated that we do not seek solely our own interest, but that we also have in view, *so to speak*, the well-being of the entire country." etc.

These statutes, which were already observed in 1767, and which were not intended to be made public, revealed the system perfectly: the intimate interest of the Order under the appearances of the interests of the States on every point of the globe.

Such a society which, by the capitation that is used so lucratively, would be absorbed daily with the legacies in capital and real estate that the interest and revenues would double in a short period of years, ceaselessly accumulating in a frightful progression, would, in a lapse of time shorter than one might think, after having secured, by its immense establishments, its accredited principles in a uniform and general teaching, necessarily end up invading all the possessions of the material world as true *Tubalcains*, who would seize, moreover, the existence of the workers, as sole managers of universal industry on the two hemispheres. Then this society would be master of the soul, body, and goods of men; the dream of universal and absolute domination would be realized; which should suit its members better than the supposed recuperation of the goods and wealth of the old Templars, put forth to amuse the foolish and to make dupes. They had to have perceived the danger of such a formidable association, which, in its insatiable ambition, found its dream too seductive, too beautiful to renounce it.

We omit, so as not to enlarge the volume, some interesting documents, such as:

1. The act of obedience of the brethren of the Strict Observance, such as it was sent from Berlin in 1772, a copy of which had been sent to London (under the mark A, in the memorandum) to the G.O. of France, on October 6, 1771.
2. The act of reunion and submission of the *clerical* members of the new Templars, to the provincial G.M. Baron *von Hund* and to the provisionary council of the Strict Observance.
3. The act of affirmation and recognition of the same, in the number of four, given at the prefecture of Eckhorst, on July 2, 1767.
4. The composition of the general chapter of the *Clerics* of the 7th province.
5. The composition of the 7th province and of the nineteen prefectures.
6. A list of sixty-two persons of note, having their characteristics.
7. The statutes of the Order, drafted by the chancellor of the province and published, in 1767, by the provincial council, an extract of which is above.

These documents are found in the *Fastes initiatiques*.

CLERICS OF THE LATE OBSERVANCE (RELAXED OBSERVANCE)
(1767)

High Observance and Exact Observance

A scission occurring at Vienna, in 1767, in the *Strict Observance*, gave birth to the LATE OBSERVANCE, or the *Relaxed Observance.*

This new society had as chief, among others, the Baron *von Raven*, in Mecklenburg; the preacher *Starck*, at Koenigsberg. They flattered themselves to possess, *alone*, the *secrets* of the association and to know the *mysterious* cave where were deposited riches of the ancient Templars.

This régime was composed of the following ten grades:

1. Apprentice,
2. Companion,
3. Master,
4. African Brother,
5. Knight of Saint Andrew,
6. Knight of the Eagle of Master Elect,
7. Scottish Master,
8. Sovereign Mage,
9. Provincial Master of the Red Cross,
10. Mage or Knight of the Brightness and of the Light.

The ten grades were subdivided into five parts, to wit:

1.	Knight novice of the	3rd year
2.		5th —
3.		6th —
4.	Knight Levite,	
5.	Knight Priest.	

This rite had, they say, a great success until 1800, period in which the Mother Lodge *Royal-York à l'amitié*, of Berlin, declared to renounce the system of high grades in order to henceforth follow only the three symbolic grades.

The same scission also produced:

The High Observance,

In which they occupied themselves with alchemy, magic, the Cabala, divination, evocations, etc., etc.;

And the Exact Observance

Where the teachings participated in the first two Observances, which had as its base *Jesuitism* and *Catholicism.*

CHAPTER XVII
Order of African Architects

or

THE AFRICAN BRETHREN
(1767)

This Order was formed by brethren educated and of good principles. Their lodges, in Europe, are all closed, except perhaps that of Constantinople (*Berlin*).

Only one of their Grand Masters was known; it was the war counselor *Koppen*.

Their 1st grade offered an instruction more extensive and more complete than all the grades together of the Scottish systems. They said that the *lodges of Saint John* neglected the great aim and that they could not be the least instructed therein, and that the *Strict Observance* did not know the reasons for the continuation of the Masonic Order. They occupied themselves with the *hieroglyphs*, especially those relating to Freemasonry, which they sought to know well. They made a mystery of their aim until the 7th grade, that one could obtain only by strength of zeal, perseverance, and discretion. Their secondary occupations were the sciences, especially history and antiquities, the research of which they judged indispensible to the true Freemason.

Their first grade, after the symbolic, was called the *Architect* or *Apprentice* of the *Egyptian Secrets*.

They called themselves THE AFRICANS, because their study began with the history of the Egyptians, in the mysteries of which they found indications of Freemasonry, although they placed its origin much later, upon which the crusades did not give them any light.

Their commerce was modest and noble. They did not make any case of decorations, aprons, sashes, jewels, etc., but they liked a certain luxury and sententious inscriptions of a sublime, but hidden, sense.

Their banquets were simple, decency reigned there, and they pronounced their instructive and scientific discourses.

The receptions were made without any recompense. Zealous brothers who fell into an unfortunate position received great relief.

They have published, in Germany, many important documents on Freemasonry.

This Order was established in Prussia, in 1767, with the agreement of Frederick II, called *the Great*.

Its grades, eleven in number, were divided into two temples, to wit:

1st Temple:	1. Apprentice,
	2. Companion,
	3. Master,
2nd Temple:	4. Architect, or Apprentice of the Egyptian Secrets (*manes musæ*),
	5. Initiate in the Egyptian Secrets,
	6. Cosmopolitan Brother,
	7. Christian Philosopher (*Bossinius*),
	8. Master of the Egyptian Secrets, *aletophilote* (*friend of the truth*),
SUPERIOR	9. *Armiger*,

GRADES 10. *Miles,*
11. *Eques.*

The Grand Chapter gave each year, during the life of Frederick II, a gold medal of 50 ducats, as a prize for the best treatise or discourse.

In 1806, there no longer existed but one chapter of this system, the one of Berlin (*Constantinople*).

ORIGIN OF THE ORDER

Frederick II, having attained the throne, seeing that Freemasonry was no longer what it had been, and appreciating what it could be, conceived the plan of an *Inner Order* which could at the same time take the place of a *Masonic Academy*. He made a choice of a certain number of Masons in a state to comprehend his ideas and charged them with the organization of this body. They distinguished among them the brothers *Stahl*, *de Gone*, *Meyerotto*, and *du Bosc*. They instituted the Order under the name of an extinct society: THE ARCHITECTS OF AFRICA and established statutes conforming to the views of the King, who, on his part, gave privileges, and saw, in 1768, to raise, in Silosia, by his architect *Meil*, a building specially intended as the Grand Chapter, and endowed it with sufficient assets, a choice library, and rich furniture, all of an elegance worthy of the Order and of the King.

This Order, without pretentions toward domination, teaching tolerance, professing the original principles of Freemasonry, and making of its history a particular study, prospered in the silence and in all liberty. Its principal statutes were to fear only God, to respect the King and to be discreet, to exercise a general tolerance towards all the Masonic sects, without ever affiliating with any. It is for this reason that they never submitted to the act of obedience of the Baron *von Hund*, despite all the solicitations which had been made of them. They observed, in the admission of candidates, the most severe prudence. They say that the *Duke Ferdinand of Brunswick* was refused because he mingled himself with sectarian affairs. They gave themselves to active research on the history of the mysteries, of the secret societies and their different branches, and cultivated the sciences, principally mathematics. In their works, often held in the Latin tongue, reigned morality, good form, a solid instruction without ostentation. Their library and their archives have obtained, by the protection of the King and distinguished persons, among others the Prince de *Lictenstein*, at Vienna, real treasures of manuscripts and documents, of which no Masonic branch may boast. (Discovery on the system of *the Order of African Architects*, Constantinople (*Berlin*), in-8vo of 51 pp., 1806.) This piece is extracted from the Masonic library of the very obliging brother *Th. Juge*.

KNIGHTS BENEFICENT OF THE HOLY CITY OF JERUSALEM, IN PALESTINE, CALLED KNIGHTS OF CHRIST OR OF THE TEMPLE OF SOLOMON, OR KNIGHTS OF THE HOLY SEPULCHRE

(1782)

This order was created at Lyon, in 1782, by brothers of the lodge *les Chevaliers-Bienfaisants*. It professed *Martinism* (rite of *Martinez*) and had acquired a great preponderance of the German lodges of the *Strict Observance*, whose final grade divided into three parts (see the system) was entitled *Knight of the Holy City* or of *Beneficence*. They named the Duke Ferdinand *de Brunswick* G.M. of this Order, the régime of which is *Jesuitic*, under the veil of Freemasonry.

We read in the *Biblioteque des sociétés secrètes*:

"*Les Chevaliers-Bienfaisant* originally formed the *United Lodges* of Germany, which then united with the *Strict Observance* and recognized as their superior the Duc *de Chartres*, since become Duc d'Orleans.

"Their doctrine, although it deviated much from that which was used in the other civilized lands, was nevertheless not new. Many of its ideas, as singular as they were, had already been put forth by the ancient philosophers, especially as regards the system of the *numbers*. The adherents to this philosophy formed this Masonic sect, which spread into France and Germany, and led into grave error many young, inexperienced Masons. This sect exercised a very great influence at the Convent of Wilhemsbad, and then made considerable progress.

"We also give it a *Jesuitic* origin, for the letters C.H.B. (*chevaliers bienfaisant*) give the numbers 3, 8, 2, which make 13, number indicating the thirteenth letter of their alphabet, or N, which means *Nostri*."

NOVICIATE OF THE ORDER

The candidate is called *Mac-Benack*. They put a red cord around his neck and a sign of the cross formed of nine knots, in memory of the nine founding knights; these marks are to never leave him. They have him answer the following three questions:

1st question. "The temple raised by Solomon, in the Holy City, was the general type of Freemasonry; do you think that this type had been chosen in an arbitrary manner, or that there were connections between this type and the Masonic institution, and what might these connections be?"

2nd. "According to the study that you have had to make of the symbols and emblems of Masonry, and according to the moral instructions that you have received in your previous grades, what idea have you formed on the historical origin and essential aim of the Masonic institution?"

3rd. "If Masonry is connected to some rare and essential knowledge, do you think that it would be within the power of men to communicate all the knowledge, and, in the contrary case, what would be the true means to procure it?"

EXPLANATIONS OF THE EMBLEM OF THE TABLEAU

"The seven degrees designate the seven founding gentlemen of the Order.

"The two columns, adorned with fleurs-de-lis, are dedicated to *Hugues de Paganis* and *Geoffroy* de Saint-Omer, both French, first instituters of the Order.

"The letters J.B. are related to *Jacobus Burgundus* (Jacques Bourguignon [of Burgundy] *Molai*), according to the established custom of calling knights by their names of baptism and province.

"The number 9 has a connection to the nine knights who appeared at the committee of Troyes and at that of Sens in 1310, in order to defend the interests of the order.

"The *tassel* represents the cord that the novices wear as a sign of obedience.

"The *mosaic pavement* is the image of the black and white banner carried by the knights into combat and in ceremonies.

"The *three doors* of the *temple* represent the three vows of the knights: *Obedience*, *Poverty*, and *Chastity*; they were dispensed with finally by the G.M. *Harris*, second restorer of the Order; this is why the third door is shown *closed.*

"The branch of acacia on the tomb of Hiram recalls the one that the knights, disguised as operative masons, placed upon that of *Jacques Molai*, when they transported his ashes upon *Mount Heredom*, in Scotland (*where this mount is unknown*).

"The sixty-one flames or *teardrops* around the tomb recall the sixty-one knights who were burned alive at Paris.

"The fourth grade is called *Scottish*, because it was *reproduced* and *preserved* on the isle of *Mars* (they mean *Mull*) in Scotland, by *Aumont*, first restorer. That is why the Scottish wear the green sash, emblem and hope of the re-establishment of the Order[65].

"The *phoenix* is the emblem of the novices and the most ancient emblem and symbol of Masonry, being the image of honor, which perishes only to be revived and of the Order which has perished in the flames and was reborn from its ashes.

"The *pelican* indicates the great number of subjects that the Order nourishes as its children, being hospitable and vowed to fraternal charity.

"The candidate *deprived of his metals* recalls the spoliation of the goods of the Order, and the vow of purity of the knights. - The *three journeys* represent the three caravans that the knights had to make into the Holy Land, before receiving the cross of the order."

CODE OF THE ORDER. The general code of regulations of the Order was decreed at the national Convent of the Gauls, in the month of November 1778 (corresponding to the year 465 of the secret era of the Order of the new temple, number of years elapsed since 1313), and concluded at Lyon on December 10, 1778[66].

"Thus," says the ritual, "the Masonic Order which exists today contains three epochs that it is important to never lose sight of:

1. The Primitive Order,
2. The Templars,
3. The Freemasons.

PRIMITIVE ORDER. "The knighthood existed before *David*, and this existence cannot be contradicted since David was made squire by *Saul*, and since history makes known to us that the emperors and the kings were received knights by the bishops and prelates before being crowned.

ORDER OF THE TEMPLARS. "*Garimond*, Patriarch of Jerusalem, having received, in 1118, the three vows from the two gallant knights *Hugues de Paganis*, and *Geoffroy* de Saint-Omer, from the province of Auvergne, institutors of the Order, on the day of the Trinity, confided in them all the knowledge of the ancient Order or ancient knighthood.

"*Baudoin*, then King of Jerusalem, granted them a part of his palace near the old temple of Solomon, which has caused to give to this first house, and to all those of the filiation, the denomination of *Temple*, and to the members of the Order, that of *Templars*. This motif is also the one which has always made the *Temple of Solomon* to be considered as the *image of the Order.*

"*Gilbert Norfolk*, British noble; *Philibert* de Saint-Maur, *Hilderbrand*, *Canis* (cane) *de Scala*, German noble; *Jacques Dufort de Duras*, Lyonnais noble; *Martin de Rhodes*, of Provence; *Guillaume de Gamache*, Catalonian noble; *Hugues VI*, of Paris and its vicinities, are the knights who united with the first two.

ORDER OF THE FREEMASONS. "*Jacques de Molai*, twentieth G.M., having been condemned to perish in the flames, *Beaujon*, his nephew, received from him all the instructions of the Order. He secretly gave him funerary honors and was then elected G.M. on the day of Saint John, 1313. (*It is here that begins the Roman Jesuitico-Templar Écossais that detached grades and others have uncritically spread with profusion.*)

"*Pierre d'Aumont*, provincial Master of Auvergne, succeeded Beaujon, and was succeeded by *George Harris*, who exempted the knights from the third vow, that of chastity."

The *noviciate* of the Templar Order, which has served as its model, has much relationship with it.

EXTRACT FROM THE RITUAL FOR THE USE OF THE COMMANDER OF THE INTERIOR, PRESIDENT OF THE CHAPTER

The Commander opens the works thus: *In the name of God All-Powerful, Master of the Universe, and by the permission of our legitimate superiors and with the consent of my brethren, I open this assembly.*

The First *Senior* (Surveillant) responds: "*You have opened it according to the ancient observance and with the consent of all the brethren, let it be open.*"

They extinguish the candles; a small lamp lights the assembly; the Commander says:

"*May the darkness remove every curious and indiscreet eye.*"

The aspirant having been introduced; the Commander concludes the allocution addressing him thus:

"...Humanity is the cry to arms to which the *Knights* rally; they ask of you zeal, morals, *obedience*, and discretion; the sacrifice of a part of your fortune and *of your liberty*, that you are going to make to charity and public utility, and by your firm and free will to pledge yourself thereto. - (*He responds.*)

"The veil of silence is therefore going to fall, and the *Masonic Shadows* which surround you are going to disappear, and you are going to know the respectable Order which has perpetuated its existence through Freemasonry."

The obligation being given, the Commander arms the Knight, with Latin formulas, and proclaims him, saying: *In the name of the Father who has created you, of the Son who has redeemed you, and of the Holy Spirit who has sanctified you*, etc. After the history of the Order, the Commander says:

"We disguise ourselves as Masons in order to better hide our state and to gain our sustenance. In order to conceal our motives from our enemies, let us take as emblem the name, customs, and tools of the Masons which have served us for two hundred years.

"*Transierunt vetera et cuncta nova facia sunt.*"

All the Knights remove their costume and dress as Masons, arm themselves with tools, and make their tour of the enclosure. After this ridiculous scene that it suffices to have already given an account, the Commander gives the explanation of the *phoenix* and the *pelican* and closes the Chapter in the same manner that he opened it. (See the *Tuiler général*.)

EXTRACT FROM THE HISTORICAL DISCOURSE

The lecture is made, in chair, by the senior Brother Lector. After a short narrative on the establishment and misfortunes of the Order, he continues thus:

"Here is what the historians relate of the proceedings made by the Templars. We who are their descendants have a quite certain tradition of the misfortunes which have occasioned the destruction of our Order; here is the true cause thereof: *Their wealth and the means that they have employed in order to acquire it.* I am going to teach it to you:

"Hugues *de Paganis* and the first Templars, working to repair the house that Baudoin II had given them, excavated in the ruins in order to draw materials therefrom, and encountered an iron trunk containing, among other very precious things, *the process for succeeding in the great work*, science that Solomon and his confidants possessed unanimously, and which had been taught to them by the master *Hiram Abiff*, whom Hiram, King of Tyre, friend and ally of Solomon, had sent them.

"All the historians relate the temple of Solomon to us as the most unbelievable monument of antiquity. The riches that he employed in its construction are represented to us as immense, and it is proven that all the treasures of the mines of Peron would have been necessary, and this same history teaches us that Solomon had no such mines in his States; moreover, it represents his power as very limited. What it relates to us, that the King of Tyre sent him the master Hiram Abiff with all the material proper to the construction of his temple, is none other than that the King and Master Hiram Abiff *possessed the secrets of nature*[67].

"Hugues de Paganis and the first Templars profited from their discovery and acquired great wealth. They transmitted the secret to thirty of their members, and, from that moment, the general chapter possessed it alone; it was created the chief and trustee thereof. Jean *de Montfaucon* and his accomplices were not yet initiated into the final mysteries; their conduct had deprived them thereof. But these wretches knew the aim of the *works of the Order*, while giving advice to the Pope *Clement V* and *Philippe-le-Bel*. These two princes resolved to destroy the Order in order to seize its wealth and in the hope of obtaining the secret thereof[68]." - (*But this destruction was decided by the king well before the Archbishop of Bordeaux became pope, since it was the secret cause of his election.*)

"Three of our ancestors, *possessing the great secret*, found the means to escape the general and particular searches that they made against them. They wandered for a long time from kingdom to kingdom. They finally stopped in some caves, *near Heredom*, in Scotland, where they received welcome and relief from the *Knights of Saint Andrew of the Thistle*, the ancient friends and allies of our ancestors. These three Templars made a new alliance with the Knights of Saint Andrew and transmitted to these wise men *the tradition* that I have just taught you, and *their secret*, which had been possessed by the ancient Knights of Saint Andrew, at the time of the crusades.

"It is today the ancient Knights of Saint Andrew who are also our brothers (since our two orders are united), who *possess the secret.* They are known, among us, under the title of *Grand Rose-Croix*, or *members of the Grand Chapter.* The Knights of Saint Andrew and the brethren of this final grade are the only ones who may hope to attain to this eminent degree, and who had certain notions of the true good, and to whom nothing lacks but to be *guided by the practice of the operations*, and to be initiated thereby into the *grand* and *final mysteries* possessed by all the chiefs of our Grand Chapter, and which is *the physical aim of allegorical Masonry*, through which they have had him pass. You know too its moral aim; you will embrace and traverse the career which will be suitable to you.

"The number of initiates having grown, in order to hide the aim of their institution, they imagined these allegories of the *Order of the Freemasons*, which was created in 1340, after the destruction of the Order at Heredom, in Scotland; and all those who date Masonry back to the construction of the temple of Solomon do not know the true history." - (*This is as true as it is true that Masonry was created in 1340.*)

"The first grades: *Apprentice*, *Companion*, and *Master*, which have really been created at the institution of the Order - (*We have demonstrated the contrary.*) - in order to serve as *proving grades* to those of our *interior*, are the *only true ones* that the instructed Masons ought to recognize; the others (*of the Scottish rite*) have been instituted by intelligent persons who have wished to delve deeper, and who have sought to unravel the allegories of the first three grades, and who have deceived themselves. There are even those that are entirely foreign to Masonry and that cupidity has invented in order to extract money from those who wish to possess them. You see, my brother, that the classes through which you have passed, in this lodge, have served only to try you and to prepare you to receive the favor of being admitted among us, and that in our Order, spread upon the whole earth, are the allegories of Masonry.

"You are too prudent not to perceive how essential it is to *hide your operations* even unto *your name*. It is for this reason that we bear that of *Knights Beneficent* (or of *Beneficence*) of the *Holy City of Jerusalem, in Palestine.*

"The whole earth teems with Masons: few know how to unravel the allegory which leads them; few are worthy of such. Here, my brother, are the true secrets which have devolved upon you. It is thus necessary to teach you what our Order has conveyed, in this century, at the moment of reappearing in all its lustre, and this era has been set back by an event that prudence and wisdom could not have foreseen nor warded off. (*The French Revolution of 1789.*) - I will instruct you verbally. Grand Sovereigns support you; some of them are our brothers."

"We have two aims, *the physical and the philosophical works*: *the moral* is to re-enter, one day, into our goods and to see the Order enjoy all its possessions of honor and glory that injustice has wrested from it. They have prepared this event for two centuries with a wisdom that renders its secret impenetrable to the eyes of mortals, etc."

(This aim, which is far from being moral, ought to have long appeared to these knights to be but a true chimera.)

CHAPTER XVIII
Swedenborg

"One of the most illustrious reformers of the Masonic rites was the scholar *Swedenborg*, born at Stockholm, of the Lutheran bishop de Skara, at Upsala, city of Sweden, which figures in the Masonic legends. He was born in 1688 and died at London on March 29, 1772. He possessed philosophy, metaphysics, minerology, astronomy; in his works, he has treated on God, the infinite, the spirit, matter, and creation. He has left writings on all these sciences and had a profound knowledge of ancient languages. He performed very scholarly research on the Masonic mysteries. He believed and wrote that their doctrine was of the greatest antiquity, emanating from the Egyptians, the Persians, the Magi, the Jews, and the Greeks.

"Swedenborg also created himself head of a new religion. He reformed that of Rome, and his reform was followed with a brilliant success in Germany and in England, where there are cities which count from 14 to 15,000 of his adepts. To this end, he wrote his *Celestial Jerusalem*, or his *Spiritual World*; he mixed with his reform some purely Masonic ideas.

"In this Celestial Jerusalem, is found the word that God himself has communicated to him, as formerly to Moses; this word is *Jehova*, lost upon the earth, but which he invites to seek in Tartary, land which is still, in our day, ruled by the patriarchs; meaning by this, allegorically, that these people must approach the primitive state of the perfection of innocence; which has been followed by *Weishaupt* for the development of his system of illuminism[69].

"Swedenborg established his creative being in *Jesus Christ*, only God, life, love, wisdom, heat, light; he explains the books of the Jewish religion, as writings of a continual allegory[70] having always a double meaning. According to his system, death exists in man only in appearance, for it is in this moment that he is reborn into an eternal future life, and that he resurrects forever, *in becoming an angel.*

"Swedenborg has given the idea to *Martinez Pascalis* of his rite of *Elus Coëns*, which is related to biblical and Christian theosophy, and which is rather widespread in Germany and in the more considerable cities.

"Genesis has furnished to the rite of Swedenborg the program of his first three grades, and the whole process of initiation. In it, the *All-Powerful*, allegory of the Great Archit. of the Univ., gives life to the neophyte who comes out of the chaos, makes an oath of discretion, to flee from debauchery, games, prostitutes, adultery, and to be faithful to the Order. Now, as, *according to the Bible*, man is formed from mud and clay, this instituter has added to the Masonic symbols those of the elements which are: *a vase containing kneaded earth, a second full of water, and an earthen dish with lit charcoals*[71]. The rite counts eight grades, divided into two temples:

1st Temple:	1. Apprentice,	2nd Temple:	5. Companion Coën,
	2. Companion,		6. Master Coën,
	3. Master,		7. Grand Architect and Knight Commander,
	4. Elect [Élu],		8. Kadosh.

"The doctrines of the first temple are related to the creation of man, his disobedience, his punishment, and the pains of the body and spirit, which is actually represented in the initiation.

"In the mysteries, it is said that when man, by a new, holy, and exemplary life, had been reintegrated into his primitive dignity, and that by these useful works he has recovered his primitive rights, then he is reconciled with his Creator by a new, speculative life, animated with the divine breath, he is initiated *Élu Coën*; in the instructions that he receives he learns the *occult sciences* in all their parts, which make known to him the secrets of nature, high chemistry, ontology, and astronomy.

"At the time of admission, circles are traced in the middle of the temple, representing the universal planetary system, and the sun at the center.

"The great All-Powerful explains and reveals how the mystery of creation has been operated, etc." (*Reghellini*, 2nd vol., p. 434.)

Here is the opinion of *Buret de Longcahmps* on this reformer, whom they reproach, with reason, for having been too credulous and too enthusiastic.

"*Emmanuel Swedenborg*, after having given several works on mathematics, physics, astronomy, and after having meditated on the mysteries of Christianity, ended by believing himself transported into the spiritual and celestial world; he converses with his deceased friends, who appear to him under the form of angels, and believes that God himself reveals himself to him, with the charge to re-establish the Christian Church. He abandons, from this moment, all terrestrial things, and makes his customary society of angels; voyages into the planets and into the stars, and he holds frequent conferences there with the celestial spirits who, at what he claims, appear to him.

"This man with revelations and with singular visions, who believed to have found the keys of the Apocalypse, is author of the *Marvels of Heaven and Hell and of the Planetary and Austral Lands*[72]: he claims that all that he relates therein has been done in the world of the spirits, which is between heaven and earth. He has left enthusiastic partisans[73]. The physicians, naturalists, and philanthropes are still, in Sweden, more or less attached to this sect, not that they occupy themselves with seeking a new terrestrial Jerusalem, not that they regard Swedenborg as a man animated by the spirit of God, nor that they believe that he has been transported *alive* into other worlds: but they are persuaded that by means of his dogmas and the beneficent moral that flows therefrom, they may do good to men, propagate useful virtues, accredit beneficent institutions; and it is in this view that they are associated with the confraternity of the *Swedenborgians*. These sectaries are very widespread, not only in Sweden, but in England, in Holland, and in the North," (*les Fastes universels*).

What Buret de Longchaps ignored, is that Swedenborg was a somnambulist and had visions.

SYSTEM OF ZINNENDORF

(1770)

ZINNENDORF was named *Ellerman*, but he was adopted by his uncle. Morsdorf called him *Ellerberger* (*Encyclop.* of Lessing, v. III, p. 664). He was Knight Commander of the Strict Observance, director of the lodges in France, member of the lodge *Les Trois-Globes*, and surgeon-in-chief at Berlin. In the system of the Templars, he had the title of *Prior* under the characteristic of *eques a Lapide nigro*. In 1768, he founded a lodge at Potsdam. The following year, he founded at Berlin the lodge *Les Trois-Clés* both of the Templar régime. He had been stricken, in 1766, from the rolls of the *Strict Observance*, which put no obstacle to the projects and progress of Zinnendorf, because the Duke Ferdinand of Brunswick, at the Convent of Wolfenbüttel, had suspended the *Inner Order* for three years, in the hope that the true *unknown superiors* would make themselves known for the good of the Order. Abandoning this régime, Zinnendorf created, around 1770, *his rite*, of which he claimed to have received the powers, documents, and instruction from the Duc de Sudermanie and from the Grand Lodge of Sweden[74]. It is said that he held this rite from a Swede named *Cklach* or *Chlach*. It is based on the reveries of Swedenborg and presents many an analogy with the Swedish rite. It is composed of the following seven degrees:

A. Blue Masonry or grades called Saint John's:
1. *Apprentice,*
2. *Companion,*
3. *Master.*

B. Red Masonry:
4. *Scottish Apprentice and Companion,*
5. *Scottish Master.*

C. Chapter:
6. *Clercus* (Cleric) — Or *Favored of Saint John.* That is to say *Frater Societatis Jesu* — Swedish grade.
7. Brother Elect.

We read in the *Bibliotèque de sociétés secrètes*:

"The founder of this system claimed to have drawn his Masonic knowledge in Sweden; he said that *the origins* of the Strict Observance *were false* and *contrived.* Although this latter treated Zinnendorf as an infidel and apostate, though the Swedish lodges declared that the obtaining of his patent was the effect of fraud, and though the G.L. of London maintained that his English privileges were the fruit of deceit, his system, nevertheless, made great and rapid progress in Germany."

We are going to enter into some details on these grades, in order to give an idea of its *mysticism* and that of the Templar Masonry of Sweden.

In the instruction of the 3rd grade, the three white rosettes, on the apron of the Companions, are presented as a symbol of the *three blows* under which Hiram (read *Molay*) succumbed.

In the 4th grade, *Scot. App. and Comp.* (M. Elect of the Swedish system), the lodge is called the *Dark Cave*; the brethren are vested in black and wear a black cloak on which is a cross and a hood where are embroidered crossbones. *They* have from the left shoulder to the right hip a wide black ribbon, edged with *three white stripes*, on which is a crown traversed by a silver dagger. Upon the altar is a Bible opened to the 6th chapter of the Gospel of Saint Mark.

In the 5th grade, the *Scottish Master* (in both systems), the altar and the throne are draped in white with crosses of Saint Andrew (those of the *crusades*).

The candidate wears the cord of honor of Hiram.

The tableau has a red background; in the four corners are the heads of the four evangelists, a key, a globe, etc.; on the key, which is triangular, is read the motto: *Aperuit ut nemo me claudat, claudit ut nemo me aperiat.*

The 6th grade, *Favored of Saint John* or *Intimate of Saint John* is part of the *illuminated* chapter; in the rite of Sweden, it is also called *Knight of the East* or *Novice.*

The brethren wear, besides the red cross of the Templars, suspended from a wide ribbon, an *ecce homo*, on the one side, and on the other, a lamb with the triumphal standard (*signal of springtime*), and the motto: *Ecce agnus Dei qui tollit peccata mundi*. They interpret here the 60th chapter of Isaiah, and the remarkable words: *Crusade, Zion*. They have said that the secret doctrine of this degree was that of the *Carpocratians*.

In the Swedish rite, the tableau represents the New Jerusalem with its twelve gates.

The 7th grade of *Perfect Elect* (*adoptus adoptatus, adoptatus coronatus*) is alchemical. The brethren wear, besides the Templar cross over the bare chest, four other crosses embroidered on a ribbon which turns three times around the right wrist, in memory of the wounds made to Jesus by the nails of his crucifixion.

- Here are some questions drawn from the instruction:

Question. - *What is the aim of the Masonic works?*

Answer. - The knowledge and profound study of the most hidden secrets of nature. The seven letters J.B.M.B.G.I.M. (*Joakin, Booz, Mac-Benac, Ghiblim*) indicate the surest path in order to penetrate into the Hermetic medicine (which means that *the first three grades make the whole of Masonry*).

Q. - *What is signified by the death of Hiram and the Master's word lost with him?*

A. - Corrupted nature, the lost knowledge of its secrets, the events occurring to Masonry, and a salutary allegory of an event which awaits us.

Q. - *What is the true aim of Freemasonry?*

A. - The propagation and conservation of its principles, until it can renounce its existence, that is to say until Masonry agrees with the times and the times with Masonry.

Zinnendorf obtained, in 1771, from the G.L. of England, which he recognized as the premier institutive authority of Masonry, a patent to the effect of erecting a G.L. at Berlin, which, under the name of GRAND NATIONAL MOTHER LODGE OF GERMANY, became the headquarters of his system; but the G.L. of England, having reserved the right to name the provincial Grand Masters thereof, instituted, at the same time, the Duke *Charles de Mecklembourg-Strelitz* as provincial G.M. at Hanover, and the Duke *Exter* as provincial G.M. of Basse-Saxe.

Zinnendorf has claimed, *they say*, that the Order possessed four gospels lost from the Bible.

This Order of Templars being established, they occupied themselves with a system of Rose-Croix, *makers of gold*. *Plumenoeck* made the COMPASS OF THE WISE, that is the Magic Rose-Croix. - Jean-Guillaume Zinnendorf died at Berlin in 1782.

SWEDISH MASONIC SYSTEM

From 1135, they have believed to be able to indicate the existence of Freemasonry in Sweden, under King Ingon II. This can only be a confraternity of operative masons, Masonry not then existing.

1736, April 15. Masonry, come from England into Sweden, where it propagated itself rapidly among the high classes of society, would be practiced there a little before this date, since on this date the G.L. of England names the Comte *de Scheffer* provincial G.M. for the lodges of Sweden. (See our *Précis chronologique historique*.)

The true Swedish system (*not that of Zinnendorf*) worked originally according to the principles of the Strict Observance. King *Gustav* and his brother were successively the chiefs thereof. This system also lent every assistance to the prince, in the revolution which would see it recover its independence; which, once assured, was engaged in publicly re-establishing the *Order of the Templars*.

At the Convent of Wilhemsbad, where the Strict Observance offered to make known the true origin of its system, the united Swedish lodges announced that they were in possession of the true secret; that they were in communication with the *true superiors*, and that they were ready to fulfill the vows of the brothers of Germany, *if they wished to name the Duc de Sudermanie G.M.* of the 7th province; which took place, indeed, and which convinced the Duc de Brunswick to return to Sweden in order to be instructed there. He related thereof only some insufficient additions to the history of the Order and some ceremonies.

In this same era, the brother *Wachter* (eques a ceraso) discovered, in Italy, a letter which proved that the Swedes had themselves sought instructions. The Germans found themselves offended and named the Duke Ferdinand of Brunswick for G.M. of the 7th province.

The Swedish system confers twelve grades, to wit:

A.	1. Apprentice, 2. Companion, 3. Master.	called Saint John's; same grades as in the various systems
B.	4. Master Elect,	forming, in the system of Zinnendorf, the *Scottish Ap. and Comp. of Saint Andrew*. Thory says it is the same as the *Secret Elect* of the French régime. They give to the candidate some slight blows of the dagger, in order to remind him *that he would not be in security anywhere in the world, if he were to betray the secret.*
	5. Scottish Master,	It is also called *Master of Saint Andrew*, or again *Scottish Grand Elect*. This grade grants civil nobility.
	6. Knight of the East,	or Novice (Zinnendorf called it the *Favored of Saint John*). It is formed from the *Kn. of the East* and a part of the *Knight of the West*. Thory calls this grade *the Sturart brethren*, and says it is formed from the *Kn. of the East* and the *Prince of Jerusalem*. The tableau represents the New Jerusalem with its twelve gates.
	7. Knight of the West,	or the *True Templar*, also called *Favorite Brother of Solomon*. According to the system of Zinnendorf, which has only seven degrees, it is the *Perfect Elect*, formed from the other part of the *Kn. of the West* and from the additions of Zinnendorf, of which they have later made the *Adeptus Coronatus*. This grade is also called *True Capitulat, the Templar Master of the Key*. We see upon its green ribbon, and from which is suspended the triangular key, *five red rosettes*, which recall the five wounds of J. C. They speak in this Cabalistic grade of the re-establishment of the temple of Solomon. The Grand Prior gives the benediction to the newly received and cuts from his right side a lock of hair.
	8. Knight of the South,	*Commander, Magister Templar, Grand Dignitary, Elect.*

	He is part of the superiors, and wears upon his bare chest the red cross of the Templars attached to a white ribbon upon which are embroidered in gold V.V., initials of the response to this question: *Rabbi, ubi habitas*? – R. *Venite vesum*. The ceremony of installation of a candidate resembles that of the alchemists of the first centuries of our era. This grade is also called *Favorite Brother of Saint John* or of the *Blue Cord*.
9. *Favorite Brother of Saint Andrew or of the Violet Cord*,	also called *Kn. of the Purple Cord*; there they explain the *Mac-Benac*, as *Messias Benedictus*.
D. *Brother of the Rose Croix*,	divided into three classes:
1st 10. *Non-dignitary*	member of the Chapter,
2nd 11. *Grand Dignitary of the Chapter*,	presided over by the royal prince (in 1812, by the Pr. *Bernadotte*).
3rd 12. *The Reigning Master*	(the King of Sweden)[75]. This grade and the Master have as title: *The stathounder* or *vicarius Salomonis, sanctificatus, illuminatus, magnus Jehova*. Only one bother may be invested with this grade.

The members of these three classes united form the *Illuminated Chapter*, in which no one may be *Grand Dignitary* (2nd class) unless he has four quarters of nobility.

This rite, whose degrees are composed on the *abolition and re-establishment of the Templars* and on the *Qabalah* and *alchemy*, is recognized by the Grand Lodge of Stockholm.

The King *Charles XIII* created, on May 27, 1811, a public order and a special decoration on behalf of Freemasonry in his States, under the name of *Order of Charles XIII*; here is its description:

It is a ruby red cross, embroidered with gold and surmounted by a crown in gold; they wear it on a wide red ribbon, one side of which presents, on a white background, the initial letters of the name of the founder, and, on the other, the letter B in the middle of a triangle (initial of *Bernadotte*).

Since 1755, Swedish Masonry, by the admission of the high grades, became something entirely different from what it had been at its introduction before 1736. This was no longer English (*Symbolic*) Masonry in its purity. A certain spirit of *Templars* and *Rose-Croix* was mixed therein, mixture by which the Jesuits had profited in order to make themselves Masters of the lodges, and, under this pretext, achieve their goal in a manner more prompt and more sure; which explains the failure, in the workshops of Stockholm, in 1758, of the brother *Rosa*, charged by the G.L. at the *Trois-Globes* of Berlin, to communicate to the Swedish lodges the grades of the Chapter of the *Emperors of the East and West*, and to cause to be recognized, on this subject, the jurisdiction of that G.L. (See our *Précis hist., Fastes initiat.*)

While the chivalric spirit of the Templars found in Germany ardent sympathies, the Swedish, abundant in common metals, inclined more towards the *Rose-Croix* and the *alchemists*; which had been skillfully calculated by the Jesuits. "It is even to these latter that would seem to belong the idea of the foundation, in 1753, of the *House of the Orphans*, at least to judge by the eagerness to seize every occasion to inoculate their principles and their doctrines to the youth." Some accidental modifications occurred unexpectedly in the form of the government giving to Freemasonry a particular direction which therein prepared the future prosperity of the association. Thus, the Swedish, frightened of the temerity of Charles XII, had, in 1719 and 1721, contained the royal power within such restrained limits, that there remained nearly nothing left but the title. In vain, the Queen *Ulrique-Eléonore*, assisted by her husband and co-regent (*hereditary Prince de Hesse-Cassel*), had been forced to flee the burdensome protectorship of the States of the kingdom. It was reserved only to *Gustav III*, in 1771 and 1778, to achieve this aim with the cooperation of the army. Rousing the bourgeoisie against the nobility, he saw to abolish throughout his states the majority of the political laws of 1719 and 1721, and to pronounce the suppression of the senate. The occasion of this coup d'état was furnished to him by the Freemasons, into the association of which he had himself received and which had spread throughout the kingdom. In this manner, the projects of the Jesuits were overthrown, the alchemical conceptions reduced to silence; and henceforth the restoration of the *Order of the Templars*, accorded to the association by Gustav III, occupies all the Masons exclusively. The King named his brother, the Duc *de Sudermanie*, provisionally as G.M. of the Freemasons, which already produced a fortunate impression. But the credit of Masonry was increased again when *Charles XIII* had founded, in 1811, an order intended to be displayed publicly by deserving Masons. This order, which replaced the discredited Order of the Templars, was called *Order of Charles XIII*. Presently, it constitutes the grade of *Knight* in the assembly of Swedish Masons, and it counts thirty Knights (27 civil and 3 ecclesiastical), besides the princes of the royal house. The sign of the Order consists in a crown from which a cross is suspended, and the Knights of this Order enjoy the same consideration as the commanders of the other Swedish orders. Freemasonry has lost nothing of its dignity under the government of King *Charles-Jean* (Bernadotte), and the Crown Prince, Oscar I, ruling today, is, since 1816, either adjunct G.M. or titular G.M. of Swedish Freemasons.

But, toward the end of the last century, Freemasonry took on a particular character that must be attributed to the metaphysical reveries and religious enthusiasms of *Swedenborg*. These influences have exercised themselves since 1783 over Masonry. The disciples of Swedenborg seized all the seats, and the search for the *New Jerusalem* (see above the notice on this illuminatus) became the dominant idea of the Masons. There resulted therefrom a new Swedish system which extended unto England and even unto Moscow, where a lodge of this régime was constituted. Germany was also no stranger to it; for it was in part copied by *Zinnendorf*, who made it, as we have seen, the basis of the doctrines of the *National G.L. of Germany* founded by him at Berlin, and of forty-six workshops instituted by this G.L. - However, says the *Latomia*, from which we borrow a part of these details that it produces not always without error, the lodges soon saw themselves forced to modify the régime of Zinnendorf according to the exigencies of the period, and to assimilate it more and more to the dominant systems in Germany.

There exists in Sweden a *clerical* branch which does not recognize the system of Zinnendorf. It is probable that these Swedish clerics have some analogy with the *Adepti Coronati*; they claimed to know *their superiors* and to descend from the congregation of Florence. They preserved and venerated a *so-called* Testament of Jacques Molai, filled with fictions and of which there exist in several lodges copies which render it no more authentic. They flattered themselves to possess many historical documents on other orders.

According to this testament, the *Comte Beaujeu*, nephew of Jacques Molai, found the means to gather the ashes of his uncle and give them burial, engraving upon an oblong flagstone this inscription:

J.B.M.B.
A-DO-N-I-J-C.
M CCC XIV
XI MARTIS

That is to say: JAKIN BOAZ MAC BENAC A-DO-NAI-JEHOVA CRUSADE (Jacobus Burgundus Molai *Bustus anno Domini nostri Jesu Christi*, 1314, March 11).

This Beaujeu withdrew then into Scotland, with some knights who escaped the French tribunals. There they continued, in 1319, the Order of the Temple, under the name of *Rose-Croix*; which would have done likewise in Scotland, under the name of the *Order of the Thistle*; in Portugal, under that of the Order of Christ; and in France, under that of the *Order of the Blazing Star*, which had spread in the 15th century into Bohemia and Silesia, etc.

RITE OF SCHROEDER
(1766)

SCHROEDER, called the *Cagliostro of Germany*, because it is at his school that Cagliostro took lessons on theosophy, evocations, and the secret sciences called *occult*, established at Marburg (*Hesse-Cassel*), in 1766, a chapter of the TRUE AND ANCIENT ROSE-CROIX MASONS, and in 1779, it opened, in a lodge of Sarreburg, its school of *magic*, *theosophy*, and *alchemy* in seven grades (3+4).

This rite, which was also called *Rectified Rose-Croix*, is composed of Symbolic Masonry and four high grades, which have as their basis the three sciences that we have just cited. It was not practiced much but in two lodges of the constitution of the Grand Lodge of Hamburg.

RITE OF SCHROEPFFER
(1768)

SCHROEPFFER was the son of a café-keeper. He reformed the Order of Freemasons at Dresden: it is he who, at first, illuminated the princes of Germany, by means of phantasmagoria or the apparition of specters. He threw terror into Berlin and into all of Prussia, by making predictions, through phantoms, of the impending death of some great personages, *death which was always realized*. He had so stricken their minds, that the scholar *Gleditsch* could not go to the academy of Berlin without imagining that he saw the shade of the deceased president sitting in his place.

The Queen of Prussia forbade him from performing his evocations.

We read in a notice that he had just established himself as a cafe-keeper at Leipsick (Saxony), and that he had the opening of his café on October 29, 1768. He instituted his system, based on *magic*, *evocations*, etc., in a lodge of the city. He had few partisans. Later, he was persecuted and killed himself with a pistol shot on October 8, 1774, in the *Rosenthal*, near Leipsig, at the age of 35. His system disappeared with him.

His works are at Berlin.

MASONRY OF THE 72

One may only designate under this name an association called *Masonic*, the special denomination of which is unknown, or perhaps it did not have one.

One could boldly, *they say*, exchange, for its *grade of Apprentice*, all the other grades of all the systems; it was therefore a high grade, divided into three classes, rather than that of a Masonic sect, whose origin, that they suppose *German*, is not indicated.

It gave itself to the study of the *occult sciences* and claimed, without doubt in order to throw off the curious, that its Grand Master lived in Spain and bore, in the Order, the name of *Tajo*.

The number of its members could not ever exceed 72, of which there were 24 Apprentices, 24 Companions. and 24 Masters.

The youngest were charged with distributing the alms, performing research, and determining whether, in the lodges, there were brethren who were worthy of being, one day, received among them. They had to make detailed reports on these brothers.

If a Master died, he was replaced by the most senior Companion; this one by the most senior Apprentice, and this latter by one of the Freemasons recorded according to the reports.

They were not received before the age of maturity into this mysterious order, whose ritual is unknown to us.

This notice figures in some collections under the title of *A Masonic Branch* or *Anonymous Society*.

Its number 72 could imply some connection with the following order, of which it could be, perhaps, the final expression.

ORDER OF THE INITIATED KNIGHTS AND BROTHERS OF ASIA IN EUROPE (1780)

This order was founded at Berlin in 1780, others say at Vienna. Its members, of which the German papers, in 1786, had spoken much, had adopted a mixture of *Jewish*, *Mohammedan*, and *Christian* ceremonies, in order to indicate, without doubt, that they admitted all religions. Their costume is Spanish; their passwords and the names of their grades are Hebrew, such as *Melchizedek*, *Thumim*, *Lurim*, *Sanhedrin*. They made great use of the *harmonica* for their initiations and had recourse to evocations, in which a spirit, called *Gablidone*, played one of the principal roles.

We find the relating of a reception in a booklet that M. *Roellig*, a non-initiate, had printed at Berlin, in 1787, at the same time as the description of its harmonica. According to him, the ceremony would be sepulchral and bloody.

Note xv, p. 212 of the *Essai sur les Illuminés*, gives various details on this Order, *to wit*:

The supreme direction was called *the lesser and constant Sanhedrin of Europe*. The Order has five degrees:

2 grades of trial: 1. *Seekers*,
2. *Sufferers*.
3 principal grades: 3. *Initiated Knights and Brothers of Asia, in Europe*,
4. *Masters and sages*,

5. *Royal Priests*, or *True Rose-Croix Brethren.*

Having attained to this final grade called of *Melchizedek* or *Principal*, one is obliged, by oath, to remain and to live in the Order, according to the statutes.

The superiors in dignity, merit, and wisdom are *Fathers and Brothers of the Seven Unknown Churches of Asia*, provided that the fathers are not unknown.

The Sanhedrin consists in seventy-two members; same number for the degree of Melchizedek which has some connection with the *Masonry of the seventy-two* above, the aim of which is likewise hidden under the Hermetic veil (*Jesuitic ruse*).

The initiate promises, among other things, to instruct, without delay, with truth and honesty, for all that which will come to his understanding, the venerable Order, the very respectable *Lesser and Constant Sanhedrin*, the *General Chapter* of the Order and the *Chapter* of the province.

THE GERMAN UNION, OR THE XXII

Charles Frederick BAHRDT, doctor of theology, born at Bischofswerda (*Misnia*), in 1741, author of a great number of works on *polemics*, especially remarkable for the elegance of style, and become celebrated for the persecutions sown by his career as a Protestant minister, was the founder of the *German Union of the XXII*, association which, for its four years of duration, made much noise in the Masonic world and occupied the greatest minds of Germany.

Bahrdt had made, in 1777, a voyage to England. He had been commended by the Prince Louis de Hesse-Darmstadt to the brother *Hesselstein*, *G. Secretary* of the G.L. of London, by the intermediary of whom he had been received into the three symbolic grades. Upon his return to Germany, he claimed that he had learned more at London than any brother invested with the highest grades could teach him on the continent.

Cautioned against German Masonry, he long remained outside of all Masonic activity. But, in 1781, at Wetzlar, he made the acquaintance of the Baron *von Ditfurth*, highly educated Mason who was initiated into all that was then done in German Freemasonry. This brother convinced him to have himself received *Illuminati.*

Bahrdt resumed a taste for Masonry; he became one of its most ardent and enthusiastic chorus leaders; he threw himself head long into the ideas of interpretation which then reigned (1786) in Germany. Then, sharply wounded for not being able to become one of the *unknown superiors*, he conceived the idea, in imitation of *Weishaupt*, to found a new order for the Protestant part of Germany, under the mantle of Freemasonry, and which would have for its aim *to enlighten the human race and to annihilate prejudice and superstition.*

He met with some other Masons, and sent out, in 1786, from his country home near Halle, in Saxony, a *circular to the friends of reason*, *truth*, and *virtue.* It was signed by him and by twenty-one confederates. From here is given the name to the association of *German Union of the XXII.* He laid out there in the necessity to create the order that he announced, and the advantages that one would draw therefrom. He presented the *Union* as being an infallible means of contributing to the *great aim of Christ*, of increasing the light, of annihilating superstition, and of perfecting the human race; and he invited those who wished to join this secret and peaceful union of persons who honored God in his works, to make themselves known to an address indicated. He wanted, in order to achieve this, to gather the most esteemed authors and artists, to secure the book trade, journalism, and literary practices in Germany, and in this way to assure themselves the greatest influence over the entire nation. Every honest man could be admitted thereto, save the princes and their ministers. But this exception extended neither to their favored nor to the governors of the young princes; for their cooperation would be useful for acting upon the spirit of the reigning princes and inheritors of thrones and bureaus.

Bahrdt sacrificed his time and his fortune to the organization of this union and to putting it into activity. He took an interest in the Prince of *Anhalt-Bernburg*, and, strengthened by his support, he delayed not to establish, in this residence, his center of action. He had soon organized an administration which would occupy itself actively with the printing and dispatching of the works of its members, and he devoted himself entirely to the correspondence which was widespread and very costly.

In 1789, the Union caused to appear its first work under the title of *Ueber aufklærung und die Befœderungsmittel der selben von einer Gesellschaft* (*On the enlightenment and the means to contribute thereto*), in-8vo, Leipsig. - In the appendix, it protests publicly against the commotion which hastened to its disadvantage, and declared that its members had only for their aim the well-being of the human race, that they had gathered only to this end in writing, spreading, and recommending good books, in assisting enlightened persons, and in perfecting each other, through an intimate commerce and a fraternal communication, of the *discovered truths*. They protested at the same time against every other aim or intention that could be brought against them.

However, the reputation of *atheist*, that powerful enemies of Bahrdt had given him, rendered the *Union* suspect to the governments and to the persons invited to join, and opposed the desired success.

The publication of the work *Mehr noten als text*, etc. (*more notes than text*), or the *German Union of the XXII*, in-8vo, Leipsig, 1789, which divulged the whole organization and all the details, removed it beyond the attraction of the mystery. Then finally the imprisonment of the doctor Bahrdt, for having written a supposedly defamatory libel, entitled: *Religious system of the Prussian minister Wœllner*, deprived him of the first line of his activity; so that the *Union* separated itself in 1790; its members withdrew and the greater part joined the Illuminati.

The doctrine professed was: *to accustom men to making use of their own judgment, in order to appreciate the moral and economical truths, and to regard nothing as true, before forming a precise idea thereof, supported by solid reasons.*

Starting from this point of view, the Union recommended to its neophytes, and as the first study, natural religion. It was permitted to them to treat this subject in their assemblies and to discuss all that may lead to the truth, however removed the subject may be from Freemasonry or from the generally accredited opinions of the world.

Its teaching was distributed in six grades:

1.	*The Adolescent*,	composed of persons without employ or without particular destination.
2.	*The Man*,	composed of authors, artists, merchants, travelers, etc.
3.	*The Elder*,	composed of authors, artists, businessmen, and persons of position, of the 1st rank.
4.	*The Mesopolite*	chosen among the 2nd and 3rd degrees, for the different dignitaries.
5.	*The Diocesan*,	
6.	*The Superior*,	

The brothers possessing the last three grades formed the government of the Union. Their assemblies were called Synods, and they held Agapes there.

As to the first three degrees, this was but the preparatory school to the last three; thus were the members of this school obliged to make reports on their readings, on their opinions, and on their various relations.

(Extract from: Der *Frey maurer*, Gottingue and Halle, 1790 to 1795, in-8vo; communicated by the brother Th. Juge.)

SYSTEM OF FESSLER

(1796)

The lodges of Berlin had received with distinction the brother FESSLER, professor of law, and had him named Deputy G.M. of the lodge *Royal-York a l'amitié*, which, through its attentions became G.L. He tried to abolish the high grades; but, finding too many obstacles, he accepted, in 1796, the mission to review and rectify the manuscripts which serve as their basis. In this work, he preserved therefrom all that it was possible to keep, by infusing a moral and coherent sense, based on the ancient origin of the institution, and by adding to the modern historical knowledge, that which his studies had let him acquire.

Up to the moment of the establishment of his system, the *Royal-York G.L.* worked the three symbolic grades. The lodges of its obedience preserved the symbol of a temple; but each temple had a *holy of holies*, where were held the most educated and most proven adepts. Just as the temple of Masonry represents the universe, so too was the holy of holies an allusion to the perfect moral towards which the Masons ought to work to attain.

The system admits the three symbolic degrees, that all the rites present, with some slight variations; then come six superior degrees called of *high knowledge*. Here is the nomenclature of the nine grades:

1.	*Apprentice Theosophist*,	modified symbolic grades.
2.	*Companion id.*,	
3.	*Master id.*,	
4.	*The Holy of Holies*,	1st degree of high knowledge.
5.	*The Justification*,	2nd ———
6.	*The Celebration*,	3rd ———
7.	*The True Light of the Passage*,	4th ———
8.	*The Fatherland*,	5th ———
9.	*The Perfection*,	6th ———

In order to appreciate this system, we are going to give an idea of the last six grades:

4th grade, the *Holy of Holies*: the ritual is entitled *Reception of the Perfect Architect.* The lodge represents the temple of Solomon and the Master takes the title of *Superior Perfect Architect.*

HISTORICAL KNOWLEDGE: Exposition, critique, and redressing of the hypotheses spread on the origin and continuation of the Order of Freemasons, of which some educated Masons alone have the knowledge, and on the origin of:

1. The Order of the Templars;
2. The Construction of the Munster of Strasburg;
5. The construction of Saint-Paul at London;
6. The construction of the castle of Kensington;

3. The Rose-Croix and the scholars of the 17th century;
4. The times of Cromwell;
7. The Jesuits.

MORAL SENSE: Indifference, idleness, and inactivity are the shortcomings of the best men. The construction of the Holy of Holies (*symbol of the disposition of man towards perfection*) advances only slowly. The *architects* neglect their duty and fall back into a culpable inactivity: they are, for this reason, called before the tribunal of the law, and pass thus to the following grade:

5th grade, the *Justification*: the title of the ritual is: *Accusation, absolution before the tribunal of the law, and the necessity for new efforts and a new activity*. The tableau bears these words: *Nosce te ipsum*. The Master is called *Superior Just Judge*. The sacred word is *conscientia* and the password is *justificatio*.

KNOWLEDGE: Exposition, critique, and redressing of the hypotheses spread on the origin of the Order and which have given place to the creation of the following high grades:

1. The old Scottish grade of Knight of St. Andrew,
2. The new grade of Écossais.
3. The system of Clermont.

MORAL SENSE: They work with greater zeal and effort towards the construction of the *Holy of Holies*; but the workers have need of a *sublime ideal*, which ought to be symbolized in an historical personage, in order to produce the necessary effect, and no one is more suitable thereto than the noble, great, and worshipful *Jesus*. He has sacrificed himself for this Holy of Holies, and his memory deserves to be preserved and honored by the perfect architects. This celebration is their reward, and the aspect of the noble model, symbolized in Jesus, in an encouragement to their work.

6th grade, the *Celebration*: the ritual bears: *Celebration of the memory of the great ambassador of the light and truth*.

KNOWLEDGE: Exposition, critique, and redressing of four systems:

1. The Rose-Croix,
2. The Strict Observance,
3. The African Architects,
4. The Initiated Brothers of Asia.

MORAL SENSE: Despite all the efforts of the architects, the Holy of Holies cannot be achieved in this world; but death does not interrupt their works; it only makes them transform. The good and just conception of this transformation gives hope in this life.

7th grade, the Passage of the *True Light*: RITUAL; 1st point: *Consecration to death*; 2nd point: *Consecration to immortality*. At the Orient, a transparency represents *Psyche* rising to the heavens. The sacred word is *logos*; the password, *athanesia* (immortality).

KNOWLEDGE: Exposition, critique, and redressing of:

1. The Swedish system,
2. The system of Zinnendorf,
3. The system of the Royal Arch, the highest grade recognized in England.
4. The succession of the mysteries,
5. All the systems and their ramifications.

MORAL SENSE: Beyond the tomb begins our proper activity. Here below is the land of errors, doubt, and belief. It is beyond that reigns the certitude and conviction that is the true fatherland of man, according to his faculties and his needs.

8th grade, the *Fatherland*. The ritual takes this title: *Explanation of our activity, our faculties, and our whole being in our fatherland*.

KNOWLEDGE: 1st, the origin of the mysteries of the divine kingdom, introduced by Jesus;

2nd, the exoteric doctrine that Jesus communicated, in its mysteries, to his most intimate adherents;

3rd, the fate of that exoteric doctrine after his death, until the *Gnostics*.

MORAL SENSE: We labor in this world, but we only very rarely enjoy the fruits of our noblest works. Here is united the work to its enjoyment, and the sentiment of privation and resignation is unknown there.

9th grade, or the 6th and last of the *high knowledge*, THE PERFECTION. No ritual.

KNOWLEDGE: Critical and complete history of all the mysteries up to and including present Freemasonry.

The candidate makes a moral confession before submitting to a species of baptism: the G.M., while sprinkling him on the head, says: *I purify you* in the light; *the eyes*, says: - in wisdom; *the forehead*, says: - in truth; *the hands*, says: - in immortality.

They invest the candidate with the habit of the grade and the G.M. anoints him with three fingers, on the head, while saying: *I bless you and consecrate you as servant of the Most High*; then, on the forehead, while saying: As an initiate in truth, reason, and wisdom.

This grade has remained unachieved, which explains its lack of ritual; it has been conferred on no one.

The six grades were drawn from the rituals of the *Golden Rose-Croix*, the *Strict Observance*, the *Illuminati Chapter* of Sweden, and the old *Chapter of Clermont*. The system was, they say, adopted (though incomplete), and it would have received, in 1797, the approbation of the King Frédéric-Guillaume; but its practice (if it took place) did not last, for, since 1800, the *Royal-York* G.L. declared publicly to renounce all the high grades, and to hold itself exclusively to the three symbolic degrees, as well as the G.L. of Hanover and of Hamburg, with which it made, the following year, a federative pact.

ECLECTIC MASONRY (from the Greek *eklego*, I choose)

"Sensible Masons seeing how the *high grades*, into which were introduced Templar reveries, mystical speculations, the deceptions of alchemy and other secret sciences (*regarded as falsehoods, since the key to them is lost*), had harmed the action of Masonry, by making it lose sight of the aim that it proposes. How they had disfigured, ridiculed, and divided, by propagating within its bosom the spirit of rivalry which breaks every fraternal bond, and a foolish credulity which makes of the institution an inexhaustible mine of illicit products for the schemers, imposters, and swindlers. Sensible Masons, *say we*, believe to remedy such ills, by extricating Masonry from these heterogenous conceptions, and by leading it to its primitive simplicity. But this work was difficult: pride of the ones, cupidity of the others, the love of the marvelous in the greatest number, were to put an obstacle to them renouncing the ostentatious titles with which they were decorated, to the riches of which they dreamt, to this fantastic world of elementary beings that they had created for themselves, and in the midst of which *certain brothers* hoped to enjoy a life without end. They believed to achieve it, in Germany, by the establishment of ECLECTIC MASONRY which, recognizing, as a rule to follow in an absolute manner, only the original three grades, permitted however to each lodge, *separately*, to adopt as much as it pleased of the ulterior grades, of whatever species they were, provided that it did not make thereof a general business of the régime, and that it did not change, for them, the original uniformity of the three Masonic grades."

The Eclectic Rite, followed in Germany and Switzerland, is that of the G.L. of Francfort-sur-Nein. The Baron *von Knigge* conceived, at first, the idea of this reform. He was an officer in the service of Breme in the era when the lodges of Poland and Germany were confederated, in order to withstand the tyrannical usurpation of the circles of the *Strict Observance*, and in order to enlighten Masons on the fanaticism of the high grades and to accelerate their decadence, by demonstrating their uselessness and their dander.

To realize this reform, the Baron von Knigge had an understanding with the G.L.'s of Frankfort and Wetzlar, and, in 1783, its bases were posed in a general assembly... The sensible reformers, who formed the *Eclectic Association*, drew up a *Manifesto*, dated from Francfort-sur-Mein and from Wetzlar on the 18th and 21st of March, 1783, which they addressed to the Masons of Germany and of foreign countries, in order to engage them to cooperate in the aim that they proposed to attain. They developed therein their principles, they explained the motives of their *absolute tolerance*, and the reasons for which they renounced all theosophical, Hermetic, magical, Qabalistic, mystical, and Templar speculations, in order to hold themselves to the practice of the three symbolic grades:

1. *Apprentice*,
2. *Companion*,
3. *Master*.

And to the observance of the old rules dictated by the English constitution of 1723.

The lodges of these two reformer cities took the name of *Eclectic Lodges*, and adopted immediately, for the system of their union, an absolute tolerance of all Masonic beliefs.

Thus, the members of the *Eclectic Union*, attaining to the degree of *Master*, arrived at the final echelon of knowledge adopted in the rite; but then they are allowed to know, study, and investigate more deeply the immense quantity of Masonic grades of which the lodges are inundated. Complete collections in this genre are put before their eyes; they can see everything; they can learn everything; they may, without betraying their duties, adopt one or several of these systems, tie themselves to such Masonic bodies as they wish *to choose*, without the eclectic order taking umbrage. It adopts, in this regard, no particular opinion; it considers this knowledge as *a subject which has no relation to Freemasonry*.

With such a system, THE ONLY REASONABLE ONE IN MASONRY, the Eclectic Masons are sheltered from all those pitiful rivalries which divide the Masonic world by cords, crosses, jewels, and titles, which are, very often, but symbols of madness and folly.

"We have before our eyes," *says Thory*, "the list of the members of this society composed of scholars and philanthropists; we have read its regulations, and we would be inclined to believe that the eclectic system is the only one suitable to reasonable men, to friends of humanity, and finally to all Freemasons of an independent character, and whose soul is inaccessible to those petty vanities which bring shame to the majority of Grand Orients and Grand Lodges of Europe.

"The authors of this reform followed the principles of the *eclectic philosophers*, whose spirit was to *choose*, among all the political and religious systems, those which best suited them. We know that there were eclectics in medicine as in philosophy; that, scorning prejudice, tradition, antiquity, and all that was adopted by the generality of men, they thought for themselves, rose to the general principles, examined them, analyzed them, and admitted nothing but on the evidence of experiment and their own reason[76]." (*Hist. de la fond. du G.-O. de Fr. Appendix IV.*)

In 1844, educated brethren, animated by the true spirit of Masonry, at the head of which was the brother *Juge*, old editor of the *Globe*, had the project to create, at Paris, a *G.L. of the Eclectic Rite*, according to the wise and philosophical principles that we have just read.

This plan was, without doubt, too reasonably simple for French Masons; it was not realized. But the good general sense wished that the execution thereof be only deferred[77].

Already, on April 30, 1819, seven good and honorable Masons, officers of the G.O., the brothers: *Benou, Porie., Caille, Delaroche, Geneux, Pagès, and Vassal,* animated by the same Masonic spirit, *had founded*, at Paris, the lodge of the RIGID OBSERVERS, *a title sacred to them, for they observed rigorously the Masonic dogmas and customs.* Indeed, whatever was the superiority of their grades, the members of this lodge were never decorated but by the Symbolic insignia, or that of the first three degree, *the only ones that they recognized as true.*

But, we are going to cite even better an anterior and constant protestation against the high grades, since their fatal origin, by one of the old and respectable workshops of Paris; it is the lodge of *Les Neuf-Sœurs*, which dates from 1769 and which has always been able to preserve itself from the dissolving drugs of the charlatan Masons[78]. What would the partisans of these latter say, if all the lodges providing *high grade workshops*, imitating the wisdom of the *Neuf-Sœurs*, took up the resolution to close them, in order to confer, as in *eclecticism*, only the first three degrees, *the only ones which are really Masonic*, but with all the developments that they might include, and to receive as visitors, in imitation of the *Rigid Observers*, only brethren decorated by the spotless apron or cord of the Master, excepting only that *dawn-colored* one of the G.O.?

At the occasion of an article on the trials of the *Eclectic Rite*, which are more moral than physical, the editor of *la Revue de Lyon* (year 1850, p. 142) expresses himself thus:

"In the initiation into the first grade, when the Venerable asks the candidate if he wished to take an oath of fidelity to the Order and to seal this obligation with his blood, the swords of the president, of the orator, and of the secretary are crossed over the head of the neophyte: *the clanking of these weapons which coincides with the request of the Venerable produces a vivid impression on the aspirant.*

"At the end of the trials, when the candidate, placed between the two columns, receives the light, he sees not swords turned against him, *ready to pierce him if he betrays his oaths*, but all the brothers present *forming the chain of union*, striking image of Masonic fraternity."

The chain of union concludes a fraternal session in a happy manner; but we very strongly criticize the use thereof here, because this contrast of the *rose-water* with such energetic expressions of the oath, which recalls, at all times, the *sign of Apprentice*, dulls, according to us, the solemnity which concludes the reception.

Original Organization

"The deputies of several united lodges form a *directory*, or district seat.

"The deputies of several united directories form the *Provincial Grand Lodge.*

"The Provincial G.L. names, if this suits it, and for the time that it wants, a superior or *Provincial or Directorial Grand Master.* This office is not considered as essential to the organization of the rite; it is the reward for zeal and services."

(It is thus that they raised to this dignity the venerable brother *Broenner*, senator, who merited this honorable distinction by his virtue, his philanthropy, and his zeal, for which the lodge *l'Union*, at Francfort-sur-Mein, has had stricken, in his honor, a very beautiful medal.)

"The Prov. and Directorial G.M. has no other right than that of presiding over the Provincial G.L."

With regard to the other ulterior establishments, they have been formed only as centers of communication between the lodges of the *Eclectic Union* and foreign lodges. They are not considered as superior to the ordinary lodges: the most perfect equality, as well as the most entire independence, are the precious apanage of the workshops of this system.

CHAPTER XIX
Écossisme

OR RITE, CALLED OF PERFECTION, OF TWENTY-FIVE GRADES, BECOME SCOTTISH RITE, CALLED ANCIENT AND ACCEPTED, IN THIRTY-THREE DEGREES

Our aim in this work, which is, as we have said, but a short summary of a longer work still in manuscript, is to initiate the young Masons into the knowledge that it is indispensible to have in order to know how Freemasonry has been established, and to appreciate what this institution really is, considered by the initiates as a continuation or a renovation of the ancient mysteries of India and Egypt, the doctrines and symbols of which, modified through the centuries, serve as its base.

We have said that between the period of their extinction in the Gauls, by the Roman persecution, toward the beginning of our era, and the public renovation, at London, of the ancient and secret philosophy, it slumbered for around sixteen centuries. The small number of initiates who escaped the merciless massacres ordered by Caesar had to take refuge in the various associations formed after these disasters, and in which the *secret doctrine* was, at long intervals, propagated with discretion and only in order that it not be lost.

At the time of *Ashmole* (1646), the number of initiates had become rather considerable, and powerful enough to no longer fear the great day; and, under the pen of the alchemist scholar, all the oral traditions were regularized. They took a form, a body. From here came the *three symbolic grades* and their initiation rituals which did not exist before this period, since Freemasonry was unknown, whatever may be said by deceived authors and sectarians, strangers to the Order, in their grades and in their historical falsehoods.

The re-establishment of the ancient doctrine of the mysteries took place publicly, at London, on June 24, 1717, a memorable year in the Masonic annals. Its beneficent manifestation spread into all the states of Europe and of the world with an electric rapidity, under the auspices of a universal fraternity, the need of an intimate bond, of a mysterious initiation unknown until then.

This Grand Lodge, to which the Masons shall give thanks, at all times, for the blessings of the institution, was the sole and unique point of origin of the true Masonic light: all the establishments that it has constituted are regular, like it. Those which have separated themselves in order to become, in their turn National Grand Lodges or foreign Grand Orients, have lost nothing of their regularity nor of the value of their constituting power. According to these incontestable principles, all the Masonic workshops created by this G.L. or its delegates, and by the National G.L.'s or foreign G.O.'s, originally emanated from it, or from authorities established by it, and their delegates, are regular and work truly. But every establishment formed outside of this principle ought to be designated as irregular, clandestine, subversive to the Order, and not Masonic.

Moreover, the G.L. of England, depositary of the true Masonry, in three grades, the transmission of which it has made to the workshops that it constituted, could not have established any other Masonries with new grades, since there is but one true one, and since the supposed high grades have been introduced only clandestinely, by fraud, by capitation, and in a spirit of speculation on the vanity of the Masons, among whom they foment the passions that *they had promised to vanquish*, and finally have established themselves only on behalf of a culpable tolerance on the part of the regular Masonic authorities that they have constantly troubled in their administration and in their jurisdiction.

Consequently, the Royal G.L. of Scotland, professing a Masonry other than the symbolic, the branches that it has created, the chapters, councils, tribunals, colleges, consistories, etc., established outside of the true Masonry by whatever authority it may be, ought to be considered as null, irregular, and anti-Masonic, and the lodges ought to withdraw the mantle of institution from them, with the aid of which they make dupes everywhere.

In fact, all these establishments, called *high grades*, are irregular, in that none may justify a serious title arising from a primitive origin valid in the eyes of the true Mason.

How? Because a coterie of fabricators of grades, that a G.L. or a G.O. will have neglected to destroy at its birth, succeeds in the sale of its drugs and prospers; that G.L. or G.O., very regular otherwise, secures its false grades, in order to distribute them, for payment, under the names of *Chapters*, *Councils*, etc., and may believe to have founded regular Masonic establishments! We do not think so; for, instead of one sole illegitimate power, *the coterie*, there are two; and, for the true Mason, the constitutive titles of the one have no more value than those of the other. Only, one of the sources is more honorable than the other, for its motives of action are laudable.

When the G.O., legal successor of the G.L. of France, received into its bosom, in 1786, the *Grand Chapter General*, formed in 1782 from the debris of the old *Council of Emperors of the East and West*, *Sovereign Prince Masons*, formed in 1758 from the debris of the *Chapter of Clermont*, founded at Paris by the Chevalier de *Bonneville* in 1754, would the G.O. believe itself the authentic possessor of the high degrees practiced by a *disappeared body*, and especially of the *Rite of Perfection* in twenty-five degrees, that was administered by the Council of Emperors? Yes, without doubt; but this legitimate possession should have served only to forbid every trespassing body from the illegal practice of these high grades: such was its right and its duty. But far from that was the right to administer these super-Masonic rites.

Let us go back to the source: the Chevalier de Bonneville instituted his Chapter (Templar system of Ramsay), in the name of the G.M.; but, above all, from whom did he hold his powers? *From himself alone.* Here, then, was a new Masonry established very irregularly and which should have been prohibited immediately by the G.L. of France, as Sovereign guardian of the interests and dogmas of the true Masonry. The debris, members of this irregular chapter, instituting therefrom the Council of Emperors, and the debris of this latter creating the Grand Chapter General of France, could they have founded any regular and truly Masonic establishments? No, assuredly. The G.O., by inheriting them, has received grades for its archives; - but it could not have inherited the right to practice them, since this right was illusory and false with its predecessors who could not have transmitted what they had never possessed.

It is the same with the *écossisme* of thirty-three degrees, which is only a reheated version of the Rite of Perfection, increased by eight grades. In securing this *Scottish* rite, practiced nearly everywhere, except in Scotland, the G.O., sole regular Masonic authority in France, has only reclaimed its property; but this should have only been done in order to oppose themselves to what usurpers might abuse.

And if, in spreading this rite, the G.O., legitimate regulator of the true Masonry (in three grades, there are no others), has not formed but super-Masonic establishments of an imaginary, or at least contestable value, we ask what name has it given to the *establishments* instituted by Masons who hold their chimeric power only from themselves or from Masons of like value?

The history of the *écossisme* substituted for the Rite of Perfection is going to prove this truth as far as the evidence.

It is therefore clear that it is for want of examination, reflection, and without doubt knowledge, that Freemasons let themselves be abused and desert the cult of the true, in order to journey, covered with baubles, into the land of fictions.

It is to preserve the young Masons from every deceitful illusion, that after having given the exposé of the establishment of Freemasonry, based on the ancient mysteries, we have put them in a position to appreciate the various rites that sectarians and impostors have come to add to the three symbolic grades, which have no need of these superfluities, so imperfect that each rite contests in the others the superiority that each of them attributes exclusively to themselves. We have also made known the principal reformers, among whom we always see the last to believe themselves superior to their predecessors, whose Masonic works cannot satisfy him; his vanity forbids it.

Our readers should have noticed that in the midst of these false creations, these shocks of divergent opinions, these combats, these misled ambitions, SYMBOLIC MASONRY remains standing, intact and pure as the truth; feeling no damage and receiving, on the contrary, the homage of those who come to profane its temples by practicing fantastic works therein.

By means of this exposé, our readers ought to find themselves initiated enough in the ruses and intrigues employed by the inventors of grades, systems, and false Masonries, to truly appreciate the merit, value, and authenticity of the SCOTTISH RITE called *Ancient and Accepted*, of which we have reproduced the history of its formation and of its advent, though already known in part.

RITE OF PERFECTION IN TWENTY-FIVE GRADES, BECOME, IN AMERICA, ANCIENT AND ACCEPTED SCOTTISH RITE IN THIRTY-THREE DEGREES

Let us go back to the historical brief of the Council of Emperors of the East and West. We see there (page 53) that, on August 27, 1761, this council delivered a patent of *G.M. Inspector*, the tenor of which we give, to the Jew *Stephen Morin*, whom business matters called to San Domingo. The aim of the council was to propagate overseas its Masonry, called of *Heredom* or *of Perfection*, in twenty-five grades. It did not suspect that audacious tricksters would come, forty-two years later, to reproduce it at Paris, place of its birth, under another name and with an addition of eight degrees, attributed falsely to a Sovereign, Frederick II, King of Prussia, who had a taste for the high grades[79].

Stephen Morin, in his excursions to San Domingo and in the vast continent of America, communicated the twenty-five degrees of the Rite of Perfection. In his quality of G.M. Inspector, he created, according to his right, Inspectors. These titles did not designate grades, as writers have believed (there did not yet exist any grades of this name), but they announced dignities with the power to constitute (see his patent, note).

He founded, *at first*, Chapters and Councils at Different points – various places in America, then an English colony, which had, for the most part, only an ephemeral existence, and were never attached to the general organization. It is therefore in error that a modern author, in his *Défense du rite écossais*, hazards to say, according to Reghellini, the majority of whose historical facts that he reports are inexact:

The brother Stephen Morin has not introduced the Scottish Rite into America. It was practiced there before he set out, "for, in 1755, several Masons of the Scottish Rite residing at Boston presented a petition to the G.L. of Scotland, in order to be authorized to profess publicly their *rite*, and to propagate it regularly throughout all America. The G.L. acceded to this request, and the G.M. Lord *Aberdour* signed a patent for them on December 30, 1766, to establish a regular Scottish Lodge at Boston, under the title of Saint Andrew, no. 82. - The Scottish Rite of Heredom of Kilwinning prospered throughout all of America and even in an unexpected manner," (*la Maçonnerie considérée comme le résultat des religions égyptienne, juive et chrétienne*, v. II, p. 163 and 164).

This citation is full of errors. The Scottish *Rite of Heredom* did not exist in America before its introduction by Stephen Morin. As to the *Scottish Rite*, it was not yet invented. The English G.L. had instituted, in this beautiful English colony, provincial Grand Lodges. The G.L. of Scotland then established them, and in order to distinguish their origins, they said: *English Masonry, Scottish Masonry*, which were and still are the same Masonry, *Symbolic Masonry*. The G.L. of Scotland did not recognize the high grades, for, in 1803, a G.L. of America, calling itself Scottish[80], addressed a circular containing the nomenclature of a great number of Masonic grades, that it authorized. The G.L. of Edinburgh declared:

"That such a number of grades could only inspire the deepest scorn for *Scottish Masonry*, and that it did not recognize it, wishing ever to preserve its rite *according to its primitive simplicity.*"

The lodges of its jurisdiction then rose to one hundred thirty-five[81].

The history of Scottish Masonry makes known that, on June 11, 1757, the colonel *J. Young* who, for thirty years, had exercised the functions of Deputy G.M., received from the G.L. a commission of Provincial G.M., for all the lodges of America and the East Indies (of its obedience) with power to introduce Scottish Masonry there (*that is to say* to establish symbolic lodges there in the name and under the auspices of the G.L. of Edinburgh).

To this so simple a fact, the *Defense du rite écossais ancien accepté* replies:

"It is therefore not from France, as they seek to have it believed, that the Scottish grades were *exported* into America. The allegation of the G.O., in this regard, is consequently false. It will be appreciated in its true value by all the enlightened Masons who shall know henceforth what to believe on its LEGITIMATE, POSITIVE, AND UNASSAILABLE RIGHTS," (p. 49, Paris, 1811).

Presumption in history goes badly for the one who does not know how to read it. In expressing oneself in this way, one is isolated from all polemic; this style is no more Masonic than the *Scottish grades* that it claims to defend, and of which it was not, then (1757), a question in Scotland.

Let us return to America, where occurred, in 1776, the war of independence which interrupted all the Masonic works until there was peace, that is to say at the recognition of the United States in 1782 and 1783. The Rite of Perfection suffered this common necessity: it slept. But if it went to sleep with its twenty- five degrees, it awoke with thirty-three.

With peace, the brother *Morin* resumed the work. He erected, in 1783, at Charleston, a Grand Lodge of Perfection, and attempted, without success, to found similar establishments in the other States of the Union. But it must have been to the Masons of Charleston that the perfection of the *Rite of Perfection* did not appear perfect, since they brought to thirty-three degrees the rite practiced by the G.L. This *American* creation was called a Scottish rite, and by another contradiction, worthy of the work, the *new rite* took the name of *Ancient* and Accepted. This title suits well only the *symbolic* rite, the first and consequently the most ancient of all; and as nearly all the reformers place it at the head of their systems, it is indeed truly *accepted*[82]. Whatever it is, the new 33°, without any other power than their will, and without other ceremony, made use of this rite in order to instituted the *Scottish Supreme Council of the French possessions in America.* And it is this trickery, continued to our day, which still captivates the good faith of serious men. O ignorance! When will you cease making dupes?
And you, pride, when will you make no more swindlers[83]?

The Comte *de Grasse-Tilly de Rouville*, having left San Domingo, was, in 1802, received into the 33rd degree, in this *Supreme Council* that some Masons, without legal titles, had just formed at Charleston. The scheming Comte returned no more to San Domingo, and yet he created himself, by his own authority, *Grand Commander ad Vitam of a supreme Council of the Puissant and Sovereign Grand Inspectors General for the French Windward and Leeward Islands of America, 33rd Degree of the Ancient and Accepted Scottish Rite*, seated at the Cap Français, San Domingo isle. This Supreme Council, at the Cap Français, has never existed but in the speculative ideas of the Comte and of his associates. What strange courage ambition gives which inspires such effronteries!

The Ancient and Accepted Scottish Rite was practiced only in the United States, when the Comte de Grasse received his patent, and it is established by evidence that the *supposed Supr. Coun.* which delivered it to him did not yet have a public existence.

"What appears long since demonstrated, is that this rite does not go back further than 1797, the period in which it was created, at Charleston, by four Jews named *John Mitchell, Frederick Dalcho, Emmanuel de la Motta, and Abraham Alexander*, who, with purely mercantile views, appropriated the functions of *Grand Commander, Lieutenant Grand Commander, Treasurer, and Secretary*, and thus held the entire administration in their hands. In these beginnings, the degrees were not yet definitively decreed, and the system, such as it is constituted today, was fixed only in 1802, after the admission of the Comte de Grasse."

We see, indeed, that on December 4th of this year, the *Supreme Council of Charleston* resolved to make known, by a circular, its foundation and the names of the degrees of its régime; without indicating, however, by what path this *supposedly ancient* rite had been transmitted, or with what body, *of like nature*, it was related to. It is to this circular that the G.L. of Edinburgh responded, in 1803, *that such a number of grades could inspire only the most profound scorn for Scottish Masonry and that* IT DID NOT RECOGNIZE THEM (page 128 above)[84]. It is in this same year, 1802, that the Comte de Grasse and some other brothers of the French islands of America received from this *Supr. Coun.* patents which gave them the power to establish a Supr. Coun. at the Cap Français, isle of San Domingo (see above), and to propagate the *Ancient and Accepted Rite* everywhere that seemed good to them, except in the American Republic and in the English Antilles. This Supr. Coun. of San Domingo was the only one which figured in the annual of the

Supr. Coun. of Charleston, published the following year, as being in correspondence with it, ALTHOUGH IT DID NOT EXIST[85].

There has circulated in France more than forty copies of the register of the *Deputy Inspector*, the brother *de Grasse-Tilly*. According to document no. 1 of this register, the brother *Stephen Morin* has conferred the title of Deputy Inspector to *Franklin*, who gave it to *Moses Hyes*, who transmitted it to *Spitzer*, at Charleston. The Deputy Inspectors, gathered (on January 15, 1781) at Philadelphia, gave it to *Moser-Cohen*; this latter invested with this title *Isaac Lelong*, who, at Charleston, gave it to the brother *de Grasse-Tilly* and others. These brothers were therefore regular possessors only of the twenty-five degrees of the Rite of Heredom, divided into seven classes. But, according to the precise terms of the patent of Stephen Morin, from which derives their title of Deputy Inspector, this brother has been authorized to spread the Masonry of Perfection and to create Deputy Inspectors only *in all the places where official substitutes are not established*. Thus, the rights of those who have granted this patent, or of their legitimate representatives, remain ever the same in France, or rather are the *only ones* by virtue of which all the degrees of the Rite of Heredom may be given. And who are the legitimate successors of the brother *Chaillou de Joinville*, of the Prince *de Rohan*, and the other *Princes of the Royal Secret*? The G.O. of France; since, in 1773, the G.L. of France, which possessed the Masonry of Perfection, was dissolved into the G.O. and gave it all its rights. However, some dissidents had refused this union, which was carried out entirely on February 17, 1786, by that of the Gr. Chap. General of France which contained the remains of the old G.L. and subsequent chapters. Thus, the G.O. has become, since this time, the sole legitimate possessor of the twenty-five degrees of the Rite of Heredom. No other Masonic power, in France, may confer them, nor assume the jurisdiction and oversight thereof. Thus has the G.O. failed in its duty, in a strange manner, by allowing the practice of this rite, in 1803, by the lodge of *Les Sept-Écossais* at Paris, by the brother *Hacquet*, ex-notary arriving from San Domingo and who was clever enough, the following year, to have his twenty-five grades of Heredom accepted into the G.O., which, for this gift, named the crafty brother *President of the Grand Consistory of Rites*!

The turpitudes of Charleston exercised their deadly influence over the *supposed* Écossais of France; we say *supposed*, for it is evident, the G.L. of Edinburgh has declared that there is nothing Scottish, nor anything recognized by it, in this new hodgepodge. Thus, the G.O. drew up, on November 12, 1802, a circular inviting the lodges of the correspondence *to repel the insidious insinuations of the brothers who, forgetting their oaths and guided by an innovating genius, have attempted to overtake the religion of the lodges and chapters, by inviting them to unite themselves with so-called Scottish lodges, in order to follow the rite thereof.* This circular is principally directed against a small number of Masons called *Scottish*, qualified as *ultra-insular*, and in the aim of turning away from the Masonic temples a germ of discord which, during the most tempestuous times, seemed to have respected them.

The Scottish lodges, anathematized by this decree of November 12, united themselves into dissident fractions and established, in the basement of the home of the restaurant-keeper *Mauduit*, on the Poissonière boulevard, the nucleus of the Gen. Scot. G.L. of the *Ancient and Accepted Rite*, which, on October 22, 1804, proclaimed its organization in the locale of the M.L. of the Philosophical Scottish Rite, and proceeded to the election of its officers, the number of which is fixed at forty[86].

In November, the G.O. expressed some uneasiness. The brother *Rottiers de Montaleau*, Grand Venerable, whose every concern is for the peace of the Order, instead of dispersing and annihilating this nascent authority, interposed himself between it and the G.O., and he enters into conference with the brother *Pyron*, in order to devise between them the means to unite these two bodies.

On December 3rd, the respective stewards held an assembly in the hotel of the Marshal *Kellermann* and signed: 1st, a concordat which unites the two associations;

2nd, the act of a new organization of the Masonic Order in France.

On the 5th of the same month, the concordat is accepted by both bodies assembled, and the act is sanctioned, in the middle of the night, in an extraordinary meeting of the G.O.

The Comte *de Grasse-Tilly*, having recently arrived from America, and *Roettiers de Montaleau*, take an oath as particular representatives of the G.M.: the one, the brother de Grasse-Tilly, for the *Grand Chapter General of the Ancient and Accepted Rite*; the other, the brother Roettiers de Montaleau, for the *Symbolic Grand Lodge General* established within the bosom of the G.O., which thus accepts, by a role reversal, the patronage of the Scottish Rite and unites it to its administration, which already included all the recognized rites!

It resulted from this operation that the *Scottish Grand Lodge General of the Ancient and Accepted Rite*, as well as its *Grand Chapter General*, have existed only forty-five years. This act of fraternal concern did not obtain the results that sound reason would expect therefrom.

In this first session of the gathering, the G.O. decreed the adoption of the project concerning the recognition of all the different Masonic Rites, and, because of the joining to this body of the Scottish Grand Lodge General of the Ancient and Accepted Rite, it decreed the common organization between it and the lodges and chapters of this regime; all, save definitive wording which remains confided, as well as that of the regulatory articles which will complete it, to the care of the commission which did the preparatory work of the project adopted this day[87].

On December 14, the G.O. decided that the lodges whose name would have been omitted in the rolls of its correspondence, because of difference of rite or Masonic opinion, are reintegrated into their ranks.

On December 19, it addressed to the lodges this manifesto:

"The desire to propagate the Masonic light and the love of the Order have convinced the G.O. of France to declare, to the university of Masons, that it shall henceforth profess all rites.

"The Scottish Masons, the Masons of all the rites known upon the two hemispheres, gathered under one same banner and fortified by the protection of the government, form now an alliance *that nothing may break*.

"The G.O. of France shall address you at once, with the details of its new organization, the statutes and regulations that this union necessitates..."

In our *Histoire chronologique du G.O. de France* (*Fastes initiatique*), this citation is followed by a *note*. We believe it necessary to reproduce it here; it is perhaps a restatement, but the subject permits it:

"MOTIVES OF THIS UNION. The G.O., central point of Masonry in France, trustee, for thirty years, of the confidence of the regular lodges, which it has never abused; enjoying the consideration of the foreign Orients and the protection of governments; sole legitimate possessor of the *Rite of Perfection* in twenty-five degrees, and strong by its right and its recognized power, sees, suddenly, to raise by its side a bastard association taking the title of *Scottish G.L.*, announcing new light, more refined grades, emanating from *Heredom* in Scotland, under the denomination of *Ancient and Accepted Rite.*

"With more education, the members of the G.O. would not have met with the fear of seeing its columns threatened by a great collapse; they would have known that they had nothing to fear from so incoherent a rite, and whose fiction, audacity, and falsehood had recently raised to thirty-three degrees the number of grades emanating from a fabulous mountain, called *Heredom*, unknown in Scotland. They could have, from the origin of its appearance, annihilated with a breath this pretended rite, by proving and proclaiming, as we have done, the vain falsity of its pretentions, it would have prevented very honorable brothers from becoming dupes of trickery. Yet, they could not have been unaware that, better enlightened, the Grand Masonic bodies of Scotland, London, and Prussia had rejected it. Instead of imitating them, and thus rendering an immense service to Freemasonry, they have thought that, in order to prevent the troublesome consequences of this new establishment, it would suffice to make conspicuous the nomination of its Grand Officers, proclaimed in its midst for more than a year, not suspecting that the subtlety, the pomp of the grades, and the attraction of the decorations had corrupted a part of it, of which several noble brethren had even accepted offices in this new association. Then, sensing the necessity to stop at its source a germ of division, the G.O., after negotiations, named a commission which met, in equal number, with deputies of this rite, under the mallet of the Marshal *Kellermann*. After several conferences, the act of union was decreed and signed, save definitive wording. In order to obtain the *bill of indemnity*, that is to say the approbation that it requested of the lodges, the G.O. told them that: 'one of the most powerful motives which have decided it, is the positive hope which has been given to it, and guaranteed by the very respectable brother Marshal *Kellermann*, that, from the present operation, would infallibly result the general reunion into the G.O. of France of all the lodges which are qualified, in this empire, of the G.L.'s, MOTHER LODGES, or SINGLE SCOTTISH LODGES, and which are not, nevertheless, yet united with the correspondence of the G.O., nor even with that of the *Ancient and Accepted Rite*.'

"The brave Marshal believed in good faith; but the discord introduced into this sanctuary delayed not in bringing out therefrom more discord than ever.

"ON ÉCOSSISME: Écossisme, rejected by Scotland, by England, and by Prussia, had introduced itself into France furtively. Timid in its attempts in the provinces, it presented itself with more assurance in Paris, where the time nearly always lacked to examine new things with care.

"It was received with little ardor, because besides the charm attached to all that is new, and the interest powerfully excited by an addition of twenty-two degrees to the *three in use*, they found that, in the majority of its numerous and brilliant grades, incoherence, absurdity, ridiculousness, or terror dominated. But the French, more courteous towards foreigners than prescribers, tolerated this novelty, then received it with benevolence.

"Later, we see écossisme admitted on par with the other rites, honored by Masons, and researched by some of them. Then believing itself infinitely above the modest French Rite, the confraternity of which it was only willing to tolerate, delayed not in showing, until around 1793, an invasive spirit which tended towards domination. But the courageous energy of the Masonic authority of France has always, most fortunately, preserved it in the fraternal share that it had let it take.

"Moribund at the restoration of the Order, at the close of the revolution of '89, the Masonic life rendered to the lodges by the G.O. withdrew écossisme from its lethargy: from 1798 to 1803, it recovered a part of its strength, and, in 1804, it found itself entirely on its feet.

"Dazzled from this return to existence and presenting itself with new advantages: *thirty-three grades* (instead of twenty-five) fabricated, the Comte *de Grasse* says in America, others say coordinated at Paris, it had need of a support for its definitive foundation; the G.O. offered that to it, it accepted and was invigorated to its usual strength. Soon it was no longer considered as an adopted son: it believed itself to have innate rights, and wanted to speak as master, as if *the house belonged to it.* And under the pretext that the G.O. had not put into activity quickly enough the new general constitutions of the Order, decreed on December 5, 1804, and which were found to be forcibly delayed by the unfinished work of the drafting committee, the Scottish associations separated from the G.O."

On July 21, 1805, discussions arose between the G.O. and the members of the G.L. of the Ancient and Accepted Rite. These latter denounced several of their officers that they accused of having signed an act of union only in order to paralyze the works of the G.L., but with the pronounced intention of having no regard of it, etc.

In fact, the leaders of this rite acted without good faith and with mental reservation: they claimed that *union*, in a case such as this, is not *fusion.*

On July 29, debates arose, after which the brother *Pyron*, secretary of the G.L. of the *Ancient and Accepted* Rite and one of the promoters of the union, is stricken from the rolls of the G.O., under the charge of *slanderous accusations.*

On September 6, the G.O. pronounces the breaking of the concordat of December 5, 1804, between it and the G.L. of the *Ancient and Accepted* Rite; and on the 16th of the same month, the representatives of the G.O. and those of the G.L. signed an agreement which declared broken, *de facto* and *de jure*, this act of union[88].

CHAPTER XX
Foundation of a Supreme Council of the 33rd Degree at Paris

Shortly after the return from San Domingo to Paris, in 1803, by the brother Hacquet, of the Rite of *Heredom*, in twenty-five degrees, that France had sent there in 1761, by *Stephen Morin*, there arrived from America the Comte de *Grasse-Tilly*, son of the Admiral of this name[89], presenting himself, at Paris, as *supreme head* of a new Masonry in thirty-three degrees, which was called *Ancient and Accepted Scottish Rite*. This system included nearly all the degrees of the Rite of Heredom, and some grades borrowed from other rites or of new creation. According to the Comte *de Grasse*, the author of this latest reform was the King of Prussia, *Frederick the Great* (declared enemy of the high grades), who had instituted it on May 1st, 1786, had drafted, by his own hand, the regulations thereof in eighteen articles, called the *Grand Constitutions*, and had founded, in Prussia, a Supreme Council of the 33rd Degree.

These assertions which were since recognized as falsehoods in all points, have made this Comte *de Grasse* to be classified among the most dishonest charlatans of the super-Masonic institutions.

The Supreme Council of the 33rd Degree is erected at Paris and organized provisionally on December 22, 1804. Its definitive constitution was decreed and published on January 19, 1811 (*printed* in-8vo).

In the beginning, this council was formed of nine members; this number was then brought to eighteen; finally, by article 1 of its constitution, it is composed of twenty-seven members.

The brother *Thory*, joyous to see arise a rival (we were going to say bastard) authority, hostile to the legitimate power, says, in his so-called *Histoire de la fondation du G.O.*:

"This establishment is formed by the consent and request *of all the lodges* of this rite, represented by their Venerables or by deputies," (p. ,147).

"This régime, says the Golden Book of the Comte *de Grasse*, existed in America, from where it has been brought to France in 1804. The regulations which govern it, and which it considers as its *Grand Constitutions*, are: 1st, those decreed by the representatives of Paris and Bordeaux on the 6th day of the 3rd week of the 7th moon of the Hebrew era (September 24, 1762)."

This title, without signatures, which certainly has not been drafted for the Scottish Rite in thirty-three degrees, which was yet to be born, and in which are not even announced the names of the nine supposed representatives, contains a materially false fact, namely: *that the deliberation of these representatives has been transmitted to the Ill.·. B.·. Comte de Grasse-Tilly, Sov.·. G.·. Insp.·. of all the lodges of the two worlds.*

"2nd, the statutes that Frederick II, King of Prussia, decreed in eighteen articles, completed on May 1, 1786."

This second historical falsehood no longer needs to be proven.

That, then, is the basis upon which rests the *Ancient and Accepted Rite of the 33rd Degree*. How have its founders been able to become so audacious, with these coarse allurements, so as to make dupes and to recruit them, in great part, from the elite of civil society and from the G.O. itself? Would their continuators have not played a more noble role by unveiling the fraud and renouncing its exploitation?

On December 29, there was a large meeting: forty officers of the G.O. were initiated, they say, to the Grade of Rose-Croix (18th degree); some of them were admitted to the 29th and 32nd, and others were elevated to the 33rd degree; here is the oath signed, *manu propria*, by these latter:

"We the undersigned declare to have accepted and received with recognition the eminent grade of Grand Inspector General of the 33rd and last degree, From the V.·. P.·. and V.·. Ill.·. B.·. Alexandre-François-Auguste de Grasse-Tilly, Grand Commander *ad vitam* for France, President of the Sup.·. Coun.·. of the 33rd Degree, the assembled Grand Council.

"We swear authentically on our word of honor and on all our promises and oaths pronounced in the face of the G.·. A.·. of the Un.·., and to the Grand Council of Sov.·. GG.·. Insp.·. Gen.·, of the 33rd Degree, *to obey* said Supreme Council, *to have its secrets respected* and to conduct ourselves in the duties of our charge as Sov. G.·. Insp.·. G.·. of the 33rd degree, in a manner to have the Royal and *Military Order* of Freemasonry cherished and respected, and to conform ourselves, entirely, to the credentials which we have been given.

"In faith of which we have, by our own will, signed the present oath. - Given and delivered at the Or.·. of Paris, on the 29th day of the 10th month of the year of the T.·. L.·. 5804 (December 29, 1804).

"*Signed*: Bacon de la Chevalerie, Challan, Roettiers de Montaleau, Burar."

If these officers of the G.O. had been as anxious to educate themselves as they appear to have been eager to adorn themselves with vain titles, they would not have shamefully fallen into the attractive snare which has been so cleverly laid for them. This act, fatal to their memory, can only be the effect of an unpardonable ignorance: Seeing as that their body, which is the legitimate possessor of a rite that alone, in France, it has the power to administer, if it desires, how are they going to take these degrees, *with recognition*, among intruders who, according to their patents, have no right to practice them in France, and, which is inconceivable, blindly *accept* new grades, without examining whether this addition to the twenty-five of the Rite of Perfection is not a superfluity and an audacious speculation! One is pained to see figure among these *obedient* and faithful servants of the new rite so distinguished a Mason as the Br. *Roettiers de Montaleau*: it is therefore that it is easier to agree perfectly with the good administration of the Order, than to investigate the basis and the dogmas thereof[90].

Moreover, what matters, in the eyes of the true Mason? These concordats, sworn and undone, then renewed and broken; these prizes of the high grades; these more or less solemn oaths of brethren seduced, for whom they are, by bonds and even acts of recognition of rites? Do these promulgations of *super-Masonic* constitutions matter; these erections of chapters, tribunals, consistories, and all that pleased the fantasy of these *beribboned* men to produce? Does this prevent him from regarding as irregular the nebulous origin of the Sov. Coun. of the Emperors of the East and West and its rite as non-Masonic, or rather the régime of a coterie formed in the shadow of Symbolic Masonry? Does this prevent him from regarding as irregular and shameful the clandestine fabrication of the eight grades upon the rite of twenty-five degrees by the tricksters of Charleston, and to regard, consequently, their work as an impudent *trickery*?

Is it that all these concordats, past or to come, and all these grades wasted on illustrious and very honorable personages, can make it so that fraud and deceit are not the basis of all these systems in twenty-five, in thirty-three degrees, more or less? Certainly not: the works of these high grades will never be *Masonic works*. A good policy would be to prohibit them in each state; for they harm the true Freemasonry, they trouble it, debase it, and although tolerated for it, they have often been the cause of the persecutions that they have experienced.

If the G.O. of that time, as was its duty, had had archives confided to an honest and educated brother, charged with increasing them each year, would it have lacked any documents in order to appraise at their value all these pretended Masonic conceptions[91]?

Would it not necessarily have what some curious brothers have: collections of grades, of rites, with the names of the authors, the indication of the places and dates of their creation? Has a new rite emerged? An attentive examination would have made known its formation, whether it had as its basis some new truths, or, only, some modifications, or the falsehood. Its duty was thus to enlighten itself by writing to the Masonic bodies, from where the presenters said that these rites emanated. Then, armed with their response, and especially by the infallible knowledge that the collections give, the G.O. would have ruined, annihilated, for ever, all the shameless charlatans whose misshapen works dishonor the institution. What service this body would have rendered to the Order in general, and what tribulations it would have spared the brethren who have succeeded it! In Freemasonry, as elsewhere, ignorance and pride have produced all the evils.

Before returning to the operations of the *Supr. Coun.*, we are going to give the synoptic table of the two rites, to get a better sense of the similarities and differences of the grades in both series. We recognize clearly that the eight added grades are a superfluity which disfigures the *Rite of Perfection*, which serves as basis to the new system, improperly called *Ancient and Accepted Scottish Rite*.

If we make a comparative recapitulation, we find that the number of parallel degrees in the new system is 22.

The number of grades falsified, composed, or arranged by the inventors of the 33rd is 9.

Then, they have taken from other régimes the *Écossais of Saint Andrew* and the *Sovereign Tribunal*[92], two grades, 2.

Total of the degrees: 33; in which the 31st, 32nd are the 25th and last of the 7th class, according to the old nomenclature. As to the 33rd, it is an absurdity worthy of the rite: we have never seen a charge, a dignity, whether or not it bears the title *Supreme* or *Sovereign*, taken as a grade; it has long remained to be seen what the password would be. (See hereafter, note no. 98.)

NOMENCLATURE

Rite of Perfection in 25 grades	Ancient and Accepted Scottish Rite
1st Class	1st Class
1. Apprentice,	1. Apprentice,
2. Companion,	2. Companion,
3. Master.	3. Master.

2nd Class	2nd Class
4. Secret Master,	4. Secret Master,
5. Perfect Master,	5. Perfect Master,
6. Intimate Secretary,	6. Intimate Secret. Or *Master by Curiosity*[93],
7. Intendant of the Buildings,	7. Intendant of the Buildings or *Master in Israel,*
8. Provost and Judge.	8. Provost and Judge[94], or *Irish Master.*
3rd Class	3rd Class
9. Master Elect of the Nine,	9. Master Elect of the Nine,
10. Master Elect of the Fifteen,	10. Master Elect of the Fifteen,
11. Master Elect, chief of the 12 Tribes.	11. Sublime Knight Elect.
4th Class	4th Class
12. Grand Master Architect,	12. Grand Master Architect,
13. Knight Royal Arch,	13. Royal Arch,
14. Grand Elect, Ancient Perfect Master.	14. *G. Écoss. Of the Sacred Vault of James VI, or G. Écoss. Of Perfection*, or G.-Elect Ancient Perfect M. *and Sublime Mason.*
5th Class	5th Class
15. Knight of the Sword or the East,	15. Knight of the East or the Sword,
16. Prince of Jerusalem[95],	16. Prince of Jerusalem, *Grand Council Key of the Lodges*,
17. Knight of the East and West,	17. Knight of the East and West,
18. Knight Rose-Croix,	18. Sov. Prince Rose-Croix.
	6th Class
19. Grand Pontiff or Master *ad Vitam*,	19. G. Pontiff or Subl. Écoss. Called of the Celestial Jerusalem.
6th Class	
20. Grand Patriarch Noachite,	20. Venerable G.M. of all the Lodges, Sov. Prince of Masonry or Master *ad Vitam*[96],
21. Grand Master of the Key of Masonry,	21. Noachite or Prussian Knight,
22. Prince of Lebanon, Knight Royal Axe.	22. Knight Royal Axe or Prince of Lebanon,
	23. Chief of the Tabernacle,
	24. Prince of the Tabernacle,
	25. Knight of the Brazen Serpent,
	26. Scottish Trinitarian or Prince of Mercy,
	27. G. Comm. Of the T.·. of Jerusalem.
7th Class	7th Class
23. Knight of the Sun, or Prince or	28. Knight of the Sun or Prince Adept,

Prince Adept, Chief of the Grand Consistory,	29. G. Éc. Of Saint Andrew, or Patriarch of the Crusades; Knight of the Sun; Grand Master of the Light,
24. Ill. Kn., G. Comm of the Black and White Eagle, G. Elect K.H.	30. Knight K.H. G. Inquis. G. Elect, or Knight of the Black and White Eagle,
	31. Gr. Insp. Inq. Commander (of the Sovereign Tribunal),
25. V. Ill. Sov. Pr. Of Masonry, G. Kn., Sub. Comm. Of the Royal Secret.	32. Sov. Prince of the Royal Secret,
	33. Sovereign Grand Inspector General.

On July 9, 1805, they established at Paris a *G. Consistory of Princes of the Royal Secret, 32nd Degree of the Ancient and Accepted Rite.*

On September 5, same year, the leaders of the Supr. Coun., no doubt not finding it to their advantage to unite themselves freely with the G.O., continue to not act with Masonic sincerity: the possession of their rite arising from fraud, the spirit of truth did not inspire them; that is why the word *union* signified for them *separation, division*, and not *fusion*; from here came their debates between themselves and with the representatives of the G.O.

Considering a rupture, they based it on the supposed delay that the drafting committee of the G.O. made to produce its work on the organization of French Masonry. Consequently, the concordat of December 5, 1804, was declared *null* in the session of the day.

The next day, there was a particular meeting with the Marshal *Kellermann*. Here, the representatives of the Supr. Coun. notified those of the G.O. of the decree of annulment bearing that if, by the 15th of that month, the draft of the organic statutes is not present, the treaty of December 15, not being executed, shall be considered as null, and the Scottish G.L. Gen. will resume its works.

September 16, agreement between the representatives of the G.O. and those of the G.L. of the Ancient and Accepted Rite, which declared annulled, *de facto* and *de jure*, the act of union of December 5, 1804.

September 24, installation of the Grand Consistory of the 32nd Degree of the Ancient and Accepted Rite, erected the previous July 9th.

October 1st. The Supr. Coun. issues a decree concerning the organization of its dogmatic power. This decree occasions long and interminable discussions between the G. Consistory, which complains strongly that its rights are infringed, and the Supr. Coun. which ends up, on December 29, 1810, suppressing the *G. Consis. of France.*

June 10, 1806, demission of the Comte *de Grasse-Tilly* of his dignity of Sov. G. Commander of écossisme, in favor of the Prince Cambacerès, who is recognized in this dignity on the following July 1st, and solemnly installed on the 16th.

ADMINISTRATION. The Supr. Coun., which, with the G.O., administers this rite in France, is constituted in a spirit which, as the majority of the grades of the regime, is removed from the true spirit of Masonry; for, its dignitaries, named for life and who are irrevocable, personify an *oligarchical* power, foreign to the true Masonry.

The constitution of the Supr. Coun. attributes all the dogmatic, legislative, administrative, and other powers, to the members of the 33rd degree, which recruits from among themselves. Whereas with the G.O., all the powers reside in the hands of the representatives of the lodges, from which this body is uniquely formed.

It resulted from this difference of organization that all the decisions made by the sections of the Scottish G.L. and the G.L. itself, in general assembly, are submitted, in the last resort, to the Supr. Coun., which may annul them, if they displease it, whether in a meeting of all the members of the degree, or even in administrative committee, where three members present can validly deliberate, and where, consequently, the deliberations may be taken by the majority of two votes against one.

In the G.O., on the contrary, the decisions of the chambers in general assembly, have a definitive character and no one has more power to modify them.

We understand the inappreciable benefit of *Masonic unity*, which cannot exist where two independent administrations are found, even when they would be bound by intimate and reciprocal relations.

The practice of this ostentatious rite, in the present lodges, gives reason to the Modern Rite, and goes even further, since today they no longer work, after the first three degrees, but the *Rose-Croix* and the *Kadosh*. The other grades are threadbare and no longer figure but in the Tilers; *vanitas vanitatum*!

SUPREME COUNCIL OF AMERICA, AT PARIS

In 1812, some Masons, invested with the 33rd grade that they had received, in America, from a supposed Supr. Coun. of this degree, and, consequently, all as *regular* or *irregular* as the Comte de Grasse-Tilly, took on several persons with whom they claimed to erect, at Paris, another Supr. Coun. of the 33rd Degree, under the title of COUNCIL OF AMERICA, in rivalry with the one of France.

There resulted therefrom for nine years, scandalous conflicts which had no end. There was up to three *Supr. Couns.* at Paris. The Comte de Grasse became G. Commander of the one from America which took, at this occasion, the name of *Council of the Comte de Grasse or council of Pompei*, place of its sessions, in order to distinguish it from that of the Prado, name of the place of this latter. The Comte de Grasse having retracted the act of creation of the Council of the Prado, that he declared schismatic, this latter suspended the Comte from his functions of G. Commander of the Scottish Rite, he and some of his partisans. This shameful spectacle for the actors and for the *play*, but which the practice of the high grades, called philosophical, has produced too often, spectacle unknown to the modest Masons of the symbolic grades, came to an end only on May 7, 1821, by the treaty of union and fusion between the Supr. Coun. of France and the one of America, called *of Pompei*. (See the *Historical Summary* on each of these councils.)

ESTABLISHMENT OF ÉCOSSISME AT NEW YORK (America)

The number of charlatans inspired by écossisme has been considerable. Thirty- three degrees indeed! The field is vast and suitable to the speculative genius. If, leaving Paris for a moment, we transport ourselves to New York, we will learn how the *Ancient and Accepted Scottish Rite* was introduced there.

A Frenchman, Joseph *Cerneau*, Jeweller, had established himself at San Domingo, where he was initiated into the mysteries of the *Rite of Perfection* that *Stephen Morin* had brought there. Forced to leave this island at the time of the insurrection of the blacks, he crossed the Spanish Antilles, the United States, and came to fix himself at New York. Here, he founded, in 1806, a *Supreme Council* of the 33rd Degree, of which he instituted himself Grand Commander, Secretary, and above all, Treasurer. He made a multitude of receptions, especially among the South Americans. He delivered diplomas and sold aprons, sashes, and jewels to the Masons that he initiated. He even attempted the fabrication of those tin boxes which serve to contain and protect the seals that are attached to the diplomas. To these various branches of industry, he joined the speculation of bookselling: he was the author and publisher of a *Masonic Manual* in Spanish, with which he inundated Mexico and the other colonies of this part of America. Later, he succeeded in engaging a correspondence with the G.O. of France, which recognized his *Supr. Coun.*, and aided, thus, without knowing it, in the traffic that he made of the Masonry called *Scottish*.

The news of these successes arrived at Charleston; and jealous, apparently, of the profits that he drew from the initiations, the Jews of the *Supr. Coun.* of this city dreamed of giving him competition. To this end, they dispatched one of their own to New York, *Emmanuel de la Motta*, already cited on page 129, who, upon his arrival, elevated to the 33rd degree several brothers and went with them to the brother *Cerneau*, in order to make him submit to an interrogation on the origin of his powers. This brother refused to give the explanations requested of him, and it appeared to the Masons who interrogated him, that he was, said the Jew Emmanuel, *completely unacquainted with the sublime knowledge of the 33rd degree*.

After having made an ample harvest of dollars and constituting on August 5, 1813, the *Supr. Coun.* of New York, which had for its first Grand Commander the brother *Tompkins*, Vice-president of the United States, Emmanuel de la Motta went to propagate, at other points of the republic, the mysteries of the *Ancient and Accepted Rite*.

The establishment of the new council prevented the brother Cerneau from giving himself to his business; so, he just lowered his prices and multiplied the receptions among the foreigners who landed at New York. But the indecency of his actions had removed from him all that this counted as honorable Masons. He had become there, by 1830, the object of such profound scorn, and he had fallen into such great distress there, that he dreamt of quitting this theatre of his past splendor, and to go finish his days in the land which had seen to give birth to him. Moved with compassion for his misfortune, the G.L. gave him, in 1831, a sum of money to pay for his passage. Since then, we no longer hear talk of him.

The men with which the *Jew de la Motta* had surrounded himself in order to found a *Supr. Coun.* at New York were also traffickers of Masonry, more skillful and less indecent than Cerneau. They were made up of some honorable persons, whose names served them as recommendation and cloak. Sheltered by these names, they turned away, to their credit, the fees arising from the receptions and the diplomas; and, in order to dispense with the rendering of accounts, they convoked the *Supr. Coun.* only at distant and irregular periods, and only to proceed with initiations whose ceremonial, prolonged by design, filled every session and did not allow them to occupy themselves with anything else.

They repeatedly fulminated against their competitor, the brother Cerneau, accusing him of abusing the confidence of Masons by conferring to them a false écossisme (*as if the Jeweler Cerneau had not had as well as the Jews of Charleston, the right to add eight grades of fantasy to the twenty-five of the Rite of Perfection*) and of appropriating to himself the sums resulting from the collation of grades and the deliverance of diplomas.

The last manifesto that they published against him is from the beginning of 1827. However, there transpired something at an address that they had employed to hide their embezzlements. An investigation took place, after which they were eliminated, without commotion, from the *Supr. Coun.*, by the honest members who, in this body, were in the majority. But the selfish zeal of the banished was the sole motive force of this Masonic authority; and, when they no longer took part therein, it fell into a complete apathy. It was scarcely that, at greater and greater intervals, some meetings took place, and still only a small number of people assisted there. Properly speaking, this *Supr. Coun.* no longer existed.

Into these circumstances arrived at New York, in 1832, a Mason, (*the pearl of the genre*); he had himself called *Marie-Antoine-Nicolas-Alexandre-Robert-Joachim de Sainte-Rose*, ROUME DE SAINT-LAURENT[97], *Marquis de Santo-Rosa, Comte de Saint-Laurent, and he took the title of Very Puissant Grand Commander* ad vitam *of the Sup. Coun. of the 33rd and last Degree of the Ancient and Accepted Scottish Rite*, SUPREME CHIEF *of Ancient and Modern Freemasonry, for Terre-Ferme, Southern America, Mexico, etc., from one sea to the other; the Canary Islands, Puerto Rico*, etc., etc. etc.

Well done! Here is a brother who is good at it; and, leaping with feet together over Masonic equality, he left far behind the *de la Mottas*, the *Cerneaus*, the *Grasse-Tillys*, the *Pyrons*, and other *ejusdem farinæ*. Long live the *Ancient and Accepted Rite* for transforming a simple Mason, barely received Master, into a Sovereign Prince, a Grand Commander, superior even, in titles and dignities, to the Masters of the earth!

This *myrionym* Mason presented himself as invested with the full powers of the *Supr. Coun.* that he foretold, in order to negotiate its reunion with the one of New York, to form thereof only one, which embraced all those of America, and to thus succeed in making cease all the *schisms* which divided écossisme in this part of the world. His propositions were accepted, and they established, consequently, at New York, a Masonic authority which took the name of UNITED SUPREME COUNCIL, *for the western Hemisphere, of the 33rd and last Degree of the Ancient and Accepted Scottish Rite*, and which had as its Grand Commander the brother *Elias Hicks*, judge of the court of police. He fulfilled the same functions in the last Supreme Council of New York.

The new body published a manifesto in which it announced its establishment, made known its motives, and called to it all the *Scottish* Masons of America. After, was the text of the treaty of union, in sixteen articles, dated April 5, 1832, and a profession of faith whose principal dogmas were the independence of the rites and Masonic tolerance.

Despite all the commotion that its foundation made, this Supreme Council fell asleep nearly immediately, the Comte de Saint-Laurent, who was the soul thereof, having left the country in order to return to France; so that at the very moment when this Mason negotiated at Paris for the alliance of the Supr. Coun. of this capital with the Supr. Coun. of New York, the latter no longer existed but in name. (See Masonic institution in the State of New York, *Fastes initiat.*)

- We read in a booklet, published in the French language at Philadelphia, in 1810, "that a council of *Barracoca*, in the country of Cuba, constituted by the metropolis of Kingston, had itself been authorized to create a particular council at New York; that this council has been promulgated October 28, 1808, and that there have been raised in its midst some doubts on the legitimate powers of the body which constituted them. In order to remove all the difficulties," *they add in this writing*, "the council decided that it would solicit its regularization with a superior authority.

"Without doubt, the brethren, irregular in their opinion, are going to address the Sovereign Inspectors of the 33rd Degree of the *Ancient and Accepted Rite* in America, and the Supreme Council, the great regulator of this regime, the supposed head of the

Consistories, the composition of which they would most certainly know. Not at all, the 33rd degree and the Supreme Council are entirely ignorant in America.

"These brothers determined (page 7 *of the printing*) that they will address a supplication to the Very Illustrious and Very Puissant Grand Consistory of Kilwinning, in Scotland. They are writing, consequently, to the *Prince of Wales*, in order to obtain his support in this circumstance." (HERMES maçonnique, volume I, p. 301.)

CHAPTER XXI
On the Brother Pyron

This Mason, of sad memory, has taken too great a part in the intrigues employed to the end of establishing, at Paris and in France, écossisme in thirty-three degrees, for us not to relate here some facts which ought to find their place in the history of the Order. Let us examine first the legitimacy of his titles in this rite that he extols.

We find, on page 76 of the register of the Comte de Grasse-Tilly, that *Jean-Baptiste-Pierre-Julien* PYRON, *old agent general, intendant of the domains and woods of the house of Artois*, has taken an oath as *Deputy G. Inspector General of the 33rd Degree, for the French Windward and Leeward Islands.* This article is signed Pyron, *de Grasse-Tilly*[98]. The heading is no. 28; we read there the date of the 25th day of the 8th month, 5804 (almost two months before the erection of the Supr. Coun. which took place on December 22). Such is the unique title that the brother Pyron could produce in this rite, and one has wondered:

"Where was, in 1804, at Paris, the mysterious temple of the initiations into the 33rd degree? There was none. And yet the Br. *Pyron* is secretary of the Holy Empire, in other words, of the Supr. Coun. 33rd Degree. In what Lodge of Perfection, in what Chapter, in what Council may a simple taking of an oath ever take the place of an initiation? But in supposing that this form was admitted in this new Order, it still remains to examine whether the Br. *Pyron* is Grand Inspector for France.
Assuredly not; his own title expresses the contrary. he may still less take the title of G. Insp. of the 33°. He is, according to his title, *Deputy G. Insp. Gen. of the 33°, that is to say, appointed by the 33°*, intended by the G. Insp. to represent them *in the French Windward and Leeward Islands*," (HERMES, p. 310).

And it is this illustrious deputy in America, who has no regular title, who cannot justify his initiation, and who, later, declared *irregular* the works of a Sovereign Chap. erected by the G.O. of France, sole legitimate authority which may create and organize it. See the printed DISCOURSE, pronounced on February 27, 1812, at the Scot. Sov. Chap. of the Ancient and Accepted Rite.; of the *Père de famille*, valley of Angers, in response to the *fulminant* decree attributed to the brother Pyron, (*in order to console himself*, it says there, *for the interdict thrown upon him indefinitely by the G.O. of France*), at the occasion of refusing to pay the Supr. Coun. , whose regular existence is proven impossible, the trifling sum of 3,308 francs, that the brother Pyron demanded by his letter of January 30, 1812, in order to provide *for the great expenses that the Supr. Coun. has to make*. By means of this sum, the Chap. of the *Père de famille*, instituted by the G.O., would have been *regularized* and elevated to the 32nd degree. What brave brethren, these founders of rites!

We have seen, p. 133, that, on July 29, 1805, the brother *Pyron*, secretary of the Scottish G.L. General of France, was stricken from the rolls of the G.O. under the charge of *slanderous accusations*. Here is how the unfaithful historian of the G.O. recounts this event.

"July 29, debates after which they strike from the list of officers of the G.O. one of the members of the G.L. of the Ancient Rite, the very one who had brought about the meeting, and *whose influence and zeal they feared*. - This decree, injurious for the person who was its object, as for the Ancient Rite, became one of the *accessory* causes which *convinced* the Supr. Coun. of the 33rd Degree to separate from the G.O. to which it had united itself by the treaty in question. The decree taken out against the brother suppressed from the rolls has been posted, unanimously, by the G.O. assembled on March 8, 1811," (*Acta Latam.*, v. I, p. 225).

Where has *Thory* seen the report of this decree? On April 29, 1806, the G.O. upheld the exclusion pronounced against the brother *Pyron*, then secretary of the Supr. Coun. of the 33rd Degree, and this, *for serious reasons*; in fact, it is said (note, p. 87), *the brother Pyron remained trustee of the act of union, and they were far from presuming that this brother would abuse it one day*. We have just seen his insane conduct toward the Chapter of Angers, he would not have pursued this, unless he had been reintegrated upon the rolls of the G.O. Thory is therefore here, as in many discussions between the G.O. and its adversaries, a narrator, not only unfaithful, but of bad faith, and giving, at the expense of the truth, nearly every reason to its adversaries, to maintain their hostility against the G.O. The subject which occupies us is going to give us an example.

It is recognized that every inventor or introducer of a rite is desirous to exploit it in order to draw a profit therefrom. The request for *union* with the G.O. had for its aim to make itself known by recruiting from the true center. There they seduced officers of this body and other honorable Masons. They admitted them into the highest grades, under oath. Since that time, the fraudulent rite has passed as being *recognized* and *legitimate*. The turn was played, a pretext was then necessary to break this union: they put forth the supposed delay of the committee of the G.O. in the drafting of the new organic laws. The impatient ones of the Supr. Coun. limited its presentation to fifteen days. But as they did not extemporize any general statutes, like the titles of eight grades, the rupture was pronounced and the treaty of union declared null.

What does the *veracious* Thory say in this regard, some lines before the article that we just cited? It must be read to be believed.

> *The concordat of 1804 is not, he says, executed by the G.O.*, WHICH REFUSED *to put into activity the new general constitution of the Order, decreed on December 5th of the previous year* (that is to say seven and a half months before).

This mention is as accurate as the transformation of the Pyronian slanders into *influence* and *zeal*. But this falsity, wittingly written, is most unskillful, since it claims then that the striking of the brother Pyron was one of the causes which *convinced* the Supr. Coun. to separate itself from the G.O. For if this latter *refused* truly to fulfill the conditions of the union, it would be found *de facto* broken by it, and the Supr. Coun. would have no need of other *causes* to convince itself or rather to consent to this natural separation.

This fault of logic is remarkable and pains one to see in a writer such as *Thory*; it is that in him were found two men: the good Masonic man, and the head of a sect. This latter is always the enemy, *nevertheless*, of every authority which wants to limit his power, that is to say his ambition. Outside of the *Philosophical Scottish Rite*, of which he was the intelligent soul, the amplifying historian, and the very faithful trustee of *undiscoverable* archives (see p. 73), the other rites or Masonries were but secondary. But the G.O., having several times to hinder the indiscreet progress of the invasive rite, the pride of the secretary suffered therefrom. (See the *historical brief* of the M.L. of the PHILOS. SCOTT. R., *Fastes initiat.*) And being unable to openly revolt, the Mason avenged himself largely in the *Acta Latomorum*, an incomplete work where the chronology and the facts are too often incorrect, and especially in his *History*, very partial, *of the foundation of the G.O.* In neither of these two works do we find the extract from the booklet of the Chapter of Angers which had made so great a sensation in 1812[99], because it was revealing the turpitude of the adversaries of the G.O. Thus, may the G.O. be assured that its most perfidious enemy was the brother *Thory*, who nevertheless figured among its officers. Indeed, his books, because of a great reputation that the author has enjoyed, have seeded and rooted in the minds of many readers the most vexatious prejudices against the G.O. of France. We have tested them ourselves. It is only in a serious examination that *scratching*, so to speak, the Mason, we have found the sectarian who avenges himself; and that in unveiling the historian we have laid bare the *Zoile of the G.O.*, in clever, calm, and nearly guileless forms. With more care and less hatred, the brother *Thory*, so well assisted by numerous archives, would have been capable of producing two good works.

Returning to the brother *Pyron*, we will find this bold innovator incubating grand projects for the future of his rite, which, unfortunately, had ever for its basis the fable of Berlin, which is to say that he worked *for the King of Prussia.* - Let us open with an indispensible citation:

"EXTRACT *from the Golden Book of the Supr.·. Council for France of the Sov. G. Insp. Gen. of the 33rd and last Degree of the Ancient and Accepted Scottish Rite.* - Session of the 1st day of the 5th month, 5806.

"Considering that the elevation of the resp. brother *Lecourt de Vallière* renders vacant the dignity of *Sovereign of Sovereigns* in the G. Consistory of the *Subl. Princes of the Royal Secret*; that this dignity resided in the person of *Frederick II, King of Prussia, as Supreme Chief of High Masonry*; that this Prince having delegated his Sovereignty to the Supr. Council of the 33rd. Degree, in order to exercise it after his death, considerations of the highest importance, known by all the Prince Masons, make it desirable that the *Sovereign of Sovereigns* be chosen henceforth from among the depositaries of the Sovereign power."

We extract from the *Hermès* an anecdote which gives the complement of this project, here it is:

"The brother *Pyron*, malcontent, no doubt, for having fallen from his quality as Mason by a solemn judgment of the G.O. of France, dreamed up and made enter into the high conceptions of his dignity as secret. of the *Holy Empire*, that the regular power of Freemasonry, which had passed from the family of the *Stuarts* into the hands of *Frederick the Great*, would be sustained in France by *Napoleon the Magnanimous*, the *Sovereign of Sovereigns.* He remitted, consequently, by himself, to this emperor, a note, supposedly *historical*, containing this filiation in which he said further more:

"The general dogmatic regulative administration of High Masonry belongs to the president of the Supr. Council of the 33rd Degree who ought to be a very powerful Sovereign, a grand commander, and who, in this quality, represents the King *Frederick.*

"The inspectors, members of the same council, have the right to annul, to reform, or to modify what appears to them contrary to the dogma.

"The grades of *Elect* and *Kadosh* ought no longer be given but by communication, because the *Masonic vengeance* has been accomplished since the ascension of Napoleon to the throne of the French Empire, and because the revolution has left nothing more to desire to the descendants of the Masons," (pages 336 and following).

In relating this fact in the *Hermès*, we would add:

"We feel that this proposition was of no consequence; but it makes known the opinion of the Br. Pyron on the aim of écossisme, an opinion unfortunately shared by many Masons, and even by some eminent officers of the G.O., opinion which, if it were true, would have thrown out the words of the high grades. which make allusion to events and projects entirely foreign to the Masonic spirit. We prefer to believe that it symbolizes only a natural fact, and consequently, the *cry of the ancient initiates*[100]."

We see how this Mason set to thinking and stirred himself to founding and propagating his supposedly *Scottish* rite; and despite the terrible lesson given to him, in 1812, by the Chapter of the *Père de famille* at Angers, which caught him in the very act of imposture, and demonstrated to him, even to obviousness, that the regular existence of his Supreme Council was an impossibility, he continued no less, with the persevering audacity of a quack doctor, to offer his drug to the workshops of France. Here are the two circulars that we received as president - founder of the three workshops of the *Trinosophes*, at Paris (*we copy faithfully*):

"Extract from the Golden Book of the Supreme Council for France of the Puissant and Sovereign Grand Inspectors General, 33rd and last Degree of the Ancient and Accepted Rite.

Ordo ab Chao

"Session of the seventh day of the sixth month, five thousand eight hundred eighteen, August 7, 1818.

"The Supreme Council for France of the Puissant and Sovereign Grand Inspectors General, 33rd and last Degree of the Ancient and Accepted Scottish Rite, instituted at Paris for France in 5804, by virtue of the Grand Constitutions.

"To the V,V,V.·. Ill, Ill, Ill.·. Lodges, Chapters, Colleges, Tribunals, particular Councils, and Grand Consistories

S.·. S.·. S.·.

"The Supreme Council for France taking into consideration the Good of Masonry and not wishing to allow an Extended stagnation which could only be harmful to it, We have the high Favor of informing you that it has resumed its Labors in the session of the day; Consequently, it counts on your Cooperation, your Zeal, and your Fidelity. The Lodges, Chapters, and Consistories are invited to resume their correspondence as in the Past, and at the usual address, to the Ill.·. Secretary General of the Holy Empire for France, the Br.·. Pyron, rue Basse-du-rempart, no. 40. This correspondence will be followed on our part with the promptness and accuracy that we always place to draw closer more and more the sacred Alliance of our Union.

"We have the High Favor in the sentiments of the most intimate fraternity V,V,V.·. Ill, Ill, Ill.·., V,V,V. and R,R,R.·. B,B,B.·. and Scottish Kn. *the signatures follow.*

Signed: Pyron de Chaboulon.

"To the V.·. R.·. Lodge and Chapter Trinosophes, under 2 rites, O.·. of Paris.

"V,V,V.·. R,R,R.·. B,B,B.·. and Kn.,

S.·. S.·. S.·.

"I have the High Favor to announce to you that the Supreme Council for France, instituted at the O.·. of Paris in 5804, has referred me to announce to you in its name the expedition Hereafter; I pray you, V,V,V.·. III, III, III.·. B,B,B.·. and Kn., to admit the reception thereof, and to address me for the Supreme Council the response that you will have intended to make to it.

"The first 18 degrees of the rite composed of 33 degrees which have been separated therefrom according to the Particular Considerations, are Reunited under its Power from which they are inseparable; and will be henceforth Conferred by the Lodges and Chapters already Constituted, and which it is going to Constitute in The extent of France, in giving to the Rite all the Consistency, and all the activity which belongs to it, and which it enjoys over the whole surface of the Globe.

"The III.·. Secretary of the Holy Empire for France, Puissant and Sovereign Grand Inspector General, *Signed*: Pyron de Chaboulon.·. Old General agent of affairs, and old Intendant of the Woods and Domains of *Monsieur*, Son of France, Comte D'artois, brother of the King. - Rue Basse-du-rempart no. 40." (The whole thing is the writing of Pyron, the orthography of which we reproduce.)

This piece bears in the margin: WITHOUT RESPONSE, *the Br. Pyron having no legal character, nor his Supreme Council.* Signed: RAGON.

On all this, we leave to the readers the care of making considerations; but we, while abstaining therefrom, cannot help but say to them: *Risum teneatis*!

The brother Pyron, whether fortunate or unfortunate for his memory, died at Paris at the end of September 1818. He occupied himself with establishing a new Consistory of the Ancient and Accepted Rite: it was, then, the ninth Masonic power in Paris, without including the *Persian Rite*; which ought to appear reasonable for an Order whose essence is *unity*.

CHAPTER XXII
Various Opinions on the Scottish Rite and on the High Grades

"Several Masonic bodies have disputed the possession of this (*Ancient and Accepted Scottish*) Rite, and each of them extols the sublimity of its initiations. It is necessary to believe, however, that on the one side and the other, one may try so lively an enthusiasm for these admirable mysteries only on the faith of the Masons who have brought them; for, with the exception of some grades, such as, for example, the *Rose-Croix* and the *Kadosh*, the series of degrees of écossisme is given only by communication and in a most succinct manner. Very few brothers, furnished with high grades, know in what consists the marvelous knowledge that they attach thereto; and it is most certainly not those who show the most pride in possessing them. Indeed, as to the doctrine, it is all trivial, or inconsequential, or absurd in these superior grades; and as to the ceremonial, it consists in insignificant formalities, when they are not foolish or ridiculous, and even degrading for the dignity of the candidate," (*Hist. pitt. de la Francm.*).

The Baron *de Tschoudy*, in his *Etoile flamboyante* (v. I, p. 168), said, in 1766, that the mechanism of all the Masonic grades had no other source, motive, nor means than the desire to distinguish themselves in the eyes of their fellow- men, and after to be posed this question:

"Why, renouncing thus the simplicity, the essence of their institution, are the Masons lost in imaginary spaces?" He adds: "Adorned with the mosaic, charged with useless decorations, which are only the livery of pretention and vanity; would this vanity not be *the germ of all these same grades that they announce with emphasis and treat with gravity...*" And further on (page 167): "It is to ambition, to that cruel vice, the weapon of the strong, the oppressor of the weak, that *must be attributed without hesitation, all the excesses* which are committed daily in the whole of things of general society, the disorder of particular societies, and *notably the abuse which has slid into Masonry through the multiplicity of grades*, the modern invention of which is the effect of the *pretentions* and *envy to dominate*."

And yet, this distinguished and conscientious Mason extolled three grades called superior: the *Écossais of Saint Andrew*[101], the *Kn. of Palestine*, and the *Unknown Philosopher*. He enumerates (p. 174) up to forty of these so-called *superior* grades, which were practiced then.

The brother *Beyerlé*, counsellor at the parliament of Nancy, in his *Essai sur la Francmaçonnerie* (2 vol. in-8vo.), published in 1784, says (p. 13 of the preface):

"The second principle which serves as basis to this work, is that the germ of all Masonic knowledge is contained in the first three grades. Thus, this multiplicity of grades which has been brought forth by *cupidity*, *charlatanism*, and extravagance, ought to be, for ever, *excluded from the Masonic régime*; and if they are permitted to preserve the documents thereof, it ought only to be in order to serve as the history of Masonic extravagance. They ought, consequently, to be carefully shut up in a place that the less educated Mason may not approach."

The brother *Vernhes*, of Montpellier, after having made a just criticism of the innovations of Ramsay in his *Parfait Maçon* (1 vol. in-8vo, 1820-21), writes (p. 197):

"Children of *pride* and *greed*, a multitude of grades even further removed from the ancient Masonic spirit joined themselves at once to those that Ramsay had introduced, each arrogating to himself the right to create new ones."

Chemin-Dupontès, in his *Encyclopédie maçonnique* (4 vol. in 12-mo, 1820 to 1825), after having said (v. III, p. 174) that in France Masonry was *frivolous* and *vainglorious*, did not delay to add:

"They are but a trifling Mason in the Symbolic Lodges: beyond, there is no longer but *puerility, foolishness, vanity, Masonic absurdity, feudality, and despotic titles and forms.* They disdain there the beautiful name of *Brother*; they give themselves there the title of *Knight.* They are no longer under the sweet and benign law of the *level and the mallet*, where the head is but the first among equals, and which recalls the golden age of the good King Saturn[102] they are under the absolute empire of the scepter and the sword, where ridiculously ostentatious titles are borrowed from the iron or middle ages. They do not occupy themselves there, or nearly so, with the relief of the misfortunate. They learn nothing more there than in the symbolic grades. They give themselves there only to practices that may only be called, conservatively, *insignificant.*"

Let us cite the following passage from the COURS *des initiations*, p. 193:

"The all but modern system of the high grades, regarded by some as a useful amplification, and by many others as an arbitrary creation and a true superfluity, does not have the great import of the first three degrees. These latter make all the nations into one sole nation. On the contrary, in the high grades, each nation wishes, among itself, to be among itself; it isolates itself from the Masonic world, and arranges, in its manner, for its customs and its needs, the so-called *superior* system of *écossisme*, or any other speculation of the spirit.

"A visitor presents himself with elevated grades in order to participate in meetings *superior* to those of the lodges. They occupy themselves less, in order to admit him, with his quality of high Mason, that a *variant* in his high grades could have him rejected, than with the direct interest that he may inspire in the national Masons, with his profane position, and with the deportment of his country with the one that he visits. In foreign lands, more than in France, these scruples, or rather these abuses, are pushed far away.

"Whence we many conclude that if the capitulary and philosophical grades are superior to the first three degrees in pompous denominations and in working apparel, they are altogether inferior in humanitarian and even philosophical results."

All has been said on the incoherence of the grades which compose the Ancient and Accepted Scottish Rite in the Masonic courses of *Ragon*, *Vassel* and *Chemin-Dupontès*, but we will make here an observation on the instruction of the *Scottish Apprentice*, the first question of which, according to us, ought to be suppressed. Let us examine the dialog between the Venerable and the First Surveillant.

Q.: What is there between you and me?	A.: *A cult.*
Q.: What is a cult?	A.: *It is a secret.*
Q.: What is this secret?	A.: *Masonry.*

First of all, Masonry is not a cult, its ceremonial proves this. If this (invisible) cult is a secret, it is well guarded, for the Jesuits, authors of these questions, have revealed it only in their Rose-Croix, a Catholic grade and not at all Masonic. But they had a goal, from there the ridicule of this commencement.

Here are these three questions reduced to one:

Q.: What is there between you and me? A.: *Masonry*.

Is not this question from a Venerable to a Surveillant ridiculous, for not saying more? What! Masonry is between these two brothers? What is it doing there, and what are they doing with it? The catechism says not a word.

The modern Apprentice, created in England and adopted in 1786, by the G.O. of France with slight modifications, does not have this defect. we have seen many Apprentice manuscripts, anterior to this date, which do not present this anomaly, that one does not find either in the 24th edition of the symbolic grades published by Samuel *Prichard* in his *Masonry Dissected*, bearing the date of October 13, 1730, although this author had written under the Jesuitic influence. *Ashmole*, who died in 1692, original author of the manuscripts, had not introduced therein these strange questions that Prichard would have reproduced; it is therefore only later that this stain has soiled the ritual called *Scottish*[103].

CHAPTER XXIII
Universality and Unity of Freemasonry

Freemasonry has as its fundamental character, *universality*. This character is indispensible to its essence. It is ONE, and every rite or every nation which strays from this principle loses its way and departs from the Masonic path.

We do not conceive of a true Masonry which may be called *English*; another *Scottish*; a third *French*; another *American*, etc., etc. All these Masonries, which draw their titles from what their partisans call the *high grades*, are no more Masonic than the Masonry of *vengeance* or *with the daggers* of the Templars and the Jesuits; than the useful Masonry called *Forestry*; or than the innocent Masonry of *adoption*, which, all of them, are Masonic in form and name only.

Are there *English* mathematics, *Scottish* mathematics, *French* mathematics? No, there is *mathematics*, as there is Freemasonry. Some nuances in the wording of the rituals, in the ceremonial, or in the mode of reception (though uniformity were preferable), does not suffice to *nationalize* a Masonry at the expense of its universality.

It is said: *Universal fraternity engenders unity*. What is this universal fraternity really, if it is not Freemasonry, whose members dispersed among all the peoples of the globe tend towards making thereof one day but one sole family of brethren, in order to achieve the *unity of humanity*.

But this *hominal* unity may be realized only when Masonic unity will truly exist, that is to say what there will emanate from one unique center, an immense superior congress which will give the intellectual and administrative impulse to the secondary unique center of each State, or nation, which will communicate this impulse, we do not say to the *Chapters*, *Councils*, *Consistories*, etc., etc., these centers of discord are to be abolished, but to the lodges of its jurisdiction.

In order to achieve this goal, conceived for centuries, that is to say in order to succeed in the formation of a unique *universal* center, it is indispensably *necessary* that there is only one sole direction in each State, and as there is but one Masonry, there may exist only one sole hearth. An authority, no matter the age of its usurpation, which will have come, by fraud or by tolerance, to abuse the good faith of the Masons, and to raise altar against altar, by exciting disunion[104] cannot be truly Masonic, and its abolition must be pronounced[105]. Do we wish to preserve and restore honor to Freemasonry? It is necessary to return to the principles and no longer depart therefrom.

Freemasonry, for more than a century and a third that it has existed in France, has constantly given enough proofs of order and wisdom to the different governments which have succeeded one another during this long period, to aspire to be finally recognized as a useful association of *morals* and *beneficence*. We have seen that the revolutions stopped its progress and suspended its works. If, at the appearance of a new government, the Masonic authority has been eager to bring its felicitations and prayers to the new head of France, it was not to make an adulation, Masonry enlightens and does not flatter; but, composed of the elite of the citizens, it bears the homage of its constant fidelity to the laws and to the Sovereign, with the expression of its joy at the recognition of the Order and the well-being of its homeland.

We may without doubt hope that, under a GRAND MASTER as enlightened as the one who presides over the supreme administration of the institution, and who has not ceased to show the active interest that he brings to its prosperity, it will be possible to obtain the protection highly accorded by the emperor Napoleon I; and the benevolent tolerance accorded today by a strong government, whose head put all his ambition into creating and founding an authentic recognition which will place Freemasonry at the rank of the institutions protected by law, under the direction of the Minister of the Interior.

But then, it will be of every necessity that the G.O. be in fact, as it is lawfully, the unique regulator of the Masonic Order in France, under the high oversight of its G.M., and that the other supposedly *Masonic* authorities arrange themselves under its banner, if it is suitable for it to admit them there, because it will have to be (as it should have been, if it had been able to uphold its rights) the SOLE power responsible for Masonic acts and deeds before the civil authority.

In this hypothesis, we would counsel it to return to the pure and simple administration of true Freemasonry, symbolic Freemasonry, summed up in its three grades, reviewed and completed.

For this it would only be necessary to remember the solemn deliberation, made by its predecessors on October 3, 1777, and to set into action, for ever, these principles of an incontestable truth:

"This multitude of grades, whose form varies to infinity, which, *all*, mutually oppose one another, and whose aim escapes at each instant the penetration of the most enlightened Mason, *is contrary to the true spirit of our Order.*"

Let the G.O. return from the fear that has inspired in it the badly informed and not very logical opinion of its commission of 1848, which *has unanimously pronounced for the upholding of the high grades.*

"Although we are not unaware," *it adds*, "that they constitute in Masonry a nonsense; that this nonsense, which created *Pontiffs*, *Princes*, and *Sovereigns* is absurd and shocking; we fear to weaken the G.O., to place it in a state of inferiority vis-à-vis *Scottish Supreme Councils.*"

But we have shown that the basis of these *Supr. Couns.*, like every system of high grades which replaces fraternal equality with individual Sovereignty, that is to say union with perturbation, is inhumanitarian and anti-Masonic. It belongs, then, to the G.O. to renew the example given in 1783 by the provincial lodges of *Frankfort* and *Wetzlar.* To enlighten the workshops, by freeing them from the shameful yoke of the false systems, ought to be the role of the G.O. which, in rendering to the Order this immense service, could not but add to the high consideration that it enjoys. The G.L. of Edinburgh which, from the beginning, has stigmatized by its scorn all the high grades, and the majority of the G.L.'s of Germany which have rejected their practice; have they lost their consideration? They have been, on the contrary, elevated into the spirit of the true Mason.

We think, therefore, that the commission of the G.O., after having laid bare the hideous wound with which the high grades have covered, distorted, and deformed the Masonic body, would counsel the rejection of it, not the support. But as it is proper to rebuild when one destroys, it should have proposed a model of instruction so that French Masons, raised to the 3rd degree, could no longer be placed in supposed inferiority of *knowledge* among the high grade brethren in any country. It could have proposed, as we propose, to decree, after purifying all, that there will be established in one of the principal lodges of each city a *school of general instruction* for each of the degrees.

In the 1st, the professor would explain all that is known of the ancient initiations, from *Zoroaster* up to the extinction of the mysteries in the Gauls and at Rome.

In the 2nd, he would demonstrate that after a slumber of many centuries, the renaissance of the ancient doctrine is due to the scholar *Ashmole*, whose rituals have been put openly into practice by the G.L. of England on June 24, 1717, certain date of present Freemasonry. And that the architect-builders who have had for their successors the monks, and after these latter the associations of stonecutter masons, to whom have succeeded societies of trade-guilds, have never had any connection with the philosophical and secret doctrine of the *initiates* who, later, have taken as a veil the denomination of *Freemasons*, especially because of the symbolic interpretation of the tools. The professor would then make known the progressive march of the institution in each land, according to the impulse given by the G.L. of England, its establishment in France, under the direction of the G.L. to which has succeeded the G.O., sole regular authorities which have had the true Masonry. Finally, the moral, philanthropic, and civilizing aim of the Order.

And in the 3rd, he would treat, after the interpretation of the grade, on the invention of the super-Masonic rites and systems, on the laudable or condemnable aim of their authors. He would initiate his listeners into the most important grades of these régimes, by means of the rituals which would be placed at their disposal.

The result of these instructions would be similar, with more perfection, since each professor would bring thereto the contribution of his knowledge, to the FASTES INITIATIQUES which, at first, could serve as guide.

At the end of a year or two of professorship, who would be, in any land, the very highest graded Mason who would dare to compare the vanity of his title, the futility of his decorations, to this ensemble of positive knowledge of a *French Master*? This intellectual revolution, begun in France, would be universalized very quickly. - Then, the Mason honored with the grade of Master would see, as formerly, only equals around him, and would no longer have the shame of counting, like today, thirty classes of superiors so pompously and ridiculously titled, and who, for the most part, have not even gained in ribbons what they lack in instruction.

CHAPTER XXIV
On the Reform of the Symbolism

We have made known, in the chapters which precede:

1. The rites and the numerous grades that, since *Ramsay*, innovators, inspired by charlatanism, pride, and speculation, have spread into the world of the Masons;
2. The systems, more or less philosophical, that reformers, animated with the desire to do better than their predecessors, have produced, principally in Germany;
3. The anomaly, in true Masonry, of the *Rite of Heredom*, in twenty-five degrees, whose system is Templar and the origin unknown;
4. And the fraudulent addition of eight incoherent grades, made to the Rite of Heredom, in order to make thereof a new régime, under the false denomination of *Ancient and Accepted Scottish Rite in Thirty-Three Degrees*, which addition is tarnished by a deceitful origin well proven.

All have wished to add, to ameliorate, to make anew, and have produced only misshapen *superfluities* with the ancient Masonic symbolism, which needs only to be recast, especially in the third part, altered, for political cause, towards the end of the 17th century.

We have uttered the vow to see all these systems, of which the least fault is not being Masonic, relegated to the libraries of the lodges, to aid in the general instruction of the brethren, who will find some good wheat in this immense heap of chaff, and who, in view of so many aberrations and impotent attempts, will be healed, if they are so inclined, from the sickness of *imitation*.

We invite the erudite Masons to draw their inspiration from what they might find of good in this book, in order to improve the *first three grades*, which are and ought to be the whole of Masonry, and to give them every regular complement that their nature demands; which the high grades have in vain attempted to do, because their authors, instead of going back to the source of things, have, in the interest of a sect, consequently non-Masonic, stopped half way, by speaking only of the *crusades*, which are a digression in Freemasonry, or of the *Temple of Solomon*, imitated form the temple of Tyre, which was but the reproduction of that of Memphis, symbol of the eternal temple of nature.

We are going to reproduce a rather pleasing attempt which has been made in the laudable aim of completing the *Mastership*. We do not approve of this work in its entirety; but as we find, in its few pages, much more of true Masonry than in the entire collection of the hundreds of grades called *Scottish*, we think that it may be useful to consult this attempt, which has for its title THE DECORATED MASTER, *in three parts*.

In every hypothesis, the reading of this grade may only be agreeable to the young Masons who will find here a fruitful supplement to their instruction. All that one reads here has already been said, but has not been, like here, presented in a body of doctrine orthodox enough.

The Decorated Master in Three Points

First Point

FIRST CHAMBER, CALLED SECRET OR OF MEDITATION

There must be two contiguous chambers for the two receptions. The first chamber, hung in black, is lighted by a sepulchral lamp. The brethren here are vested in black.

JEWEL: a silver sun; in the center, a gold triangle in a crown of acacia.

The president having been assured that the chamber is covered within and without, says: With me, my brothers! By the sign (of horror)! By the battery (secret)! The secret chamber is open.

RECEPTION. The introducer leads the candidate and knocks at the door as a Master.

Question. - *See who knocks.* Answer. - A simple M., having the name *Gabaon.* Q. - *Let the tomb of Hiram be open to him.* (The candidate is introduced by the steps and comes to order as a Master.)

The questions that we omit are those of the Mastership.

Q. - *What do the five perfect points of the Mastership signify?*

A. The junction of the feet signifies that I am to march to the relief of my brethren; the bending in of the knees, that I am to adore the G. Arch. of the Univ.; the junction of the hands, that I owe assistance to my brethren; the application of the hands upon the shoulders, that I must enlighten my brethren with my council; the fraternal kiss is an image of the tender and intimate union which ought to reign between us.

Q. - *What good has been bequeathed to the children of Hiram by the crime which has deprived them of their father?*

A. - Hope. Q. - *On what is it founded?*

A. - On the power and goodness of the G. Arch. of the Univ.

Q. - *Gabaon*, receive as a token of the esteem of the secret Masters this key which assimilates you to them. It opens the tabernacle of the mysteries of Masonry. Remain a few moments in the tomb of Hiram, and meditate here on his death.

All withdraw, with the exception of the introducer who remains with his, without speaking to him.

Second Point

SECOND CHAMBER CALLED OF PERFECTION

This chamber, hung in green, is lighted by twenty-seven lights; one upon each altar, seven in the south, five in the north, and twelve in the east. It is adorned with shrubs, garlands, and flowers. In the middle, a tripod with fire; upon the altar of the Master, a box of incense. The brethren are vested with white robes.

Q. - *Ven. Brother First Surv., what do you come here to do?*

A. - To adore the G. Arch., and to perfect the temple.

Q. - *What do you bring?* A. - Zeal, fervor, and constancy.

Q. - *Where do you seek the materials for the completion of the temple?*

A. - In the heart of my brothers.

Q. - *Are you a decorated Master or a simple Master, secret and perfect?*

A. - I know the triangle, the circle, and its quadrature.

Q. - *Why are we no longer surrounded by darkness? Whence comes that our brows are no longer imprinted with sorrow?* A. - The work is accomplished, the day succeeds the night, and life succeeds death. Q. - Let us thank, therefore, the one who fills us each day with his blessings.

Stand and to order! Invocation to *Jehovah*. They respond *amen*.

The Very Respectable throws incense on the cassolette. All turn towards the east, bend the right knee, bow the head, and meditate for a moment.

CLOSING. *With me*! *By the sign* (of admiration, by lifting the hands and the eyes toward heaven)! *By the battery* (three times three blows)! ACCLAMATION: *Vivat* (three times)!

Third Point

The introducer leads the aspirant to the door of the *green* chamber, called *of perfection*, and has him knock three times.

Q. - *See who knocks*.

A. - It is a simple and secret Master, named *Moabon*, who wishes to pass from the chamber of meditation into the chamber of *perfection*. Q. - *Ask him when he comes*.

A. - From the lodge of Apprentice, where he rough-hewed the coarse stone, symbol of ignorance; from the lodge of *Companion*, where he whetted his tools on the pointed cubic stone, symbol of emulation; from the middle chamber, called chamber of *revelation*, where he worked on the tracing board, symbol of genius; and from the secret chamber, or chamber of *meditation*, in which, after examination on his Masonic knowledge, the Very Respectable has given him a key which opens the tabernacle of the mysteries. Q. - *Let Moabon be introduced*.

Q. - *Moabon, are you a secret Master*? A. - I have passed from the square to the compass, I have mingled my tears with those of my brethren, I have meditated in the tomb.

Q. - *What do you seek*? A. - The secret of the Masters.

Q. - *How will you find it*? A. - By means of this key.

Q. - *Where do you keep it hidden*? A. - In a coral chest, surrounded by ivory.

Q. - *Of what metal is it*? A. - Of any, without being less precious thereby.

Q. - *What keeps you from using this key*?

A. - I am waiting for you to show me how to use it.

I consent thereto, if you yourself consent to renewing, at the foot of the altar, the promises that you have already sworn in the Order. A. - *Order it, Respectable Master*.

He takes his obligation. The president says to him:

"Receive, Moabon, with this kiss, sign of the fraternal alliance that you have just contracted with us, the insignia of perfection and the name of *Johaber*."

PROCLAMATION. Vener. Brothers 1st and 2nd Surveillants, proclaim upon your columns that the architect *Hiram* is replaced, in the Masonic works, by *Johaber*, his son, his emulator, and his avenger, whom we shall henceforth enlighten with his brilliant lights.

INSTRUCTION … Q. Whence come you?

A. - From the lodge of Apprentice, etc. (See above, and add: and from the chamber of perfection, where I am using this key.)

Q. - *What does this key represent?*

A. - The work which leads to knowledge, meditation, and even perfection.

Q. - *What names do you give to the principal ornaments of the temple?*

A. - Beneficence, virtue, friendship, knowledge.

Q. - *What is the grade of Apprentice?*

A. - It is the birth of a Mason; we have not confided in the Appr.; but we have studied his inclinations and his character, in order to know what may be obtained from him eventually. We have proceeded toward him by physical and moral proofs, before attaching ourselves to him more directly.

Q. - *What does the Apprentice Mason Do?* A. – He wanders in the darkness, the thunder rumbles over his head, the murderous swords clash around him; he crosses the waves and the flames; then, the agitated elements calm and the light appears to him.

Q. - *Explain yourself.* A. - Darkness is the emblem of the prejudices which obscure the judgment of the profane; the thunder and noise of the weapons, of the catastrophes that ambition, falsehood, and ignorance prepare for the right-thinking man; the waves and the flames strip the neophyte of the errors and vices of a perverse world, and the appearance of the light signals his entrance into a new world, where reigns virtue and truth.

Q. - *What is the grade of Companion?* A. - The youth of the Mason: the Masters let the Companion advance by himself and show him a confidence which excites him to good works.

Q. - *What does the Companion do?* A. – By five mysterious journeys, he is led toward the sanctuary, where the brilliant glimmer of the Blazing Star enlightens his heart and animates him with a noble ambition.

Q. - *Explain yourself.* A. - The five journeys represent the five phases of life; the neophyte receives, for each of them, wise instructions. He learns, by the mallet and the chisel, that it is with the love of labor; by the compass and the rule, that it is with a just heart and an ordered mind; by the crowbar, that it 1s with the strength of soul; by the square, that it is by the perfect regularity of his works; by the liberty of his hands, that it is with a soul free of prejudice, that one arrives in the sanctuary of the temple. The letter G instructs the Comp. that knowledge, as well as virtue, is the path thereof, and the blazing star sees to present to him that a glorious reward will be the prize of his labors.

Q. - *What is the Mastership?* A. - An edifice divided into three distinct parts.

Q. *What are they?* A. - The chambers of revelation, meditation, and perfection.

Q. - *What is the chamber of revelation?* A. - The middle chamber, where the Companion receives the first point of the Mastership, that is to say, important revelations.

Q. - *What is the chamber of meditation?* A. - The black or secret chamber, called the tomb of *Hiram*, where the simple Master receives the second point of Mastership, comes to meditate on the revelations which have been made to him, and to seek the key of the tabernacle of the mysteries.

Q. - *What is the chamber of perfection?* A. - The green chamber or council of the decorated Masters, where the simple and secret Master receives the third point of Mastership, by making use of the key of the tabernacle of the mysteries of Masonry.

Q. - *What is the grade of simple Master?* A. - It is the mature age of the Master, and the type of the mysterious ceremonies of all the ancient and modern cults.

Q. - *What does the simple Master do?* A. - He learns gratifying and distressing truths that may be deposited only in a discreet, firm, and magnanimous heart, truths which would trouble the spirits of a child and of a young man that misfortune and bliss have not yet tried.

Q. - *What is the grade of secret Master*? A. - It is the intermediary age between maturity and old age.

Q. - *What does the secret Master do*? A. - He reflects, calculates, and questions. He is afflicted, he hopes.

Q. - *What is the grade of perfect Master*? A. - It is the old age of the Mason.

Q. - *What does the perfect Master do*? A. - He acquires the experience of men and of things; he establishes himself to the point where there is no longer uncertainty, and, reaching the apogee of philosophical power, he leaves the path in order to be seated at the end, between wisdom and truth.

Q. - *What is the secret of Masonry*? A. - I divide it into five distinct parts.

Q. - *What is the first*? A. - The exposition of the natural, universal, and immutable religion, by means of the symbols and maxims.

Q. - *What is the second*? A. - The secret of the operations of nature.

Q. - *Would you have discovered it*? A. - Far be it from me to believe so; but we explain, by the *quaternary* and the *monad*, what the Great Architect has left to man to divine. The quaternary represents movement, which is the *cause*; fermentation, which is the *means*; putrefaction, which is the *effect*; death and life, which are the *results*. By joining to the quaternary, the monad, which is the *matter* or *subject*, we represent the five elements of generation, whose operations are expressed symbolically in the middle chamber, which in this sense, is the *womb* where is accomplished the mystery of the reproduction of beings.

Q. - *What is the third*? A. - The perfection of the temple, that is to say the perfection of the human heart, of which, under this point of view, the temple is but an allegory.

Q. - *What is the fourth*? A. - The victory of darkness and winter over the sun, and that of the sun over the darkness and winter, represented by the death and resurrection of *Hiram* (who is the SUN), minister of Solomon, the most powerful and wisest of the monarchs (who is GOD), conservator of the *temple* (which is the EARTH), and master of the *workers* (who are the MEN); Hiram is stricken by three villainous Companions (which are the *three wintry months*), drawn from the tomb and avenged by nine virtuous Masters (which are the *nine months of spring, summer, and autumn*, which give the flowers, harvests, and fruits).

Q. - *What is the fifth part of the Masonic secret?*

A. - The victory of errors and passions over the truth or virtue, and that of truth or virtue over the errors and passions, represented likewise by the death and resurrection of Hiram (who is *truth* or *virtue*); also, Hiram is stricken by three villainous Companions (which are *ambition*, *falsehood*, and *ignorance*), drawn from the tomb and avenged by the nine virtuous Masters (which are the *virtues* and the *Masonic duties*).

Q. - *What is the aim of the ceremonies retracing the movement of the stars, the vicissitudes of the seasons and the operations of nature*?

A. - To render homage to the G. Arch. by celebrating the wonders of his power and his wisdom, and to inculcate in the heart of the initiates, by these representations, the love, veneration, and recognition which are due to him.

Q. - *What is signified by the jewel of the simple, secret, and perfect Master, or Decorated Master*?

A. - The three points of the triangle signify *past*, *present*, and *future*; the entire triangle, *eternity* or *Eternal God*. The three angles signify again *strength*, *wisdom*, and *beauty*, attributes of God. They signify also *salt*, *sulphur*, and *mercury*, principles of the work of

God. The three angles represent too the three kingdoms of nature, empire of the Creator, and the three phases of the perpetual revolution: *birth*, *life*, and *death*, revolution that God governs without being governed. In short, the triangle is the emblem of the Divinity. The crown in the form of a circle which surrounds the triangle symbolizes the immense expanse, the infinite power of the G. Arch., and the sun is the sign of his unity and beneficence.

Q. - *Why does the Decorated Master say that he knows the circle, the triangle, and its quadrature?*

A. – Because he effectively knows the meaning of these symbols. The first two have been explained. The third recalls to us the four duties of perfection: fraternal love, doubt in what cannot be demonstrated, to do only what we would want ourselves to do, and to await the final hour with all confidence in the goodness of God.

Q. - *What is the origin of Masonry?*

A. - The human intelligence, in developing itself, gave birth to a multitude of goods and evils. Men erected to the faith altars of truth and falsehood. The sages were forced to gather secretly in order to render a faithful cult to this deity soon forbidden upon the earth. Thus, was born INITIATION or the *allegorical cult.* It rendered illustrious the rivers of the Ganges and the Nile, Greece and Italy. *Moses*, raised in the Egyptian wisdom, modified it and gave it to the Hebrews; the crusades and the pilgrims brought it, they say, into Europe.

Q. - *What proof do you have of this long transmission?*

A. - The similitude existing between all the religions and their legends: the Indian *Vinayuyen*, the Egyptian *Osiris*; the *Adonis*, *Hercules*, and *Bacchus* of the Greeks; the *Atys* of the Phrygians, the Jewish *Hiram* and the modern *Christ*, are but one sole and same allegorical personage.

Q. - *What is signified by the sign of the simple, secret, and perfect Master?*

A. - *Horror* in the chambers of revelation and meditation, and *admiration* in the perfect chamber.

Q. - *What does the number SEVEN signify?*

A. - The seven planets, the seven metals, the septenary periods of man.

Q. - *What does the number TWELVE signify?* A. - The three Companions and the nine Masters of the legend of Hiram; the twelve apostles of the legend of Jesus, or the twelve months of the year, the twelve works of Hercules, the twelve tribes of Israel.

Q. - *What is your name?* A. - In the middle chamber, Gabaon; in the tomb of Hiram, *Moabon*; in the green chamber, *Johaber.*

Q. - *Why are you called child of the widow?* A. - Because man is the son of the earth, which is the widow of the sun in the hibernal season.

Q. - *What are the duties of every true Mason?* A. - To glorify God, to love his brothers, and to render homage to the truth.

This instruction is followed by a rather long discourse by the Orator, that the *Abeille* maçonnique (1831) reproduces with the ritual. We note here this passage:

"Since Masonry is the natural, universal, and immutable religion; since Mastership in its three points of revelation, meditation, and perfection, is the crowning of the edifice, and since you are a simple, secret, and perfect Master, there you are invested with the high priesthood of the cult never soiled with the blood of men, which affirms the belief in God by the ingenious ceremonies retracing his wonders, and consolidates in the hearts love and virtue by a system of touching and expressive symbols. Our mission is *to travel in order to spread the light and reunite what is dispersed.*"

CLOSING. - *Vener. Brother 1st Surv., how old are you?*

A. - As a simple Master, seven years; as a secret master, twenty-one years; as a perfect Master, I no longer count.

Q. - *What is your situation*? A. - A perfect quietude; for the trials are passed, and we have no more but to reflect.

The president has it announced that he is going to close the chamber of perfection; he strikes three blows (*repeated by the Surv.*) and says: *Glory to God*! All repeat while striking three blows: *Homage to the truth*! (all, etc.) *Love to our brothers*! (all, etc.) *The Council is closed.*

We see that this attempted complement of the Mastership has been conceived well enough to have to be reproduced in its entirety, as being able to guide the brothers so disposed to attempt a similar perfecting in the projected reform.

CHAPTER XXV

The following régime, called ORDER OF THE UNKNOWN PHILOSOPHER JUDGES, IN TWO GRADES, belongs to the Jesuitico-Templar system, continued in the *Order of Christ.* It is interesting, in that it makes known the means employed by a powerful Order to choose, attract, and retain its adepts. The introduction would not be out of place in the discourse of a lodge orator, on the day of initiation. There is truth in the judgment borne upon the high grades, and upon the *Ancient and Accepted Scottish Rite.* They acknowledge here that the modern Templars and the Jesuits have taken, in order to better propagate themselves, the veil of Masonry. The interpretations on some grades, made from the Templar point of view, are not without interest. It summarizes, by itself alone, many of the grades relating to the *Order of the Temple.* That is why we have deemed it fitting to reproduce it nearly in its entirety. This remarkable ritual is Masonic only in form: the jewel of the adept is a *dagger*, and his *work is vengeance.* Finally, it is a high grade: it alone is the truth, all the others are in error; it is in this way that the fabricators of all these productions mutually render justice to themselves.

Order of Unknown Philosophers, in two points

First Point

GRADE OF NOVICE

INTRODUCTION

The human race enjoyed in peace the blessing of life. Directed by the simple laws of nature, he passed serene days. In these happy times reigned innocence, and all preserved, without wishing to depart therefrom, the equilibrium that the Creator had given him. The bliss was general and perfect, nothing could be added thereto, as also no anxiety had yet caused tears to flow. The golden age, at last, flourished, and Pandora had not yet brought the fatal blow. This calm did not last long; soon *ambition*, impure mother, gave birth to the monster which would be the mother of so many other monsters and give death to humanity. The infernal *tyranny*, fruit worthy of such a mother, fixed its stay upon this earth formerly so happy, and established is régime there. It set all in order in order to enslave all and succeeded only too much therein. Hiding its abominable designs under the appearance of protection and benevolence, it easily seduced the simple and upright men. Its success endured beyond its expectation; it was itself astonished with the progress that its domination made, and with their rapidity. Nothing stopped it any longer and it surpassed itself. Through rewards artfully distributed, it could increase the number of its adulators. This number became prodigious; it could impose upon all so well; it could so well enchain them in bonds that it soon no longer hesitated to lift the mask and show itself uncovered.

It was then that they took notice of the artifice; but it was already too late. The chains were clinched; the blessing had disappeared and even unto the hope to see it reborn. The age of iron, in a word, had taken the place of the first, vice dominated virtue, and, even unto our day, all the efforts have been impotent to recall the bliss of the first age, that happy age so worthy of our regrets, that age that the poets teach us as the happiest of times, and in which the arts flourished and where the destructive art of Bellona was yet unknown.

However, all hope was not lost. In the midst of general slavery, some sages escaped the power of despotism and were able to keep themselves free. These intrepid philosophers preserved faithfully the precious deposit confided to their keep, and, from age to age, they transmitted it unto us. May the spirits of these illustrious ancestors see from their celestial retreat and applaud the efforts that our Order renews ceaselessly in order to accomplish the great work, the elements of which they have left to us.

It is in the view of recalling these happy times, it is in view of forever perpetuating the history thereof, as well as the fatal events which have made them vanish, that the triple power has undertaken to raise a tabernacle supported by 26 iron columns, each bearing the name of one of the letters of the alphabet of the philosophers. These columns are destined to receive the golden rings that the adepts are to furnish on the day of their initiation, so that the first column called *Abraxas* received all the rings sent by the brethren whose names begin with A, and so on.

By the exactitude of this correspondence, the Masonic world will see the day arrive when, by the infinite number of its workers, it will have contributed to the edification of an altar, whose columns will be of the purest metal, though they had been of iron in their origin, which will then symbolize the great era of regeneration.

In this fortunate era, the Order will distribute rewards to the brethren whose names will be found in the Holy of Holies, and who shall be known by the hieroglyphs inserted into their rings, after having served at the construction of an eternal temple, which will be revealed to the chapters enjoying nine years of installation.

Such is the aim of this sublime grade. Let the new initiates be well permeated with the principles that it contains; the grand and sublime truths that it contains will contribute not a little to console them in adversity and to make shine in their soul some ray of hope for a better future.

PRELIMINARY INSTRUCTION

When one has been well assured of the moral qualities of the brother that one wishes to initiate, they research his capacities... etc... It is necessary that he be at least Rose-Croix, that he be already instructed in the royal art, and that he has shown dispositions towards receiving the impressions which are going to be given to him.

As he ought to be unaware of our sublime grade, he could not have desired to be admitted hereto but by whatever glimpse thereof may have been allowed to our friend and brother. It is necessary not to anticipate his desires. he must be left to want, for some time, to be further instructed ... His admission decided, his friend tells him that his mission is finished, and shows him a mark, the bearer of which will be the one (*an unknown*) who will come to take him and whom he is to follow.

RECEPTION

The reception room is an underground vault into which one descends by a trap- door which shuts the vault, and by means of a ladder that they remove and which is replaced after the reception. The cavern is lighted by only a single lamp; upon the walls, painted black, are the following hieroglyphs:

South Side

A. 1. A rock.
B. 2. A bull's head.
C. 3. A crocodile.
D. 4. A medal; at the center, the sun; around, the six planets and the legend: *Sol solus in medio.*
E. 5. A harpy, half woman, half serpent, holding two lit torches.
F. 6. A five-pointed radiating star.

North Side

G. 1. A trowel in a radiant circle.
H. 2. Sabre or Phrygian harpé, gold hilt, one reads here *Adonai* in gold letters.
J. 3. A closed right hand; the index finger raised indicating the heavens.
K. 4. The bust of Janus upon a square house.
L. 5. The full moon.

East Side

M. 1. A radiant goat's head.
N. 2. A vase from where comes out a whitish liquid.
O. 3. A dog's head.
P. 4. A square pedestal resembling marble.
Q. 5. A *quadrifons* head of Janus.
R. 6. A wheel surmounted by an evil genius and a cupid which stops it course.

West Side

S. 1. A serpent forming several folds.
T. 2. A sun with nine very luminous rays.
U. 3. A weapon in agate.
V. 4. A caduceus.
X. 5. The figure of *Xantus*, the brow girt with a diadem, placed above a painted door.
Y. 6. The head of *Argus*.
Z. 7. A faulx.

Each of these figures is preceded by the letter which, in the writing of the grade, corresponds to the hieroglyphic number indicated in this table:

1	2	3	4	5	6	7	8	9	10
a	i	x	l	e	g	f	p	s	n
11	12	13	14	15	16	17	18	19	20
r	h	j	c	k	z	v	t	m	q
21	22	23	24	25					
d	b	o	y	r					

The members of the chapter are vested in a black robe with a hood which may veil the figure.

The candidate having been introduced by the ladder into the underground vault, they give him a clear view, so that he can consider the objects which surround him and make some reflections.

The president breaks the silence, questions him on all his grades and says to him:

"My beloved brother, the multitude of grades, some incoherent, through which you have been obliged to pass in order to arrive at this place, are, we may tell you with frankness, as so many baubles that the supreme chiefs of our initiation have left to the grandchildren condemned by them to vegetate upon the gilded benches of a Masonry which is so only in name. If you have sometimes reflected upon the divergence which reigns in the multitude of inferior degrees, you will have noticed, without doubt, that the general aim of the Order is to *see change take place* in the *ignorant multitude,* and to purify, so to speak, in the crucible of the cup, the true Masons, and to prepare them so that the essential secret of the association may be confided to them without danger, and even to give them the keep of that sacred deposit, which is to be transmitted from age to age, up to the moment when the divine Trinity will ordain the accomplishment of the great work.

"The grade that you are going to receive, very worthy brother, is the first rung of the true ladder of the philosophers. You are not unaware of its existence, and it is through the intimate conviction that you have acquired from your eminent virtues, that, by unanimous consent, we have called you to us. In rending the veil with which your eyes were covered, we offer you the knowledge of the sublime art which leads to the discovery of the true philosopher's stone, vainly sought by the common Masons. These men, in their profound error, and in the delirium of the most vile cupidity, taking literally the mystical language of the sages, wish to obtain a metal, an object worthy of their desires, and they consume their fortune and their life in unfruitful research. Far from us are those who attach to the pursuit of our secrets so vile a passion, the thirst for gold, or so indiscreet a curiosity! We choose our adepts only among the enemies of foolish pride, vain cupidity, and culpable ambition. If, in the symbolic lodges, we make use of extraordinary costumes; if we employ a sometimes-bizarre language, it is only in order to distinguish more easily, in these nurseries, the bad plants, and to avoid choosing them for election. You have long been the object of our observations and our study; you have earned our solicitude, and the difficulties will be leveled under your steps. You ought to be all the more flattered to see yourself carried, all at once, to the pinnacle of the knowledge of the sublime art, where the adepts are very few in number. But, before going further, we must give you a glimpse of our obligations. There is no longer anything symbolic among us. The blindfold of illusions no longer veils the eyes, it is the truth alone which is going to dictate my words. When you will have pronounced your new obligation, you will cease to belong to yourself, your very life will have become the property of the Order. The most absolute obedience, the entire abnegation of your will, the prompt execution, without reflection, of the orders which will be transmitted to you on the part of the supreme power, such shall be your principal duties. The most terrible punishments are reserved to the perjurers… and what is a perjury in the eyes of the Order? The one who, in even the slightest matters, disregards the orders that he has received from his chief, or refuses to execute them; for nothing is indifferent in our Sublime Order. I ought, however, to reassure, on one point, your conscience; it is that never will the orders that you receive be contrary to your duties towards society. Far from it, our association tending only towards the bettering of men, carefully avoids all that may wound their rights. Shortly, my brother, you will know more on our Sublime Order, and you will gain the conviction that the major part of the elevated Masons, with what they think, with the highest discoveries of the Masonic art, deceived by a vain science, are still very far from the truth, *multi vocati, pauci vero electi.*

"Know how to read our sacred code, and soon, uniting your efforts to those of your brethren, you will hasten the moment of the general bliss, sole recompense that you may expect from our painful labors. (*A pause.*)

"Are you persuaded, my brother, that the Masonic Order professes that the Scottish Rite is in possession of the Sovereign principle of the royal art, and that it knows, alone, the greatest secret of Masonry?" (*They respond*; he continues.) "The grade that you are going to receive is the *ne plus ultra* of Masonry, and it is here that the order is absolutely exposéd; here, that the hieroglyphs which will have been presented to your view, in the various grades, are explained and entirely revealed. There are no more declamations of schemes to impose such upon you, the truth alone shall be employed to seduce you. Your employ, in the future, will be to form men and to reward the virtues that you recognize in them. You are to learn here how one may tie the hands and feet of the usurpers of the rights of man. You will learn to govern humans and to dominate them, not by fear, but by virtue. It is necessary, in a word, that you consecrate yourself entirely to an Order which has undertaken to re-establish man in his primitive dignity. This is the domination of virtue. It is necessary that its secret, but no less powerful, government conduct the other governments toward this noble aim, without, nevertheless, allowing itself to be noticed, other than by the opinion and universal assent of society.

"There exists a considerable number of our brothers; we are spread into the most remote lands, all conducted by an invisible force. We labor, in concert, towards the great regeneration; and, united in body and soul, nothing may prevent the execution of the plan of architecture which has been traced for us by the divine Trinity. It is through a constant assiduity and in the most profound secret that we have already sketched out numerous works; we must achieve them for the welfare of humanity.

"Fix you sights, my dear brother, on the vast field that we open to your activity. Become our worthy collaborator and assist our efforts with all your means. There are no works, with us, without reward. In us, you see a part of the unknown legions united by indissoluble bonds to fight on behalf of the oppressed virtue. We owe the sublime knowledge that we teach only to the benevolence of our chiefs, who have been willing to grant it to us in order to excite our emulation and to engage us in new research. Imitate us, beloved brother, and merit the esteem of the *illustrious unknowns* who govern us." (*A pause.*)

"Have you quite decided, my brother, to render yourself worthy to keep watch, with your brethren, for the defense of the rights of nature and our Order?" (*They respond.*) "The step that you make today is the most important of your life. By receiving you into our Order, I expect of you two noble achievements, grand and worthy of you and of the glorious title of UNKNOWN JUDGE GRAND INQUISITOR. If you are good, honest, and faithful, you will respond to our vows and to our spirit; but if you come to be but a perjurer and a false brother, do not pledge yourself to us, you would be miserable and unhappy! Our vengeance would reach you anywhere. Reflect, there is still time. I am going to return your metals to you; withdraw yourself, if you feel repugnance towards entering among us. I caution you that this is not a vain trial, and that I speak to you very seriously. I repeat to you, reflect well on this, I await your final will..." (If he hesitates, they cover his eyes and lead him outside of the area of the locale, which he must not know. If he persists, he kneels at the feet of the initiating Sovereign Commander, the chest uncovered and holding with his left hand the point of a dagger to his heart, and his right hand in the left hand of the president, he pronounces his obligation.)

OBLIGATION. "I... promise obedience to the very perfect and holy Trinity, to the Grand Commander, First President, Supreme Judge of the Unknown Tribunal, Sovereign Grand Prince in this final grade, and, as much as it will depend on me, to admit no brother unworthy of this holy grade. I promise to work for the triumph of our Order; to defend it against all the false systems that they could attempt to introduce thereto. I promise particularly to assist my brother Philosopher Judges, to protect their innocence, as well as that of any other man unjustly accused. I swear to never defend the cause of a tyrant, and to give up all claims to the favor of the great. I promise to fight courageously for the regeneration of society, for virtue, and for the liberty of all the brethren; to aid in destroying superstition and annihilating the usurpers of the rights of men, who enjoy today in peace goods that they have usurped from us; to never prefer my particular interest to the general good; and to follow in all the precepts of the Order. I oblige myself furthermore, and I promise solemnly to inform my initiating Grand Commander of all my discoveries and to keep him in my open heart, from this day forth; to consider all my brethren, elevated to this sublime grade, as my most sincere friends and worthy of the greatest respect, above the common Masons; finally, to be inclined toward the better will and without strange preoccupation. I promise to keep as holy all my domestic, social, and civil duties. So, help me God, for the happiness of my life and the repose of my soul!!!"

The initiator makes felt the point of the dagger which causes a slight prick, and resumes thus:

"Here you are, my worthy brother, well advanced in the career of illustrious men. You have just made the first step prescribed to all those who have the true desire to attain to the high knowledge of *Scottish* (Jesuitic) Masonry. You are, from this moment, a POSTULANT in the career of the *UNKNOWN PHILOSOPHER JUDGES*. From this day, keep yourself from kneeling at the feet of your equals, and even less still from those who pretend to be your superiors. Think maturely and remember that you belong presently to the great establishment which works for the welfare of humanity." (Then, taking into both hands those of the candidate, he adds:)

"By virtue of the powers which have been transmitted to me, and that I have merited by my long journeys, by my discretion, and by my zeal and my constancy, I receive and constitute you, very regularly, UNKONWN PHILOSOPHER JUDGE, GRAND INSPECTOR GENERAL; may you be ever worthy of this high favor." (He has the aspirant rise and resumes thus:)

"All that you have learned, very worthy brother, is not in order to attract those who, like you, have aspired to the grade that I have the right to confer, nor to inspire in them an indiscreet ardor; they must await the day of the light in silence. Confidence is the most authentic mark of a sincere friendship; we must increase the number of our brethren, but with discretion; we must avoid rendering this grade too common, and initiating too easily a person that we will have believed to be our friend. It is necessary that he be proved beforehand, and that we are most assured of the discretion of the one that we admit: *There are many called and few elected.*

"The obligation that you have just contracted instructs you on the first notions of this grade, which is the last of Masonry. If, in what I have said, or in what you have pronounced with me, you have had reason to make some remark, open yourself to me; it is my duty and in the interest of the Order to remove all your doubts and all your qualms." (If there are objections, the initiator combats and destroys them; if they are serious, they are referred to the supreme power and the reception is suspended; if there are none, they communicate to the candidate the *words*, *signs*, etc.[106], and invite him to prepare himself for the study that he is to make for the three years of his noviciate.)

Subject of the Studies OF THE NOVICE UNKNOWN PHILOSOPHER JUDGES

As the aim of the Order is the perfection of society, its first care is toward the choice of its members. All the initiates are employed at the research and study of those of the Masons who are worthy to be admitted among the *Unknown Philosophers.* They ought therefore, to have constantly their eyes about them, to follow the men since and even before their entrance into Masonry, which is the channel of proof. They must no longer neglect to *observe the conduct and the bearing of those of his brethren initiated into the sublime grade of Philosopher Judges*, who are known to him, and give an *account thereof* to his initiating Commander *with whom he must preserve his agreements of obedience and submission that he has promised to him*, as well as to the Order, in his obligation.

"The Unknown Philosopher Judge is to make a particular study of the art of knowing and judging the inclinations of men by their exterior air, their tastes, their manners of being, their affections, and even their clothing. Let him read *Lavater* and the works of the doctor *Gall*; let him familiarize himself with the art of *physiognomy*."

We are going to give here some of the inferences that may be drawn from the choice of *colors in clothes*, in supposing, however, that the choice is not obliged by profession, rank, or custom. There are first the *primitive colors*, which announce, in general, in their choice, more frankness in the character than he something more pronounced. The *false* colors, or those arising from mixture, are signs of indifference, frivolity, or instability, which, often, arises as much from education as from the foundation of the character. These impressions are susceptible to vary often and for a mere trifle. One may hope, however, to fix these characteristics.

ON THE PRIMITIVE COLORS

1. GOLDEN-YELLOW. - Color dedicated to the SUN (in Hebrew *schemesch*, sol or *Hhamah*, heat); it is the indication of the grandeur of the soul, of penetration.
2. BLUE. - Color consecrated to JUPITER (*Tsedek*); it is the general indication of magnanimity, promptness, emulation for all that is good and just.
3. WHITE. - Color consecrated to the MOON (*jareah*, or *lebanah*, because of its whiteness); it is an indication of modesty, of timidity. If a man wears a blue dress coat over white clothes, they will say that he seeks the truth; if the coat is of any other color, one may think that he is a suspicious, ambitious, avaricious character.
4. RED. - Color dedicated the MARS (*Maadim*, because of its reddish color). A blue coat and underneath the color red is an indication of immoderate ambition, a spirit of revolution, inclination towards cruelty, callousness.
5. GREEN. - Color consecrated to VENUS (*nogah*, scintillating). It is the indication of a character difficult to satisfy, of an impatient spirit, full of self-love, quick

to betray a cause, if he cannot obtain what he desires therefrom.

6. PURPLE. - Color dedicated to MERCURY (*chochab* [kokab], swift in travel). Indication of dexterity, intelligence, suppleness, but without delicacy; illegitimate ambition and covetousness.

7. BLACK. - Consecrated to SATURN (*schabethai*, who rests). Indication of laciturnity, profound reflections, curiosity, and prattling.

ON THE COMBINED COLORS

PURPLE AND BLUE. - Very liberal, envious.
PURPLE AND ROSY RED. - Greedy, cruel, fiery, haughty, subject to despair. WINE DREGS. - Slow, dull, poor discretion.
FLESH. - Libertine.
ROSE. - Inconstant, of an ambitious prodigality, disdainful[107].
LILAC. - Ignorant and avaricious.
DULL RED. - Sanguinary.
DAWN. - Friend of man.
CAPUCHIN. - True hypocrite.
PUCE. - Capricious.
BROWN-YELLOW. - Bad subject.
VIOLET. - Malicious, litigious.
OLIVE. - Easily moved to tears, lowers the eyes at the request of a service.
DAWN-MARIGOLD. - Prompt, choleric.
CLEAR YELLOW. - Knavish.
PALE YELLOW. - Distrustful.
CHAMOIS. - Good heart, compassionate, generous.
ROSY-WHITE. - To be excluded from the Order.
DRAB GREEN. - Incapable of great undertakings.
PEARL-GRAY. - Prodigious, lacking order, impatient.
HAZEL-GRAY. - Fine, subtle.
GRAY-WHITE. - Evil heart, wicked, imbecile, machine proper to many things.
AQUA-GREEN. - Active and frank.
IRIDESCENT. - Inconstant.
BEDIZENED. - Ignorant, arrogant, brutal.
AZURE-WHITE. - Elevated spirit, genius carried toward the high sciences.

One cannot deny that, in general, the color indicated by the predominant taste is a very great indication of the inclinations of the individuals. However, this rule is not infallible, and it is necessary that it be confirmed by other observations.

A man who wears only a single mark of his true taste, announces sincerity and the propensity towards virtue. No choice is the indication of a false or uncertain character. To allow others to impose their tastes upon oneself announces weakness and an inclination towards making bitter reflections. As we have just said, the colors of choice of an individual do not always suffice for gaining an accurate idea of his character. It is still necessary to study his customary manners; to grasp well the traits of his countenance. Man is before you, examine him: is he brown? Is he reddish? Is he pale, yellowish, or whitish? Are his eyes fixed or wild? Is he lively or languid? Is his gaze languishing, superb, ardent, or down-cast? How does he look at the face, boldly or to the side? Can he withstand a gaze with steadfastness? Has he a sprightly air? Does he look up or down? Is his brow unwrinkled, and in what sense, horizontally or vertically? Is his countenance noble or common, easy or affected? How does he carry his head, straight or inclined? Is his language regular, disordered, or interrupted? While speaking, does he agitate his hands, the body, or the head with vivacity? Does he approach those to whom he speaks, does he take them by the arm or by the coat? Is he a great speaker or taciturn? How does he walk, quickly or calmly? To whom does he owe his education? Has he always been under the eyes of his parents? What was his education? Has he traveled? In what lands? Is he constant and firm in his resolutions? Are the obstacles something for him? How may one win him? Is it by praise or meanness, by women, by money, by friends? Does he love his attire? Upon what does he exercise his will? Does he love good living? Is he sober, greedy, sensual? Is he discreet or copious in the wine? What is the character which dominates in his drunkenness? Is it tender or furious? Is he gay or sombre?

It is also necessary to seek to know whether the subject that you have in view sleeps little or much; whether he is a dreamer, a sleepwalker, if he talks in his sleep; whether he is difficult to wake; what kind of impression a sudden waking makes on him. *All these observations are to be noted with care* by the Unknown Philosopher Judge, *in order to be able to give an exact account* of a subject proposed by him.

After this outline of the objects of study, the initiating Commander resumes in these words:

"Among all the knowledge that you have just acquired, you will find, I think, the highest wisdom. There yet remains much else that I cannot give you in this day, but that you will obtain after the expiration of the three years of your noviciate, which may be abbreviated in consideration and reward for the good services that you will have been able to render to the Order in general and to some of our brethren in particular.

"It remains for me to give you the origin of the *Symbolic Ladder*, a more extensive explanation of which will be given to you when the time will have come for it."

ORIGIN OF THE SYMBOLIC LADDER

"The instructed Masons are not unaware that our Order was the first of the world, and that the religion which has emerged therefrom is the essence of all the civil associations, as well as the moral principles which have purified all the cults; that it is from the sanctuary of Masonry that have shot forth the rays of light which enlighten the universe. These Masons can no longer deny that, in the first times, there have never been recognized but *five degrees of knowledge*; that the number of twenty-five or thirty-three degrees, which form the framework of *écossisme*, is an effect of the love of innovations, or the product of some self-love; for it is constant that, of the reputed thirty-three practiced today, there are twenty-eight *apocryphal*, which merit no confidence.

"The Jesuits, who appropriated the hierarchal system of Masonry, increased the ladder by two degrees and brought it to seven. These skillful masters had, without much trouble, their innovations adopted by the *Adonhiramite* Masons, who, without further examination, regarded it as the true symbol of the mystical science. Here is the ladder:

1st	rung	Jakim,	The Jesuits interpret	Jnitiatio,
2nd	—	Tubalcain,	the initials of these	Temporalis,
3rd	—	Booz,	words as representing	Beneplacitus,
4th	—	Schibboleth,	the seven grades of	Scholasticus,
5th	—	Mac-benac,	their Order, to wit:	Magister,
6th	—	Ghomel,		Generalis,
7th	—	Nekam.		Noster.

"If you are zealous, my brother, as I am pleased to believe, you will read the history of *Ignatius of Loyola*[108] and of the *institution of the Jesuits*, and you will recognize there, not only the symbolic ladder, but even the reception of our Adonhiramite Masons; like them, *the novice* makes three journeys; he is neither naked nor clothed; he has the left breast uncovered, the right knee bare, the left shoe slipshod, etc. In what views have the Jesuits calculated the system of their organization on the Masonic ladder? Is it not because they had recognized the excellence thereof, and that this gradation was most proper to form men, as they wished to have them, and to achieve that unity of action that we seek in our Sublime Order?

"Will the Masons be less constant than these men, whose superiority one is forced to recognize that they have acquired, and by means of which they could have made the happiness of society if they had not turned all their views toward its domination? Will the Masons, having a more purified aim, have less success, if they wish to place therein all the zeal of which they are capable, if they wish to make use of all the knowledge that the age has bestowed upon them? We do not think so, and that is what we encourage, that is what excites us into the efforts that we make to enlighten men on their true interests, by recommending to them all the social virtues. You are called, my brother, to contribute to this truly divine work. Here is the true philosopher's stone with which all the metals are changed into gold. It is by the gathering of all the knowledge that the royal art furnishes that we can turn to the profit of society even unto the passions of men, by directing them and employing them, each according to his means and his faculties.

"Such are the lessons that we have received from our ancestors and from our predecessors, the too unfortunate Knights of the Temple, from whom we hold our institutions. If Europe has been enlightened, if the times of barbarous ignorance and superstition have disappeared for ever, it is to them that is due this blessing, and we cannot have too much recognition of them. Thus, do we hold the honor of succeeding them, and we do not want to deprive them of the glory which is restored to them. And as you have entered, like us, into their Order, I do not think that it is irrelevant to give you a summary of the deadly catastrophe which has stricken them in the most iniquitous and least merited manner."

ABRIDGED HISTORY OF THE DESTRUCTION OF THE KNIGHTS OF THE TEMPLE

"After the death of Benedict XI, occurring on July 31, 1304, the cardinals gathered to elect a new pope, and formed themselves into two factions, the one French the other Italian.

"Philippe-le-Bel, King of France, had projects that he could not accomplish without the assistance of the Pope who would be elected. His party formed divisions in the conclave in order to favor his designs. He sent to seek Bertrand de Goth, then archbishop of Bordeaux and, in the conference that he had with him, he informed him of his designs and of the power that he had to have him elected Pope, and that it would be him, if he swore to execute *seven propositions*, which he would make known to him, except the seventh, which he reserved until the moment of its execution, which was accepted by the ambitious prelate. Consequently, Philippe laid out to him the *six conditions* unknown to our history, and, after having exacted and received his oath for the execution of the seventh, he took as hostages the brothers and the nephew of Bertrand, who was elected Pope under the name of Clement V.

"He established his see at Lyon, where he carried out the first six conditions. When the favorable moment for the execution of the seventh had arrived, Philippe declared to him that it was to join with him in order to totally exterminate the *Knights of the Temple* within the entire expanse of Christendom.

"The motive of this cruel project was that some time before the death of Benedict XI, there occurred a sedition at Paris, occasioned by the alteration of the coinage, that Philippe had fabricated from a low alloy. The people mutinied, pillaged, and demolished the house of Etienne *Barbet*, Master of the Mint. Then, they went to the palace of the King, where they committed much violence.

"The knights, against whom envy had raised powerful enemies, were suspected of having excited the disorder. From that time, their ruin was resolved and sworn by Philippe. He no longer wanted but for a pretext. As with authority and force all becomes convenient, he easily found it; he created it. To this end, he chose two adventurers, named *Gérard Habé* and Benoit *Mahuc* (a ritual says *Monluc* or *Montluc*), to whom he proposed, under the hope of great rewards, to have themselves admitted among the Knights Templar, in order to then accuse them of the greatest crimes.

"Indeed, these two wretches, having an outward honesty, titles, and apparent qualities, were admitted. A short time later, they accused the whole Order of the greatest abominations, and demanded to be separated therefrom. It was here that they awaited it.

"As the wicked employ betrayal, yet do they fear the traitors. King Philippe let the two denunciators perish in the most cruel torments; and, under the pretext that they had provided him, he had arrested, on the same day, in all of France, all the Knights Templar who could be found. This order was executed on October 13, 1307, two years after the accusation brought by the two traitors. Their papers, their titles, their treasures, and their property were seized. The King *Charles d'Anjou* did the same in Provence. The Knights arrested in France were imprisoned at the Château de Melun in order to be judged. The Pope sent representatives to judge Jacques *Molay*, G.M., whom he had enticed to France with sixteen Knights, among whom were found *Guy*, brother of the Dauphin de Viennois, Hugues *Pérald* and Théod-Basile *de Menoncourt*. The G.M. and his companions were arrested, and the most cruel torments were exercised upon them, in order to force them to confess the crimes of which they were accused and of which they were innocent. Their trials concluded without success. Fifty-seven were burned alive in one day, and fifty-nine the following day; and they continued until the entire destruction of the Order.

"Jacques Molay and the three Knights, Guy, Péralde, and Menoncourt, were not included in these first executions, the Pope having reserved the judgment thereof. All the Knights were arrested, but all were not put to death. Jacques Molay and his three companions, after having suffered for seven years in the irons, were burned alive on March 11, 1314. They drew the pity and the tears of the spectators by their steadfastness and their heroic constancy, protesting their innocence, which was then demonstrated by a memorable event. The G.M., ready to die, said, addressing himself to God: 'Permit us to reflect on the torments that injustice and cruelty cause us to endure; forgive, O my God, the false accusations which have caused the entire destruction of the Order, of which your providence had made me the head, and permit that one day the undeceived world know better those who strove to live for you. We hope in your goodness, the reward for the torments and death that we suffer, to enjoy your divine presence in the abode of happiness.' Then, addressing the people, he said: 'You who see us ready to perish in the flames, you will judge our innocence; for I summon the Pope Clement V, within forty days, and Philippe-le-Bel, within a year, to appear before the legitimate and terrible throne of God, in order to give an account of the blood that they have unjustly and wickedly shed!' - They were precipitately dragged off to the scaffold, in fear of the movements of the people. The prophecy of Jacques Molay was accomplished: Clement V died around the following April 20 (1314), and Philippe-le-Bel, November 29, 1314, at Fontainebleau, at 46 years old[109].

"Very illustrious brother, for what concerns this prophecy and all the remarkable events of this frightful persecution, you may read the history of the time. You will find there more particularized details. It would remain for me now to teach you why the Masons ought to take such an interest in this illustrious society, and why we regard the Knights Templar as our predecessors and our instituters. But it is not permitted to me to bring unto here my revelations: I will tell you, however, and I am authorized therein, that after your noviciate has ended, all will be revealed to you.

"I must now give you the knowledge of the regulations of our Order, so that you will take care to conform yourself thereto. I implore you to give me the greatest attention; for it is not yet permitted to me to leave them to you in writing. Try therefore, to engrave them well into your memory."

REGULATIONS OF THE ORDER OF UNKNOWN PHILOSOPHER JUDGES

Art. 1. Reckoning from the day of his initiation into the sublime grade of *Unknown Philosopher Judge*, the adept shall recognize as chief only the Judge Commander who shall have received him.

Art. 2. An aspirant is to deposit, before his admission, into the hands of the brother preparer, who makes the remittance to those whom it may concern, the sum of 300 fr., included therein 60 fr. for the diploma.

Art. 3. The initiation is but the opening of a noviciate which is to last three years, which cannot be abbreviated but for imminent services rendered to the Order, and by special authorization of the Sup.·. Pow.·. The third year having been completed, the novice shall obtain the recompense due to his patience, his perseverance, and his good conduct. He shall be admitted to the supreme rank of the Commanders, and enjoy the prerogatives attached to this grade. The certificate or diploma (payed in advance) shall be delivered to him.

Art. 4. From the second year, the novice may present a candidate, the qualities of whom he shall be assured, according to the studies indicated. In the third year, he may present as many as he shall have recognized worthy of this favor.

Art. 5. Beyond the above fixed fees, each initiate remits into the hands of the Commander who receives him, a gold wedding ring in alliance, in the interior of which one shall have engraved, on one side, the first and last name of the novice with the date of his initiation; on the other side, the name of the brother preparer who presented him. This ring is transmitted to the Supreme Power by the initiating Commander, and it is deposited upon the column to which it belongs.

Art. 6. For the duration of his noviciate, the initiate may know only the brother preparer and the Commander who initiated him, and through whom, alone, he may forward his requests and his propositions to the chapter under the oversight of which he is found.

Admitted to the rank of Commander, he is admitted to the chapter and the members thereof are known to him. He has, from then on, the oversight of the initiates whom he is charged to receive. They give him the explanation of the letter E, engraved in the heart of the eagle (*Eternity*, that is to say, *extermination*).

Art. 7. Every judge or novice must be ever furnished with his jewel (*dagger*).

Art. 8. Every novice entering the Order chooses a *characteristic* name, which he preserves all his life, and under which alone he corresponds with his superiors.

Every Judge Commander being authorized to deliver certificates of his receptions, ought to have, in order to legalize his characteristic, a seal of the order, bearing a distinctive sign of its possessor, an imprint of which is deposited in the archives of the Supreme Power.

Art. 9. Five Judge Commanders, gathered in a place where there is no chapter established, may form one, with the approval of the Supreme Power, which shall be granted freely, save the cost of shipping and postage, which is fixed at twenty francs invariably.

Any chapter whose members are reduced below the number of five, be it by death or prolonged absence or change of domicile, is dissolved de jure, and may no longer act as a chapter.

Art. 10. The president of every chapter is named for life by the Supreme Power, upon the presentation of three candidates by the chapter.

No chapter may exceed the number of eighteen members, the president included therein.

Art. 11. The precedence of the chapter is regulated by seniority. Thus, the first chapter established in a province or in a department, in whatever place it is found, becomes the *Metropolitan* thereof, and has under its inspection all those which will come to be established in its district.

Art. 12. Where there exists a chapter, no judge may act on his own movement, outside the preparation of the candidates, which is left to the discretion of all; but for the initiation, it is necessary that the chapter be consulted and gives its consent. If there is no chapter, the judge must give an account to the last chapter to which he belonged, and this latter to the Supreme Power, of all his operations.

Art. 13. Every judge must answer for his actions before his chapter. He cannot disobey its mandates or refuse to submit to the penalties which may be pronounced against him, in case of culpability.

Art. 14. Every chapter that wishes to be constituted sends to whichever one of the chapters is known to it, and this latter to the Metropolitan or to the Supreme Power, the table of its members, and it deposits, at the same time, into the treasury of the Order, the sum of *three thousand francs*[110].

Art. 15. Every chapter constitution emanates from the Supreme Power. The Metropolitans may deliver them, but always by letter of authorization from the Supreme Power, without the cooperation of which, nothing of importance is to be done.

Art. 16. Every chapter is responsible, toward the Supreme Power, for each of its members. That is why it alone has the right of jurisdiction over them.

Art. 17. Every judge or novice must go to the convocation which may be made for the good of the order, except for legitimate grounds for dispensation, of which he shall give an account to his immediate chief, and the validity of which shall be examined. If the excuse given appears to be a pretense, they will keep watch over the conduct of the suspect. If he is missing at a second call, he shall be informed, in order to submit himself to a trial of judgment; and if he refuses this, *he is recognized as a perjurer and condemned as such*[111]. His judgment is indicated to him by the president of the chapter, if he is a Judge Commander, and by the initiating Commander, if he is a novice. If the condemned subject returns with penitence and submits himself to the punishment pronounced against him, one may, and even ought, to reduce the punishment, and, sometimes, grant a full pardon. In the contrary case, the judgment receives its full rigor.

Art. 18. Perjury is the most serious fault that an Unknown Philosopher may commit. To be unfaithful to one's oaths, is to be a perjurer: *the punishment of this crime will reach the guilty in whatever part of the world he had counted on taking refuge.*

Art. 19. He is forbidden from publishing the book of the constitutions of the Order, as well as its regulations, under penalty of being considered as a perjurer.

Art. 20. It is only permitted to give a reading of the regulations to the adepts, according to the following rule: 1st, to the Novice, from the 1st art. to the 23rd; 2nd, to the Judge Commander from art. 24 up to the 34th; 3rd, to the newly installed chapters, from art. 35 up to art. (blank), etc.

The regulations are deposited in the tabernacle, the keep of which is entrusted to the Supreme Power and shall be communicated to all the members of the Order, at the day of the great regeneration.

Art. 21. In the case where a member of the Order who, by his functions, would be the trustee of all or part of our secrets or of our written regulations, would come to lose them, he shall inform consecutively his superiors thereof, and, these latter, the Supreme Power, in order to employ all means possible to recover them. In all cases, the copies or extracts which shall be delivered therefrom to whom it may concern, shall not bear titles, or they shall be written in hieroglyphs. Their authenticity will be attested only by the stamp of the power who will have delivered the documents.

Art. 22. In case of a serious illness of a member possessing the secrets of the Order or only a part, he will form a sealed package of the documents which concern the Order, with the address of the Judge Commander nearest his residence, to be transmitted, under a new envelope, to the chapter to which he belongs, or to the Supreme Power, if he is attached to it. This package shall be deposited into the sure hands of a third party, the fidelity of whom may be counted on, in order to reach its destination, in case of death.

Art. 23. The great feast of the Order is celebrated at Saint John of summer. We also celebrate Saint John of winter; but this feast has less solemnity and is not obligatory. The Novices owe, on this day, an honorary visit to the Judge Commander who has initiated them.

"Here, my brother, concludes the communications that I am authorized to give you. Work to make yourself worthy of the other knowledge, and to elevate yourself to the rank of *Judge Commanders*, and you will receive the just recompense of your zeal and of your labors."

Order of Unknown Philosopher Judges

Second Point
GRADE OF JUDGE COMMANDER

PREAMBLE. The Novice having been tried for three years of postulance, and being judged worthy to be elected to the dignity of *Judge Commander*, is notified thereof by his initiating Commander. In order to be assured of his dispositions, he sees to know from him the opinion that he has taken of the Order. He shall ask him by writing his reflections on all that he may have seen, on all that has been taught to him on the sacred mysteries, and the promise to submit himself to all that will be prescribed to him in the new degree that he is going to obtain. He shall also pose some philosophical questions to him on which he will ask him, also by writing, for his responses. Finally, he shall employ all means which may put him in a position to judge the means, cast of mind, and opinions of the Novice. All his responses shall be remitted to the chapter, and by it transmitted to the Supreme Power, which will judge whether it is appropriate to admit him. In the case where the dispositions of the Novice would not suit the expectation of the Order, one is limited to communicating to him the second part of the history of the Templars, starting from the point where they left off at the 1st degree, and such as it is found hereafter, and they tell him that there is no other secret than the one which has just been revealed to him. If, on the contrary, he shows suitable dispositions, they proceed with his admission as we are going to see. The Novice is apprised that he is to furnish himself with a black robe, necessary in order to assist in the chapter. He entrusts it to his initiating Commander, who places it upon the table of the president. He is led into the chapter with the same precautions as in the 1st degree of reception.

RECEPTION. The Novice having been introduced; the president says to him:

"My respectable brother, you have seen, since your admission into the Order of *Unknown Philosopher Judges*, how necessary it is to apply oneself to knowing men, and how indispensible a study of philosophy is in our laboratories. Since your initiation, three years have elapsed; in this you have been assimilated to the disciples of Pythagoras, who were obliged, for a similar lapse of time, to keep the most profound silence; to observe nature in its effects, in order to go back more easily to the primitive cause of what was offered to their view. You have had, during the time of your noviciate, to familiarize yourself with all the duties that our Order imposes, and on which a part of its regulations has instructed you. You have been placed within range of judging the views of the Order and its destination, you must know by now what you are in for. A gold tabernacle is presented to your eyes. It is surrounded by twenty-six columns decorated with capital riches; all that architecture possesses of the most majestic and most sumptuous ornaments serve to enhance the lustre and magnificence thereof. These twenty-six columns present to you an equal number of tribes, which watch and surround the *Holy of Holies*, into which the oracles of nature are deposited. In vain, they have endeavored for a long time to raise a temple consecrated to the study of the holy philosophy. This goal can only be attained by us, only by the solid institution of our Order. Each of the tribes knew its children; it watched over their philosophical education; it is through its care that they attained to some perfection in so difficult an art as true wisdom. You are going to enter today, my brother, into the second tribe, and you must work there to perfect yourself in the art that the unknown workers profess, and whose means are drawn from sound philosophy. In the new career, which is opened before you, you are going to be charged with instructing and guiding the solitary travelers who seek the true knowledge. If you notice among them tepidity and little desire to be instructed, abandon them to their sad state. The study of our sciences requires an elevation of the soul and some enthusiasm for the beauties of nature: the weak minds are incapable thereof. Before expounding further on this subject, it is indispensible, my brother, that you take between my hands a new obligation which may assure me of your discretion. This oath is to render you more dear to our hearts than you have been up to this day. Do you intend to give this new token of your fidelity towards the Order and of your attachment for your brethren? (They await his response; if he consents, he kneels with the same circumstances of the *Novice* who is going to take his obligation.)

OATH, 1. "Do you promise and swear, on what you hold most sacred in the world, to practice mercy, and to never reveal the name of anyone who has received you, nor the place, nor the mode of your reception?" (At each interpellation, the aspirant responds:) *Yes, I promise and swear it.*

2. Do you promise likewise, and swear to me to be modest in your actions; to never initiate into this grade any brothers, unless he be your intimate friend, or without the consent of your chapter, or at least that of two of your brethren if you are too far removed from a chapter, or without a special power emanating from the Supreme Power?...

3. Do you promise and swear to have, at all times, a gentle character; to assist your brothers and more particularly the *Philosopher Judges*, in the Order from which you are going to acquire a degree moreover, to aid them in their needs, to relieve them in sickness, and to never arm yourself against them under any pretext?...

4. Do you promise and swear to take truth as the basis of your discourses; to guard respectfully the secret of this Order, and to confer only with the greatest circumspection the grade of *Unknown Grand Commander Elect Philosopher Judge*?...

5. Do you promise and swear to work towards the propagation of the Order as well as to its security and its preservation; to do, to say, and to write at all times, in all places, and at every hour, what will be prescribed to you by me or by your superiors, most certain that you are not being deceived, and that the orders which will be transmitted to you shall emanate from a legitimate power, to which you swear obedience, although it be up to the present unknown to you and that it may yet be for a long time; do you swear that you will respect in me the organ of the supreme chief of the Order, *Philosopher Judge*, first worker of the great laboratory?...

6. Do you promise and swear to me to be patient in adversity, and to admit into this grade only men free in their actions and in their will?...

7. Finally, do you promise and swear to keep inviolably the secrets that I am going to confide to you; *to never forgive the traitors and to make them suffer the fate that the Order has reserved for them*; to have the greatest consideration for the Masons invested with the high grades, paying attention that our Order cannot and must not be conferred but to a Mason of the 30th degree, to whom this sublime grade will have been conferred according to the forms required by the statutes of Masonry? Do you promise and swear to keep yourself from the excess of wine, the table, and women, the most common causes of indiscretion and weakness? Do you promise and swear to *consider the Knights of Malta as no more than cruel enemies*, as the usurpers of our rights, the despoilers of the goods, titles, and dignities of the Knight Philosopher Commander Templars, our

ancestors and our predecessors, and of whom we are the legitimate heirs? Do you swear it, beloved brother? RESPONSE: *Yes, I promise and swear it.*

Repeat with me: WISDOM, PRUDENCE, JUSTICE, GOODNESS... (The candidate raises only the left knee. The Commander-President says to him:)

"With the seven conditions that I have just imposed on you, in the name of the Order, by virtue of the powers which are delegated to me and that I have merited by my long journeys, by my discretion, by my zeal, and by my constancy, I receive you very regularly into the number of *Philosopher Judges Grand Inspectors General, Unknown Grand Commanders.* May you never forget this glorious title!"

EXPLANATION OF THE LADDER. "You have without doubt not forgotten, my brother, the first moral point of the hieroglyph of the ladder, an explanation of which was given to you on the day of your initiation. I will add to what you know, that the common Mason is still, in this regard, in the greatest error. This ladder belongs to us particularly; it is the mystical type of our Order: it is composed of two uprights which recall to us the union which took place between Philippe-le-Bel and the Pope Clement V, and the strength that this union gave them against our unfortunate predecessors. The assemblage of these two uprights by the seven degrees of which it is composed gives an accurate idea of the seven conditions that Philippe imposed upon Bertrand de Goth, in order to sit upon the throne of Saint Peter. These seven degrees also represent the seven points of the obligation that you have contracted at my hands, in the same manner in which the King of France acted with the Archbishop in order to force him to participate in the annihilation of the Knights Templar. *As you yourself have just promised and sworn an implacable hatred for the enemies of this Order, you are expected to unite all your efforts for their total ruin, in order to resume possession of our rights that they have usurped.*

MORAL. After such care, my brother, you have merited a greater reward than all those which have been granted to you up to this day; it is the revelation of the secret of all the emblems of Masonry. Bring your memory back to the first grades that you received therein: you will perceive that the aspirant to the *grade of Companion* must hold the trowel in one hand, and if this formality is not fulfilled in all the lodges, it can only be attributed to the profound ignorance in which the majority of the Venerables live, and with which they practice the royal art. Consider the *grade of Elect*, you will see the Mason armed with a dagger, and with a sword in the grade of *Knight of the East.* Pay attention to the response made, in this last grade, to the Sovereign Master for the interpretation of the dream which has disturbed him: 'This is the voice of the Great Architect which, for a long time, has called you to govern the East and which orders you to render liberty to the captives... See the lion, which is ready to devour you, this is the image of the fate, which is reserved to you, if you remain deaf to the voice which has spoken to you.'

"The instructions that you have received are the proper means to aid you in tearing off the blindfold of error and to know the truth in its full extent; which is the unique aim of our Order. By the end of this dream, you learn the fate which is reserved to those who would be unfortunate enough to be unfaithful to their promise towards us and would be deaf to the orders emanating from the Supreme Power. You may now, my brother, enlighten yourself through your own research; a vast field is opened to your study, you have the key of knowledge. The veil has been rent for you from the first day of your initiation into our mysteries. Go back to your thoughts on what you have seen since that moment. Reflect on the ceremonial that you have seen us practice; meditate well on the moral which has been taught to you, and, without doubt, you shall soon acquire all the knowledge that I may possess. You will convince yourself, by yourself, of the aim of Masonry.

"Let us return to the grade of Knight of the East: in one hand, he is armed with the sword, in the other, he holds the trowel. Under this emblem, you are to see the Masons after the persecution. Before it, they acted without mystery; but when it arrived, they were pursued on every side, the sword became necessary for their just defense, and they wore it in order to make use of it at the first attack. This is what is represented allegorically in this action. But if you examine the shape of the trowel and that of the cross, which serves as ornament to all the high chivalry, you will recognize there the dagger, necessary in order to defend oneself against an unforeseen attack. If you pay equal attention to the questions and answers of the grade, as well as to the color *aqua-green* affected in this degree, you cannot misunderstand the class of men that our Order requires[112]. Soon you will conceive, with us, the hope to see arrive the great regeneration, to see the *Philosopher Judges* reintegrated into all their rights; which cannot, nevertheless, take place without the strength, courage, constancy, and unshakable steadfastness that we demand of all those that we admit to share our sublime works.

"Through this brief survey, you sense how much care we must take in the choice that we have to make of our new brethren, and you must see that *lacking land to construct our temples materially, we must raise them in our hearts*. You must, then, my beloved brother, recognize that we find in you all the qualities that we seek, since we have admitted you among us. We hope that this will be for your happiness and the prosperity of the Order."

CONTINUATION OF THE HISTORY OF THE KNIGHTS TEMPLAR

Portugal is the place where the respectable Order has been most worthily preserved. King Denis, called *the Liberal*, who reigned in this country, was the only Sovereign who refused the persecution of the Templars. He protected them, preserved their goods and perpetuated the Order under the name of *Knights of Christ*. If in the time from your admission to the noviciate, you had not obtained the entire knowledge of what has relation to the destruction of the Templars, give me today your attention. You shall discover not only how this illustrious Order was destroyed, but also how it is found that the interests of the Masons are so directly bound to theirs. You will see that all Masons, in fact, are Templars; of which it is not permitted to us, and of which it would perhaps not be wise to instruct them.

The news of the persecution of the Knights of the Temple had reached Cyprus, where the Order had its principal establishment. In the absence of the Grand Master, detained in France, they had been vanquished by the Turks, who took from them Saint-Jean-d'Acre and several other strongholds. A part of the goods of the Knights of the Temple were given by Clement V to the Knights of Saint John of Jerusalem, on May 22, 1312, in the period of the closing of the Council of Vienna, which had been opened on October 16, 1311. These knights are yet today in possession of these goods thus despoiled, and this is the cause of the just hatred of the *Knights of the Black and White Eagle, Unknown Philosopher Judges, against the Order of Malta*, sentiments that they still make us promise today in our obligation. Now, as the number of Templars to escape the murderous sword of the persecution was very small, and as, in order to avenge themselves of the unprecedented crime of which they were the victims, they had need to repair their loss, they admire, in our Order, people of a recognized merit, that they seek and that they find among the Masons. Knowing all the virtues that this class of distinguished men professed to practice, they thought that they could do not better than to attach themselves to them, by offering them initiation into the Order, which was accepted with promptness, and, in exchange, they admit the Templars to the initiation in the Masonic mysteries.

The Knights of the Temple instructed their new brethren on the barbarous atrocities that they had had to endure, as well as the first causes of the terrifying persecution which had been directed against them. They declared to them the resolution that they had taken secretly to repair the loss of their brothers by new admissions, in order to re-establish the Order and to resume possession of their goods. They invoked the assistance of their new brethren in order to achieve this goal that they proposed. The Masons applauded this generous design and accepted with enthusiasm the offer which was made to them. They agreed that in place of the cross, with which the Knights were decorated, they would adopt a *double-headed eagle*, wearing a crown, and that, in order to shelter themselves from searches and perfidy, it was very important to hide the secret of their Order from all those who would not be sufficiently proven, and of whom they would not be sure of themselves, after having studied them while they traversed the various grades of Masonry. They decreed too that, in order to avoid every surprise, it was necessary to put into use signs and words which would have some analogy with their history.

When you received the grade of Master Mason, you shed tears upon the tomb of the *Master Hiram Abi*; you have been rendered indignant in the most stark manner at *Abiram*, his murderer. Is it not the image of the conduct of Philippe-le-Bel and that of the two villains who joined him in order to bring him the destruction of the Templars? Were they not the murderers of our Respectable Master? Did not these three infamous companions call into your heart the desire for vengeance, as they teach you that it was carried out upon the three murderers of Hiram? The grades through which you have passed in order to teach the knowledge of the historical facts of the Bible[113], do they not dispose you to make a just application of the death of Hiram to the tragic and deadly end of *Jacques Molay*, Philosopher Judge, Grand Commander of the Order? Is not your heart prepared for vengeance, and do you not feel the implacable hatred that we have sworn to the three traitors, upon whom we owe to avenge the death of Jacques Molay? Behold, my brother, the true Masonry, such as it has been transmitted to us. Know how to sit in the midst of men whose bravery and good morals make up the whole doctrine. This doctrine is the rule that you must impose upon yourself. It is that which imposes on us our constitution.

Here you are now, placed at the level of the zealous Masons who devote themselves to us for the common vengeance. You will have envy and persecution to dread. You will not be able to escape this but by observing carefully your obligations and hiding from the vulgar the high destiny which is reserved to you. Since you have attained the final degree of light, and since you have justly merited it, by your qualities and your morals, I dare to hope that you will justify the confidence I have placed in you, and that the Order will never have to reproach me for the admission of a useless or harmful member. I have not hesitated to enlighten you on the true motives of our conduct towards you, and on what interests the Order in general, no more than on the precious advantages that you may draw therefrom. I like to believe, my brother, that in you uniting with us by the sacred bonds of the most sincere friendship, you will acquire, by your submission to our institutions, the perfection merited by your zeal, and which makes up the basis of the sublime grade of *Philosopher Judge*, *Unknown Grand Commander*.

You are now at the rank of the elect called to accomplish the great work. Your name is, from today, deposited in the urn of elections, and your actions will lead you, I hope, to the happiness which makes up your hope and to which we all aspire… *Amen*!

The Judge-President gives the accolade to the new Judge and communicates to him the true words, etc.[114].

DIALOG TO BE RECOGNIZED

Q. - Are you Grand Commander, Unknown Philosopher Judge?

A. - My brother, I only know *Abatos*, *Mendes*, and the *Crocodile*.

Q. - To whom were you presented in order to be admitted into this knowledge?

A. - To the throne of the All-Powerful, upon which was seated justice.

Q. - What did you see out of the darkness?

A. - Superstition, usurpation, tyranny, hypocrisy, barbary; the five furies ready to sacrifice the innocent.

Q. - What did they demand of you before creating you adept?

A. - An oath containing this condition, of which I have promised the entire effect, and I am going to reiterate it with you.

Q. - What can protect you against your enemies?

A. - Firmness of my character, the promptness of my *work*, and the power of my *jewel*, against which nothing may resist.

Q. - Where do you wear this precious jewel?

A. - Over my heart.

CONTINUATION OF THE REGULATIONS

Art. 24. A constituted chapter may institute another, with, however, the authorization of the Supreme Power.

Art. 25. Half of the fees, fixed for the constitutions and initiations, is payed into the general treasury of the Order, established with the Supreme Power; the other half is deposited into the treasury of the chapter, in order to be distributed, in virtue of relief, to the brethren who shall be in need, and to pay the expenses of the chapter.

Art. 26. The treasury presents its accounts, each year, at the summer solstice, and it is examined forthwith, the remaining funds determined, and the expenditure documents delivered consecutively to the flames.

Art. 27. In the places where there is no chapter, or at least in five leagues from any chapter, half of the initiation fee, which would had to have been deposited into the treasury of the chapter, belongs to the initiating Judge Commander.

Art. 28. It is forbidden to every Judge Commander to go perform initiations outside of the place of his domicile, unless by a special mission, which would be given to him by a chapter or by the Supreme Power. In this case, he receives an indemnity for his displacement.

Art. 29. No chapter preserves any outline of its operations; this outline is sent to the Supreme Power by the means indicated further down, at pain of nullity of what would have been decided. To this end, there will be acknowledgement of receipt, following the protocol which shall be regulated. This document shall be preserved by the president of the chapter.

Art. 30. Every chapter may regulate interior discipline; but this regulation is always subject to the approval of the Supreme Power, which has the power to reform or modify it at the presentation, but may no longer change anything after, without the consent or request of the chapter.

Art. 31. To encourage the zeal of the members of a chapter, they may accord attendance dues, if the situation of the treasury permits it.

Art. 32. The penalties pronounced against the brethren who render themselves guilty of some misdemeanor, whatever it may be, are: reprimand, admonishment, stricken out from the rolls, and *even more serious penalties, if the crime is of a nature to compromise the society. The sentences of the latter nature may not be executed without confirmation and judgment by the Supreme Power.*

Art. 33. Whatever be the type of correction that a chapter shall have judged appropriate to inflict upon one of its members, it is expected to inform the Supreme Power thereof, which sees to keep an account thereof by the name of the brother that it concerns.

Art. 34. In general, all that tends to enlighten the Supreme Power on the morality and the conduct of the members of the Order, is to be addressed exactly and included in a report, which is addressed by the president of the chapter, every three months.

PHILOSOPHICAL AND HERMETIC ALPHABET

♓	Pisces.	A. 1.	ABATOS, name of a rock separated from the isle of Philé, in the Nile, which formerly served the Unknown Judges.
♑	Capricorn.	B. 22.	BACCHIS, allegory which shall be applied hereafter.
♒	Aquarius.	C. 14.	CROCODILE, image of the tyrants and of the persecutors of the Templars.
△	The Triangle	D. 21.	DANAÉ, name of a coin, image of the greatest means of seduction employed by the persecutors of the Templars.
∧	The Compass	E. 5.	ECHIDNA, name of one of the furies. It recalls to us the instigations of evils that the Templars have suffered, and the usurpers of their goods and

			their rights.
✠	The Cross.	F. 7.	FIRE, image of the envy of the most just vengeance, the love of glory, the hope of triumph and victory.
♉	Taurus.	G. 6.	GNOSIA, the pentagon, indicating the part where ought to commence our exploits.
♐	Sagittarius.	H. 12.	HARPÉ, dagger.
☆	The Polar Star.	I. J. 2. 13.	JANUS, figure which indicates to us that nothing can fail us under the conduct of wisdom and time.
♄	Saturn.	K. 15.	KRODO or CODRUS, first divinity of the Saxons. In Saxony and in Belgium are many of our brethren; there have been three at *Moscow*, at the Kremlin, whose initial is K.
♎	Libra	L. 4.	LUNE [MOON], symbol of ignorance. It is also the initial of laurel, the juice of which, taken moderately, enlivens, and, in a strong dose, kills.
♏	Scorpio	M. 19.	MENDES, god of the East, where was the greatest power of the Templars; initial of the name of our G.M. Molay assassinated and burned inhumanely, and of whom we will be the inexorable avengers.
☉	The Sun	N. 10.	NAPHTÉ, name of fish, hieroglyph expressing the love of order and peace.
☾	The Moon	O. 23.	ORTHUS, dog, emblem of fidelity; activity in undertakings and in the accomplishment of our duties.
♈	Aries	P. 8.	PUTEAL, sacred pedestal which contains the ashes of the innocent victims, and upon which the tyrants are to be immolated.
□	The Square	Q. 20.	*Quadriformis*, signifies taking all the figures, employing all means in order to succeed. It also signifies the extirpation of our enemies spread into the four parts of the world.
—	The Straight Line	R. 11.	ROUE [WHEEL], it is necessary to keep watch on the course of the years. It will be easy for you to stop that of the time which ought render unto us the laurels, dishonored by tyranny. Avoid the accuser; fear him above all.
╲	The Oblique Line	S. 9.	SERPENT, supple animal which folds in upon itself under the grass; which, in the sun, changes color, like the chameleon. It deceives the shepherd who pursues it, it rises up, darts forth, and is lost under the foliage. It is thus that ought to be the Unknown Philosopher Judge.
♊	Gemini.	T. 18.	TITAN, sun, the sole God, author of good and evil. The unknown judge is the sun, the God who must govern all, who must rule the world, and

		make the happiness of the human race.
⊥ The Inverted Cross.	U. V. 28. 17.	URN; Tabernacle which contains the destiny of men; it is the emblem of our heart which contains the secret which must restore vigor to the Universe. *Wodan*, emblem of commerce. Promptness in execution assures nearly always the success of an undertaking.
× The Cross of Saint Andrew.	X. 3.	XANTHUS, river which stood in the way, with the *Scamandre* and the *Simois*, of the descent of the Greeks, by the flooding of their waters. It is thus that the three columns of the Order oppose with all their strength, the powers of tyranny.
‡ Double Cross.	Y. 3.	YEUX [EYES], like *Argus*, we must not ever close our eyes on our proselytes and our novices; like another *Gorgon* with wings filled with eyes, we cannot carry too far our view in order to make a choice of men proper to spread the spirit of liberty and concord. The Unknown Judge must be at once as vigilant upon himself as upon others; to be, in his house, father and minister; in all places, the *director* of the *courses*; to give the example of the love of glory and to electrify the souls of the aspirants.
♃ Jupiter.	Z. 16.	ZANCLE, or the *Faulx of Time*, emblem of death; it is time which cuts the wings to victory; it is the Unknown Judge who, in his just wrath or in the extent of his recognition, always knows the moment to punish or to reward.

(This alphabet differs a little from the one published by Tacxsi.) [115]

We notice, in the ritual, many passages which indicate the *Hermetic work* and show that the occupation of the adepts was the study of the operations of nature, under the name of *secret science*. We shall speak of this science and of the *occult sciences* in the chapters which are going to follow, as having formed in Egypt the high initiation or the *greater mysteries*. We do not think that a studious Mason may reasonably dispense with taking cognizance thereof, in order to form an idea thereof and to be in a position to understand the ancient hieroglyphs.

We ought also take note of the support that the opinion of the UNKNOWN JUDGES gives to all that we have written, in this work, on-the high grades, and particularly on *écossisme*. But écossisme is Jesuitic and Templar, and yet the Unknown Judges, who had the secret of this régime, which they practiced, say, on page 156 above:

"We have never recognized but five degrees of knowledge; the number of twenty- five or thirty-three degrees, which form the framework of *écossisme*, is an effect of the love of innovations, or the product of some self-love; for IT IS CONSTANT THAT, OF THE REPUTED THIRTY-THREE PRACTICED TODAY, THERE ARE TWENTY- EIGHT WHICH MERIT NO CONFIDENCE."

What should the present partisans of écossisme think of this final judgment? We arrive at OCCULT MASONRY.

END OF MASONIC ORTHODOXY

OCCULT MASONRY
OR TREATISE ON THE OCCULT SCIENCES
Being the continuation of
MASONIC ORTHODOXY

"Weaken, little by little, all the old superstitions, and do not introduce any new ones. - If the imbeciles still want the acorn, let them at it; but think fit to present them with bread."
(*Indian maxim.*)

SECOND PART
OCCULT MASONRY
OR
TREATISE ON THE OCCULT SCIENCE

CHAPTER XXVI

Let the children of darkness
become the children of light.

The occult sciences reveal to man the mysteries of his nature, the secrets of his organization, the means to achieve his perfection and his happiness, finally the decree of his destiny. Their study was that of the high Egyptian initiations. It is time that they become the study of the modern Masons.

We have not yet spoken, in *Masonic Orthodoxy*, but of the *three degrees* of *Symbolic* Masonry, being the continuation of the ancient initiation, and of the *high grades*, which tend to misrepresent the nature thereof. It remains to us to occupy ourselves with *occult and philosophical Masonry*, likewise in three grades, emanating from the ancient *greater mysteries.*

The primitive instituters had two aims in their mysteries, which were not without some identical connections to one another; which has caused one to believe, with reason, that they had a *dual doctrine.*

The first aim was to draw man from the state of barbary in order to *civilize* him, and to take the civilized man in order to *perfect* him, to bring back the man that they believed fallen from his first nature. According to them, man was to begin anew, it was necessary to restore him even unto humanity; initiation alone could regenerate him. From here come the *lesser mysteries*, imitated in present Freemasonry.

The second aim was to research the means to restore matter to its first nature, which they also believed to be fallen.

GOLD was deemed, for matter, what the ETHER of the eighth heaven was to the souls; and the seven metals, known then, each called by the name of a planet, formed the ascending scale of material purification which corresponded to the moral trials of the seven heavens.

Thus, the mystagogy or *initiation* into the mysteries had its two divisions.

In the first, they only *purified* man of the inclinations; only passed him through the *crucible.* It was an alchemy of the spirit, a human mystagogy.

The second was the initiation into the mysteries of the operations of nature, a mystagogy of the body.

In the one, they sought the *cubic stone* or the *angular stone* of the temple of philosophy, capable of gathering, by this ingenious symbol, all of humanity into one same faith, one same hope, one same love.

In the other, they sought what may bring back the golden age: the *philosopher's stone* and the *elixir* which prolongs life.

The one would serve as a veil to the other, as it still serves today, as one may be convinced by some comparisons that it is easy for us to make.

1st GRADE. Freemasonry is called the *royal art*: art, because every work is done only by a certain combination of principles tending toward the accomplishment of the subject that the artist proposes; *royal*, because Ashmole, scholarly alchemist, payed homage to the wise king, which the laws of the philosophical work possessed at its base[116].

The perfect knowledge of the philosopher is sufficiently analogous to that of the Mason: the philosopher must understand the true germ of nature, before commencing his work. Likewise, the Mason must truly understand the core of the heart of man, before admitting him as a brother.

When the philosophers speak of the GOLD and the SILVER (symbolized in the lodges by the SUN and the MOON), from where they extract their matter, they do not intend to speak of the common gold and silver, because they are dead, whereas those of the philosophers are full of life.

The object of the research of Masons is the knowledge of the art of perfecting what nature has left imperfect in the human race, and to arrive at the treasure of the *true moral*. - The object of the research of the philosophers is, likewise, the knowledge of the art of perfecting what nature has left imperfect in the metallic genre, and to arrive at the precious treasure of the *philosopher's stone*.

Life resides uniquely in the radical humid. In order not to fail in the work, it is necessary to *strip* the matter of its husks, in order to have the nucleus or center, which contains the whole virtue of the composite. - This depuration has its symbol in Masonry, when the candidate must be *stripped* of all the mundane prejudices and of the error of the dangerous passions, in order to lead him to virtue and perfection.

ROUGH ASHLAR. The artist must work upon a body created by nature, in which he will have joined the *sulphur* and the *mercury*, which he must separate, and then purify in order to rejoin them. This body is called the *rough stone*. This is the same as the rough ashlar that the Masons labor to smooth out and from which they seek to remove the superfluities, which in moral Masonry they called *destruction of the vices*.

The word *vulgar*, translated in Masonry as *profane*, designates every subject which is not proper to the work, such as the *vulgar* quicksilver, the sulphur, the mercury of trade, the *vulgar* gold and silver; we add sometimes the epithet *stupid* (stupid vulgar) when the subject has no life in itself.

2nd GRADE. They prove here the truth of Masonry. They explain here the meaning of things, the *blazing star*, etc. What institution is as much in the way of truth as Masonry? It has adopted the primitive doctrine, proclaimed the G.A. of the Universe that it honors by homage pure from every cult and superstition. It recommends the love of neighbor, the practice of virtue, of equality, and of beneficence, the horror of vice, falsehood, and hypocrisy, tolerance in opinions, submission to the laws, respect of the rights of others, universal benevolence, and the perfecting of oneself through instruction and the spirit of fraternity.

They show likewise the truth of the philosopher's art: it is founded, *firstly*, upon this: that the physical powder, being made from the same material from which are formed the metals, namely the *quicksilver*, has the faculty to mingle with them in the fusion: *one nature embracing a nature which is similar to it*.

SECONDLY, on this: that the imperfect metals remain such, because all quicksilver is raw, the physical powder, which is a mature and cooked quicksilver, and, properly, a *pure fire*, may easily communicate the maturity to them and transmute them into its nature, after having made the attraction of their raw humidity, that is to say of their quicksilver, which is the only substance which is transmuted; the rest being only shells and excrements, which are rejected in the projection[117].

An artist may risk undertaking the work, when he will have, by means of a vegetable menstruum, united with a mineral menstruum, dissolved a third essential menstruum, with which united it is necessary to cleanse the earth, and then to exhale it in *celestial quintessence*, in order to compose thereof their sulphureous lightning, which, in an instant, penetrates the bodies and destroys the excrements.

We designate, in masonry, this celestial quintessence by the *five-pointed blazing star*, called by the philosophers the *central fire of nature*, symbolized also by the letter G, which means *generation of the bodies*. It is necessary not to confuse the Hermetic philosophy with alchemy.

The philosopher's matter exists everywhere; but it must be sought especially in the metallic nature, where it will be found more easily than elsewhere. It is the *angular stone*, which may be designated only by the double triangle ✡, which also symbolizes the two hemispheres. - This figure is the emblem of the sentence of Hermes, which says that *what is below is like that which is above*. It is also the stumbling-block against which thousands of men have run aground.

3rd GRADE. We know the present *Mastership*. It is not, in tis summary, but a pale reflection of the primitive initiation, the allegorical drama of which has been disfigured by the series of political events at the period of its renovation. Although the moral symbolism leaves there a great part to the *philosophical* symbolism, the alteration of the system is such, and the developments thereof are so incomplete, that today, all the ability of an instructed Venerable is necessary in order to give any interest to the interpretations of the *cropped* hieroglyphs (even the *Phoenix* has disappeared) of this beautiful grade.

If, as we would desire it, they wished to double the three symbolic degrees, true grades of trials, commented and elaborated in the *three schools of instruction* that we have proposed (p. 153) with three corresponding grades called philosophical or greater mysteries[118], in which would be developed the ancient secret doctrines, they would open to the adept therein the deposit of the most useful knowledge and truths; he would recognize the truth of the alliance of the two systems, the *symbolic* and the *philosophical* in the allegories of the monuments of all ages, in the symbolic scriptures of the priests of all nations, in the rituals of the mysterious societies. He would see therein a constant series, an invariable uniformity of principles which proceed from a collective, vast, imposing, and true, and which would not really be as coordinated as that. The charm of the seduction and the ardent desire to know would push the adept to penetrate into the sanctuary, by traversing the thorny path which leads there, and, assisted by a strong will, a constant perseverance, and a study without prejudice, he would succeed in lifting the veil; and the secret of these allegories, of these emblems, of these symbols, of these sacred enigmas, would cease to be a mystery for him; for nature would be revealed to him.

It is thus that in the initiatic schools, the adept gave himself to the most profound studies: mathematics, interpretation of the numbers, navigation, architecture in its three divisions: *sacred*, *civil*, and *nautical*, etc. The privileged adepts, or those recognized worthy, were initiated into the most secret doctrines and into the *occult sciences*. Philosophers of modern times have drawn from these intellectual sources. It will be no different with the studious Masons who love to know the various speculations or conception of the human spirit, to find here the most striking ideas, the principal aphorisms, bases of the systems of these mysterious authors[119].

THE GOLDEN CHAIN. According to *Hermes* and his disciples, from the center of the archetype (the highest of the heavens) shoots forth, without interruption, the universal spirit, inexhaustible source of light and fire which, traversing all the celestial spheres, and finding itself gradually condensed, flows continually toward the earth. Likewise, by the action of the *central fire*, of the terrestrial sun, there escape from the earth continual emanations which, soon sublimated, rise toward the vault of the heavens in order to there be freed from their impurities. In a word, the *condensed* fire becomes *air*, the air becomes *water*, the water contains the *earth*. Likewise, the purified earth is converted into water, the sublimated water escapes into the air, the exalted air is disseminated in *fire*[120]. This eternal rotation of ethereal emanations, of the vital molecules, is depicted, in Genesis, under the emblem of the *mysterious ladder of Jacob*, by which ascended and descended the *angels*. This is the brilliant *golden chain* which, according to the ancient allegory, ties all bodies to the earth. They ordinarily represent it by the sign X: to express the effluvium of the igneous atoms from the heavens into the earth, and V depicted their return toward the ethereal places. Indeed, the *luminous triangle* depicts, among the philosophers, the *catabathmic* movement of the igneous atoms towards the earth, because at the point of their departure, they are in their brilliance, in all their purity. The *black pyramid* or *dark triangle* expresses, on the contrary, their ascension or return toward the heavens; for, in leaving the globe, they are charged with all the terrestrial impurities.

Hermes represented knowledge by the *sacred fire* that his disciples fed and that they could not let extinguish *under penalty of death*. It is terrible to have to depict, by human torment, the misfortune caused, in the intellectual and moral world, by any interruption in the transmission of the sciences from one generation to the other. That entirely initiatic idea is a proof that the modern Masonic knowledge, well-conceived, is a transmission from the ancient knowledge. The light may travel under the bushel (in the heart and in the intelligence of some initiates), but it is never extinguished: transmit it likewise.

CHAPTER XXVII

Power of the Numbers According to Pythagoras

The numbers are *intellectual* or *scientific.*

The *intellectual* number existed before all in the divine understanding. It is the basis of the universal order and the bond which enchains things.

The *scientific* number is the generative cause of the multiplicity which proceeds from the unity, and which are rejoined thereto.

It is necessary to distinguish the unity from the art. The *unity* belongs to the numbers; the *art*, to the numerable things.

The scientific number is *even* or *odd.*

It is only the *even* number which undergoes an infinity of divisions into parts, always even. However, the *odd* is more perfect.

The *unity* is the symbol of the identity, equality, existence, and the conservation of harmony in general[121].

The *binary* number is the symbol of diversity, inequality, division, separation, and vicissitudes.

The *dyad*[122], origin of the contrasts, represents for them matter or the passive principle.

Each number, like the unity and the binary, has its properties which give it a symbolic character which is particular to it.

The *monad* or unity is the final end, the final state, the repose of the state in its decreasing.

The *ternary* is the first of the odds. The *triad*, mysterious number, which enjoys so great a role in the traditions of Asia, and in the Platonic philosophy, image of the supreme being, unites within it the properties of the first two numbers. The ternary represented to the Pythagoreans not only the surface, but also the principle of the formation of the bodies[123].

The *quaternary* is the most perfect number and the root of the other numbers and of all things. The *tetrad* expresses the first mathematical power. It also represents the generative virtue from which derive all the combinations. The initiates consider it as the emblem of movement and the infinite, representing all that is neither corporeal nor sensible. It is as symbol of the eternal and creative principle that *Pythagoras* communicated to his disciples, under the name of *quaternary*, the ineffable name of God, which means *source of all that which has received being*, and which, in Hebrew, is of *four* letters.

It is in the *quaternary* that is found the first solid figure, the universal symbol of immortality, the *pyramid*[124]. For, if the triangle, represented by the number *three*, makes up the triangular base of the pyramid, it is the *unity* which makes the point or summit thereof. Thus, *Lysis* and *Timeus* of Locres said that not one thing can be named which does not depend on the *quaternary* as its root[125]. There is, according to the Pythagoreans, a connection between the gods and the numbers, which constitutes the kind of divination called *arithmomancy*. The soul is a number, it moves by itself; it contains within it the *quaternary* number.

The number FIVE was considered as mysterious, because it is composed of the *binary*, symbol of what is false and double, and the ternary, so interesting in its results. It expresses therefore, energetically, the state of imperfection, of order and disorder, of happiness and misfortune, of life and death, which is seen upon the earth.

It even offered to the mysterious societies the terrifying image of the EVIL PRINCIPLE, throwing trouble into the lower order, and, in a word, the *binary* acting in the *ternary*.

Yet the *quinary*, under a different correspondence, was the emblem of marriage, because it is composed of *two*, first even number, and *three*, first odd number. Thus Juno, presiding over wedlock, had as hieroglyph the number *five*[126]. Finally, the *quinary* offers one of the properties of the number *nine*, that of reproducing itself by multiplying it by itself; there always comes a five to the right of the product, result which made it employed as the symbol of material vicissitudes.

The number FIVE designated the *universal quintessence*, and symbolized, by its form ς, the *vital essence*, the *animating spirit* which winds through all nature. Indeed, this ingenious character is the union of the two Greek accents ῾᾿ placed over the vowels which are to be, or not, aspirated[127]. The first sign ῾ has the name of *strong spirit*, it signifies the *superior spirit*, the spirit of God aspirated (*spiritus*), respired by man. The second sign ᾿ is called *gentle spirit*, it represents the *secondary spirit*, purely human spirit[128].

The number six was, in the ancient mysteries, a striking emblem of NATURE, as representing the *six* dimensions of all bodies; the *six* lines which compose the shape, to wit: the four lines of direction toward the north, south, east, and west, with the two lines of height and depth, corresponding to the zenity and nadir. The sages applied the *senary* to the physical man, whereas the *septenary* was, for them, the symbol of his immortal spirit[129].

Never has a number been so well received as the SEPTENARY, whose celebration is due, no doubt, to the number of which the planets are composed. Thus, does it belong to the sacred things. The Pythagoreans regarded it as formed from the numbers *three* and *four*, the first of which offered them the image of the three material elements, and the second depicted to them the principle of all that is neither corporeal nor sensible. It presented to them, under these correspondences, the emblem of all that is perfect. Considered as composed of the *senary* and the *unity*, this number served to designate the invisible center or spirit of each thing, because there exist no bodies whose six lines constitute the shape, which exist without a *seventh* interior point, as center and reality of this body, whose exterior dimensions give only the appearance. The numerous applications of the septenary confirmed the ancient sages in the use of this symbol[130]. Moreover, they exalted the properties of the seven, as having, in the second place, the perfection of the *unity*, which is the *number of the numbers*; for if the unity is uncreated, if no number produces it, the *seven* is no longer engendered by any number contained in the interval of the *ten*; and the *four* offers an arithmetical middle between the *unity* and the *seven*, since it surpasses it by the same number, *three*, of which it is surpassed by the *seven*, since *four* is above *one*, as seven is above *four*[131].

The number EIGHT or the OCTARY designated the natural and primitive law, which supposes all men equal. From the heavens, from the seven planets and the sphere of the fixed, or from the eternal *unity* and the mysterious number *seven*, is composed the *ogdoad*, the eight days, the *first cube of evens*, regarded in arithmetical philosophy as sacred[132].

The number *eight* symbolizes perfection, its figure 8 or ∞ indicates the perpetual and regular movement of the universe.

On the NONARY or TRIPLE TERNARY. If the number *three* has been celebrated among the first sages, that of *three times three* has had not less celebrity, because, according to them, each of the three elements which constitute our body is *ternary*: the *water* enclosed by the earth and the fire; the *earth* containing igneous and aqueous particles, and the *fire* being tempered by the globules of water and terrestrial corpuscles, which serve as food. None of the three elements finding themselves thus extricated from the other two, all the material beings composed of these three elements, each of which is triple, may consequently be designated by the figurative number of *three times three*, become the symbol of all corporatizations. From this comes the name *nonary envelope* given to matter. Every material expanse, every circular line has as representative sign the number *nine*, among the Pythagoreans, who had observed the property that this number possessed to reproduce itself unceasingly and in its entirety in every multiplication, and which offers to the spirit a most striking emblem of the matter which forms itself unceasingly to our eyes, after having undergone thousands and thousands of decompositions.

The number nine was consecrated to the spheres and to the muses. It is the sign of every circumference, since its value in degrees is equal to 9, that is to say to 3+6+0. However, the ancients did not see this number without experiencing a sort of terror. They considered it as a bad omen, as a symbol of versatility, of change, and the emblem of the fragility of the human things. Thus, they avoided all the numbers where 9 appeared, and principally 81[133] which is the product of 9 multiplied by itself, and the addition of which, 8+1, presents again the number *nine*.

If the figure of the number 6 was the symbol of the terrestrial globe animated by a *divine spirit*, the figure of the number 9 symbolized the earth, under the influence of the *evil principle*. From here comes that terror inspired by the nonary. However, according to the Qabalists, the numeral 9 symbolizes the generative work, or the look of a small, conglobed being, the lower part of which seems to make an effusion of its spirit of life.

The ENNEAD is the first square of the odd numbers[134].

The number TEN or DENARY is the measure of all and it leads back to the unity of the numbers multiplied. Containing all the numeric and harmonic correspondences, and all the prerogatives of the numbers which precede it, it concludes the *abacus* or the table of Pythagoras. This number represented to the mysterious societies the assemblage of all the marvels of the universe. They drew it thus: ⊙ that is to say the unity in the middle of the zero, as the center of a circle, symbol of divinity. They saw in this figure all that is worthy to fix the thought: the *center*, the *radius*, and the *circumference* represented to them *God*, *man*, and the *universe*.

This number was, for the sages, a sign of concordance, love, and peace. It is also, for the Masons, a sign of *union* and *good faith*, since it is found expressed by the junction of the two hands or the *Master's grip*, of which the number of the fingers is 10[135].

The number TWELVE, like the number *seven*, is celebrated in the cult of nature. The two most famous divisions of the heavens, that by *seven* which is that of the planets, and that by *twelve*, which is that of the signs, are found in the religious monuments of all the peoples of the ancient world, unto the ends of the Orient. Although Pythagoras does not speak of the number *twelve*, it is no less a sacred number. It is the image of the Zodiac, and, consequently, that of the sun which is its chief.

In the Pythagorean doctrine, the system of the numbers resolved the problem of cosmogony.

This science of the numbers represented not only arithmetical qualities, but every grandeur, every proportion. By it, they were to arrive at the discovery of the source of things, which we would call today the ABSOLUTE[136].

The ancients and Pythagoras himself, whose true principles have not always been grasped, have never had the intention of attributing to the numbers, that is to say to abstract signs, any particular virtue; but the sages of antiquity had agreed to recognize a *first and unique cause* (material or spiritual) of the existence of the universe. From this, the UNITY has become the symbol of the Supreme Divinity. It has been used to express and to represent God, but without attributing to the number ONE any divine or supernatural virtue.

They have said with truth:

"Philosophy is the reason spoken or written, and its action is manifested only accompanied by the science (or the knowledge in practice).

Applied to nature, it has produced physics.

——	life,	——	hygiene
——	matter,	——	chemistry.

Applied to legislations, it has produced jurisprudence.

——	wealth,	——	economy.
——	intelligence,	——	psychology.
——	certitude (truth),	——	method, etc.

"Instead of saying *knowledge* (faculty of knowing), we say *philosophy*, or the reason which operates by its own virtue (*faculty*), which experiments, which compares, which draws the fact from its element in order to group it, to generalize it, to elevate it to the state of law, and from the state of law to the state of science. Every discovery arises from philosophy. It is therefore the first science, the science of sciences. Every man of genius or scientist has begun by being a philosopher.

"Philosophy destroys error."

The philosophical principles of the ancients, which made up the basis of the secret teaching in the greater mysteries, have been transmitted, from age to age, by the initiates. We find them reproduced in the works dated from the last centuries, and especially of the 14th, of which we are going to cite the opinions of three renowned authors in the secret sciences. In so important a matter, it is unnecessary to fear any repetitions; for they announce a conformity of ideas and aim and cannot but serve as confirmation of the ancient wisdom.

CHAPTER XXVIII

Occult Philosophy of Agrippa[137]

There are three worlds: the elementary, the celestial, the *intellectual*.

Each subordinate world is ruled by the number which is superior to it. It is not impossible to pass from the knowledge of the one to the knowledge of the other, and to go back even unto the archetype. It is this ladder that we call MAGIANISM, profound contemplation which embraces the nature, power, quality, substance, virtues, similarities, differences, the art of uniting, of separating, of composing; in a word, the entire work of the universe.

This is a sacred art which must not be divulged. The universal connection of things confirms the reality and the certitude of Magianism.

The four elements, principles of composition and decomposition, are each triple. The *fire* and the *earth*, the one active principle, the other passive principle, suffice for the production of the marvels of nature.

The *fire* by itself, isolated from any material serving to manifest its presence and its action, is immense, invisible, mobile, destructive, restorative, inclined toward all that borders it, flambeau of nature whose secrets it enlightens.

The *earth* is the support of the elements, the reservoir of all the celestial influences. It has all the germs thereof and the reason of all the productions: the virtues from on high assist it.

The germs of all the animals are in the *water*.

The *air* is a vital spirit which penetrates the beings and gives them consistency and life: uniting, agitating, filling all, it receives immediately the influences that it transmits. It escapes the spiritual and natural images which strike our senses.

In the archetypal world, *all is in all*: proportion retained, it is the same in the latter.

There is one sublime, secret, and necessary cause of the condition, which may lead to the truth.

The world, the heavens, the stars have souls which are not without affinity with our own.

The world lives, it has organs, it has senses.

The *imprecations* have their efficacies. They attach themselves to beings and modify them.

The names of things have their power. The magical art has its language. This language has its virtues: it is an image of the signatures. From this comes the effect of the *invocations*, *evocations*, *adjurations*, *conjurations*, and other formulas.

It appears that the *number* is the first reason of the series of things.

The *numbers* have their virtue, their good or malevolent efficacy.

The *unity* is the beginning and end of all. It has neither end nor beginning. The *binary* is evil.

God is the *monad*. Before it extended itself outside of *itself* and produced the beings, it engendered within itself the *ternary* number which, like the unity, represents in God, the soul of the world, the spirit of man.

The *quaternary* is the base of all the numbers.

The *quinary* has a particular form in the sacred expiations; it is all. It stops the effect of venoms. It is redoubtable to the evil geniuses.

The *septenary* is very powerful, be it for good or evil. The denary number is the measure of all.

Man has *all* within him: number, measure, weight, movement, the elements, harmony.

The characters of these words are not their virtues. We may hold the knowledge of the properties and events thereof.

The intelligence of God is incorruptible, immortal, eternal, insensible, present to all, influencing all.

The human spirit is corporeal, but its substance is very subtle and of a free union with the particle of the universal spirit, soul of the world, which is in us.

- Few persons have understood his treatise on *Occult Philosophy*, for there was a key which he reserved for his friends of the first order (19 *epist...* lib. v.).

He said, with reason, that all that the books teach concerning the virtue of magianism, astrology, alchemy, is false and deceitful, when taken literally; that it is necessary to seek a *mystical sense*, sense that none of the masters had yet developed. (We refer to the *Fastes initiatiques*, the various hieroglyphs of Agrippa.)

CHAPTER XXIX

Principles of the Rational Philosophy of Cardan[138]

There is a first matter in all that exists in fact. This matter remains existing when the present form of the body is destroyed, for nothing is annihilated.

It is evident that there is, in nature, something hidden under the form, and which is the *substratum* thereof. This *substratum* is not engendered and is not annihilated by corruption. Now, it is that which is called *first matter*, unproduced matter, eternal, infinite, indestructible.

The first matter always exists under some form.

There is no void in nature.

Matter is everywhere: it cannot exist without some form, whence it necessarily follows that form is everywhere.

There is no space without body. Space is eternal, immovable, and immutable. The principles of the natural things are of the number of *five*: *matter*, *form*, *soul*, *space*, and *movement*.

There are two primary qualities: heat and *humidity*.

Time is not a principle, but it approaches it, because nothing is done without it. *Rest* is not a principle either, but the prevision of a principle, like *death*, *cold*, *dryness*.

There are three things eternal in their nature: *intelligence*, *first matter*, and *space* or place. The quantity of matter is always the same in the universe.

Our soul is representative as a *mirror* (*anima enim nostra tanquam speculum*). Leibnitz, a century and a half later, said that each soul or *monad* is a living *mirror* or endowed with internal action, representative of the universe, according to every point of view, and as regulated as the universe itself.

- Cardan became *ecstatic* at the age of fifty-three. This is the most celebrated ecstatic that modern history presents after *Joan of Arc*. Under several accounts, he recalled *Socrates*: like him, he fell into ecstasy at will, and saw, with the eyes of the spirit, strange and far away objects. He asserts, like the sage of Greece, that nothing had happened to him, good, bad, or even indifferent, that had not been previously foreseen. During his ecstasies, which were short in duration, he did not feel the violent pains of gout, and did not hear the din made around him. He died at the age of seventy-five, as he had predicted. Socrates, who had had before his judges the presentiment of his condemnation and his death, told his friend *Criton* that he would die in three days. Cardan did not believe, like Socrates, that he was favored by a *particular genius*. He attributed this extraordinary faculty to the strength of the imaginative virtue, to the subtlety of his sight, and, above all, to a particular nature of his soul.

In 1431 they had condemned, in *Joan of Arc*, revelations and apparitions, as being works of the demon. A hundred years later, they canonized *Therese* for the same causes.

CHAPTER XXX

Philosophical and Medical System of Paracelsus[139]

The Holy Scripture leads to all truths.

The Bible is the key of the theory of illnesses.

One ought to consult the Apocalypse in order to understand the medicine of the mages.

All the beings, even the minerals and the fluids, take food and drink, and expel excrements.

His physiological theory is founded upon the application of the laws of the Qabalah in the demonstration of the functions of the human body.

The vital force is an emanation from the stars:

The *Sun*	is found in relation	with the	*heart,*
The *Moon*	———	———	*brain,*
Mars	———	———	*bile,*
Mercury	———	———	*lungs,*
Jupiter	———	———	*liver,*
Venus	———	———	*kidneys* and the *organs of generation,*
Saturn	———	———	*spleen*[140].

Leaves are the *hands* of the vegetables. Their lines (*signatures*) indicate the properties that they possess.

The physician ought to know the planets of the microcosm, its meridian, its zodiac, its orient and its occident.

CHAPTER XXXI

Iatricy or the Art of Healing

(From iatreao, Gr. I heal)

For the *iatric* philosophers, each plant and each constellation correspond, on the one hand, to some tree, some plant, some mineral, and, on the other, to such or such part of the human body.

The application of this principle to the art of healing was quite simple: the seat of an illness being known, iatric astrology, in order to destroy it, uses plants correlating to the part of the body affected. It is thus that *basil*, *lavender*, and *saffron* were indicated for healing the pains of the *stomach*, because this vital organ was under the empire of *Leo*, and because these three plants corresponded to this sign.

Others, in order to heal, employed plants whose configuration of parts had some similarity with that of the affected part of the human body. Thus, *anthora*, representing by its roots two hearts united, was indicated for maladies of the *heart*, and *anthemis* (chamomile) passed for an ophthalmic plant, because its flower has some similitude with the organ of sight, etc. The efficacy of these anthropoid plants (*anthropos*, man, *eidos*, imitation, *that which resembles man*) has often given reason to this method.

The observation of the similarities went so far as even the color of the juice of the plants, their flavor, their aroma, their touch, etc., and finally the number of their coupled leaves, that of the petals, of the stamens, that of the knots of the stem, etc., went under the domination of such plant, and presented even more resources to the astrologer physicians.

The relation of the three kingdoms to the astrological fictions of the hierophants, who had determined these concordances between man, the elements, the celestial bodies, and the numerous individuals of these three kingdoms, proves that, if they sometimes erred in the interpretive systems that they established, they had at least pushed the observation of nature much further.

The harmonies, so admired, of *Bernardin de Saint-Pierre*, between the animals, the vegetables, and the great mineral masses, were all known by the Egyptian priests. They were found disseminated in their religious fables. This naturalist philosopher has rediscovered only what existed four thousand years before him. It would be easy to reproduce the table thereof[141].

IATRIC MASONRY

This Masonry was instituted in the 18th century. The adepts sought the universal medicine. We know of only one grade, entitled:

THE ORACLE OF COS. - Sacred words: *Adonai*. They respond: *Solomon*.
Passwords: *Eloah*. Id. *Stibium*.

Cos was the capital of an island of this name, in the *Sporades*, near Asia Minor, homeland of *Hippocrates*, *Appelles*, and the poet *Philotas*. The celebrated physician, called the *father of medicine*, in whose honor this grade was composed, was born around 460 before our era, and died at a very advanced age.

You will find in the *Tuileur général* the emblems of the *Oracle of Cos* and its two columns.

EXEGETICAL[142] AND PHILOSOPHICAL SOCIETY

This society was founded a Stockholm (Sweden), in 1787, for the secret teaching of the doctrines of *Swedenborg* and *Mesmer*. They also taught there the occult sciences.

CHAPTER XXXII

Mesmerian Masonry
OR THE RITE OF UNIVERSAL HARMONY

There has been recognized, in nature, a universal, occult, and imponderable agent or fluid, governing and modifying all the beings, and which, specialized in the human organism, has received the name of ANIMAL MAGNETISM. It is a vital force that every organism possesses and can emit.

This essentially communicable agent, at the desire of the will, causes the living bodies through which it is permeated to undergo infinitely remarkable and, most of the time, beneficent transformations by its eminently curative and always sedative properties.

MESMER[143] discovered it at Vienna around 1772, and proclaimed the existence of a *universal fluid*, capable of being disengaged, transmitted, and becoming a means of healing in a multitude of various ailments; he called it MAGNETISM, because of its attractive analogy with the magnet. It follows from here that magnetism is, in some way, the *science* of attractions. Treated as a visionary and insane, he came to Paris in 1778 and operated there marvelous cures, which greatly excited the public curiosity. In 1784, the government named a commission of *scientists* to examine the means that Mesmer employed and to state the results obtained; but the report was not favorable, despite the efforts of the celebrated *Jussieu* to support the existence of the marvelous effects of the magnetic fluid, recognized publicly by the scientist *de Puységur*[144] and by the doctor Cloquet[145]

Mesmer instituted at Paris, in 1782, the rite of *Universal Harmony*[146], based on animal magnetism. They believed then, and with reason, that no doctrine capable of striking the spirits by some mysterious circumstance ought to be foreign to Freemasonry.

Indeed, if the Mason, worthy of the fair title of *père de famille* ought, in order to merit it, to be at once, in his house, the *legislator*, *Priest*, and *physician*, his medical knowledge, unsupported by observation and experimentation, may only be very incomplete. Let him become a *magnetizer*, and the art of healing, in many cases, becomes with him a fact useful to all.

Thus, in the high grades, if the present *Rose-Croix*, instead of *playing at sacrilege*, and the *Knights Kadosh*, at philosophy, under the anti-Masonic Templar veil, occupied themselves seriously and religiously with studying and learning to apply a science intended for the well-being of the human race, it would be most worthy of these Masons who are yet but *half* the benefactors thereof. But this science was not to be communicated, in the first degree of the *greater mysteries*, but to the brethren devoted to humanity, and whose morals and discretion would have been proved and recognized in the three *symbolic* grades, scrupulously given[147].

These considerations bring us to entering into some details on magnetism and somnambulism, in the aim of interesting and enlightening a large part of our brethren; foreigners, unfortunately, to the magnetic notions.

A Freemason ought not be unaware that the ancient sages, after having studied the phenomena of nature and the laws of all creation, have believed to perceive the existence of two worlds: the *material* and visible world, and an *incorporeal* and occult world; the one limited in its effects, and whose apparent and manifest causes in their eyes could be explained; the other, infinite in its essence, incommensurable in its power, and whose often impenetrable causes remain, for them, enveloped by a mystery whose depths they could probe only at long intervals. They sought a common, *absolute criterium*, with which they may relate these two orders of phenomena, in order to explain the greater part of the wonders and the operations which seem supernatural. You will see further on that these two worlds are but one; and we hope that magnetism will lead to the discovery of that *absolute criterium*[148].

CHAPTER XXXIII

On Magnetism

All is possible in magnetism.

MAGNETISM, practiced in antiquity by the gymnosophists of India, by the Magi of Persia, and by the initiates of the greater mysteries, appears to have been only under the iatric (*medical*) bearing and under other names[149].

There has become again, since MESMER, a new, beautiful, extraordinary thing, worthy of the highest interest and of the serious study of the philosopher and Mason[150]. We do not believe to exaggerate in saying that at the point, though yet imperfect, to which the magnetic science has arrived, it is the path which opens a vast future to the *world of truth and light.* It illumines, it enlightens its adepts and, ALONE, it may fix them in the *belief of the true*, and resolve, later, the great problem of the *absolute.*

It has for support the universal substance, in which all is unveiled for the SEER (the *omnivoyant*). In his *magnetic* state, there is a complete absence of all distraction, an entire suspension of the dealings of the soul with the body, and, during its intimate union with the universal soul, nature has no more secrets for it. The step that remains to be taken is immense, without doubt, but the prodigious effects, acquired from the studies made, do not leave the result doubtful, result in which man may find even unto the *accomplishment of his destiny*, so misunderstood up to the present.

This physical agent or *magnetic fluid* is the vital or nervous fluid which, emanating from man, partakes of his heat, of the principle of his vitality, and of his intelligence.

To magnetize or make use of one's *magnetic fluid*, is to make use of one's existence, of one's vital principle, of one's life, in order to add, momentarily, to the existence of others. The doctor *Chardel* said, with reason, that "the vital magnetic fluid is with man that final modification of the light called the *spiritualized life.* It serves as agent to the soul for the execution of all its actions. The impulse that we give it, in our movements, stops at the limits of the organism, whereas in magnetizing, the *will* projects it outwardly. That is, as concerns the use of the life force, the primary difference which exists between magnetizing and acting," (*Essai de psychologie physiologique*, p. 205, 1831).

To magnetize someone, is therefore to deploy, extend, and augment within him this principle of vitality and intelligence of which it is already provided.

All heat comes from the sun, which thereby impregnates all the bodies. We draw our own from the atmosphere where it is in principle. All heat which disengages itself from a body or from a fluid bears within it a principle and an aroma which are its properties. Thus, our blood, provided, in its circulation, with a normal heat and a very strong aroma, may, *by our movements*, project them outside of us[151], and, *by our will*, penetrate the bodies and the individuals upon whom our intention directs them. The individual, thus impregnated, has a vitality and an intelligence *in addition*, that the magnetizer directs, under the influence of which he finds himself, and whose *will*, that greatest lever that man has at his disposal, is perhaps, itself, in the fluid state[152].

In order to act magnetically well, it is necessary to have *strength*, *energy*, *will*, and to employ much gentleness and benevolence toward the magnetized, that one saturates with his fluidic and caloric aroma, by which, through its radiation, the atmosphere itself is aromatized.

As soon as the organic and intentional molecules, escaped from the magnetizer, mingle with the subject, if he is suitable and disposed, there is established between them an intimate, mysterious connection, and the phenomena that they expect delay not to manifest themselves, not only upon the organ bestirred, but upon the whole system, and the fluidic union is such that the subject experiences in the same part of the body the pain that the magnetizer feels, or the person with whom he is put into contact.

Magnetism is an art which, for the happiness of humanity, will soon be generally practiced; it is a *work of charity*, but it is also a work of patience and devotion.

The magnetic effects are certain and always the same, because the universal substance is invariable. They are exercised equally upon animals sleeping or awake, and even upon inanimate objects.

The common conductors of the magnetic emission in the medicative work are the hands and the gaze, the voice and the breath.

The known gestures are called *passes* and last ten to fifteen minutes in order to make the subject enter into somnambulism[153]. The fluid is directed and descends by following the nervous strands unto the extremity of the fingers, and leaping beyond this limit in order to strike and penetrate the bodies upon which the *will* directs it.

"The being who finds himself in this state acquires a prodigious extension in the faculty of sense: several of his exterior organs, ordinarily those of sight and hearing, are made supple, and all the operations which depend therefrom are operated internally…," (doctor HUSSON).

When somnambulism arises from magnetism, as simple as it was, the magnetism becomes compounded.

The thought, although unpublished, conceived in the brain, before a *seer*, is made into a daguerreotype in a manner to become readable for him. Does the magnetizer read a letter, a journal in the next room? The *seer* repeats the contents that he sees clearly in the mind of the magnetizer; which appears to him even easier (*less fatiguing*) than reading at a distance. (See *Magianism.*)

The unfeeling indifference of the Indian prisoners, acclaiming their *song of war and death* in the midst of tortures; that of the martyrs of all times, are the result of the ecstasy caused in them by a magnetic reaction.

Man, by the energy of his personal virtuality, has a certain power to modify many things and their circumstances. Indeed, magnified by the enthusiasm of a powerfully excited passion, he wins over and dominates all that surrounds him and changes, consequently, the conditions and customary productiveness of life; and his power of *will*, carried to its highest energy, occasions inexplicable phenomena. This will exists in the *first cause.* From here, the origin of all phenomena: if you frequent sad, gay, spiritual, or violent men, you will find yourself inclined toward melancholy, gaiety, the spirit, or violence. The *intimates* who habitually frequented Socrates participated in his intellectual faculties, which abandoned them some weeks after they were separated from him.

There are many things of the domain of the senses which yet surpass the limits of science.

The experimenters, up to this day, have not arrived at any complete result; and the professors, in their privileged chairs, have all been impotent to discover the truth of the facts, because their studies have not led them to appreciate the magnetic effect, so powerful, which emanates not only from the *terrestrial* magnetism, fed by the solitary action, but also, and more powerfully perhaps, by the astral magnetism which inundates our atmosphere and permeates all that has life and action.

Let the scientists deign to study this idea and to submit themselves thereto, they may only progress from discovery to discovery for the well-being of humanity and for their personal glory.

ON MAGNETIC ELECTRICITY

They claim today, as being verified *by experiment*, that magnetism and electricity are one and the same thing. For the *seer*, the color of the magnetic fluid is that of the electric spark.

However, M. the Comte *de Szapary*, in his *Magnetothérapié*, establishes a difference.

He considers man as an *electro-magnetic* machine: the electricity flows in the blood, the magnetism in the nerves, it is the nervous fluid. All the functions of the body and the soul are operated by the magnetism; all the disorganizations by the electricity. In renouncing the theory of the magnetic fluid in the nerves, and that of the electric currents in the blood and the organs, they no longer give an account, *he says*, of the mechanism of the functions of the human machine and of its orders. According to this author, the illnesses arise from a struggle of the superabundant electricity with the magnetic force, of the latter with the electricity. The persons among whom the magnetism predominates experience the chills; they are difficult to warm; and it is with difficulty that one brings a coolness to persons dominated by too much electricity.

The principal electric current flows from the brain to the hollow of the stomach (*solar plexus*), and from there to the brain. The first current takes place in the day, by the movement that is given to the body, and the second at night, through the dream. The stomach and the brain are in a continual rapport, the one sustained by the other. It is because of this that if one experiences too sharp of an impression, for example, a sudden fright, one touches oneself involuntarily on the head and stomach, in order to draw back there the fluid withdrawn too quickly. This oscillatory movement is the magnetism of the man who has his poles of affinity in his fellow-creature. The indefatigability of the body comes from the spiritual activity which causes the magnetic fluid to reascend to its source.

The magnetic force comes from the sun, it penetrates the earth and comes back out of it, and from this encounter or friction of its own force with itself *arises heat.* From the absorption of this emission of the earth results the chemical decomposition and the growth of the bodies which are found there; from the physical heat results vegetation.

The moon has an electric, *destructive*, *putrefying* influence. It diminishes the magnetic force of the sun, cause of the *semi-sleep* among the somnambulists, disquiets and troubles the sick. *Cholera*, *plague*, and *typhus* are electrical illnesses.

Man does not fortify his magnetic vigor by contact with the earth, since it attracts the magnetic force of the sun. It takes his superfluous vigor. That is why the lively and petulant children love to roll around on the ground.

WAKEFULLNESS AND SLEEP: The exterior revelations of life are different in sleep than in waking: in the first case, the polarity (*property of the magnet to be directed towards the poles*) changes place, and while the senses of the exterior are resting, those of the interior are awake (*the soul dream*). From this changing of rest and activity comes, for the body, refreshment and strength.

We will consider the book of M. the Comte *de Szapary* as one of the more complete works on the magnetic science: it is a reasoned manual, full of facts and indispensible to every magnetizer.

We know that this group of electric sparks which escapes in a luminous aigrette from a voltaic battery possesses a salutary influence over a great number of hopeless nervous illnesses. M. Theodore *Courant*, disciple of *Beickensteiner*, author of the *Etudes sur l'électricité médicale chez les anciens*, employed, with success, for the magnetic science that he perfects, and with happiness, for the afflicted that he relieves or heals, *magnetic electricity*. His manner of operating is quite simple.

He places the sick upon the stool of an electric machine. He places himself in the sphere of action in order to secure the electric fluid, appropriate it to the human organism, vitalize it, and, thus centupling its magnetic forces, he acquires a power great enough to re-establish, in a nearly immediate manner, with the subject on whom he operates, the *circulation of the fluids*, the perturbation of which gives rise to the majority of sicknesses and sometimes death. In this case, a magnetizer may wrest from death an individual who, in the impotent hands of the best physician of the faculty, would infallibly succumb.

The most constant effect of magnetic electricity is to re-establish this circulation and the increasing of the energy thereof by the emission of a vivifying fluid. We would restore pith and vigor to the elderly who had become dull, if the vital fluids recovered, within him the energy which, in his youth, operated the general circulation. Science may, perhaps, supplement this in part; all is not discovered: magnetism is still only at the state of glimmering.

MESMERIAN APHORISMS

The *immaterial does not exist*: the light, the universal soul are incorporeal fluids, but essentially material; for all that is, is something, since upon the metallic sheet of the guerroetype, the images fixed there invariably produce something.

The universal substance is *one*; it is all at once, *light*, *heat*, *intelligence*.

There is no space *without body*.

Cold *does not exist*: it is a *lesser* heat.

The opacity of the bodies *does not exist*. (For the *seer* the light is everywhere.)

The immensity is *without distance*.

For the eternity, time *does not exist*.

Speaking on the sun: *all by it*, *nothing without it*.

God is the *universal substance*, he is *light*, *heat*, *intelligence*.

But the sun is the author of the universal substance, and yet it is not God. Would it be the residence of God from where God animates the universe?

Not daring to write that *God is all* and that *all is God* or *all in one* and *one in all*, in fear of passing as *pantheists* or as *naturalists*, although they recognize, like *Agrippa*, that the *immaterial does not exist*, the magnetist authors say that God, which they consider as the *universal substance*, the soul of the world, is *omnipresent*, *omniscient*, and omnipotent: but omnipotent up to the limit of the *nothingness*; for God has *all power*, *except over the nothingness*, which is *non-being*. The non-being author of God necessarily implies the forfeiture of his qualities of omnipresent, omniscient, and *God cannot consider himself in the abstract*.

God cannot do *nothing*; God cannot cease to be; two barriers raised against his omnipotence. Man can, in some manner, cross this final barrier; for he can destroy himself, cease to be man. He becomes something else, but *it is no longer man*.

Nothingness cannot, therefore, take place as long as God will be. God cannot make it. Nothingness would limit his *infinity*, God would be *finite*: *he would no longer be God*, which cannot be; for nothing, in the universe, would be renewed any longer.

God, then, can neither make nor experience *nothingness*, because God cannot cease to be. He is all, he is all-powerful, the universal intelligence which creates, animates all. The visible universe, of which he is the conductive and conservative genius, is *God manifested*[154].

CHAPTER XXXIV

On Somnambulism

"Those who see only with the eyes of the flesh are very near to being blind."
(CLAUDIA RACHEL)

SOMNAMBULISM is produced either by natural dispositions, or, among the sick, during the *magnetic* action; it ceases then after the healing. In this state, the sick has a particular feeling keen enough to see, comprehend, and indicate what may be salutary to him and to others.

Somnambulism is a mixed state between sleep and wakefulness. We will distinguish two species thereof, the *natural* or *spontaneous*, and the *artificial* or *magnetic*[155].

The first expresses the state of a subject who rises spontaneously, *during the night*, *walks* and carries out certain actions; this is the *noctisurgium* of the Romans, that it would be better to translate as *noctambulism*.

The second is the state incited in a subject by the *will* or the processes of the one who magnetizes, or by the subject acting on himself or receiving an impression from a magnetic body; this is the *somnus medicus* of the Romans. But as in this *sleep* it is no longer a question of *walking*, but of healing, the expression *somniatricism* would have been fitting.

There are individuals who, *awake* and falling into ecstasy, are endowed with the power to be entirely *absorbed* (after *absorption*, there is magnetic nutrition) and to project their sight into space: they are the best *seers* who know the *past*, the *present*, and even the *future*; thousands of facts attest to this[156]. These individuals thus magnetized, and unknown to them, must hold principally this faculty of *terrestrial* magnetism with which their nature is found *en rapport*.

What is remarkable, is that, in their beginnings, these *seers*, most lucid and most astonishing in their ecstasies, do not believe in somnambulism, and do not put any faith in the extraordinary facts that they have revealed with the greatest exactitude. They are unaware of their magnetic power. We know a person who claims to draw from the atmosphere the element of these always justified revisions, and which, for her, is found traced there. She was also long in disbelief of her power.

A *lucid* somnambulist, a SEER, does not resemble a sleeping being any more than an active man who is in a state of sleep. His matter becomes torpid, but his intelligence is expanded beyond; it lives in the *ether*, that spirit of eternal life. His soul, nearly *fluidified* in unison with the elasticity of the *universal substance*, soul of the world, *living and regenerative fire*, from which it emanates, receives infinite perceptions. He embraces all, he enjoys *ecstatically*, he is happy and pleased in this state: nature and all its marvels are revealed to him at any distance.

All the bodies are moved within the midst of the light that the sun radiates. All light disengages infallibly from the heat to which are pervious all bodies and all fluids. It results therefrom that the solar rays, at once luminous and caloric, permeate, transpierce all the bodies which, exteriorly and interiorly, remain enlightened by the light, which is disengaged from their relative heat, according to their nature and porosity. From here come two sorts of light: the light *apparent* to our sight, and that which is *invisible* to our organs, when the sun, source of life, is hidden from us. Heat being inherent to the light, as the light is to the heat, all the bodies permeated with the solar heat are therefore enlightened by a *phosphorescent* light which is disengaged from the heat of the bodies, and which, in the darkness, guides and enlightens certain animals, such as the *mole*, the *owl*, etc.

This continuity of invisible light that pervades the perception of the seer, with greater rapidity than is able the reputed electric spark sliding over its iron filament, shows that, for it, the bodies have lost their opacity. - Every individual may be a magnetizer, but every individual is not a somnambulist.

In antiquity, somnambulism was called *prophecy*.

ON THE UNIVERSAL SOUL OR ANIMATION

The UNIVERSAL SOUL, source of the life of all beings, and the ANIMATION of the three kingdoms and worlds, is, according to the Hermetic physicists, light, heat, electricity, and magnetism, both terrestrial and astral, intelligence and movement, all supreme effects submitted to one same cause.

Friction, whence comes the discovery of the electric fluid, produces, at the same time, electricity and heat, and, at its exterior point, light, three effects which have a common nature, since one same cause engenders them.

DEDUCTIONS. The universal soul being *light*, it is intelligent; being, by its universality, without interruption, it is *all-seeing*, *omniscient*. As all light has its relative heat, and since all heat, by its incessant movement, exercises in the body a penetrative action, the light is *omnipresent*. Finally, as by its concretion under various aspects and its alternate and perpetual disconcertion, it produces and renews all, the light is *omnipotent*. From here it results that the *universal soul* (substance) is all, is everywhere, that it sees all, knows all and produces all. Then, being *light*, *intelligence*, *heat*, and *movement*, it unites all the attributes of God.

The intelligence or spiritualization decorated with the name of *soul*, sensibility or sentiment are produced by the constant action of the universal fluid elaborated by the encephalon (the brain), whose differences of organization cause the intellectual differences.

ON THE OCCULT (invisible) WORLD

This extraordinary sight of the somnambulistic *seer* ought not make one believe in the *real* existence of *two worlds*, as credulous commoners think. There can only be one world, the one where we live and that we are still far from knowing well. The air, the odors, the fluids, the terrestrial and atmospheric influences, etc., etc., are invisible; they belong to our world, and are improper to form thereof a second.

The *soul of the world*, uncreated, universal, generative, of which all the bodies are permeated, and of which our animation takes part under the name of *human soul*, does not form a second world. It is invisible, incorporeal, but not immaterial, according to the magnetist authors.

The *soul*, in the state of *ecstasy*, whether natural or caused by the addition of a fluid analogous to its nature directed by a magnetizer, is accumulated in the cerebral reservoir at the expense of the other parts of the body, deprived not of *life*, but of *sensation*. The soul, no longer existing but in the brain, can put to work all the cerebral faculties, without employing ordinary and material organs. This soul, thus disengaged, enters into immediate communication, since it is a part of it, with the universal soul. As this latter penetrates all bodies, the human soul penetrates therein too; it sees and gives an account thereof. And as the universal soul forms one all without interruption, it is easy for the human soul to likewise see everywhere and at considerable distances. But all these things, as extraordinary as they are, do not constitute a *new world*, a *second world.*

The *visible objects* which comprise our world are so many parts concretized by absorption and assimilation of the universal substance, of which they are then the *manifestation*. After their discretion by emanation and decomposition, they are fluidified, etherized, and universalized. Thus, returned to the great all, every manifestation disappears; they become invisible. From here it results that the two worlds are but ONE, since it is always the *universal substance* with or without manifestation, that is to say the *materialized* fluidic substance or the fluidic material substance.

CHAPTER XXXV

On Thaumaturgy[157]

Magnetism, developed by science and by the knowledge of the *occult world*, was called THAUMATURGY. A thaumaturge, to the eyes of the vulgar, was a performer of miracles. Ignorance has caused since, these denominations to be taken amiss. The sciences which follow are of the domain of thaumaturgy.

ON THE PROHPETS[158]

Progressive spirits, accustomed to the contemplation of the astral and terrestrial phenomena, regenerated in a deep and incessant meditation, exalted, in the silence of retreat and in the peaceful contemplation of study, by the austerity of a life of application and by a violent contention of the soul, experienced long *ecstasies* (see Somnambulism) during which their intellectual sight, leaping across the intervals, the spaces, and even the obstacles placed between them and the reality, plunged into the future. It was read therein the immutable destinies of the empires and the nations, and their mouth proclaimed them with the sublime accent of inspiration, without them comprehending the chain of causes from which they derive.

The college of the great initiations was, in antiquity, a school of *prophecy*.

ON DIVINATION

"Nothing of importance has occurred in
this world, without having been predicted."
(MACHIAVELLI)

Divination (from *divinare*, to divine) is the science of the future.

According to the opinion of the mystics, all beings, from God down to the atom, have a particular number which distinguishes them, and which becomes the source of their properties, as well as their destiny. Chance, according to Cornellius Agrippa, is, at its foundation, only an unknown progression, and *time*, but a succession of numbers. Now, the future being a composite of chance and time, they ought to make use of the Qabalistic calculations in order to find the end of an event or the future of a destiny.

Many have thought that *Pythagoras* was so named because, in the predictions of the future, he gave answers no less certain and true than those of the Pythian of Apollo. His name is derived from *puthon*, diviner, and *agoras*.

He discovered and taught the power of the numbers which, in his system (see p. 191), resolved the problem of cosmogony. "There is," he said, "a connection between the gods and the numbers which constitutes the species of divination called *arithmancy* or *arithmomancy*. The soul is a world, it moves itself by itself. The soul contains within itself the quaternary number."

His science of the numbers was based on the Qabalistic calculations. The astronomy that he taught mysteriously was astrology; but his most secret science was alchemy.

The Greeks, like the Egyptians, had divided divination into *artificial* (augurs and aruspexes) and natural (by dreams[159] and oracles[160]. They called the first *mantike* (knowledge through the augurs and aruspexes), and the second *manike* (knowledge through the delirium of the spirit).

The Romans only knew the artificial divination: the *augur* and the *aruspex*, that they regarded as uncertain or deceitful; from here come the strange contradictions of *Cicero* in his opinions on this science and in his treatise on Divination; yet he was from the college of augurs and placed this dignity above all those with which he was invested.

CHAPTER XXXVI

On Psychology[161]

PSYCHOLOGY is the part of philosophy which treats on the soul, on its faculties, and on its operations. The psychological science, science of the soul, is the first rung of that immense ladder that it is necessary to learn how to *climb* in order to know the truth. But, in order to attain thereto, *it is necessary to be as*, in the beginning, man was, in the presence of the nature from which he received directly the impressions in the fullness of their action. It is necessary to be entirely free from scientific and religious prejudice. The science, in general, makes an abstraction of politics and religion, in order to be ONE AND UNIVERSAL.

ON PHYSIOLOGY[162]

"The philosophy of the future will be psychology perfected."

BALZAC.

PHYSIOLOGY is the science of the principles of the animal economy, of the usage and play of the organs. It is the science of life and animated nature. It is by it that *Lavater* and *Gall* have succeeded in *physiognomic* and *phrenological* discoveries. *Vegetable* physiology is the science of the vital functions of vegetables. *Mineral* physiology occupies with success, at this moment, some privileged scientists.

ON PHYSIOGNOMY[163]

PHYSIOGNOMY teaches the knowledge of the inner moral of man through his exterior; and his character, his inclinations, etc., through the inspection of the countenance, because the magnetic fluid, that life of the thought, imprints upon the countenance the moral sensations which characterize the distinctive traits thereof. Indeed, says M. de Ségur, "the habit of certain affections of the soul gives to the muscles of the face a contraction which allows the character to be read upon the appearance."

The talent or art of distinguishing things by their look is the feat of the *physiognomist.*

We often see that the one who does not believe in physiognomy distrusts a man or an animal on its appearance, a mushroom on it look, and a plant on its color.

LAVATER, born at Zurich in 1741, is the creator of this curious science. We have from him: *Essais physiognomoniques*, in 4 vol., in-4to, 1775-1778. He died in 1801 from the effects of a wound received at the time of the retaking of Zurich by the French in 1799.

ON CHIROMANCY

The science which teaches the knowledge of the future of a person at the inspection of his hand, is called CHIROMANCY (from the Greek *cheir*, hand, and *manteia*, divination). Main [hand] (*manus*) comes from the Arab verb *mana*, to count;

whence comes *manach*, calculation; *al-manach*, the calculation (of the days of the year according to the revolutions of the stars); *mene* (the moon); *mensis* (the month, *measure* of the year); *moneia* (money, in order to regulate the *accounts*). The Greeks called the 5, *pente*, all (*the whole hand*); because of the *five fingers*, and they expressed this number by the letter V which represents the four fingers separated from the thumb.

Although the hand does not seem to offer the importance of the skull, it is however, like it, a sort of register where are traced the various vicissitudes of life. The numerous lines which streak the palm are so many hieroglyphs which, joined with its shape and that of the fingers, indicate the human destiny and the good or vicious inclinations that it is necessary to cultivate or combat. This is an *original* book, the reading of which ought to be learned at the same time as ordinary reading. More simple than that, it does not stop being useful, for it informs the adolescent of his destiny, according to his *written* inclinations, as well as of the connections that would be useful or dangerous to him to make with such persons who extend their hand, and that he should only take with knowledge of cause.

We read in the book of *Job*, written 1800 years before our era, and 200 years before Moses:

"God then placed as a seal upon the hand of all men, so that all the mortals that he employs as his workers know their dependence (*destiny*)."

It is a truth, long recognized, that the hand differs according to the professional class of the individuals, and that it is transmitted thus for several generations: a lawyer or a doctor, son of a laborer or an artisan, will bear the hand of his fathers, and transmit it, slightly modified, to his son, and so on. The hand is therefore the characteristic sign of the race and serves marvelously the science of prognostics. It was, in antiquity, a bond of union and friendship. It was transmitted by the Gnostics, admitted by the English, and it cannot but be perpetuated everywhere, because a hand is the symbol of the future. A handshake expresses confidence, the hope that one places in the person who receives it; it is thus that, in order to indicate the intimate, indissoluble union of marriage, they say of a young woman that she has *given her hand*, that she has been united forever.

Two hands united and gripped symbolizes *good faith* (grade of *Master*).

Each profit of the unceasing service that the hand procures without appreciating the infinite merit thereof:

The hand commands, accuses, calls, sends away, approves, disapproves, affirms, denies, receives, and repels; it is the auxiliary of the teacher in the chair, the lawyer at the bench, the orator at the tribunal, among whom it doubles the power to move; finally, how would one operate without it in the magnetic work? But the msot noble of its privileges is its movement of supplication towards heaven in order to address our vows to the Creator of the worlds[164].

ON THE PHYSIOLOGY OF THE HAND

The infinite number of fibers which gather together, form, upon the surface of the human body, the organ of TOUCH. They comprise three membranes called *epidermis* (outer skin, cuticle), *ritivale*, and *skin*. Their concussion, transmitted to the *sensorium* (brain) by the nerves, produces there these two great movers of life: *pleasure* of *pain*.

The organ of touch, which the five senses enjoy, resides particularly in the hand, as being the most flexible part of the body, and the one which best lends itself to the various caprices of the will. If it were possible to increase the articulations thereof, that is to say the number of fingers, no doubt they would add, in proportion, to the power of sensation[165].

How admirable is the structure of men! Further, he is endowed with this vast intelligence which embraces the infinite, plus his brain is spacious and his hand is furnished with ganglions[166]. The functions of the hand are nearly universal. The principal agent of the fifth sense (*touch* is superior to all those that they have invented: the hand feels and measures the most voluminous bodies as the very smallest; it analyzes, models, manufactures, transforms, all that exists; creates all that the genius suggests to it; provides a living, prepares the food that it conveys to the mouth; protects, defends against obstacles; serves as guide in the darkness, makes known the real state and the property of bodies: shape, size, resistance, temperature, etc., from where arises other knowledge. Ever-active messenger of the intelligence, the hand is the exclusive portion of man. Many animals are superior to him in sight, hearing, scent, and taste; the touch of man erases them all by its perfection, since it is consecutive to them and rectifies their errors: we touch, because we have seen, heard, smelled, and tasted the objects.

Thouch is voluntary; it supposes a reflection in the one who exercises it. The other senses do not require such. Sound, light, and odors strike the respective organs without one expecting it, whereas one touches nothing without an act of will. Touch is the geometry of the spirit, the sense of the reason. The hand permits the spirit to *solidify itself*, by detaching our being from all that surrounds it. It hollows out the space, establishes the expanse, measures the distance, exercises all the arts, realizes all the materials of the globe, the expanse of which it makes known to us, and places us in a position to traverse space.

Those who have examined the ascending scale of the hominal series, and of the animals, have seen that intelligence shines everywhere, and grows in proportion to the sign of perfection of that organ. Here are the observations made among the idiots, cretins, and imbeciles:

IDIOT (who is without idea, nor understanding). The thoracic member and the hand of the idiot are misshapen and atrophied (emaciated) like their brain. Their forearm is deprived of movement of rotation; the small hand, supported by a large wrist, sometimes lacks a palm (the inside of the hand between the wrist and the fingers), or the wrist remains inclined toward the palm.

IMBECLIE (weak of spirit, incapable). The hand of the imbecile has a little more development, but it is considered badly conformed, and the muscles of the arms, although less restrained in their movements, do not have much more extent than those of the idiot.

CRETIN (imbecilic and deformed). The hand has nothing normal with the cretin. Its movements are restrained. It is mounted upon a large wrist at the base, and at the extremity of the fingers, the coverings are absent or under-developed. Too voluminous and too slender, and always badly formed, this hand and the arm seem to communicate to the deportment and the bearing an uneasy and constrained air.

Among the men of ordinary intelligence, the hand has nothing abnormal. It permits sometimes a certain beauty; but its movements are no less constrained, being mounted upon a large wrist. Dupuytren has remarked that the tactile part of the hand is meagre and that the coverings, at the end of the fingers, are under-developed or absent.

Among those of a superior judgment, the thoracic member and the hand are models of perfection. This hand, always supported by a fine and slender wrist, is particularly organized and *en rapport* with the art or science that they cultivate.

The modern physicians have indicated other facts: the hand is tuberculous among consumptives and the scrofulous. The avaricious have crooked fingers, and the prodigious have the inverse.

All these observations are worthy of fixing the attention of the philosopher and the Mason.

ON CHIROLOGY

CHIROLOGY is the science of language with the aid of the hands; for, one of the precious advantages of the hand is to be the auxiliary of the speech and to serve as lingual organ and expressions among the *deaf and mute.*

The hand, instrument ceaselessly in communication with the brain, that temple full of mystery and marvels, that abode of the thought and understanding, is always fashioned upon his greater or lesser perfection, that is to say, according to the brain in its development, it is more or less well-proportioned.

We know that the fingers are called: the *thumb* (*pollex*, the sign of power)[167], the *index* (the indicator), the *medius* (middle finger), the *ring finger* (which receives the ring)[168], and the *auricular* (the little finger, the only one which may be introduced into the ear); their language is called *chirology.*

The celebrated *Abbé de l'Epée*, born at Versailles in 1712, dying in 1789, was the first who turned this ingenious language to his advantage by founding the *Institution of the deaf-mutes*, eminent philanthropic establishment, created in the aim of giving to the arts, the sciences, and to society, a number of individuals who, without this fortunate invention, would have been unhappy and a burden to the social body instead of being useful to it.

One may supplement by *digitation* (the touch of the fingers) the loss of sight. We could cite a multitude of examples which verify that the blind have indicated colors, coins, cards, etc., and others who have succeeded in reproducing, with clay, statues perfectly similar to those that they had *under the hand.*

CHAPTER XXXVII

On Phrenology [169]

> "The glorious era approaches when philosophy and morals will be founded on phrenology."

PHRENOLOGY teaches the discovery of the natural dispositions and the elements of the character of each individual. With its aid, one may succeed in knowing, with some certitude, the passions, inclinations, sentiments, and faculties of intelligence of the man.

Life continues in the organs by two things: the FORM (*type*) or the mold into which matter incessantly fashions itself, and ANIMATION or the vivifying forces which renew that matter regularly, by conforming itself to the type, whence comes a moral change at some such period of life, a change always more notable than that of the physical, because, above all, of the continual exercise of the intelligence over the connections between those of the exterior or visible objects.

This interesting science, more complete than physiognomy, has an immense scope which is balanced only by its evident and moral utility. Its interest is general and such that it should be part of the public instruction. When everybody, from the age of reason, shall be a *phrenologist*, each will know all his inclinations, he will cultivate the good ones and combat the bad ones. They will mutually connect one another. They will no longer be but little deceived, because they will be willing, since they will always know with whom they have business. One would confide without danger, or distrust whomever, without need of sanction, one might watch. Then, we shall see the mass of misdemeanors and crimes diminish gradually. The happiest consequences will proceed from this theory applied to general education, and what was, in principle, the laughing-stock of small-minded or short-sighted men, will become the admiration of the philosopher, and one of the best safeguards of society. If this science had had more doctors and partisans, such heads would have never governed.

The celebrated physiologist GALL is the founder of phrenology. Aided by his disciple *Spurzheim*, distinguished physician, he created his system and published his discoveries in 1808. Both having continued their works with the perseverance and sagacity of the genius of observation, the numerous facts that they collected on the aptitudes and innate dispositions of a considerable number of individuals whose moral portraits have all been recognized and avowed as accurate, established formally this curious science, into which the judges especially ought indispensably to be initiated, in their *baccalaureate*, in order to be able to penetrate the mystery of the motives which determine the majority of human actions, according to characterized types. Those who deny the revelations of physiognomy and phrenology, do not know how to read the countenance nor surmise anything from the exterior of the body, or rather they fear being unveiled[170].

The study of the philosopher and Freemason ought always to be completed by accurate notions on the *psychological*, *physiological*, *physiognomical*, and *phrenological* sciences, the intimate relationships of which seem to form but one alone. We do not doubt that, if phrenology were seriously practiced by an examination committee of each lodge, the Masonic body would be better composed, and masonry more brilliant and more sought, for its splendor holds only to its good composition. It is this consideration which has led us to give these notions, in order to excite the study in the spirit of our readers.

ON FREE WILL

> "The form of the material organs which determine the penchants, inclinations, and instincts of the living beings may always be modified, for upon the earth, every generative and free being is essentially mutable."

The liberty of man consists in *willing what he may*. One author has said: "The will [volonté] is to the free will [libre arbitre] what the wright is to the balance," (*Baron Massias*).

Man cannot completely enjoy his *free will*, unless he is enlightened by the light of occultism. In order to correct oneself, it is necessary to know oneself; and one does not know oneself but very imperfectly.

The response to the third French Masonic question: *What do we come to do in lodge*? is: *Conquer our passions, subdue our wills, and make new progress in Masonry* (the moral)[171]. Masonry also says indeed, as the inscription of the temple of Sais: Know thyself, or as the Indian maxim: *Know thyself and the Being* (the soul of the world). But it does not indicate to its adepts, as is otherwise done in initiations, the means to attain this noble aim. The Mason is therefore forced to have recourse to the instructive sciences that we have just expressed.

Although they are still imperfect, they shed enough light to make known one's passions, the tendencies of one's intelligence, the penchants of one's heart; in order to lead him to combat them, if they are deadly, and to develop them and direct them, if they are good; in order to labor, with resolution, to perfect his moral and his intelligence, he attains, at the same time, to the perfection of his entire being. The traits of his face, the protuberances of his brain, the shape of his hand, his gait, his demeanor, will become modified. Thus, after having attained the ideal moral that will have been proposed, he will realize his physical perfection. With such a system of conduct, the human race would not have degenerated.

The material substance that the parents transmit to their descendants being of the same nature and the same form as their own, the configuration of the organs which arises therefrom nearly always renders hereditary the intellectual faculties, the moral penchants, the corporeal traits, produced by an identical nature, bringing too often with it the predispositions to some such family sicknesses.

It is this plastic study and the rectification of the essential parts of the human organism which caused the institution, among the Magi and among the Egyptians, of a reasoned mode of physical and intellectual perfecting. They called the first EDUCATION, and the second INSTRUCTION. But, among the mature men, it is a new instruction which ought to modify the acquired education: "Upon the ocean of life, to what would serve that the reason were the rudder, if passion was the pilot?"

Epicurius said, and Lucrecius repeated:

"Philosophy alone delivers from every vain fear the one who gives himself thereto: to serve it, is to devote oneself to liberty. By it too one succeeds in mastering oneself. This one alone is sure to be superior to his passions, who has been enlightened by this science, and to whom the knowledge of causes and effects has revealed beforehand by what path he may attain the aim of his life, happiness. Thus, three serious motives militate in favor of the philosophical studies: the remedies that it offers against all the ills of the body and soul, the security that they inspire relative to the exterior world, and the moral power that they give to the man over himself.

CHAPTER XXXVIII

On the Occult Sciences

"Ignorance renders men credulous, the knowledge of the mysteries of nature renders them believers."
(H. DELAAGE).

In the FASTES INITIATIQUES, we see to precede what we have to produce in *Qabalistic*, *alchemical*, and *Hermetic* grades, with some rudimentary explanations on the OCCULT SCIENCES. We are going to extract therefrom some of those which will suffice to give an idea of these sciences, practiced, formerly, with such great reserve, in the ancient mysteries and in the Pythagorean schools, as complement to the high initiation or secret doctrine.

We think that capable professors, Masonry counts some of them, would give much interest to the *first two degrees* that we invite to establish, by basing them on the development of the philosophical sciences that we have just cited with sufficient details to convey the conviction thereof into the spirit of instructed Masons, devoted enough to the expansion of the useful knowledge to undertake this noble task. Then, we would no longer come out of our temples without profit for the intelligence:

The occult sciences would be reserved for the *third philosophical degree*, in which would be completed, with the corresponding *symbolic* grade, the education of the modern initiate who, with enough practice, would find himself having attained the summit of the ancient initiatic knowledge.

Those who declare such feat impossible do not know how to extend the possible.

The occult sciences were, in all times, the apanage of the privileged intellects; they were to be studied in themselves and for themselves; they wished a sustained zeal and an indefatigable perseverance[172]. The principle is ONE, therefore the light is ONE, and initiation (*practice*) is reserved to the one who wills firmly, according to the axiom: WILL IS POWER.

The elite geniuses who have made themselves the instituters and civilizers of the human race have wished to cultivate in man intelligence, moral and physical, in order to see humanity attain to happiness and to the perfectibility that his nature permits him to achieve, and to aid him in his irresistible penchant to expand the limit of his power.

ON ASTROLOGY

The knowledge of the phenomena of the sidereal world, of the influence of the stars over the terrestrial bodies and the scientific inductions which were drawn therefrom, gave rise to ASTROLOGY. Intimately bound to the study of the stars and their revolution, it is certainly the first and, consequently, the most ancient of the sciences and of the superstitions. The aim of the astrologers was to predict the future by the inspection of the heavens. They attributed to the constellations and to the twelve signs of the zodiac, under the influence of the planets regarded as arbiters of our destiny, qualities and virtues or various influences over men, over empires, and over future events. The inductions drawn from the twelve signs, called the *twelve houses of fate*, each of which had its particular influence, comprised the *genethliac* art (from the Greek *genthle*, birth) or the art of the horoscopes (from *hora*, hour, and *skopeo*, I look).

Ptolemy was an astrologer, for he believed in its influences.

The astrologers divided the physical existence of all that breathes into four temperaments: the *sanguine*, the *bilous*, the *melancholic*, and the *pituitous*.

Astrology, applied to the *microcosm*, human body, has given rise to *physiognomy*, that it divides into *chiromancy* (from *cheir*, hand, and *manteia*, divination), and *metoposcopy*, (from *metopon*, brow, and *skopeo*, I look), which teaches to predict the future by the inspection of the lines of the hand, and by the examination of the configuration of the face.

It gave rise likewise to *magianism* or *magic*, and this is divided into an infinity of divinations: by the proper names, by the four elements, by the evocation of shades, by the fish, etc.

Astrology, practiced in the Pythagorean school, disappeared at the annihilation of the initiatic colleges in the Gauls, by Caesar. Since, there have only existed the abuses thereof. In the 16th century, the celebrated Tycho Brahe, who had faith therein, made vain efforts to rediscover it. The charlatans and the almanacs of Liege have exploited his renown.

ON THE KABBALAH OR QABALAH

Felix potuit rerum cognoscere causae.
(Virg.)

The mysterious laws which rule the invisible world, known from the remotest antiquity, gave rise to a science which, later, was called QABALAH or SACRED TRADITION. This science is independent of the epochs and the religious forms: the Orientals, whether Indians, Arabs, or Hebrews; the Europeans, Catholics, Greeks, or Protestants, admitted likewise the principles thereof and the combinations.

The Qabalistic doctrine was long the religion of the sage and scholar, because, like Freemasonry, it tends, ceaselessly, towards spiritual perfection and toward the fusion of beliefs and nationalities between men. In the eyes of the Qabalist, all men are his brethren, and their relative ignorance is, for him, but a reason to instruct them. There have been illustrious ones among the Egyptians and among the Greeks, the doctrines of whom the Orthodox Church has accepted; the Arabs have also produced many, whose wisdom has not been repelled by the Church of the Middle Ages.

The sages wore with pride the name of *Qabalists*. The Qabalah contained a noble philosophy, pure and non-mysterious, but symbolic. It teaches the dogma of the unity of God, the art of knowing and explaining the essence and the operations of the Supreme Being, of the spiritual powers, and of the natural forces, and to determine their action through symbolic figures, by the arrangement of the alphabet, by the combinations of the numbers, by the reversal of the letters of the Scripture, and by means of the hidden meanings that they claim to discover therein. The Qabalah is the key of the *occult sciences*.

The *Gnostics* are born of the Qabalists.

CHAPTER XXXIX

On Magianism (Magic)

"Neither young man nor elder ought to remain a stranger to the study of philosophy. One is never so young that they may hesitate to be initiated into the practice of this science. Otherwise, it would be to say that there would not still be time to be happy, or that, it is too late to be happy." (EPICURIUS.)

The MAGI, those sages of the ancient Orient, observed and studied the nature of man, the mechanism of his thought, the faculties of his soul, his power over nature, and the essence of the properties and the occult virtues of each thing. These investigations, reduced to a body of doctrine, took the name of MAGIANISM, basis of the religion of ZOROASTER and of his initiatic science. Magianism is found in his sentences, in the hymns of Orpheus, in the invocations of the hierophants, and in the symbols of Pythagoras. It is reproduced in the *Occult Philosophy* of Agrippa, in that of Cardan, and it is recognized, under the name of MAGIC, in the marvelous effects of magnetism.

There are no longer any *magicians*, or there are magicians without magic; but we know of scholarly *magists*, whose works are remarkable[173].

Let us move on to the initiation of Magianism.

MAGIANISM is the science of sciences, or rather it is the ensemble of all the sciences or human knowledge. That is why, in antiquity, the magi were the most scholarly philosophers. Indeed, a magist ought to be initiated into the principal sciences: 1st, the preparatory science is the knowledge of the ancient languages, that of the Qabalistic signs, characters, alphabets, talismanic hieroglyphs, and others, in use within occultism.

2nd, in order to predict and announce the tremblings of the earth, the storms, the great inundations, the appearances of comets, it is necessary to have astronomical notions.

3rd, as the *lucid* subjects are the first instruments of prediction, and as, in order to render one lucid, the magist must employ a vegetable fluid, the study of botanicals and natural history is indispensible.

4th, these plant juices (or *subtle fluids*), attacking particularly the intellectual organs, as we are going to see, they necessitate the deeper study of anatomy and physiology.

5th, in order to foresee the epidemic diseases: plague, cholera, influenzas, fevers, etc., it is necessary to understand pathology, physics (which contain the fluids) chemistry, etc.

6th, as all diseases are but the result of miasmatic (*fluidic*) emanations of the body, the appropriation of medicaments, as means of healing, ought to have the same proportion in the vegetable fluids as their opposite. It is therefore homeopathy, as law of similars and true epitome of the medical or allopathic sciences, that must be known.

The deep study of all these sciences comprises *magianism*, which has need of comparative facts, so as not to err.

Some magical drawings or figures may lead some impressionable persons into a magnetic state, such that they are subjected to the mute will of the capable magist who operates upon them. These persons often have strange visions; they carry out what the magnetizer mentally orders them. The causes, the forces which produce these curious effects are, we have said, the idea, the strongly concentrated will, that is to say the animic influence of the spirit over the spirit of others, because of the homogeneity of nature. This effect of magianism is only the result of another form of magnetization but limited to a small number of individuals. It is this extraordinary result which has given rise to the *magical disks*.

MAGICAL DISKS

They employ, in the experiments of magianism, cardboard disks, covered with colored papers. At the center of each circle is the number of order that the color occupies in the solar ray. To the left is written the action that the colors ought to produce upon the subject, and, to the right, is found the sign of the planet from which each disk draws its protection.

These disks are in the number of *nine*: seven represent the original colors. Disk no. 8 is *white*, and no. 9 is *black*; they signify *beginning* and *end*. The action of each consists in striking with force the imagination of the subject. They produced different phenomena from one another; here is the table:

DISK	PLANTS	EFFECTS PRODUCED
1. Violet	*Hydrociam. nig.* *Adrop. bellad.* *Dat. starmon.* *Cannab. ind. hashish.* *Strychn. colubr.*	Continual movement of the arms and legs; desire to touch something or to walk over some objects; cries, barking, imitating well those of the dogs; desire to bite and attack someone with a knife; complete intoxication; appearances of all sorts of blessings; all that he desires, he possesses in illusion (*he has remembrance of all that has occurred and all he has seen*).
2. Indigo	*Pip. nig.* *Veratr. sabad.*	Feverish excitation; weakness in the abdominal members. The subject kneels and wishes to make his prayer of which he cannot recall a single word. Loss of sight, despite which he walks with ease; trembling of the eyelids; the eyes end up closing; deep sleep (*one can only wake him by pouring water on his face*).
3. Blue	*Pip. cub.* *Laur. camphr.* *Ass. fœt.* *Con. macul.*	General excitation, convulsive movements; desire to sleep; loss of all reasoning; somnolence; dejection.

4. Green	*Pseu. angust.* *Lact. vir.* *Atr. Mandr.*	Abundant tears; he plays with his hands like a child; desire to run; he claims to walk more quickly than a horse. Shuddering of all the muscles of the body; he wants to say his good-byes, as if he were going to die; general numbness; lethargy.
5. Yellow	*Strychn. n. vom. Op.* *Strych, igna.* *L. sativ.* *Veratr. alb.* *Asper. office.*	Balancing of the head foreward and backward; general numbness, sleep (*while opening his eyelids, the presence of the* yellow *disk puts him in a great fury, the cause of which he cannot explain, the other colors produce no effect on him*). Voluptuous dreams, extreme chills and pallor; complete dejection; new sleep; zoomagnetic state during which he may walk, take a stroll, and see perfectly, despite his eyelids being entirely closed; he responds to questions addressed to him on different things that in his waking he is completely unaware of (*he does not retain any memory of all that he has said, or of what has occurred*).
6. Orange	*Sel op.* *Valer. offic.* *Nicoti. tab.* *Convul. jal.*	Great joy; numbness of the upper and lower members; sleep (*while opening the eyelids and presenting him the* orange *color disk, he shows a great desire to smile, uninterrupted by any moral suffering, which he cannot explain*); tears, tendency towards a great lucidity.
7. Red	*Prunell. vulg.* *Lavand. stœn.* *Lavand. ver.* *Digit. purp.*[174]	Cries pushed by fear, he fears hidden persons showing themselves to do him harm. Acute and intermittent cries; this state lasts 2 and a half hours among some, and up to 4 and 5 hours among others (*he must have enough time to re-establish himself*).

Since the plants indicated in the table produce effects analogous to the colors, the magist ought first to employ the *plants*, then the *colored disks*, in order to direct and maintain the action produced by them.

One ought to make use of these plants only in order to prepare the subjects for the great intellectual works to which they are to be subjected; then they become useless, for at the sole presence of one of the circles belonging to the class of the planets whose effects he will have already experienced, the subject will fall back into the same state; here is an example:

A young man of twenty years, of an excellent health, was, some years ago, put to sleep with chloroform in order to perform an operation on him.

Recently (1853), he was presented with a bottle covered with black paper upon which was glued the formula or the quantity necessary of *chloroform* to put a man to sleep. This bottle was completely empty, and, a bizarre thing, this young man was immediately put into a sleep analogous to that already experienced at the time of his operation; there existed among him then, no feeling or consciousness[175].

Returned to his normal state, it was asked of him what he had experienced. He answered that he knew perfectly what it was, because the doctors had already put him to sleep in the same manner. (*It would be desirable, in the hospital, to employ the same means.*)

THE HUMAN BODY COMPARED TO AN ELECTRIC PUMP

We have seen above that the human body has been compared to an *electro-magnetic* machine. Perhaps it would receive a more just denomination by comparing it to an electric pump which functions by the voltaic piles, fed by the acidulated liquids, where the two force and suction pumps (*absorption* and *emission*) correspond to the *systolic* and *diastolic* movements of the heart. The comparison would be all the more accurate, as the numerous vessels with which the human body is provided would correspond to the multiplicators of the electric pump, which multiply its force as the numerous blood vessels multiply the force of the heart, by means of the two conducting vessels (the *aortal artery* and the *vena cava*); these correspond to the two poles, *positive* and *negative*, of every electric machine, which, being deprived of one another, destroy then all respiratory function, whence derives *catalepsy* or apparent death.

In this state, the function of the lungs seems suspended, the vital (*magnetic*) fluid is concentrated in the body of the subject. He remains there as conservator of his sleeping life, that may reawaken at the approach of a metal, the contact of a magnetizer, or the effect of an electric machine, which would re-establish the action of the suspended vital functions[176]. It is thus that a cataleptic or one supposedly dead for three days and more would be restored to life (*resurrected*) if he was deposited, on the last day, in a metallic coffin, as they claim that it was done among the ancients. We know that one can render oneself cataleptic by submitting to a severe fast where vegetables scarcely figure.

Apparent death, or *lethargy*, may be artificially induced in every individual, by means of the magic disks; but it never occurs naturally, or after the organic affections, but by the accumulation of the electrical fluids, without the generative organs of this fluid, as proves a number of experiments.

Indeed, what if a man has, for several days, attained an apparent death? It suffices to approach him with a magnetizer, who will have the sick placed on a table, head towards the south; he will place himself to his right, place his hands on the sides of the trunk, fingers directed toward the aponeurotic attachments of the pectoral muscles, and will make alternately, every second, movements of pressure; then, at the end of one to five minutes, life will return and the lungs will resume their functions.

This sleep cannot be better compared than to the chloroformication and to that of the *lucids*: in the first case, the subjects operated upon experience a mental suffering and not physical; in the second, one sole faculty exists, it is that of the speech.

Some years ago, an experiment of magianism was made upon a young girl. Being asleep, they asked her if 40 grams of chloroform would be too strong a dose to put to sleep a young girl of twelve years (*that was her age, and it was a question of her*). After a moment of silence, she answered that *she saw the child, and that there was nothing to fear.* They had her returned to her ordinary state, they gave her a bottle containing the 40 grams, and she went to sleep. Twenty minutes later, they gave her the use of speech, and, posing different questions to her on the state where sleeping persons were found, she said that they never lost the use of their intellectual faculties, which, in the contrary, were found in their greatest development, and even capable of judging the more or less advanced science of the operator. After various other questions, they had this child pass into an ordinary sleep. She remained so for eight hours before awaking. This young girl never had any knowledge of the superhuman faculties she possessed.

THE SLEEP OF THE SOMNAMBULIST DIFFERS FROM THAT OF THE LUCID

Somnambulism is a true somnolence, occasioned by animal magnetism or the action of the will, directed by means of the manual passes whence escapes, according to the magnetizers, the nervous fluid. This somnolence is none other than a numbing of the senses, during which the somnambulists have the faculty of acting, walking, leaping, etc.

The somnambulists may, without the help of a magnetizer, put themselves into somnolence, catalepsy, ecstasy, and provoke upon themselves, by their own will, all the phenomena that, up to the present, the magnetizers have attributed to their vital forces.

In this state of somnolence, which is but a numbing of the senses, the vicious subjects put forth, indiscreetly and shamelessly, the secret feelings, unbridaled desires, that they experience in the state of wakefulness; an enormous difference with the lethargic sleep of the lucids, during which they cannot make any movement. They are unaware of good and evil; if they discuss with them criminal deeds or exemplary actions, they cannot tell the difference. This state is easily conceived: in the first case, the spirit and the sensory organs remain in the same disposition as in the ordinary state; in the second, the caloric is nearly suppressed; the limbs, face, all the surfaces of the body are cold, and, an astonishing thing, is that the caloric is preserved in the respiratory paths; the breath is hot and the breathing slow; the muscles of the mouth are contracted, and give the countenance a bitter expression which disappears only at the moment of waking. Indeed, in the ordinary state, the radiance of the caloric is brought about from the center to the circumference, then the skin is hot. In the state of *lucidity*, the contrary takes place, that is to say that the radiation of the caloric occurs from the circumference (the *epidermis*) to the center, where the concentrated fire makes the breath hot[177].

NO REMEMBRANCE FOLLOWS THE AWAKENING

After awakening, the somnambulist has no remembrance of what he has said or done, because the action of the soul taking place *extrinsically*, outside of the individual, does not react upon him[178]; whereas a person who has had a dream, may remember it, because the animic or spiritual action was accomplished *concentrically*.

ON RELIGIOUS MAGIANISM

The religious ceremonies of the ancients were but a spiritualized magianism: prayer, fasting, the mortifications supplemented by the plants; the religious objects, sculptures, paintings, banners, ornaments, produced the effect of the colored disks. The perfumes which the Egyptian priests burned in their temples, the sound of the instruments, the lustral water, the sprinklings, the chants, the exhortations, succeeded in conveying the assistants to the exaltation of the senses and of the soul.

Here is an experiment made upon a man in the prime of life and vigorously constituted; he submitted to this for a salary.

They had him fast for three days, not taking, evening and morning, but a glass of water in which they put two grams of hemp powder, taking care to have him say, at the same time, his prayer. On the third day, they had him read aloud some stanzas from the odes of J.-B. Rousseau, while recommending to him to execute the movements analogous to the elocution. Soon, the book fell from his hands and the declamatory gestures continued. Having nothing more to read, he repeated what he had read and finished by improvising, devoid of any instruction: this was a machine of words and gesticulations. It was only with difficulty that they succeeded in stopping his movements. His calm restored, they left him in complete darkness, the book arranged on a table. He ended up, in order to amuse himself, by performing the reading thereof, etc.

This latter phenomenon, as extraordinary as it appears, will be understood by the magists. Here is how this man, having attained to a very high degree of exaltation, can read despite the darkness: since he was deprived of light, his eyes have convulsed, the dilated pupil touched the upper part of the socket, and operated there a slight tension of the optic nerves which disengaged, in the interior of the skull, a phosphorescent light which sufficed to illuminate him.

ON THE MAGIC OF WORDS

We read in *Origen*: "There are names which naturally have virtue, such as those used among the sages of Egypt, the magi of Persia, the brahmans in India. What they call MAGIC is not a vain and chimerical art, as claim the stories and the epicurians: the name of *Sabaoth*, that of *Adonai* have not been made for created beings; but they belong to a mysterious theology which is related to the Creator. From here comes the virtue of these names, when they arrange them and pronounce them according to the rules."

We know that the sacred word Jehovah was, among the Jews, an ineffable name. So that its pronunciation would not be lost among the Levites, the high priest uttered it in the temple only once per year, on the 10th of the month of *Tisri*, day of the great fast of expiation. During this ceremony, they recommended to the people to produce a great din, so that this sacred name was heard only by those who had the right; for any other, say the Jews, would have been immediately stricken dead.

The great Egyptian initiates, before the Jews, acted likewise with regard to the word *Isis*, that they regarded as a sacred and incommunicable word.

When the Jewish high priest uttered, according to the rules, the word Jehovah[179], they said: *Schem hamm phorasch*, signifying *the name is pronounced well*[180]. These three words form the sacred word of a Scottish grade.

We find this belief at the top of the instruction of the third degree of the *Knight of the Black Eagle*, called *Rose-Croix*[181]:

"Q. - *What is the most powerful name of God on the pentacule*[182]?

A. - Adonai.

Q. - *What is its power?*

A. - To set the universe into movement. The one of the knights who would have the good fortune to pronounce it *Qabalistically*, would have at his disposal the powers which inhabit the four elements and the celestial spirits, and would possess all the virtues possible to man."

The ancients, believing that the soul of man, after his death, put on a form similar to the one that he had during his life, so that it may be distinguished from another soul, they have thought that he could, on this occasion, come to see again the places that he had lived, to visit his relatives, his friends, to converse with them, instruct them, and indicate to them the manner to evoke them. Thus, the word *abraxas*, pronounced with some ceremony, was called upon to make appear the souls with whom they desired to speak.

Virgil himself believed that by pronouncing letters according to the magical method, they forced the moon to descend to the earth: in his eighth eclogue, he says seriously:

"*Carmina vel cælo possunt deducere lunam.*" (Verse 69.)

"They make, with words, the moon fall into the earth."

"They hold of the celebrated *de Laharpe* that, in his childhood, he attended so often, by curiosity, the mass of a priest who pronounced the *hoc est enim* numerous times, until he believed that, by the aspirated intonation of these words, the descent of *his* God into the bread and wine had been successfully carried out. His mass lasted more than three quarters of an hour, and the most intrepid blessings escaped his mystification.

"This fanatic was in the state that the pagans called *autopsy* (intuitive vision); state by which they had an intimate commerce with the gods. They believed themselves invested with all their power, and they were persuaded that there was no longer anything impossible.

"The Romans also believed that by pronouncing certain sacred verses, they had the power to cause *Jupiter*, called *Elicius* (by Numan) to descend from the heavens.

"The brahmans said that the figure or figures of the supreme God became *God*, when they had consecrated it with the ceremonies necessary to that end.

"We see that, in all times, the evocation, the conjuration, and even the appearance of the gods and demons, of the shadows and saints, have been a part of the cults profitable to the exploiters of queen and country, *credulity*. But this observation is not relative, in any fashion, to the consecration of the bread and wine of the modern offering." (The *Mass* in its relation to the myst. and cerem. of antiquity, 2nd edition, p. 280, 1 vol. in-8vo.)

THE MAGIC OF THE WILL

We know that man possess a magnetic spirituality which, keenly aided by the *will*, is the most powerful lever which has been placed at his disposal. We may therefore call this vital and propulsive influence which acts so powerfully upon the soul and spirit of the magnetizer, MAGIC OF THE WILL. It sets into motion even unto the inanimate objects, according to the expression of Virgil:

"Mens agitat molem" (the mind agitates matter).

TO MAGNETIZE IS TO DO MAGIC

"Let us relegate magnetism into the religious sanctuaries, desirous to take it out of the venal hands of the

charlatans who would compromise it and the musers who ridicule it."
(H. DELAAGE.)

MAGNETISM is, as we have indicated, a constantly active, vital, and curative force, which penetrates and animates all: it is the animalized, vitalized, intentionalized, propulsive electricity, the magnetic power of which produces such extraordinary effects upon the activities, so mysterious, of the human organism, that they seem to hold as *magic*, because it is not yet given to science to explain the physical causes thereof, no more than those of the functions of life, the functions of alimentation, of reproduction, and a thousand others. But we believe strongly that magnetism well studied, or, if you will, the science of the magi, is the golden key which will open this yet impenetrable sanctuary, where the studious and persevering adept shall be initiated into the mysteries of his being and his destiny.

The study of the action of the spirit of man over matter that, by his will, he animates with his life, as, formerly, Prometheus animated the potter's clay by breathing the *celestial fire* into it that he stole from the gods, will lead the initiate infallibly to understand the action of the *universal* spirit throughout all nature, and to give an account of the eternal phenomena and of those which are only ephemeral. The source being ONE, the spirit of man is of the same nature as the universal spirit, which means, psychologically and with reason, that man (the *human* soul) has been made in the image of God.

It is because of these marvelous deeds that a skillful magnetizer passed formerly as a *magician*; because, infiltrating his life, his essence, his force, and his will into the body of another, he transmits his thoughts to him, he immediately makes him share in all his painful or agreeable impressions; he makes thereof a docile instrument of his fantasies; he lives in him to such a point that the magnetized or the *magicked* put into somnambulism likes less in himself than in the magnetizer with whom he is identified; he can make him walk, dance, kneel, take such pose as a statue which is unknown to him, but whose image is in the mind of the magnetizer, and even subject him to false perceptions, for example, drinking water, and making him say (*and he believes it*) that it is Burgundy or Malaga wine, etc.[183]. There is more: a letter, a glove, a lock of hair, may replace him, because the least part of the fluid contains a fraction of the individual which is equivalent to his whole person, so that all his impressions are immediately felt by the somnambulist, at whatever distance he may be found.

While we conclude this chapter (May 1853), a witness worthy of trust came out of a lucid or somnambulism session, who knew only French; she was put in contact with a Turkish interpreter speaking five languages. She pronounced without hesitation and simultaneously, Arabic, German, Greek, and Latin phrases, with the same ease, the same purity of sound, and even the same inflections of voice as her interlocuter, even knowing the meaning of her locutions, since, by the effect of assimilation, she read it, with the words, in the thought of the polyglot. This phenomenon has led non-enlightened individuals to believe that the somnambulists have the gift of tongues.

These strange facts appear supernatural, denomination given improperly to what one does not understand, for nothing may be *supernatural*, that is to say above nature.

Not all somnambulists have the same degree nor the same kind of lucidity, nor the same animic faculties: the one has the gift to see illnesses, to foresee and predict their return, to explore the atmosphere and predict the plague, cholera, typhus, and other malignant fevers, the other, to see at a distance through opaque bodies, to discover the courses of water which circulate under the terrestrial epidermis, the sources which may surge up therefrom, like the Abbé Paramelle[184], to read a closed book, etc.; others have the inappreciable faculty to perceive the different fluids of the plants and to indicate their medicinal properties.

It is likewise with the magnetizers, of whom they ought to be, in general, mistrustful. Their faculties differ much; which makes the good magnetizers less common. There are some privileged ones who, endowed with an exceptional character, succeed in vanquishing among their subjects their dispositions towards *diversity* which produce *divagation*, and in leading them to a perfect *fixity* of which the marvelous result is *reality*, *truth*.

Every physician who exercises, through devotion to humanity, the first of the sciences, that of healing and relieving, ought to be a magnetizer and even a somnambulist, if it is possible, or else his art, however long the experience which enlightens him, is no more than an incomplete and vulgar profession. Let us cite an example: the celebrated *Dumez* is a somnambulist physician. Upon waking, he reads the prescriptions ordered by him in the magnetic sleep. He is always confounded at the superiority of the somnambulist over the physician. Indeed, this latter can only give *human* prescriptions; they signify *perhaps*. The other announces divine prescriptions; they signify *it is this*. Such is the meaning of the mysterious recommendation of Hippocrates, so long misunderstood: *Seek the divine*!

If we enter, with some detail, into the exposé of these sciences, so filled with interest, it is certainly not, we guard ourselves well therefrom, in order to rival the knowledge of Aubin *Gauthier*, *Chardel*, *Szapary*, *Dupotel*, *Duplanty*, *Gentil*[185], Henri *Delaage*, Alexandre *Levavasseur* and other masters in these matters: their writings instruct us, and our book can do nothing to teach them. But, in extending ourselves thus, our sole aim is to initiate, as far as we are able, the studious and *elite* Masons into this high intellectual study which honors the genius of man, in order to lead them to create an OCCULT MASONRY where all the sciences would be seriously studied and professed; while awaiting the civil authority, enlightened on the importance of the benefits that humanity is to receive therefrom, to have established MAGNETIC CLINICS in the schools of medicine, where the various LUCID (*omnivoyant*) subjects are studied, directed, and classified in a manner to draw therefrom, by a *well introduced fixation*, the foresight of the scourges which decimate men, ruin empires, and even the scourge of war.

ON TABLE TURNING

The vital fluid which emanates from the hand of man, or from several hands, may set into motion inanimate objects, with the surrounding objects experiencing it. This principle applied to a vase, a hat, a table, animates them, and submits their mobility to the will of the magnetizer. This magic of the day has made thereof a more than fashionable, *universal*, pastime; and from this *fluidomania* there may result an advantage, that of putting within the reach of everybody the magnetism which had against it numerous incredulous persons that a simple game will have converted more easily than the teachings of science.

Here is the process:

The experimenters, seated around a table, take good care to be in contact with each other and with the table only by means of the *magnetic chain*. It consists in placing (*without pressing*) the hands on the table, the little finger of the right hand resting on the little finger of the left hand of the next person, and so one. After a certain number of minutes, the fluid begins to penetrate the table which renders stronger the adherence of the hands to its surface.

The head of the chain whose fluid unites with that of the other persons takes the direction thereof, in a manner that the piece of furniture is dominated only by a single fluid, or rather that it is animated by only one spirit; and the property of the spirit being movement, the table delays not to be agitated. Then, according to the will and whim of this head, and according to the form of the chain, it turns to the right or to the left, goes forward or to the side, or strikes by one of its legs the number of blows thought by him.

All these exercises may be commanded by the voice, which renders it the most extraordinary (most *magical*) spectacle. But, at the basis, the voice is powerless, if it is not the expression of a strong will.

The science will not remain here, despite the incredulous *doctors*.

M. Faraday, in experiments conducted recently at London, has attempted to weaken by cardboard the magnetic effect, and to prove that the hands, exercising a lateral pressure on the table, tend to set it into motion, and that the pressing of the fingers is *for something* in this movement. - Agreed; but has this scientist proven that the movement of the table (they have not dared to say *the rotation*) comes *solely* by the pressing of the fingers? Not at all; this was not what he wished: he preferred to wrap himself in silence rather than to freely recognize, even in his experiments, that the EFFECT PRODUCED (*the rotation*) goes far beyond THE CAUSE which, for him, is only the *pressure of the fingers*.

There must be a very great desire for the phenomena not to exist, in order to come, by means of incomplete experiments, to deny its reality. M. Faraday has too much right to public consideration to have need of seeking to deny a physiological fact well recognized, for the sole reason that the present state of science does not permit the scientists to explain it[186].

PHILOSOPHICAL MASONRY

or

HERMETIC INITIATION

"Initiation was an organized and conservative tradition of the secret scierices."

THIRD PART
PHILOSOPHICAL MASONRY
OR
HERMETIC INITIATION

PREAMBLE

The preamble that we think ought to be given to this third part of *Masonic Orthodoxy*, second part of *Occult Masonry*, is simply an extract from the Orator's discourse in the Hermetic grade of the *True Mason*; it is expressed thus:

"The science into which we initiate you is the first and the most ancient. It emanates from nature, or rather it is nature itself perfected by the art and founded upon experiment. In every century there have been adepts, and if, in our day, artists squander, in vain, their goods, their labors, and their time therein, it is because far from imitating its simplicity and following the right paths that it traces, they adorn themselves with a disguise that it cannot suffer and lose themselves in a labyrinth where their foolish imagination leads them.

"From here come the railleries of these profane who, without respect for God, without esteem for the art, turn into ridicule our most serious mysteries.

"From here come the coarsest satires of those ignorants who, too dulled by their senses to raise themselves to the sublimity of our knowledge, blaspheme all that they cannot comprehend.

"From here comes the ridicule affected by those indolents who, unless a capable spirit and a laborious hand takes for them all the trouble of discovery and work, scorn all that they have neither the strength to imagine, nor the courage to execute.

"From here come the injurious libels of those reckless persons who, with a boldness full of bad faith, dare to place the truth and the Hermetic science at the rank of fabulous inventions and popular superstitions, without any other motive than the desire to invalidate the authenticity thereof, and the impossibility of destroying the evidence thereof.

"Let us abandon these children of darkness and those enemies of themselves to all the shame of their vain and inconsequential ideas. For us, true children of the light and sincere friends of humanity, who see the truth in our teachings, let us enjoy the advantages and the sweetness that it procures for us."

BASIS OF HERMETIC MASONRY

This Masonry or science, which crowns all that the human genius has been able to conceive of the most sublime, is supported upon three columns:

FAITH: it precedes the work
HOPE: it accompanies it;
CHARITY: it follows the success of the work.

HERMETIC CITATIONS

Let us add, before entering into the material, some extracts from *Hermetic instructions*, which will prove to the Masons raised to the *Mastership*, that they do not understand well the hidden meaning of their grade until after being initiated into the science of Hermes, if they have the good fortune, by their merit and their studies, to be admitted thereto. They will also recognize, in the *Qabalistic* citations which follow, the striking concordance of the religious doctrines with the secret doctrines of the high initiates, to which they seem to serve as veil; which has caused Bacon to say: "A little knowledge makes one a skeptic, much knowledge makes one a believer."

QUESTION. - *Are you supreme commander of the stars?*

ANSWER. - *I have seen the direction of their rays.*

Q. - *What is signified by the earth which receives the rays?*

A. - That, without it, we cannot *build*, and that the vivifying fire is necessary to it.

Q. - *What does the interred body of Hiram mean?*

A. - That, within the earth, is contained the most beautiful of secrets.

Q. - *What have you encountered within the earth?*

A. - The *rough ashlar* upon which *three* were the number *seven.*

Q. - *What else does the tomb of Hiram represent?*

A. - That the first matter cannot reproduce until after putrefaction.

Q. - *What is represented, in lodge, by the Very Fortunate* (*Very Respectable*)?

A. - Hiram, or the first matter, after the putrefaction, become the living source.

Q. - *Why is he seated in the East?*

A. - Because it is necessary that all matter be exposéd to the rays of the sun, from the rising to the setting.

Q. - *Why have they made you lie down on the tableau?*

A. - Because the Very Fortunate represents the first matter in putrefaction.

Q. - *Why have they pulled you up by the finger?*

A. - To recall to me that every good *Mason* is to assure himself whether the matter is *putrid*, before passing to the second operation.

Q. - *Why do you hold your arms crossed in lodge?*

A. - In order to bear witness to the patience that it is necessary to have in order to succeed.

Q. - *What is signified by the word* FORCE [strength] *upon the blazing star?*

A. - The black matter, indicator of putrefaction.

Q. - *What is signified by the word* SAGESSE [wisdom] *upon the moon?*

A. – The white matter, sign of purification.

Q. - *What is signified by the word* BEAUTÉ [beauty] *upon the sun?*

A. - The red matter, source of all goods.

Q. - *Why have they blindfolded you?*

A. - To show me that, although a Mason, I was in darkness.

Q. - *How old are you?*

A. - The number fifteen (3+5+7).

QABALISTIC CITATIONS

Q. - *Why were you received Knight of the Qabalah?*

A. - To know, by the numbers, the admirable harmony that there is between nature and religion.

Q. - *How were you announced?*

A. - By twelve knocks.

Q. - *What do they signify?*

A. - The twelve foundations of our temporal and spiritual well-being.

Q. - *What is a Qabalist?*

A. - A man who has learned, by the tradition, the sacerdotal art and the royal art.

Q. - What does this motto signify: *omnia in numeris sita sunt?*

A. - That all lies in the numbers.

Q. - *Explain this to me.*

A. - I am going to do so up to the number twelve, your sagacity will grasp the rest.

Q. - *What does the unity signify in the number 10?*

A. - God creating and animating matter expressed by *zero* which, alone, has no value.

Q. - *What do you mean by the unity?*

MORAL ORDER	PHYSICAL ORDER
A. - A word incarnated in the womb of a virgin; a religion.	A spirit corporized in a virgin earth; a nature.
Q. - *What do you mean by the number 2?*	
A. - Man and woman.	The agent and the patient.
Q. - *What do you mean by the number 3?*	
A. - The three theological virtues.	The three principles of the body.
Q. - *What do you mean by the number 4?*	
A. - The four cardinal virtues[187].	The four elementary qualities.
Q. - *What do you mean by the number 5?*	
A. - The quintessence of religion.	The quintessence of matter.
Q. - *What do you mean by the number 6?*	
A. - The theological cube.	The physical cube.
Q. - *What do you mean by the number 7?*	
A. - The seven sacraments.	The seven planets.
Q. - *What do you mean by the number 8?*	
A. - The small number of elect.	The small number of the wise.
Q. - *What do you mean by the number 9?*	
A. - The exaltation of religion.	The exaltation of matter.
Q. - *What do you mean by the number 10?*	
A. - The ten precepts of the law.	The ten precepts of nature.
Q. - *What do you mean by the number 11?*	
A. - The multiplication of religion.	The multiplication of nature.
Q. - *What do you mean by the number 12?*	
A. - The twelve articles of faith. The twelve apostles, foundation of the Holy City,	The multiplication of nature. The twelve operations of nature. The twelve signs of the zodiac,

who have preached everywhere for our spiritual well-being.	foundation of the primum mobile, spread throughout the universe, for our temporal well-being.

The rabbi (president of the Sanhedrin[188]) adds: "From all that you have just said, it results that the unity is developed in 2, achieved in 3 within, in order to produce 4 without; whence, through 6, 7, 8, and 9, it arrives at 5, half of the spherical number, which is 10, to show, in passing through the number 11 to the number 12, and to raise itself, by the number 4 times 10, to the number 6 times 12, end and completion of our eternal happiness.

Q. - *What is the generative number?*

A. - In the divinity it is the *unity*; in created things, it is the number 2; because the divinity 1 engenders 2; and in created things, 2 engenders 1.

Q. - *What is the most majestic number?*

A. - It is the number 3, because it denotes the triple divine essence.

Q. - *What is the most mysterious number?*

A. - It is the number 4, because it contains all the mysteries of nature.

Q. - *What is the most occult number?*

A. - It is the number 5, because it is contained in the center of the compounds.

Q. - *What is the most salutary number?*

A. - The number 6, because it contains the source of our spiritual and temporal happiness.

Q. - *What is the most fortunate number?*

A. - The number 7, because it conducts us to the dead, perfect number.

Q. - *What is the most desirable number?*

A. - The number 8, because the one who possesses it is of the number of the elect and of the wise.

Q. - *What is the most sublime number?*

A. - The number 9, because, by it, religion and nature are exalted.

Q. - *What is the most perfect number?*

A. - The number 10, because it contains the *unity* which has made all, and the *zero*, symbol of matter and chaos, from which all has emerged. It comprises then, in its figure, the created and the uncreated, the beginning and the end, the power and the strength, the life and the nothingness. In the study of this number, is found the relation of all things: the power of the creator, the faculties of the creature; the alpha and the omega of the divine knowledge.

Q. - *What is the most multiplicative number?*

A. - The number 11, because with the possession of the two unities, we arrive at the multiplication of things.

Q. - *What is the most solid number?*

A. - The number 12, because it is the foundation of our spiritual and temporal happiness.

Q. - *What is the favorite number of religion and nature?*

A. - The number 4 times 10, because it puts us in a position, by extricating all that is impure, to enjoy eternally the number 6 times 12, end and completion of our bliss.

Q. - *What does the square signify?*

A. - The square is the symbol of the 4 elements contained in the triangle, emblem also of the three chemical principles; these things together form the absolute unity in the first matter.

Q. - *What does the center of the circumference signify?*

A. - It signifies the universal spirit, vivifying center of nature.

Q. - *What do you mean by the squaring of the circle?*

A. - The search for the squaring of the circle indicates that of the knowledge of the four common elements which, themselves, are composed of elementary spirits or principal principles; just as the circle, though round, is composed of lines which escape view and are grasped only by understanding.

Q. - To what belongs, as attribute, the *salt*, *sulphur*, and *mercury*.

A. - The salt is the attribute of the *Father*, the sulphur that of the *Son*, and the mercury that of the *Holy Spirit*. From the action of these three results the triangle in the square, and from the seven angles, the dead, perfect number.

Q. - What is the most confused figure?

A. - The *zero*, emblem of *chaos*, unformed mixture of the elements.

Q. - What is signified by the four mottos of the grade?

A. - That it is necessary to *hear*, to *see*, to *keep silence*, and to *enjoy happiness*.

CHAPTER XL

Hermes

Egypt saw come out of its midst a man of a consummate wisdom, initiated into the secret knowledge of India, Persia, and Ethiopia, named *Thoth* or *Phtath* by his compatriots, *Taut* by the Phoenecians, *Hermes Trismegistus* by the Greeks, and *Adris* by the rabbis. "Nature seemed to have chosen him as her favorite, and to have lavished on him all qualities necessary to study and know perfectly. God had, so to speak, infused him with the sciences and the arts, that he may instruct the entire world thereof."

He invented many things necessary to life and gave them fitting names. He taught men to write their thoughts and to coordinate their discourse. He instituted the ceremonies to observe for the worship of each god. He observed the course of the stars. He invented music, the different exercises of the body, arithmetic, medicine, the art of metals, the three-stringed lyre. He regulated the three tones of the voice: the *sharp* took the summer, the *flat* took the winter, the *mean* took the spring (there was then only three seasons). It is he who taught the Greeks the manner of interpreting the terms and the things, whence they gave him the name of HERMES which signifies *interpreter*.

In Egypt, he instituted the hieroglyphs; he chose a certain number of men that he deemed the most proper to be trustees of his secrets, and only among those who could reach the throne and the first charges of the mysteries. He gathered them and established them as *priests of the living God*[189]. He instructed them in the sciences and the arts, and explained to them the symbols which veiled them. Among these sciences, there were *secrets* thereof which he communicated to them only on the condition that they would obligate themselves, by a TERRIBLE oath, not to divulge them but to those who, after a long trial, would be found worthy of succeeding them: the kings forbade them even from revealing them *under pain of one's life*. This secret is called the SACERDOTAL ART and comprises alchemy, astrology, magianism (*magic*), the science of the spirits, etc. He gave them the key of the hieroglyphs of each of these secret sciences, which were regarded as *sacred* and kept hidden in the most secret places of the temples[190].

The great secret observed, during the long years, by the initiated priests, and the high sciences that they professed, made them consider and respect all of Egypt, which was regarded by the other nations as the college, the sanctuary of the sciences and the arts. The mystery which surrounded them keenly excited their curiosity. *Orpheus* transformed himself, so to speak, into an Egyptian. They initiated him into theology and physics. He so appropriated to himself the ideas and the reasoning of their institutes, that his hymns announced rather an Egyptian priest than a Greek poet, and he was the first who transported, into Greece, the Egyptian fables.

Pythagoras, ever desirous to learn, even consented to undergo circumcision in order to be of the number of initiates, and it is in the depth of the sanctuary that the *occult sciences* were revealed to him.

The initiates into such or such knowledge, having been instructed by the fables, the enigmas, the allegories, and the hieroglyphs, since it was a question of mysteries in their accounts, they wrote *mysteriously* and continued to hide the knowledge under the veil of fictions.

When the destruction of several cities and the ruin of nearly all of Egypt by Cambyse, King of Persia (528 before our era), dispersed the majority of the priests into

Greece and elsewhere, they brought their sciences there that they continued to teach *enigmatically*; that is to say ever enveloped in the darkness of fables and hieroglyphs, so that the vulgar, *while seeing*, saw nothing, and, *while hearing*, understood nothing. All the authors drew from this source; but these mysteries, hidden under such inexplicable envelopes, under such misunderstood fables, ended up giving rise to a multitude of absurdities which, from Greece, were spread throughout the whole earth.

Kircher, in his *Œdipus Ægyptiacus* (v. II, p. 2, *De Alchym.*, ch. 1), expresses himself thus on the occasion of *Hermes*: "It is such an established fact that these first men possessed the *art of making gold*, whether by extracting it from all sorts of materials, or by transmuting the metals, that the one who doubted it or wished to deny it, showed himself perfectly ignorant of history. The priests, the kings, and the heads of families were the only ones instructed therein. This art was always preserved in a great secret, and those who were its possessors always kept a profound silence, for fear that the most hidden laboratories and sanctuaries of nature, being uncovered to the ignorant people, would turn this knowledge to the detriment and ruin of the Republic. The ingenious and prudent *Hermes*, foreseeing this danger which threatened the State, had reason, therefore, to hide this art of *making gold* under the same veils and the same hieroglyphic obscurities, of which he made use in order to hide from the profane people the part of the philosophy which concerned *God*, the *angels*, and the *universe*."

Evidence and the force of truth were necessary to wrest such admissions from this very scholarly father who, in many circumstances, has combatted the philosopher's stone.

Every impartial reader will think like him, not only if he studies history, but if he seeks to give an account of how the extraordinary monuments, the magnificent temples, the sumptuous palaces, and the immense works which covered the ground of Egypt, could have been conceived, undertaken, and executed. All the gold in the world, in this era, would not have sufficed.

But this gold, amassed for this use, came out of the sacred laboratories. The priests, the initiates, and the kings were in agreement: they conceived, it was willed, and the most gigantic works, the most grandiose edifices were raised, without noise, to the satisfaction of the astonished populations, and to the glory of the science, and of the cities whose opulence it founded.

Has not *Pliny* said that the kings of Egypt, in their magnificence, had these marvels of the world erected only to *employ their immense wealth*? - Whence does it arise, if not from the Hermetic art?

Semiramis saw to erect, at Babylon, a temple in honor of Jupiter, at the top of which she had placed three gold statues of 40 feet in height, representing *Jupiter*, *Juno*, and the goddess *Ops*, each weighing 1000 Babylonian talents, with the exception of that of Juno, which weighed only 800. There were two *lions* and two serpents in sliver, each figure, of enormous size, weighing 30 talents; and, in one room, a gold table, 40 feet long, 12 feet wide, weighing 50 talents. The statue of Ops held in the right hand the head of a serpent, and in the other a stone scepter. Do they make stone scepters for gold statues? No. It would be ridiculous, then, if it were not symbolic. But the goddess Ops (*wealth*) was a Hermetic representation. It was natural to present her thus, because the gold of the philosophers is called stone, and their mercury serpent. *Ops* or the *earth*, which was matter, held in her hands these two symbols in order to indicate that it contained these two principles of the art, which, being the source of riches, made *Ops* regarded as the goddess (whence comes *opulentia*, opulence). The two lions and the two serpents complete the allegory, since they signify the material principles of the work during the alchemical operation.

Jupiter and *Juno*, brother and sister, were found in this room, with their grandmother (*Ops*) and before a gold table *common to the three*, because they emerge from the same aurific principle, from which are extracted two things: an aerial and mercurial humidity, and a fixed, igneous earth, which, united, make but one same thing, called *Hermetic gold*, common to the three, since it is composed thereof.

Here is the place to note how much all this sumptuousness, spread with profusion, had enriched the very people: let us refer to the *flight of the Jews*, when Moses ordered them (*probity aside*) to steal the gold and silver vases of their hosts. These Jews were slaves, poor, dirty, and leprous; they could lodge only among the least considerable of the people; and if these folks of the latter class had vases of silver and gold, what, then, must the upper classes have, the priests and the Pharaohs?

But they will ask, how have those who, in the modern temples, passed for having possessed this knowledge, lived without pomp and have died without leaving great riches?

They would have guarded it well: this knowledge commands discretion, beneficence, and modesty. Indeed, let a philosopher reveal himself, let him heal the dying, as by miracle; let his blessings (alms, relief, generosity, etc.) be known, all those who doubted or did not believe (did they not deny algebra, when it was created?) will suspect: the philosopher will be assaulted; his life will be in danger; he will be pursued by the sick, by the indigent, and what is worse, by the avaricious, the ambitious, the inventers, etc. He would have to exile himself and hide himself or live obscurely before having himself discovered by a blessing imprudently granted.

Let us cite what the learned P. *Kircher* says of the philosophical *elixir* or *golden medicine*; he continues thus:

"The Egyptians did not have in view the application of this *stone*, and if they touch on something of the preparation of the metals, and they *reveal the most secret treasures of the minerals*, they do not mean by this what the ancient and modern alchemists mean (*well then! tell us what they meant*); but they indicated a certain substance of the lower world analogous to the sun, endowed with excellent virtues and properties so surprising that they are far above what the human intelligence may comprehend; that is to say a *quintessence* hidden within all the mixtures, impregnated with the virtue of the universal spirit of the world, that the one who, inspired by God and enlightened by his divine knowledge, would find the means to extract it, would become, by its means, exempt from every infirmity, and would lead a life full of sweetness and satisfaction."

We are going to proceed to the philosophical interpretation of the *symbols*, *hieroglyphs*, and *fables* under which have been veiled, in many manners, the operations of the Hermetic work. Under this point of view, we shall examine succinctly, the history of *Osiris*, of *Isis*, and of *Horus*, including that of *Typhon*. We shall give a summary of the sacerdotal art, indicating all the operations of the *work*; the significance of the *Apis ox*, that of the various symbolic animals, finally the explanation of various hieroglyphic plants, the misunderstood traces of which are borne yet today by many religious monuments. We think it necessary to speak thereon in order to facilitate for the less initiated readers the intelligence of these representations, the majority of which figure without aim, no longer being included by the constructors themselves who, for centuries, have lost the key of these symbols.

CHAPTER XLI

Philosophical Interpretations

HERMES the THRICE GREAT, this god of ideas and writing, of intelligence and thought, of civilization and society[191] has invented the history of *Osiris*, *Isis*, and *Horus*, and has instituted the cult thereof under the name of *Mercury*; it is allusive to the Hermetic work.

FILIATION OF OSIRIS, ISIS, AND ORUS OR HORUS

The matter of the work is the radical principle of all, active and formal principle of the gold, and which becomes *philosophical gold* by the operations of the work, imitation of those of nature. This matter, formed in the entrails of the earth, is carried there by the rain waters, animated by the universal spirit spread in the air, and this spirit draws its fecundity from the influences of the *sun* and the *moon*, which are then the father and mother of this matter. The earth is the womb where this seed is deposited and is found to be its nourishment. The gold which is formed thereby is the *terrestrial sun*. This matter or subject of the work is composed of two substances, the one *fixed*, the other *volatile*: the first, igneous and active; the second, *humid* and *passive*, to which we give the names of *Heaven* and *Earth*, *Saturn* and *Rhea*, *Osiris* and *Isis*, *Jupiter* and *Juno*. The igneous principle that it contains is called *Vulcan*, *Prometheus*, *Vesta*, etc. It is thus that Vulcan and Vesta, which is the fire of the humid and volatile part, are father and mother of *Saturn*, as well as the Heaven and Earth, because the names of these gods are given not only to the still crude matter taken before the preparation, but also during this preparation and the operations which follow. When the matter becomes BLACK, it is the *Philosophical Saturn*, son of Vulcan and Vesta, who are themselves children of the *sun*. If after the black, the matter becomes GRAY, it is *Jupiter*; WHITE, it is the *Moon*, *Isis*, *Diana*; RED, it is *Apollo*, *Phebus*, the *Sun*, *Osiris:* Jupiter is therefore son of Saturn and father of Isis and Osiris. But the color gray not being one of the principals of the work, the philosophers, for the most part, have no regard for it and pass from the black to the white and bring together, from Saturn, Isis, and Osiris, who become his first-born children. They are therefore brother and sister, whether we consider them as principles of the work or consider them as children of Saturn or of Jupiter. Furthermore, Isis is found as mother of Osiris, since the color red arises from the white, and they are spouses, since they accomplish the work together; that is to say that it produces the *philosophical sun*, called *Horus*, *Apollo*, or *sulphur of the wise*, formed from the two substances, *fixed* and *volatile*, united into one entirely *fixed*, called *Orus* or *Horus*.

The philosophers hardly ever begin their treatises and their accounts before the second operation. As the *gold* or *philosophical sun* is made, and as it is necessary to employ it as the basis of the second work, then the sun is found to be first king of Egypt. It contains, within it, the fire of nature which, acting upon the materials, produces the putrefaction and the *blackening*: here again is Vulcan, son of the Sun, and Saturn, son of Vulcan. Osiris and Isis will come next, then Orus through the union of his father and mother.

It is to this second operation that they apply this expression of the adepts: *it is necessary to marry the mother with the son*, that is to say that after its first coction, one is to mix it with the crude matter *from which it has come*, and to cook it anew until they are reunited and make but one. During this operation, the crude matter dissolves and purifies the digested matter: *This is the mother who kills her child* and puts him in her womb in order to rebirth and resuscitate. During this dissolution, the *Titans* kill Osiris, but his mother leads him from death to life, and, less affectionate towards Isis than she is toward him, he causes his mother to die and rules in her place, that is to say that the fixed, or *Orus*, fixes the volatile, or *Isis*, who had volatized him; for, in the language of the philosophers, *to kill, to bind, to close, to inter, to congeal, to coagulate, or to fix* are synonymous terms, *just as, to give life, to resurrect, to open, to unbind, to travel,* signify the same thing as *to volatize.*

Osiris and *Isis* are therefore, rightfully, the well-known principal gods of Egypt with *Horus*, who reigns last, since he is the result of the entire sacerdotal art. This is, perhaps, what has made him confused with *Harpocrates*, god of the secret and of silence, because the object of this secret is none other than Orus, called the *sun* or the *Apollo of the philosophers*. The Egyptians represented him on their monuments, under the figure of a child (sometimes swaddled) in the arms of *Isis* who nurses him, because Orus is the *philosophical child* born of Isis and Osiris, from the black woman and the red man.

These very succinct explanations may help to penetrate the obscurity of the ancient fables[192] which make mention of *adulterers*, *incest* of father with his daughter (*Cynire* with *Myrrha*), of the son with his mother (*Œdipus* with *Jocaste*), of brother and sister (*Jupiter* and *Juno*), etc., etc. The *patricides*, the *matricides* are only unintelligible allegories, unveiled by the knowledge of the work, and not actions which revolt humanity.

HISTORY OF OSIRIS

This god (*chemical*) forms the design to go conquer the whole earth. He assembles an army composed of men, women, satyrs, musicians, and dancers, and puts himself at the head to teach men *what they already know*.

Although Osiris knew perfectly the prudence and capacity of Isis, to govern his States during his expedition, he left *Mercury* with her. He felt the necessity of such a counselor, since it is the *Mercury of the Philosophers*, without which one may do nothing in the beginning, in the middle, nor at the end of the work. Constituted governor of the whole empire, it is he who, in concert with *Hercules*, or the *adept*, must direct all, conduct all, and do all. It is for Orus that Osiris undertook this long and painful journey.

The two works which make the object of the sacerdotal art are represented here, *to wit*:

The first, in this expedition of Osiris, of which that of *Bacchus*, who is identical to him, is but the reproduction.

The second, in the death of Osiris, in the honors which are rendered to him, and in his apotheosis. By the first, one makes the *stone*; by the second, one forms the *elixir*.

The *coffin*, where this prince is enclosed, is the *philosophical vessel* Hermetically sealed. *Typhon* and his accomplices are the agents of the *dissolution*. The dispersion of his limbs indicates the *fixation*; it takes place by the cares of Isis or the *earth* which like a magnet, say the philosophers, attracts to it the volatized parts. Then Isis, aided by her son Horus, combats Typhon, kills him, reigns gloriously and is reunited with her spouse in the same tomb, that is to say that the dissolved matter coagulates and is fixed in the same vessel.

Osiris, dead, is thrown into the sea, that is to say submerged in the mercurial water or the *sea of the philosophers*. Isis finds the body of her husband only in *Phoenecia*, under a *tamarind*, because the *volatile* part reunites with the fixed only when the *whitening* occurs. Now, the flowers of the tamarind are *white*, and its roots are *red*. This latter color is even indicated in the word Phoenecia, which signifies *red*, purple color.

They ordinarily represented Isis holding a *sistrum* (symbol of the work) with a vase or small seal in the hand or near her, or even a pitcher on her head, in order to signify that she could do nothing without the mercurial water, or the *Mercury* that they had given her as counsel[193].

TYPHON

Let us recall that the radical humid is, in the mixtures, the seat and the nourishment of the natural or celestial fire and becomes as the bond which unites it with the elementary body. This igneous virtue, which is like the form and the soul of the mixture, makes the office of male (*Osiris*); and the radical humor makes, as humid, the function of female (*Isis*): they are therefore like brother and sister, and their union constitutes the basis of the mixture. But the mixtures are not composed of the radical humid alone; there enters into their formation in order to complete them, homogenous, impure, and terrestrial parts, which carry the principle of corruption and destruction, because of their combustible and corrosive sulphur, which acts ceaselessly upon the pure and incorruptible sulphur. These two sulphurs or *fires* are therefore two brothers, but two enemy brothers; and, by the daily destruction of the individuals, they have good reason to convince themselves that the impure prevails over the pure: it is the evil principle (*Typhon*) grappling with the good principle (*Osiris*).

They have had to make of *Typhon* a frightful monster, ever disposed towards doing evil and which even had the audacity to make war on the eight great gods of Egypt (*the seven metals and their source*). The gods had given their names to the metals, which abound in this impure and combustible sulphur which consumes them, by making them turn and rust, each in its space.

Typhon, born of the *earth*, but from the coarse earth, being the principle of *corruption*, which operates only by *solution*, must cause the death of Osiris. The plumes which covered the upper part of the body of Typhon, and his height which bore his head even unto the heavens, indicates his *volatility* and his *sublimation* into vapors. His thighs, his legs covered with scales, and the serpents which emerge from all sides, are the symbol of his corrupting and *putrefactive aquosity*. The fire which he shoots through his mouth marks his corrosive *ability to burn*, and designates his supposed fraternity with Osiris, *hidden fire*, natural and vivifying, while the other is a destructive fire called the tyrant of nature and the *fratricide* of the natural fire. The serpents are the ordinary hieroglyph of the dissolution and putrefaction. Thus, do they acknowledge that Typhon differs not at all from the serpent Python, killed by Apollo, and we know that Apollo and Horus were taken as the same god, and that *Python* is the anagram of *Typhon*.

This monster was not content with seeing his brother Osiris killed, he hurled his nephew Horus into the sea, with the help of a queen of Ethiopia (*the blackening*). Finally, Isis resurrected Horus, that is to say that the philosophical Apollo, after having been dissolved, putrefied, and become *black*, passed from the blackening to the whitening called *resurrection* or *new life*.

The son and the mother are reunited in order to combat Typhon or the *corruption*, and, having vanquished him, they reign gloriously; first Isis (*the whitening*), then Horus (*the reddening*). It is only with the aid of the Hermetic chemistry that it is possible to explain all these fables[194].

ANUBIS

Anubis, according to *Diodorus* of Sicily (*bk.* I), was one of those who accompanied Osiris on his expedition in the Indies. He has his captain of the guards and wore as war attire a *dog's skin.* The father *Kircher*, with the sharp tone which does not suit him in this matter, has, say the modern philosophers, confused, very inappropriately, as well as other authors, *Mercurius Trismegistus* with Anubis, by surmising that the Egyptians had represented him under the figure of Anubis. Let us point to the description of *Apuleus*: "Anubis is the interpreter of the gods of heaven and those of the underworld. his face is sometimes *black*, sometimes of *golden color*. He holds raised his great dog's head, carrying in the left hand a caduceus, and in the right a green palm which seems to agitate him."

EXPLANATION. Osiris and Isis symbolize the Hermetic matter forming one same subject composed of two substances, the *male* or the agent, and the passive principle or *female*. Osiris was the same as *Serapis* or *Ammon* with the ram's head, because he is of a hot nature. Isis, taken as the *bull*, had the head of a bull, heavy and terrestrial animal, whose horns represent the *crescent moon*. They represented Anubis between Serapis and Apis, in order to indicate that he is composed of the two, or that he comes from them. He is therefore son of Osiris and Isis, for this matter, composed of two substances, is dissolved in the chemical vessel in mercurial water, which is the philosophical *mercury* or *Anubis*. As Typhon and his wife Nephthys, principles of destruction, have caused this dissolution, they say that Anubis is, *occasionally*, son of this monster and his wife, though he is, *generally*, born of Osiris and Isis; which has made Raymond Lulle say: "*Our child has two fathers and two mothers*."

The dog being, in Egypt, the symbol of a secretary or minister of the State, they have put the head of this animal on Anubis, in order to indicate that he conducts the whole interior of the work, just as the caduceus makes him known as Mercury. The face sometimes black, sometimes golden colored, that Apuleus give him, expresses clearly the colors of the work. (See hereafter *symbolic animals*, the dog.)

CHAPTER XLII

On Alchemy or Hermetic Philosophy

"All is in all." (*Pantheistic dogma.*)

The study of nature, of its mysterious revolutions, of its generative powers and the reiterated observations which result therefrom, have produced a science full of attraction, which, in the middle ages, was called ALCHEMY (transcendent chemistry) or HERMETIC PHILOSOPHY, from the name of the greatest of all these sages, HERMES TRISMEGISTUS[195], founder of the Egyptian religion and the first philosopher who, in the interior of the pyramids, taught the OCCULT SCINECES, that is to say the knowledge of man, nature, and God. - All these sciences made up the secret basis of the religious wisdom of the sanctuaries of the Orient. The Egyptian priests had placed at the doors of their sanctuaries *sphynxes* and *griffons*, symbol of the silence and the *impenetrability* with which the mysteries must be ceaselessly enveloped[196]. According to the Qabalists, Syria and Chaldea would have been the cradle of this science, and, from this common center, it would be propagated over the whole globe.

SACERDOTAL ART

Seek, you shall find.

Such is the name that the *Hermetic science* bore among the Egyptians.

This science has had, and still has, prejudices against it; but these prejudices are not proofs, says *Pernety*; and it suffices that its possibility be not rejected, for the reason that it is at least rash to declare its results impossible. "If the thing is, how is it? If it is not, how is it not?" (*Avicenne.*)

The source of health and wealth, two bases upon which is supported the happiness of life, are the object of this art, which was always a mystery.

In the system of the Hermetic philosophers, one carefully scrutinizes nature in order to discover the constituent principles of the bodies, to understand the mode and the various degrees of their generation. They teach here to know each thing by its cause, and to distinguish the accidental parts which are not of its nature.

This is a science whose result follows from the miracle in itself and in its effects. That is why the possessors of so fine a secret have veiled it in the shadows of the hieroglyphs, the fables, the allegories, and the enigmas, in order to conceal the knowledge thereof from the vulgar. They have written only for the initiates and the elect.

The brahmins, to the Indians; the gymnosophists, in Ethiopia; the magi, among the Persians; the priests, among the Egyptians; the mecubales and the Qabalists, among the Hebrews; the Orpheus, Homer, Thales, Pythagoras, Plato, Prophyry, among the Greeks; the druids, among the Occidentals; Artephius, Morien, etc., etc. have spoken of the secret sciences only through enigmas and allegories. If they had said what was the true object of their works of art, there no longer would have been any mysteries, and the sacred would have been mingled with the profane.

Medicine, the art of healing, is the science of good and evil. It teaches us to know the virtue of the metals and the plants, to study the poisons whose prudent use may produce marvelous cures. This art may be confided only to *discreet* men, and they feel the necessity for a *solemn promise*.

It is certain that the *transmutation of metals* was, as well as the *universal medicine*, by the account of Orpheus, Homer, and others, the aim of the secret operations of the ancient initiation, especially in Egypt, and some schools of wisdom, such as that of Thales, of Pythagoras. Thus, they have veiled their operations, in order to assure their perpetuity, in the allegorical accounts, the ensemble of which form that collection of fables intelligible to the initiates alone, and that serious authors have taken as history, the meaning of which, in their obscure explanations, remain insoluble. Such were: the history of *Osiris*, *Isis*, and *Horus*; that of *Typhon*, of the ox *Apis*, the conquest of the *Golden Fleece*, the return of the *Argonauts*, the *golden apples* from the garden of *Hesperides*; the history of *Atlantis*, the *Golden Age*, the *Golden showers*, etc., which may be explained only by Hermeticism or astronomy, like the fable of the Trojan War: the carrying off of the beautiful *Helen* (name of the *moon*), by the young and fair *Paris* (*sun* of the springtime), to the *old Menelas* (*sun* of winter). The intervention of the divinities of Olympus through the poets, even before *Homer*, has given to this last fiction an importance to persuade that its foundation was true.

Has not *Solomon* clearly expressed this double result of the Hermetic work, by speaking, in his Proverbs (ch. 3, v. 5), of that *Wisdom* which holds, in her right hand, the *length of days* (health) and, in her left, the *wealth* and the glory?

This is what it means that there are two kinds of sciences: RELIGION, the science of God, and PHYSICS, the science of nature. The others are not but branches. There are bastards thereof which, with the exception of the *exact sciences* which help man to understand everything, are errors rather than sciences.

ALCHEMY is the art of working the secondary principles or the principled matter of things, in order to perfect them through processes suitable to those of nature. Alchemy is therefore an operation of nature aided by nature. Thus, this science places in the hands of the initiates the key of *natural magic*, physics.

The long work is always that of nature, which has time and eternity at its disposal. The work of the art is much shorter: it advances and facilitates the *progress* of nature. It operates, like nature, simply, successively, and always by the same paths, in order to produce the same things: God and nature are pleased in unity and simplicity.

The first matter of the metals, said, after the Arabs, *Albertus Magnus*, bishop of Ratisbonne, is an unctious humidity, subtle, incorporated and mixed strongly with a terrestrial matter.

The Hermetic philosophers regard the *great work* as a thing natural in its matter and in its operations, but surprising in the discoveries that they have made therein.

What has discredited this science, are those numerous bastard chemists who, under the names of *puffers*, *charcoal burners*, *seekers of the philosopher's stone*, reduce all to nothing; they have seen to apply, to their false science, the proverb, true for them: *Alchimia est ars, cujus initium laborare, medium mentiri, finis mendicare*.

"The philosophical work requires more time and work," says *d'Espagnet*, "than expenses, for there is very little to make for the one who has the requisite material. Those who ask great sums to carry it out have more confidence in the riches of others than in the science of this art." - Indeed, the matter of the art, say the authors, is dirt cheap. The fire for the work is not very costly, and there is need only of two vessels and a stove.

An instructed chemist, a *Dumas*, a *Faraday*, would not deny, today, the possibility of making gold, from the philosopher's stone; and we are led to think that some of their particular works tend toward its research; but the prejudices render them mute. It is this prejudice which has brought *Roger Bacon* to write against alchemy and astrology; who in his mysterious investigations of Hermeticism, discovered *gunpowder*, the effects of which he exaggerated ridiculously in his enthusiasm; and who was conducted by his astrological research to the discovery of the *telescope*[197].

We find truth, in the books of alchemy, only in the SOLE POINT where the authors are in agreement, and that it is necessary to grasp well, for they dare not speak the truth but in ONE THING; all the rest is symbolized under various fictions, which do not agree and that the initiates alone comprehend.

These authors, to better throw off the curious, ordinarily begin their treatises at the second operation, and when they suppose their sulphur and their mercury already made. From here come all the old fables, allegories, enigmas, etc.

The Hermetic philosophers give this key of nature: "From all material things is made the ash; from the ash they make a salt; from the salt they separate the water and the mercury; from the mercury, they compose an elixir, a quintessence."

They put, therefore, the body into *ash*, in order to cleanse it of its combustible parts; into *salt*, to be separated from its territorialities; into *water*, in order to be purified, and into *spirit* in order to be quintessence.

The knowledge of the salts is the key of the art, by means of which it imitates nature in its operations. The adept must know their sympathy and their antipathy with the metals.

There is properly only ONE SALT; but it is divided into three kinds in order to form the principle of the bodies: *nitre*, *tartar*, and *vitriol* (old style); all the others are composed thereof.

From the nitre and the tartar (which is the same nitre cooked more) is formed the vegetables. The vitriol is the same nitre salt which, having passed through the nature of tartar, becomes *mineral salt* by a longer cooking and a hotter fire. It abounds in the concavities of the earth, where it unites itself with a *viscous* fluid which renders it *metallic*.

From the vapor of these salts is made the *mercury*, called *mineral seed*. From this mercury and from the sulphur are made, in the earth, all the metals. It is the diversity of the sulphur and the mercury which form therein the numerous family of the mineral kingdom; the stones, the marcasites, and the other different metals between them according to difference of the combinations, materials, and the degrees of cooking.

There is, in all of nature, but ONE SOLE PRINCIPLE, and, in the radical humidity of the mixed bodies, but ONE SOLE FIXED SPIRIT, composed of a very pure and incombustible fire. It is more perfect in the gold than in any other thing, and only the mercury of the philosophers has the property to draw it from its prison, to corrupt it, and to dispose it towards generation. The living silver (which must not be confused with *quicksilver*) is the principle of volatility, malleability, and minerality; the fixed spirit of the gold can do nothing without it. The gold is moistened, restored, volatilized, and subjected to putrefaction by the operation of the mercury; and this is digested, cooked, thickened, dried, and fixed by the operation of the *philosophical gold* which renders it, by this means, a *metallic tincture*.

The one and the other make the philosophical sulphur and mercury; but a metallic sulphur as leaven is not enough in the work, a seed of sulphureous nature is necessary in order to unite with the seed of mercurial substance. This sulphur and this mercury have been represented as *two serpents*, the one male, the other female, entwined around the golden staff of Mercury. The *gold staff* is the fixed spirit to which they must be attached, and with which he exercises his great power, transfigures himself, and changes himself as he pleases. It is these two serpents that *Juno*, which is the metallic nature, sent against *Hercules* in the cradle, and that this hero had to vanquish and kill in order to have them rot, corrupt, and engender *at the beginning of his work.*

The hieroglyphic figures also represent this first matter under the form of *two dragons*: the one, *without wings*, expresses the *fixed principle*, the male or sulphur; the other, *winged*, signifies the *volatile principle*, the humidity, the female or living silver.

It is these symbolic serpents that the ancient Egyptians have painted *in a circle*, the head biting the tail, in order to express that they had emerged from one same thing, which alone was sufficient in itself, and that in its contour and its circulation, it perfected itself.

It is these dragons that the ancient philosopher-poets have set to guard, without sleeping, the golden apples of the gardens of the Hesperides virgins. They are the same upon which *Jason*, in the fable of the Golden Fleece, poured the juice prepared by the beautiful *Medea.*

This first matter of the philosophical work, the symbols of which are numerous, were represented in the Egyptian temples by the SUN (fixed principle), and by the MOON (volatile principle); these two emblems have been preserved in the Masonic temples.

The DISSOLUTION is the *key of the work*, which is divided into two workings, the one to make the *stone*, the other the *elixir.* The first working is the most difficult, because of the preparation of the agents which must have two qualities: *fixed* in part (the male), in part *volatile* (the female), and, from this matter, it is necessary to make one *water* which dissolves the gold naturally. From here comes the serpent which bites its tail, and the *dragons*, the *chimera*, the *sphinx*, the *harpies*, and the other monsters of fable that one must conquer and kill, like the child Hercules strangled the two serpents, so that they be corrupted, dissolved, etc.

The MERCURY of the wise, which must not be confused with the common mercury, is a *universal* solvent; it is the scythe Saturn.

VESSELS. They employ only one vessel in order to perfect the two *sulphurs.* It is of glass, equally thick in all its parts and without knots, so that it may withstand a long and sometimes intense fire. it has an oval or round base, a long neck of about 30 centimeters, straight like that of a bottle. They do not open this vessel until the end of the first work.

A second vessel is necessary for the *elixir.* It is formed of two hollow hemispheres, of oak, into which they place the egg in order to make it hatch.

The third vessel is the *furnace* which contains and preserves the other two. We call it *athanor* (from *tannour*, oven, in Hebrew), because of the fire that they maintain therein, without discontinuing, during the operation, and the degrees of which are proportionate to the capacity of the furnace and the vessels, and to the quantity of materials that they contain.

The Hermetic philosophers place these vessels at the number of their secrets and, for this reason, they have them play a role in a multitude of fables which serve only to veil the various phases of the labors of the work. These fictions appear to differ, though the basis is the same. To give an idea of this to the readers less initiated in these matters, we are going to point out the majority of the symbols under which the philosopher-poets represent these vessels. Such were:

The *ship* of Jason; the *vessel* of Theseus (*black* veils), that of Ulysses (*black* sails to conduct Chriseis to his father, *white* for the return); the *tower* of Danaeus, the *coffin* of Deucalion; the *tomb* of Osiris; the *basket* of Bacchus saved from the waters, his *leather flask* and his bottle; the *golden amphora* or *vase* of Vulcan; the cup that Juno presented to

Thetis; the *pannier* of Erichthonius; the *casket* where Tennis Trioditus was enclosed with his sister Hemithea; the *chamber* of Leda; the *eggs* whence Castor, Pollux, Clitemnestre, and Helen were born; the *city* of Troy; the *caverns* of the monsters; the *vases* that Vulcan presented to Jupiter; the *casket* that Thetis gave to Achilles, in which he placed the bones of Patrocles and those of his friend; the *cup* with which Hercules crossed the sea in order to carry off the oxen from Gerion; the *cavern* of Mount Helicon, which served as dwelling to the Muses and to Phoebus; the *bed* where Venus was found with Mars; the *skin* into which Orion was engendered; the *clepsydra* or *horn* of Amalthea (which signifies *I hide the waters*); the *marsh* of Lerne (from *larnax*, *capsa*, *casket*, or *loculus*, coffin). Finally, they signify the *wells*, the *sepulchers*, the *urns*, the *mausoleums* in triangular form, etc., etc.

The MAGISTER (the work) is, says *Morien*, the secret of the secrets of God who has confided it to his prophets (*inspired*).

PHILOSOPHICAL FIRE. This fire has received, in the fables of the initiated poets, the symbolic names of *axe*, *sword*, *lance*, *arrow*, *bow*, *javelin*, etc.; such was the axe with which Vulcan struck the forehead of Jupiter in order to make Pallas come out; the sword that Vulcan gave to Peleus, father of Achilles; the *club* with which Hercules was presented; the *bow* that this hero received from Apollo; the *scimitar* of Perseus; the *lance* of Bellerophon, etc. - It is the *fire* that Prometheus stole from the heaves; the one that Vulcan employed to fabricate the lightning bolts of Jupiter and the weapons of the gods; the *sash* of Venus, the *golden throne* of the Sovereign of the heavens, etc. It was finally symbolized at Rome by the fire of *Vesta*, so scrupulously maintained that they punished with death the *vestal* virgins charged with maintaining it, when they let it extinguish.

They have given to the Syrian and Chaldean philosophers the name of *philosophers of the fire*, because they devoted to this element a respect which seemed to be a sort of cult, traces of which we find in all the mythology and poetry of Asia and Europe. - This Hermetic and philosophical fire, considered as the marvelous artisan of the most singular metamorphoses of the physical world, that powerful thaumaturge, sole agent which may accomplish the transmutation of the metals, is none other than ELECTRICITY, penetrating all, animating all the physical bodies, and that they recognized as the most extraordinary of the occult faculties of nature. Thus, do they say that this fire, generator of the ordinary fire which produces the light and flame, is a universal, visible, and sensible essence (*fluid*): *universal*, because it is the soul of the world that it *vivifies*; *visible* in its second development, the *light*; *sensible* in its third development, *heat*.

Let us learn to respect these high initiates who, 5000 years before Franklin, knew these things, and better than the scientists of his period, and those of our day[198].

PREPARATORY PRINCIPLES OR KEYS OF THE WORK

Our intention is not to enter into details capable of leading some readers to make attempts and to *burn charcoal*, our aim is to initiate them into the curious allusions that the Hermetic science contains and to put them in a position to comprehend Homer, the ancient poems, and even the Bible, as well as the mysteries of the ancient grade of *Master*.

The alchemical operation is divided into four parts.

The first is the *solution* (liquefaction) of the matter in mercurial water by the seed of the earth. The generation begins by the conjunction of the male and the female and the mixture of their seeds. The putrefaction follows.

The second is the preparation of the mercury of the philosophers which volatizes and spermatizes the bodies, by driving out the superfluous humidity and by coagulating all the matter under the form of viscous and metallic earth. If one wished to employ the Hermetic language which becomes then *allusive* to the account of the creation of the world by Moses, which is found explained in a satisfactory manner by the- operation of the work, one would say: "In this second *digestion*, the spirit of God is carried over the waters. The *moon* and the *sun* reappear. The elements reemerge from the *chaos* in order to constitute a new *world*, a new *heaven* and a new *earth*. The little *crows* change feathers and become *doves*, the *eagle* and the *lion* unite through an indissoluble bond. This regeneration is performed by the *igneous spirit*, which descends under the form of *water* in order to cleanse the matter of its *original sin* and bears therein the aurific seed; for the water of the philosophers is fire."

The third part is the corruption which separates the substances, rectifies them, and *reduces* them. The waters have to be separated from the waters with *weight* and *measure*.

The fourth is the generation and creation of the philosophical sulphur which unites and *fixes* the substances: it is the creation of the *stone*; the mystery is achieved.

The philosophers also call these four operations: *solution* or *liquefaction*, *ablution*, *reduction*, and *fixation*.

Through *solution*, the bodies, *they say*, return to their first matter and are restored by the connection. Then the marriage is made between the male and the female, and there is born therefrom the *crow*. The *stone* is dissolved into four elements confused together. *Heaven* and *earth* are united to put *Saturn* into the world.

The *ablution* teaches to whiten the crow, and to have *Jupiter* arise from Saturn, which takes place by the changing of body into spirit.

The office of the *reduction* is to restore to the body its spirit that the volatilization had removed from it, and to then nourish it with a spiritual *milk*, in the form of dew, until the child *Jupiter* has acquired a perfect strength.

"For the last two operations," says *d'Espagnet*, "the dragon, descending from heaven, becomes furious against himself; he devours his tail and is swallowed up little·.by little until he is transformed into stone." - Such was the dragon of which Homer spoke. His account is the true image or the true symbol of these two operations: "While we were gathered under a beautiful plane-tree, said *Ulysses* to the Greeks, and while we were there to make hecatombs, near a fountain which came from this tree, there appeared a marvelous wonder: a horrible *dragon*, whose back was spotted, sent by *Jupiter* himself, came out of the base of the altar and hastened to the plane-tree. At the top of this tree were eight little birds with their mother which hovered around them. The dragon seized them with fury, and even the mother lamenting the loss of her little ones. After this action, the same god who had sent it made it beautiful, brilliant, and changed it into *stone*, to our astonished eyes." (*Iliad*, 1.2, v. 306 and foll.)

CALCINATION. The vulgar calcination is the pulverization by the fire, and the reduction of the bodies into lime, ashes, earth, etc.; it is the death of the mixture. The *philosophical* is an extraction of the substance: of the water, of the salt, of the oil, of the spirit, and of the terreous remains. It is a change of accidents, an alteration of the quantity, a corruption of this substance, but in a manner that all things may be united to produce a more perfect body. The vulgar calcination is made by the action of the common fire or the concentrated rays of the sun. The philosophical has the water as its agent, whence the axiom: *The chemists burn with fire, the philosophers with water*. It must be concluded therefrom that the vulgar chemistry differs from the hermetic chemistry, as fire differs from water.

SOLUTION. It is, in ordinary chemistry, an attenuation or liquefaction of the matter, under the form of water, oil, spirit, or humor. In transcendent or philosophical chemistry, it is a *reduction* of the body into its first matter, a natural disunion of the parts of the compound, and a coagulation of the spiritual parts. That is why the philosophers call it a *solution of the body* and a *congelation of the spirit.* Its effect is to aquefy, dissolve, open, restore, uncook, and to evacuate the substances of their territorialities, to decorporify the mixture in order to reduce it to sperm.

PUTREFACTION. It is, in some way, the KEY of all the operations, though it is not the first. It is the tool which breaks the bonds of the parts. It discovers the interior of the mixture. It renders, say the sages, the *occult* manifest. It is the principle of the changing of forms, the death of the accidentals; the first step towards the generation, the beginning and the end of life, the middle between the non-being and being. - The philosopher wills it to be done when the body, dissolved by a natural resolution, is subjected to the action of the putredinal heat. The vulgar *distillation* and *sublimation* are but the imitation of those of nature. The first is the elevation of the humid things which then fall drop by drop. The second is the elevation of a dry matter which is attached to the sides of the vessel.

Philosophical distillation and sublimation portion, refine, and rectify the matter.

Coagulation and *fixation* are the two great instruments of nature and the art.

FERMENTATION. The *ferment* is to the work what the *leaven* is to the fabrication. We cannot make bread without leaven, and we cannot make gold without gold. The gold is therefore the soul, and what determines the intrinsic form of the *stone*, Thus, it is made from gold and silver, like the baker makes the bread, which is composed only of *water* and *flour*, kneaded, fermented, and they differ from one another only by the cooking. Likewise, the golden medicine is but a composition of earth and water, that is to say of *sulphur* and *mercury* fermented with gold, but with a restored gold. For, as one cannot make the leaven with cooked bread, one cannot make it with common gold, as long as it remains common gold.

The mercury or mercurial water is this *water*; the sulphur, this *flour*, which, by a long fermentation, turns sour and becomes the *leaven* with which is made the gold and silver. As the ordinary leaven is multiplied eternally and serves always as matter to make bread, the philosophical medicine is multiplied too, and serves eternally as leaven to make gold.

DEMONSTRATIVE SIGNS. The COLORS which occur in the matter, during the course of the operations of the work, are *demonstrative signs* which make known that one has proceeded in a manner to succeed. They succeed each other immediately and in order. If this order is disturbed, it is a proof that one has operated wrongly. There are three principal colors: the first is BLACK, called *crow's head*, *serpents*, *dragons*, and many other names.

The beginning of this *blackening* indicates that the fire of nature begins to operate and that the matter is on its way to solution. If it becomes perfect, the solution is too, and the elements become mingled. The *grain* rots in order to dispose itself to generation. "That which does not blacken cannot whiten," says *Artephius*, "because the blackening is the beginning of the whitening, and it is the mark of the putrefaction and alteration. Here is how this is done. In this putrefaction, there first appears a blackness resembling pepper thrown on a clear broth. This liquid thickens and becomes as a black earth which is whitened by continuing to cook it; and just as the heat, acting upon the humidity, produces the blackening, first color which appears, so too does the heat, ever continuing its action, produce the *whitening*, second principal color of the work."

This action of the fire upon the humid does all in the work, as it does all in nature, for the generation of the mixtures. During this putrefaction, the philosophical male (*the sulphur*) is mingled with the female (*the mercury*). They no longer make but one and the same body, called *hermaphrodite*, the *androgyne* of the ancients, the head of the crow, and the converted elements.

The matter, in this state, is the serpent *Python*, which, born from the corruption of the silt of the earth, must be vanquished and put to death by the arrows of *Apollo* (the exterminator), the blond sun, that is to say the *philosophical fire*, equal to that of the sun. The *cleansings*, which must continue with the other half, are the *teeth* of this serpent, that the prudent *Cadmus* must throw into the same earth, whence arise *soldiers* who will be destroyed themselves, letting themselves dissolve into the same nature of earth.

The second demonstrative sign, or the second principal color, is THE WHITE. *HERMES* has said: "Know, son of the science, that the vulture cries from the mountain top: I am the white from the black, because the whiteness succeeds the blackness." This matter, called *white smoke*, is considered as the root of the art, the living silver of the angels, the true mercury of the philosophers, the mercury *tinged* with its white and red sulphur, mixed naturally together in their mines.

The great secret of the work, then, is to whiten the matter, also called *brass*; it is then a precious body which, being fermented and become *elixir* in the white, is full of an exuberant hue, that it has the property to communicate to all the other metals. The spirits, previously volatile, are then fixed. The new body resurrects beautiful, white, immortal, victorious. That is why they call it *resurrection, light, day*, and all the names, in the number of more than one hundred thirty that we could cite, which may indicate the *whiteness*, the *fixity*, the *incorruptibility*.

The formation of this desired whiteness is announced by a *capillary circle* of a color drawing on the orange, which appears around the matter at the sides of the vessel.

The philosophers have often represented this whiteness by the form of a *brilliant* bare sword. "When you will have whitened," says *Flamel*, "you will have vanquished the *enchanted bulls* which shot fire and flames from their nostrils. *Hercules* has cleaned the stable of Augias, full of filth, rot, and blackness. *Jason* has poured the juice (of *Medea*) over the dragons of Colchos, and you have in your power the *horn of Amaltheus* which, although it is not white, may, during your life, fill you with glory, honors, and *riches*. For the future, it is necessary for you to have fought valiantly, and like Hercules. For this, *Achelous* (son of the Ocean), or humid river (the blackness, the *Black Sea* of the river Esep), is endowed with a very powerful force, and often changes itself from one form to the other."

The black and the white may be considered as two extremes which may unite only by a medium. The matter, while leaving the black color, does not become white all at once: the color *gray*, which partakes of the two, is found as intermediary. The sages have given it the name of *Jupiter*, because it succeeds the black, which they called *Saturn*. This is what is meant that the *air succeeds the water*, after it has achieved its seven revolutions or *imbibitions*. The matter having been fixed at the base of the vessel, it is Jupiter which, having driven out Saturn, seizes the kingdom and takes over its government. At its advent, the philosophical child is formed, is nourished in the womb, and comes into the light of day, beautiful, brilliant, and *white* as the moon. This matter in white is, from then on, a *universal remedy* of all the sicknesses of the human body.

The third principal color is THE RED, which is obtained by continuing the cooking of the matter. It is the complement and the perfection of the *stone*. After the first work, they call it *masculine* or *philosophical sperm*, *fire of the stone*, *royal crown*, *son of the sun*, *mine of the celestial fire*, and a hundred and twenty other names, according to the manner of looking at it under the aspect of its color and its qualities. But it is good to know that, to throw off the *seekers of gold*, the sages, for the most part, begin their *treatises on the work* with the red stone.

In this operation, the fixed body is volatilized. It ascends and descends in the vessel until what fixes it, having vanquished the volatile, precipitates it to the bottom with it to no longer make but one body of an absolutely fixed nature.

PHILOSOPHICAL SULPHUR. For the manner of making it in the first work, *d'Espagnet* expresses himself thus; his style is symbolic, but the meaning is transparent: "Choose a red dragon, courageous, which has lost nothing of its natural strength; seven or nine virgin eagles, whose eyes are incapable of being dazzled by the rays of the sun. Put them with the dragon into a clear prison, close well, and, above, a hot bath in order to excite them into combat, which will be long and very painful even unto the forty-fifth or fiftieth day that the eagles will begin to devour the dragon which, in dying, will infect the prison with his corrupted blood and with a very black venom, the violence of which will make the eagles expire. From the putrefaction of their cadavers will arise a crow, which will raise its head little by little. The bath increasing, it will deploy its wings and begin to fly. The wind, the clouds, will flare up here and there. Tired of being tormented thus, it will seek to escape: take care that it finds no outlet. Finally, cleansed and whitened by a constant rain, and a celestial dew, you will see it transforming into a swan. The birth of the crow indicates the death of the dragon and the eagles.

"Are you curious to push even unto the *red*? Add the element of the fire which lacks in the *whitening*, without touching or stirring the vessel, by strengthening the fire by degrees and pushing its activity upon the matter, until the *occult* becomes *manifest*; the certain indicator will be its *citrine* color. Then govern the fire of the 4th degree, always by the degrees required, until, with the help of Vulcan, you see blood *red roses*, which changed into blood-colored *amaranth*; but do not stop bringing the fire to bear by the fire, until you see all reduced to very red and impalpable ashes."

This philosophical sulphur is an earth of a tenuity, of an igneity, and of an extreme dryness, containing a very abundant fire of nature, which has it named *fire of the stone*. It has the property to open, to penetrate the bodies of the metals, and to change them into its own nature. They call it then *father* and masculine seed.

The three colors *black*, *white*, and *red* must necessarily succeed one another in the order which has just been indicated. They are not the only ones which manifest themselves. They indicate the essential changes which occur to the matter, while the other colors, nearly infinite and similar to those of the rainbow, are only passing and of a very short duration. They affect the air rather than the earth; they drive one another out and are dissipated in order to make room for the three principal ones of which we speak.

These strange colors are sometimes the indication of a badly conducted operation: the blackening repeated is a certain mark thereof; for the *little crows*, say the philosophers, ought not return to the nest after having left. It is the same with the premature *reddening*: it ought not appear until the end, as proof of the maturity of the grain and the time of the *harvest*.

ON THE ELIXIR. It does not suffice to have attained to the philosophical sulphur. The *stone* cannot be perfect until the end of the second work, called *elixir*.

It is composed of three things: of a *metallic water* (philosophical sublimated mercury); the *white ferment* (in order to make the elixir in the white) or the *red ferment* (for the elixir in the red); and the *second sulphur*. Five qualities are necessary for it: it must be *fusible*, *permanent*, *penetrating*, *tinging*, and *multiplying*. It draws its *hue* and its *fixation* from the ferment; its *fusibility* from the living silver which serves to unite the tinctures of ferment and sulphur; and its *multiplicative* property from the spirit of the quintessence which it has naturally.

Its perfection consists in the complete union of the *dry* and the *humid*, so that they are inseparable, and that the humid gives to the dry the property of being fusible at the least heat. They give the proof thereof by putting a little of it on a heated copper or iron plate: if it melts at once without smoking, it is perfect.

CONFECTION. This second work is done in the same vessel or in a vessel similar to the first, in the same furnace, with the same degrees of fire, but in a much shorter time.

RECIPE ACCORDING TO D'ESPAGNET[199]: "*Red earth* or 3 parts red ferment, *water* and *air* taken together 6 parts; mix all and pulverize in order to make an amalgam or metallic paste, the consistency of butter, so that the earth is impalpable or imperceptible to the touch; add thereto one and a half parts of fire and put all in a vessel perfectly sealed. Give it a fire of the 1st degree, for the *digestion*. You will then make the extraction of the elements by the degrees of the fire which are proper to them, until they are very reduced into *fixed earth*. The matter will become as a brilliant, transparent, red stone, and will be, then, in its perfection. Put it in a crucible on a slight fire and imbue this part with its red oil, by incorporating it drop by drop until it melts and flows without smoke. Do not fear that your mercury is evaporated, for the earth will drink with avidity this humor which is its nature. You then have in possession your perfect *elixir*. Thank God for the favor that he has granted you, make use of it for his glory, and keep the secret."

The white elixir is made like the red, but with white ferments and the white oil.

QUINTESSENCE. The *quintessence* or fifth substance is an extraction of the most spiritous and radical substance of the matter. It is obtained by the separation of the elements, the purest parts of which unite and form a celestial and incorruptible essence, disengaged from all the heterogeneities.

The *philosophical secret* consists in separating the elements of the mixture, rectifying them, and, by the reunion of the pure, homogenous, and spiritualized parts, making that quintessence which contains all the properties thereof, without being subject to their alteration.

TINCTURE. The *tincture*, in the philosophical sense, is the very elixir, rendered fixed, fusible, penetrating, and *tingeing*, by the corruption and the operations that we have indicated. This tincture does not consist in the eternal color, but in the very substance which gives the hue with its metallic form. It acts like saffron in the water; it permeates more than oil does on paper; it mingles itself intimately like wax with wax, like water with water, because the union is made of two things of the same nature. It is from this property that comes it being an admirable PANACEA for the illnesses of the three kingdoms of nature: it goes to seek within them the radical and vital principle that, by its action, it disencumbers from the heterogeneous matter that shackles and grips it. It comes to its aid and joins itself to it to combat its enemies. They act then in concert and win a complete victory. This quintessence drives the impurity from the body, as the fire causes the humidity to evaporate from the wood. It preserves the health, giving its forces to the principle of life, in order to resist the attacks of the illnesses, and to make the separation of the truly nutritive substance of the aliments away from that which is but the vehicle.

THE MULTIPLICATION. They mean by *philosophical multiplication* an increase in quantity and quality, and the one and the other beyond all that it is possible to imagine. That of the quality is a multiplication of the tincture by the corruption, volatilization, and fixation reiterated as many times as the adept pleases. The second increases only the quantity of the tincture, without increasing its virtues.

The *second sulphur* is multiplied with the same matter from which it is made, by adding thereto a small part of the first, in the desired proportion.

D'Espagnet describes three manners of performing the multiplication.

The first is to take one part of the perfect red elixir that one mixes with nine parts of its red water. They place the vessel in the bath, in order to make it all dissolve in the water. They cook it, after the solution, until it coagulates into a material similar to a ruby. They then incorporate this matter into the matter of the elixir; and, from this first operation, the medicine acquires ten times more virtue than it had. If one repeats this same process, it will increase by one hundred, a third time by a thousand, and so on, always by ten.

The second manner is to mix the quantity of the elixir that one wishes with its water, in the required proportions, and put it all in a well-sealed vessel of reduction, dissolve it in the bath, and follow the whole regimen of the second, by distilling successively the elements by their own fires, until it all becomes stone. They then incorporate it, as in the other, and the virtue of the elixir increases by one hundred, from the first time. By repeating it, one increases the strength of the elixir more and more; but this path is longer.

The third is properly the *multiplication in quantity*. They project an ounce of the elixir, *multiplied in quality*, over one hundred ounces of purified common mercury. This mercury, placed over a small fire, will soon change into elixir. If one throws an ounce of it over one hundred ounces of other purified common mercury, it will become very fine GOLD. The multiplication of the elixir in the white is made in the same manner, by employing the white elixir and its water, instead of the red elixir.

The more one repeats the multiplication in quality, the more it will have an effect in its projection. As to the multiplication in quantity, its strength diminishes at each projection.

One ought to push the repetitions only unto the fourth or fifth time, because the medicine would become so active and so igneous, that the operations would be instantaneous, since their duration is abbreviated at each repetition. Its virtue, moreover, is great enough at the fourth or fifth to fulfill all desires; for, from the first, one grain can convert a hundred grains of mercury into gold; at the second, a thousand; at the third, ten thousand; at the fourth, a hundred thousand, etc. One is to judge this medicine like the grain of wheat which multiplies each time it is sown.

PROPORTIONS. The Hermetic philosophers do not grow tired of recommending to follow nature. Without doubt they know it since they flatter themselves to be its disciples; and why is nothing more confused than what they say, in their writings, on the weights and measures to be observed? The one says that his fire must be measured *clinically* (according to the oven); another *geometrically*, etc., etc.; finally an author better advised counsels to give a slow and weak fire rather than a strong one, because one risks only finishing the work later.

The compound of the mixtures and their life subsists only by the measure and the weight of the elements combined and proportioned in a manner that the one does not dominate over the others in tyranny. If there is too much fire, the germ is burned;

if too much water, the seminal and radical spirit is found suffocated; if too much air and earth, the compound will have too much or too little consistency, and each element will not have its free action.

This difficulty is not so great as it first appears: in truth, nature always has the balance in hand to weigh the elements and to make its mixtures thereof, proportioned such that there results therefrom the mixtures that it proposes to produce, save the numerous abortions, caused accidentally, of which we are unaware. But everyone knows that two heterogeneous bodies do not mingle together or cannot remain united long; that, when the water has dissolved a certain quantity of salt, it is saturated thereof, and can dissolve no more; that, the more the bodies have an affinity together, the more they appear to seek one another and even to leave those which have less in order to unite themselves with those that have more. Those experiments which are recognized as accurate between the minerals and the metals ought to serve as a guide; but one ought not forget that nature, which acts successively, perfects the mixtures only by things which are of like nature: one is not, then, to take wood to perfect metal. The animal engenders the animal, the plant produces the plant, and the metallic nature, the metals.

CHAPTER XLIII

Symbolic Animals

The most dangerous animal is:
Among the *savage* animals: the slanderer.
Among the *domestic* animals: the flatterer.

The nature of the symbolic animals, the ceremonies observed by their cult, characterize allegorically the Hermetic work, its matter, and the phases of the operation.

THE APIS OX. A *black* bull was necessary, having on its forehead or on one of the sides of its body a *white* mark in the shape of a *crescent*. It ought to have been conceived by the impressions of the lightning bolt. All these characteristics clearly designate matter of the work, daughter, according to *Hermes*, of the *Sun* and the *Moon*. The Egyptians consecrated this bull to these two divinities, because it bore the signs thereof in the colors *black* and *white*, and the *scarab* (consecrated to the sun) that it was to have on its tongue. *Apis* was more particularly the symbol of the moon, as much because of its horns which represent the *crescent moon*, as because this star, outside of its fullness, has always a dark part indicated by the *black*, and the other part, designated by the white mark, is resplendent and in the form of a *crescent*.

The ox was the most useful animal to man, by its strength, its docility, and by its work in the fields. This has caused it to be said allegorically that *Isis* and *Osiris*, who have never had human form, had invented *agriculture*. The Egyptians thought, said *Abnephius*, that the genius and the soul of the world lived in the ox, and they venerated it. But what is most certain, is that the priests, permeated with recognition toward the Creator for the eminent services that gave them the knowledge of the *sacerdotal art*, wished not only to render thanksgiving to him in particular, but by joining those of the people who, conducting themselves only by the senses and not being able to conceive of *God*, recognized indirectly the blessings therefrom in their cult for the most useful and most necessary animal. From here come the feast days and the pomp instituted for this cult, especially at *Bubaste*, city of the ox.

APIS had to be a young, healthy, fearless bull, because the material must be chosen fresh, new, and in all its vigor. They kept it only four years, number of the elements. They lodged it in the temple of *Vulcan*, name given to the secret furnace of the philosophers. After the four years which also symbolizes the four philosophical seasons and the four principal colors of the work, they drowned it in the fountain of the priests, and they sought beforehand a new one, entirely similar, to succeed it.

The Greeks, instructed by the Egyptians, also represented the philosophical matter by one or several *bulls*, as we see in the fable of the Minotaur (*bull of Minos*), shut up in the labyrinth of Crete, vanquished by Theseus with the help of Ariadne's web; by the oxen that Hercules carried off at *Gerion*; by the three thousand from the stable of *Augias*, by the oxen of the sun which grazed in Trinacria; those that *Mercury* stole; by the bulls that *Jason* was obliged to put under the yoke, in order to succeed in carrying off the *Golden Fleece*; the abduction of Europa, etc. Not all of these oxen were *black* and *white* like Apis had to be. Those of Garion were *red*. These colors are not the only ones which occur in the philosophical matter, and the others from the fables have had in view these different circumstances.

THE DOG. This animal was, because of its faithfulness, its vigilance, and its industry, the symbol of a secretary or a minister. It is the hieroglyphic character of Mercury that they represent under the name of *Anubis*, with the head of a dog. The philosophers give to their Mercury the names of *dog of Corascene* and *dog of Armenia*. Isis, in the inscription of her column, says that *she is this dog shining among the stars*; they call it the *dog-star*. (See *Anubis*, p. 246.)

THE WOLF. This animal, because of its form, appearing to be but a *wild dog*, has participated in the same honors as the dog. The Egyptians thought that Osiris had taken the form of the wolf in order to come to the aid of Isis and Horus against Typhon, because the philosophers saw, under the name of *wolf*, their matter perfected to a certain degree. Here is the explanation: the wolf was consecrated to Apollo, whence comes the name of *Apollo-Lycius* (from *lukos*, wolf)[200]. The fable says that *Latone*, in order to avoid the pursuits and the effects of the jealousy of *Juno*, had hidden herself under the form of a *she-wolf*, and that, in this state, she had set *Apollo* into the world (that is to say the *sun*, of philosophical *gold*).

"Our *wolf*," says *Rhasis*, "is found in the Orient and our *dog* in the Occident. They bite one another, become enraged and kill each other. From their corruption is formed a poison which, eventually, changes into *theriac* (elixir)."

The philosophers say that the *wolf* and the *dog* have the same origin. That is why, in the fiction of the expedition of *Osiris*, we see that this prince is accompanied by his two sons: *Anubis*, under the form of a *dog*, and *Macedon*, under that of a *wolf*. These two animals represent, therefore, hieroglyphically, but two things taken from one same subject; one of which is more tractable, the other more ferocious.

THE CAT or ŒLURUS. The cat was in great veneration, because it was consecrated to Isis. They represented it atop the sistrum that we see in the hand of this goddess. This animal was embalmed, after its death, and carried in great mourning into the city of *Bubaste*, where Isis was particularly revered. The cat would partake of the same honors as many other animals among a people who had made a study of the nature of things, and the relationships that they have or appear to have between them. Now, we know that the shape of the pupil of the eyes of the cat seem to follow the phases of the moon in its increase or in its decline. Its eyes shine at night like the stars. These connections gave, without doubt, occasion to say that the *moon* or *Diana* hid herself under the form of the *cat*, when she escaped into Egypt with the other gods in order to avoid the pursuits of *Typhon*. *Fele soror Phœbi* (Ovid, *Metam.*, 1.5.) Moreover, they say that the cat was, among the ancients, the symbol of liberty.

ŒLURUS or the *cat god* was represented, in Egyptian monuments, sometimes holding a sistrum in one hand, and carrying, like Isis, a handled vase in the other; sometimes seated and holding a cross (*symbol of the four elements*) attached to a circle.

THE LION. The lion, which is considered king of the animals by its strength, its courage, and its strong character, superior to that of the others, held one of the first ranks in the cult that they rendered to it. The throne of Horus had lions as supports. Its ardent nature, full of fire, had made it consecrated to Vulcan, symbol of the philosophical fire. The lion was, for the philosophers, the emblem of the Hermetic art.

THE HE-GOAT. It was generally regarded as the symbol of fertility. It was that of the god *Pan* or the fecondating principle of nature, that is to say the *innate fire*, principle of life and generation: when the priests wished to represent the fertility of spring, and the abundance of which it is the source, they depicted *a child seated upon a goat and turned toward Mercury*. This depiction indicates the analogy of the (*Hermetic*) sun with Mercury, and the fecundity of which the matter of the philosophers is the principle in all beings. It is this matter, principle of vegetation, universal and corporified spirit, which becomes *oil* in the olive, *wine* in the grape, *gum*, *resin* in the trees, *juice* in the plants, etc. If the sun, by its heat, is a symbol of vegetation, it is only by exciting the fire dormant in the seeds, where it remains as torpid until it is reawakened and reanimated by an exterior agent. This is what occurs in the operations of the Hermetic art, where the philosophical mercury works by its action, upon the fixed matter, where is found shut up, as in a prison, this *innate fire*. It develops it by breaking its bonds, and sets it in a state of action, in order to lead the work to its perfection. Here indeed is the *child seated upon the goat*, and the motive which inclines it to turn toward Mercury. Osiris being this innate fire is no different from *Pan*, thus was the goat consecrated to the one and the other. It was, for this same reason, one of the attributes of *Bacchus*.

THE ICHNEUMON AND THE CROCODILE. They regarded the ichneumon (*Pharaoh's rat* or *mongoose*, the size of a cat) as the sworn enemy of the crocodile; but not being able to vanquish it by force, being but a species of rat, it employed cleverness. When the crocodile slept, it insinuates itself, they say, into its gaping mouth, descends into its intestines and gnaws them. They make use of this fact to indicate something similar in the operations of the work: the FIXED, which at first appears only to be a small thing, or rather, the *innate fire* that it contains, seems not to have any form; but in the proportion that it is developed, it is *insinuated* therein so that it finally takes the upper hand and *kills it*, that is to say that it *fixes* it like itself.

The *crocodile*, as an amphibious animal, was a natural hieroglyph of the philosophical matter composed of water and earth; thus, did it often accompany the figures of Osiris and Isis. The Egyptians represented the sun in a ship as pilot, and this ship was carried by a crocodile, "in order to signify," said *Eusebius* (*Prepar. evang.*, 1.3, ch. 3), "the movement of the sun in the humid." - He should have said: in order to signify that the Hermetic matter is the principle or the base of the gold or the philosophical sun. The water where swims the crocodile is that mercury or that matter reduced into water. The ship represents the vessel of nature, in which the sun or igneous and sulphureous principle is as pilot, because it is that which conducts the work by its action over the humid or mercury. The crocodile was also the hieroglyph of Egypt itself, and especially of the Lower, as being more marshy.

THE TORTOISE. It was, among the ancients, the symbol of matter, because they had noticed upon its plates a type of representation of this figure ♄ of Saturn. That is why *Venus* was sometimes represented seated upon a goat whose head, like that of the ram, presents, nearly, this figure ☿ of Mercury, and the right foot supported upon a tortoise. We see too, in a philosophical emblem, an *artist* making a sauce with a tortoise and grapes. A philosopher who was asked what the matter was, responded: *Testudo solis cum pinguedine vitis*.

THE CYNOCEPHALUS (*dog*-faced baboon). This animal, which has a body nearly similar to that of a man and a head to that of a dog, has been one of the most frequently employed hieroglyphs. The Egyptians often made use of it as a symbol of the sun and moon, because of the relationship that they had noticed between it and these stars. They supposed too that the cynocephalus had indicated to *Isis* the body of *Osiris* that she sought, and, for this reason, they placed it with this god and goddess. The truth of these allegorical accounts is that the *cynocephalus* was the hieroglyph of Mercury and of the philosophical mercury, which is to always accompany Isis as her minister, since, without the mercury, Isis and Osiris could do nothing in the work. HERMES or the philosopher Mercury having given cause, by his name, to confuse him with the *philosophical Mercury* of which they suppose him the inventor, Egyptians and other non-initiates have confused the invented thing with its inventor and taken the hieroglyph of the one for that of the other.

When the cynocephalus is represented with the caduceus, some vases, or with a crescent; with a lotus flower or something aquatic or volatile; it is a hieroglyph of the philosophical mercury. But when we see it with a reed or a roll of paper, it represents Hermes, secretary and counselor of Isis, to whom they attribute the invention of writing and the sciences. The idea to take this animal as a symbol of Hermes has come from the Egyptians thinking that the cynocephalus knew naturally how to write the letters utilized in Egypt.

THE RAM. The nature of the *ram* which is regarded as hot and humid corresponding to that of the philosophical mercury, the Egyptians did not fail to place it among the number of their principal hieroglyphs; and, in the fable of the flight of the gods into Egypt, they say that Jupiter hid himself under the form of a ram, and, having represented him with the head of this animal, they gave him the name of *Amun* or *Ammon*. All the accounts invented on this subject serve only to designate the Mercury of the philosophers; *example*:

"*Bacchus*, being in Libya with his army, found himself," says the fable, "extremely pressed by thirst, and invoked Jupiter, who appeared to him under the form of a ram and conducted him, across the desert, to a fountain where he quenched his thirst. In memory of this event, they elevated a temple there in honor of the master of the gods, under the name of *Jupiter-Ammon*[201], and he was represented with the head of a ram." - *Explanation*:

The ram, being one of the symbols of Mercury, was to appear to Bacchus in *Libya*, the name of which signifies *a stone from where flows the water*: the mercury, whose nature is hot and humid, is formed only by the resolution of the philosophical matter in *water*. "This water," says *the Cosmopolite* (*nov. lum. chim.*), "is our Mercury that we draw by means of our magnet, which is found in the belly of the ram." - *Herodotus* relates that Jupiter appeared to Hercules under the same form; which indicates that, in Greece as in Egypt, Hercules was the symbol of the *artist* or Hermetic philosopher, whose ardent desire is to see the *philosophical Jupiter*, which can only show itself in *Libya*, that is to say when the matter has passed through dissolution, because then the artist has the mercury so desired. The ram was a victim that they sacrificed to all the gods, because the mercury, of which it is one of the symbols, accompanies them in all the operations of the *sacerdotal art*. Thus, it figures in many fables and in that of the *Golden Fleece*.

THE EAGLE AND THE SPARROW-HAWK. The *eagle*, king of the birds, was consecrated to Jupiter because it was a fortunate omen for this god, when he went to fight his father *Saturn* and because it furnished him weapons, when he vanquished the Titans, etc. The chariot of Jupiter is yoked with two eagles, and they almost never represented him without putting this bird near him. Indeed, the philosophers have called *eagle* their mercury or the volatile part of their matter, They have called *lion* the fixed part, and speak only of the combat of these two animals.

They have supposed with reason that the eagle was a good omen to Jupiter, since the matter is volatilized in the time that he won the victory over Saturn, that is to say when the color *gray* took the place of the *black*.

The philosophers have given the name of SPARROW-HAWK to their matter which, having attained to a certain degree of igneity, becomes philosophical sulphur. They had recognized that, by its nature, this bird had a relation to the eagle: both are strong, bold, daring, of a hot temperament, igneous, fiery.

They represented Osiris with the head of a sparrow-hawk, because this bird, which attacks all the others, devours them, transforms them into its nature by changing them into its own substance, since they serve as its food. It represents, therefore, Osiris, igneous and fixed principle, which *fixes* the volatile parts of the matter, symbolized by the eagle and the *sparrow-hawk*. Homer, in the *Odyssey*, calls the sparrow-hawk, which is a symbol of the sun, the messenger of Apollo.

IBIS. Herodotus relates (bk. II, ch. 75 and 76) that there were, in Egypt, two species of ibis: the one, *all black*, which combats the winged serpents and prevents them from penetrating into the land, when in the spring they come in droves from Arabia. The other species is *black* and *white* and represents Isis. The all-black ibis, which fights and kills the winged serpents that Herodotus has never seen, indicates the combat that takes place between the parts of matter during the dissolution. The death of these serpents signifies the putrefaction which is the continuation thereof and by which the matter becomes *entirely black*. We have, on this subject, spoken of two dragons, the one winged, the other without wings, whence results the mercury, which is made after this putrefaction; the matter, in part *black* and in part *white*. Mercury borrowed the form from this second species of ibis which, by its two colors, has the same relation with the *moon* as the bull *Apis* and becomes, like it, the symbol of the matter of the Hermetic art.

The great services that the ibis rendered to all of Egypt, whether in killing the serpents, or in breaking the eggs of the crocodiles, were sufficient for the Egyptians to accord it the same honors as the other animals, and the connections that we have just indicated have made it admitted among the hieroglyphs. Because of its relations with the moon, they gave to Isis, who is the symbol of this star, the head of an ibis. This bird was consecrated to Mercury, because this God, fleeing before Typhon, took the form of an ibis. Hermes, under this form, kept watch, said *Abenephius* (*De cultus Egypt.*), over the preservation of the Egyptians, and instructed them in all the sciences[202].

In vain did they make ingenious commentaries in order to explain these hieroglyphs in a sense other than the Hermetic sense. If *Vulcan* and *Mercury* are not the basis of these applications, one arrives, in imitation of *Plutarch*, *Diodorus*, and others, at forced inductions, unlikely, and which do not satisfy. We always have, before our eyes, that *Harpocrates* with the finger over his mouth, announcing that this cult, these ceremonies, these hieroglyphs, contain mysteries, that it is not permitted to everyone to penetrate, that it is necessary to meditate upon in silence; that the priests did not reveal to those who came into Egypt only in order to satisfy their curiosity. The interpretations of many historians are no more believable than were those of the Egyptian people who rendered honors of the cult to the animals, because they were told that the gods had taken the figure thereof[203].

CHAPTER XLIV

On the Hieroglyphic Plants

LOTUS and EGYPTIAN BEAN. The *lotus* is an aquatic plant which differs only by the color of its flower, which is *white*, from the *Egyptian bean*, whose flower is a rosy *red*. Its leaf represents, in some way, the sun by its roundness, and by its fibers which, from a little circle placed at the center of this leaf, are spread like rays unto the circumference. Its flower in full bloom presents nearly the same thing. This flower appears at the surface of the water, at the rising of the sun, and plunges itself back in when it is setting. Such are the analogies which have caused it to be inserted among the hieroglyphs. Because of its whiteness, the flower of the lotus adorns the head of Isis, and that of the Egyptian bean appears on the head of Osiris, Horus, and priests in their service. Without this difference of color, one of the two plants would have sufficed. The vases over the cup of which we see a child seated, are ordinarily the fruit of the lotus.

THE COLOCAISE. This is a species of *cuckoopint* which grows in Egypt, in aquatic places. Its root is good to eat. Its fruit, composed of red berries in a cluster, like a bunch of grapes, along a sort of pestle which rises from the depths of the flower, is seen on the head of several divinities, and upon that of Harpocrates, because its red color represented *Horus* (Hermetic), with which they have often confused the *god of silence*, who was only invented in order to mark the silence that one is to keep on this same Horus. Minerva was worshipped at Sicyone under the name of *Colocaise*.

THE PERSEA. This tree, which grows in the environs of greater Cairo, has leaves similar to those of the laurel, but longer. It is an evergreen. Its fruit has the shape of a pear. It has a kernel which has the taste of a chestnut, and the shape of a heart. This peculiarity, joined with that of its leaves which resemble a tongue, have made it dedicated to the god of silence, upon whose head we see it more commonly than on that of any other divinity. This kernel is represented sometimes whole, other times open to appear as an almond, but always to announce that it is necessary to be able to govern one's tongue, and preserve in one's heart the secret of the mysteries. It is for this reason that we sometimes see it upon the radiant head of Harpocrates or placed over a crescent.

THE MUSA or AMUSA. The trunk of this tree without branches is spongy, covered with scaly bark. Its leaves, wide, blunt, three meters long, are strengthened by a thick and wide rib which extends through the middle. From the top of the trunk arise red or yellowish flowers: their fruit, of an agreeable taste, rather similar to a golden cucumber. Its root, long and thick, is *black* on the outside, pulpy and *white* on the inside. It gives a *white* juice which then becomes *red*. It is not its beauty which has earned it its hieroglyphic honors, but its connection with certain Hermetic divinities: the plumes of Osiris and his priests; those of Isis, where its leaves are sometimes found; the cut fruit which is seen between the two leaves which form the plume; finally, the flowering trunk of this plant which Isis presents to her spouse, are things which are not represented without cause on the *Isaic Tablet*. These depictions are therefore mysterious; but the mystery will be easy to uncover for the one who reflects on all which precedes. He will recognize, in the description of the *amusa*, the four principal colors of the great work: the black is found in the root; now, the color black is the root, the base, or the key of the work. The black husk removed; we discover the *white*; the pulp of the fruit is also white. The flowers that Isis presents to Osiris are *yellow* and *red*, and the skin of the fruit is golden. We have seen, in our descriptions, that the moon of the philosophers is the matter attained to the white. The saffron-yellow color and the red, which succeeds the white, are the sun or the Osiris of the art. The author of the Isaic Tablet had reason, then, to represent Isis in the posture of a person who offers a *red* flower to Osiris. We may again observe here that all the attributes of this god partake, in whole or in part, of the color *red* or of the *yellow* or of the *saffron*; and those of Isis, of the *black* and the *white*, taken separately or mixed, because the Egyptian monuments represented these divinities according to the different states where the matter of the work is found during the course of the operations. One may therefore encounter with Osiris all the colors; but then it is necessary to pay attention to the attributes which accompany him. If the author knows all about the mysteries and he has wished to represent Osiris in his glory, the attributes will be *red* or at least *saffron*. In his expedition of the Indies, the colors will be varied, which was indicated by the tigers and leopards which accompanied Bacchus; in Ethiopia, Osiris dead, the colors will be either *black* or *violet*; but never will you find there *white* without mixture, as we never see any attribute of Isis purely *red*.

These hieroglyphs, so multiplied, have been, for the most part, falsely interpreted by poorly instructed historians who, in their accounts on the Egyptian cult, have taken for *gods* all the symbols placed in the temples, and, for a *true worship*, the public veneration of which they were the object.

MOLYBDENOS. The philosophers who have imagined this plant, called *Saturnian*, to represent their work, say that its root was of lead; its trunk, of silver; and its flowers, of gold. Homer, in his *Odyssey* (1.x, v. 302 and following), makes mention thereof under the name of *moly*.

SUMMARY

We have seen (note 198) that the *philosopher's fire*, that principal agent of alchemy, was *electricity*, of which the modern physicists have so well determined the mysterious laws of action.

Let us examine the nature of the elements considered as the principal causes of the Hermetic work: the *elixir of long life*, and the *philosopher's stone*.

1. The NITRE is known to be a constitutive element of the majority of the natural bodies. Combined with the alkaline principle, it produces the *natron* or natrum[204] of the ancients, and the saltpeter of the moderns. The writings and the science are in agreement in recognizing in this chemical agent the virtues of a universal solvent. The Jews use it in baths[205].

The chemists draw from this salt their *strong water*[206] and their *aqua regia*[207], which are the principal agents employed in metallurgy.

2. The second principal element is the SULPHUR; simple, universal substance, that the sacred tradition and the classical tradition mentioned frequently. The sulphur has upon the nitre, the strong water, and the aqua regia, a singular effect: it disposes them to act upon the mercury by producing metallic amalgams.

3. And the third element is the MERCURY, that the alchemists supposed to be the base of all the metals.

The combinations of these three elements would produce: in the liquid state: the *elixir*; in the solid state, the *philosopher's stone*.

The physician-alchemists know perfectly the powerful therapeutic properties of these three elements.

The elixir, that marvelous restorer of youth, and preserver of life and beauty, quite superior to all the balms invented since, was rendered even more efficacious by the adjudication of a little gold in dissolution. It then became the famous *aurum potabile*, that nectar, that ambrosia of which the poets of antiquity have proclaimed the existence.

This *potable gold* was recognized as a powerful and vivifying medicine. The energetic and medicinal ingredients were combined therein in a manner to produce a depuration, a revivification, and, in some way, a *resurrection* of the human organism.

The same substances which, combined in a certain fashion, produced the elixir, being amalgams and prepared in another manner, produced the *philosopher's stone*, whether in powder or in a state of concretion. The nitre, the sulphur, and the mercury were mixed in different proportions according to the nature of the metal that they wished to transform. Then the Hermetic fire was indispensible.

Whence it results that the composition of the stone contained such quantities of nitre, sulphur, and mercury deemed necessary to reproduce the transmutation of certain metals, with the action of electricity, when they had arrived at the state of fusion.

This definition may serve to make understood the mysterious descriptions of this stone by the Hermetic writers. One of them expresses himself thus: "The philosopher's stone, the great aim of alchemy, is a specific preparation of chemical agents, which, once found, is destined to convert the entire mercurial part of a given metal into a gold purer than that which is extracted from the mines, and this by throwing only a small quantity of gold into the metals in fusion; whereas the part of the metals which is not mercury is immediately burned and disappears. This stone has the weight of gold; it is fragile like glass, of dark color; it melts like wax at contact with fire. This is what the alchemists promised to find; but they asserted too that they would make the same stone for the silver, and this stone would transform into silver of a superior quality all the metals, except silver into gold. They have promised further, says the celebrated *Boerhaave*, to perfect the philosopher's stone to such a degree that, thrown into a certain quantity of melted gold, it would change the substance into philosopher's stone. They have asserted, finally, that they would give it a strength and a virtue such that, mixed with pure quicksilver, it would transform it likewise into philosopher's stone.

"All this, therefore, say the alchemists, is a question of doing in a short time, through science, what nature accomplishes in several years and even in several centuries. All is in all, according to the pantheist dogma. There is in the lead, the mercury and the gold. Well then! If we found a body which agitated all the parts of the lead, in a manner to consume all that is not mercury, while bearing in mind the sulphur in order to fix the mercury, is there not good reason to believe that the remaining liquid would be transformed into gold? Such is the basis of the opinion that admits as probable the discovery of the philosopher's stone, of that stone that the alchemists claim to be a concentrated and fixed essence, which, when it is founded with any metal whatever, unites immediately, by its magnetic power, with the mercurial part of the metal, volatilizes and drives out all that is found impure, and lets exist only the pure gold.

"The alchemists have employed two other means to arrive at the making of gold. The first is the *separation*: for they say that each known metal contains a certain quantity of gold; only, in the majority, the quantity is so minute, that it would not defray the expense that one would make to obtain it. The second means is the *maturation*. Indeed, the alchemists consider mercury as the base and the substance of all the metals, and they assert that by subtilizing it and purifying it with great effort and after long operations, they would change it infallibly into gold."

The fundamental question is to know: 1st, if the metals have a common base, and what that base is; 2nd, if they have a common metallic principle, and what that principle is; and if, by the action of electricity, they can, being in fusion, be transformed by the addition of certain quantities of nitre, sulphur, and mercury, well prepared, and produce the stone so desired.

The modern metallurgists, and physicists who study the phenomena of electricity, continue to occupy themselves with these important questions, persuaded that if they can decompose the metals, they might recompose them and make them undergo such transformations as they will.

The scientist *Bavy* has already made a step in this science, when he reduced, by his galvanic experiments, the generally accepted number of *simple* substances by decomposing several of these bodies regarded as *elementary*; but, among those that he had classified as such, Messrs. *Brand* and *Faraday* have indicated some of them which were also really *compounds*. This analysis, pushed to its final end, will at last cause to succeed the *decomposition* of the metals and the discovery of their first bases[208].

The alchemists, in their operations, made known that they united the power of electricity and ordinary fire, and that they applied the galvanic forces to the metals in fusion. How do we verify their assertions and demonstrate the vanity of their doctrine, if, disregarding their *practical* indications, we continue to employ only ordinary fire?

The *electricians Cross*, *Fox*, and some others, have come very close to the transformation of the metals, when they have changed the form and character thereof by the continued action of the galvanic currents of electricity. They have produced, in a short space of time, what nature accomplishes only at the end of several centuries: *magnificent crystallizations* in *mineral* substances that they had not suspected to be susceptible to such a formation. It is regrettable that they have not employed electricity to the metals in fusion, while adding thereto the chemical agents familiar to the alchemists and the metallurgists[209].

Until the alchemists of antiquity are recognized as the most sublime philosophers, science draws great profit from the conscientious labors of the mystical philosophers of modern times, such as *Cardan*, who has discovered the formidable lever of the will; *Artephius*, the secret of the vital principle; *Hortensius*, the fabrication of the diamond; *Albertus Magnus*, *Roger Bacon*, *Raymond Lulle*, *Aslin de Lisle*, *Arnaud de Villeneuve*, *Paracelsus*, *Agrippa*, *Von Helmont*, *Avicenne*, and so many others, the arcana of nature; *Mesmer*, magnetism, that other occult power of the human organism; *Leibnitz* and *Fourier*, the sublime means of universal harmony. Their prodigious works are as so many torches which lighten the path which leads to truth.

CHAPTER XLV

Effects of Barbary

"These writings, where those men superior to their centuries that they surpassed, had always consigned the immortal results of their knowledge, and made known the most secret mysteries of the human organization, and by which everything was combined, developed, dissolved, and transformed in the universal laboratory; these writings were private to the *initiates*, in order to interpret the mysteries and secrets thereof.

"The studious of that time, for whom the *book with seven seals* was found thus closed, wandering without guidance, submitted these sublime sciences to their unenlightened reasoning; the Qabalah, indecipherable for them, is lost; alchemy and iatricia become *chemistry* and *medicine*; astrology becomes *astronomy*; magianism was treated as *magic*[210], *sorcery*; even magnetism, which formerly was an essential part of the art of healing, was likewise lost; it was fortunately rediscovered by Mesmer, while studying the influence of the planets upon man; and, under this denomination, he caused this curious part of the occult sciences to pass from the secret laboratory of magianism, into the public domain of science.

"In the times of European ignorance and intolerant beliefs of the Middle Ages, they slandered and persecuted those who gave themselves to any study of these sciences so as not to lose the thread thereof; and, under the superstitious pretext that they held a sacrilegious hand over the holy ark of faith, they were excommunicated[211], they were accused of sorcery, enchantment, and were condemned to perish in the flames of a *pyre*, for the greater glory of God, of whom they were, however, the most sincere admirers and true interpreters of his works.

"Blind fanaticism and the persecutions dispersed or annihilated almost entirely these laborious workers of the ancient philosophy; and at the renaissance of the light, superficial knowledge and doubt, in the scoffing style, were impotent to produce anything capable of replacing what was lost, or seemed to be; for some great geniuses, scattered among men, occupy themselves, in secret, with enlightening the progress of humanity, despite the disdain of the men who, in the eyes of the multitude, pass as scholars.

"In this period of doubt on *occultism*, FOURIER has not disregarded the study of the stars and their influences. This superior genius has not feared to study deeply the mysteries and secrets of the ancient science, and he was marvelously rewarded by the discovery of the laws of UNIVERSAL HARMONY and UNITY, that sublime bond of the chain of causes. he has been able then to penetrate further than his predecessors and than *Leibnitz* himself, in the intelligence of the mysteries of nature. At the example of the alchemists, he has given the results of the knowledge, without making known the processes that have procured it for him."

Elite and studious Masons, walk in his steps, renounce the Masonic futilities, give your spirits to scholarly research, add to yourselves the meditations that occupied the ancient sages, instruct yourselves in order to enlighten your brethren, and let the serious study of the useful sciences become the aim of your philosophical sessions. Reveal therein the ancient mysteries, of which you shall be the glorious interpreters. I have dared you to trace the path thereof: BECOME INITIATES!

SHORT NOTICE ON FOURIER

F.-C.-MA. FOURIER, born at Besançon, in 1772, died in 1837, is founder of the *Societary* or *Phalansterian School.* He figures in our philosophical gallery as author of the *Theorie des quatre mouvements et des destinées générales*[212].

Fourier, whom one would be tempted to believe a Freemason, expresses himself thus in this theory, published in 1808 and reprinted in 1840 (1 vol. in-8vo, with a preface by the publishers).

"God is the enemy of uniformity. He wills that movement varies in perpetuity. To this end, he makes hatch periodically, in our societies, germs of beneficent or harmful innovations. It is to the reason to judge the use of these germs: to suffocate the bad ones, like the political clubs, to develop the good ones, such as *Freemasonry.*

"What salutary party could one draw from Freemasonry, which has succeeded in operating the affiliation in all the civilized religions, and to compose itself only of the well-to-do class, under the protection of the great who are at the head, and who have accustomed the people to see, without jealousy, its mysterious assemblies held in secret, far from the vulgar profane!

"This is an entirely new question for this century, which has not been able to discern the resources that this institution offers: it is a diamond that we disregard without knowing the price. Thus, the savages of Guahana tread underfoot the blocks of gold, before European cupidity taught them their value."

This light, this encouragement from a profound thinker, has not yet produced anything, such power has the force of inertia over the spirit of the Masons!

Let us say here, for the Masons who have not read Fourier, a word on his system.

This philosopher has come to complete the work of *Newton,* by discovering the law of *passionate attraction.* He has, in his vast system, as ingenious as true, found the *universal analog,* the laws of *unity* and *harmony* of the worlds. Fourier was an ecstatic, and this disposition toward ecstasy gives the key of his foresights.

Newton has developed the principle, indicated before him, of the sidereal (*material*) attraction which makes every planetary system gravitate around its pivotal star and produces the harmony of the celestial bodies.

The attraction is therefore a law (*law of love*) which rules the whole universe. For the execution of this powerful law, God has never employed constraint: he *impassions* his innumerable creatures for the thing that he wants them to do. Their liberty and their happiness are the result of their obedience to this law, that Fourier calls the *passionate attraction* or the *law of harmony and happiness.*

The character of this divine law is *unity* or the unique, universal principle, cause of the order, general harmony, and simplicity in the means of production (see note 136); whence it results that the principle which, in nature, rules the material or the *body* of things and beings, is the same which rules their mineral, vegetable, or animal *animation.*

Fourier goes further: he considers man as being instituted by God, *king of the earth,* and, according to the principle of *unity,* all that exists upon the earth is to be *modeled* on man; the earth is to *reflect* man, as man *reflects* God. Consequently, all the created beings are *en rapport* with the double nature (*material* and *animic*) of man; and this observer calls the law of these connections the *universal analogy*, *limitless* science by which he discovers the history of the future and that of the past. It is thus that, according to him, the animals and the plants are as so many *hieroglyphs* en rapport with the human destinies and as analogy teaches to decipher.

We regret that Fourier has not made a complete treatise on *passionate botanics*[213]: he has limited himself to giving the key of the system and of the classification. He has joined to the precept examples which give the allurement to this science. Let us cite:

THE BOX-TREE, emblem of *poverty*, lives in arid places and sterile terrains, as the *indigent* is reduced to the most paltry domicile. We see the insects attach themselves thereto as to the poor who have not the means to protect themselves therefrom. The indigent has no pleasures: nature has depicted this effect by depriving the flower of the box-tree from petals, which are emblems of pleasure. Its fruit is a reversed cook-pot, image of the cuisine of the poor which is reduced to nothing. Its leaf is curved into a scoop in order to receive a drop of water, like the hand of the poor which seeks to receive a farthing from the compassion of the passers-by. Its wood is compact and knotty, by allusion to the rough life and difficulty of the miserable, among whom reigns insalubrity, represented by the fetid oil that is drawn from the box-tree.

THE MISTLETOE is the portrait of the *parasite*, living from the juices of others. It develops itself indifferently in one direction or the other, like the schemer who takes on all masks. The mistletoe represents by its leaves duplicity, and with its glue it sets the trap where come to be taken the birds, like the fools are taken by the ruses of the parasite.

THE BALSAMINE: Fourier depicts in this flower the *industrious* and *fortunate adventurer*.

THE CROWN IMPERIAL is the picture of the noble industry *humbled*. It is that of *the scholar or the artist*. This flower, which has six corollas reversed and surmounted, like the balsamine, by a ton of foliage, in the form of truth (*triangular form of the lily and the tulip*). It excites a lively interest by the accessory of six tear drops which are found at the bottom of the chalice. Each is astonished thereby: it seems that the flower is in mourning; it lowers the head and sheds large tears that it keeps hidden under its stamens. It is therefore the emblem of a class *which grieves in secret*. This class is very industrious; for, the flower bears as a banner the artistic sign, the tuft of leaves grouped at the top of the stem, in a symbol of high and noble industry, sciences, and arts. This intelligent class is that of the useful scholars who are obliged to bow before plebeian vanity: thus, the plant inclines its beautiful flowers in an attitude of suffering. They are swollen with hidden tears: image of the fate of the scholars and artists, principal adornment of society. This flower is orange, which is the color of *enthusiasm*, by analogy to the class of scholars and artists, who have no other support than the enthusiasm against poverty.

It is thus that such objects, quite insignificant at first glance, are embellished by the faithfulness of interpretation and by their hieroglyphic rightness.

FIN

ENDNOTES

1. "The LAW, which is reason exempt from passions, ought to reign with the exclusion of men, the most virtuous of whom are formed from reason and passions." (Emperor Julien.)
2. We write this word and those which derive therefrom without the hyphen [referring to his use of Francmaçonnerie instead of the common Franc-Maçonnerie]; since one no longer says franche-maçonnerie, franches-maçonnes, it is a gross error against logic and grammar to write franc-maçon, francs-maçons: how do you write the plural of franc-maçonne? If you submit *franc* to the rule of numbers, you ought, in good logic, to submit it likewise to the rule of genders and say franche-maçonnerie. We think even that in imitation of many French words, whose orthography is contracted, we could suppress the *c*, the radical would be sensible enough.
3. Among the ancients, they did not distinguish between knowledge and *wisdom*, between *ignorance* or *madness*, or *foolishness*. They judged that science, that is to say the *knowledge of the true relations of things* is inseparable from a just decision; and this decision is the *wisdom*, *sapiens*, from the primitive root SAP, which marks, in the proper sense, all that relates to the sense of taste; and, in the figurative, what relates to meditation: the sage is the one who *tastes well*, who *judges well*, and who *knows*.
4. The city with two rivers: the *Ose* and *Ossrain*; a borough, today replaces it under the name of *Sainte-Reine* (Gold Coast); there are excellent water rails which give renown to its hospital.
5. There remain there some beautiful monuments of antiquity, such as the temple of Janus and that of Cybel.
6. Born at Litchfield in 1617, died in 1692. Author of the *History of the Order of the Garter*, in-fol.
7. Already, in 1641, according to the journal of *Ashmole*, the corporation took in, as *external members*, persons foreign to material architecture, by which it hoped to retain some usefulness or some relief; from here comes the expression *accepted* added to the word freemason and that, much later, jongleurs have, illegally, added to the title of an equivocal rite.
   But it is only after 1691 that has begun, in England, the denomination of *free* and *accepted*, and that they were so inclined to admit *openly* lords, dukes, jurisconsults, merchants, haberdashers, etc.
8. Extracted from the chapter entitled: *Origin of the schools or colleges of architect-builders* (extinguished in the 4th century), *and of the corporations of free-masons* (Fastes Initiatiques).
9. By casting a glance thereto, we see that the initiates, mingled with the builder-masons, saw to choose for *patrons* or protectors, powerful personages, near to whom they had access, and their choice fell principally upon members of the clergy, to better veil their intentions; but once the philosophical standard was deployed, the clergy disappeared from the *protectorate* and none of its members became *Grand Master*. Moreover, the protectorate endured indefinitely; whereas the *Grand Masters* were, in principle, renewed annually, save re-election or prolongation.
10. See our *Chronological Table* of the introduction of Freemasonry among the

various nations of the globe, and the *Historical Brief* of its institution and of its progress or failure in each State or Kingdom.

They recognized there, evidently, that the appearance of Freemasonry upon the scene of the world, gave birth spontaneously, as by enchantment, to sympathies unknown until then between the most foreign men by climate, religions, morals, opinions, politics, and language, and that twenty years has sufficed for there to be Freemasons among the principal peoples of the earth; so true is it that men have need of getting to know one another in order to understand and love one another.

11. The solstices were celebrated long before Numa Pompilius. These feasts took the name of *Saint John* only under the monk-builders, in the 4th century. We read, in the instruction of the grade of *Kadosh* called of *Sudermanie*, thirtieth degree:

    "Many brothers in the royal art believe that our lodges dedicated to Saint John, are to Saint John the Baptist or the Evangelist; this is an error: the one to whom they are dedicated is *Saint John the Almoner*, who was the Grand Master of the Knights of *Saint John of Jerusalem*, in the 13th century, and who has always been the most beautiful ornament of the Order, and the patron of the Templars."

    Would there not have been here an anachronism, shortcoming too familiar to the fabricators of the high grades: *John*, called the *Almoner*, Patriarch of Alexandria, was born at Amathonte (Cyprus) around 550 and died around 619. He could not, therefore, be Grand Master in the 13th century, unless there are two Saints John the Almoner.
12. This table is found in the *Histoire des cultes et ceremonies religieuses*, published by Prudhomme, vol. IV.
13. It is to this solemn session that we carry back the famous discourse of this reformer, inserted in several collections. Here he places erroneously, as he has expressed elsewhere, the origin of Freemasonry (see the notice which concerns this) at the time of the crusades and divides into three classes the members of the association. This interesting piece is found in *Hermès*, vol. I, p. 339 and following.
14. See our notice on the lodge *Anglaise*, number 204, of Bordeaux, in the Fastes Initiatiques.
15. The *Masonry of Adoption* was created at Paris in 1730; would it have existed if it had had to go under this name? What French person would have wished to let themselves be called *free-mason*? It is, perhaps, because of the signification that the expression Free-masonry recalls to other lands that the Freemasonry of the ladies does not exist there. Would they not have to modify the name, since they have changed the thing?
16. What is reported of this event and its results in the *État du G.-O.*, vol. I of the revival, pages 13 and 14, is of an inexactitude such as it gives notice or a complete ignorance of the facts, or the will to disguise them.
17. Expression of the brother *Lachaussée*, in his *Mémoire* called *justificatif.*
18. It is therefore wrongly and animated by a spirit of injustice that *Thory*, as unskillful proposer, has baptized this power with the name of *schismatic.* Freemasonry is essentially democratic, the majority had force of law and all legitimately. Thus, seeing the few number of brethren who remained faithful to it, but that the sentiment of progress and the need for reform did not

inspire, it is, on the contrary, the *Grand Lodge of France* which became schismatic, by resisting, in the general opinion of enlightened Masons. Moreover, it lost its *orthodoxy*, by dwelling in the old routine, whereas the new body, which followed the progress of ideas, *alone* became orthodox.

19. Circul. of the G.O., from June 26, in4to, p. 2 and 8.
20. It is to be noted that, within this whole constitutive piece, one does not see a single abbreviation. The secretariate has made use thereof only later. The first time was in the copy of the constitutions of the Order presented to the G.M. on October 22nd of this same year; this abbreviation is limited to this: T.S.G.M., Très Sérénissime Grand-Maître [Most Serene Grand Master]. The *tripunctuated* abbreviation begins only from the circular of August 12, 1774, addressed to the Lodges with the correspondence of the G.O., to announce the taking of possession of its new locale, rue de Pot-de-Fer-Saint-Sulpice, and address to them the budget of annual expenses rising to 16,000 francs. This circular is remarkable in two respects. First, the tripunctuated abbreviations begin from this day; we read, for the first time, at the head of this piece: The G.·. O.·. of France *to all the regular lodges* - Then the G.O. had, up to this period, given the dates by *day*, *week*, *month*, and *year*, and errors often resulted therefrom, especially when it took Monday, instead of Sunday, for the first day of the week. It is thus that is found, for some writers, the error of one day in the announcement of the date of the installation of the G.M.: one of the official reports says that it took place on the fifth day of the third week of the eighth month, 5773; now, the third week of this Gregorian month beginning on Sunday, October 17, it is evident that the fifth day, Thursday, is the 21st, date which is not correct, since the installation took place on Friday, the 22nd; it should read the sixth day; but they have taken Monday as the day which begins the week. - *Thory* indicates October 28, which corresponds to Thursday, fifth day of the fourth week. - Thus, does the circular say that, *in order to establish the uniformity of surety of the dates, the G. o. has decided to no longer announce the weeks.*
21. This is the first time that we hear talk of *regular* and *irregular* Masons, or *regular* or *irregular* lodges. This distinction has been explained in a writing of the G.·. O.·. published under the title of *Letter on the regular Masons*, in which we read this passage:
"...The rejected Masons continued their works; the G.·. O.·. sees itself, therefore, obliged to distinguish, by a particular title, the lodges of its association. The word regular announced the aim that they intended, the design to compose it only of exact Masons to fulfill their duties; it was consequently adopted as being more proper to *characterize* those who would form it. A *regular* lodge is a lodge attached to the G.·. O.·., that is to say to the representative body of Masonry in France, the only one authorized by the S.G.M. to work under its auspices, and a *regular* Mason is a member of a regular lodge."
22. It is the first power of the globe which had constituted *Masonic associations Freemasonic* lodges, since there existed none before it. The societies of operative masons, small or great, were only corporations or guilds, and never *Masonic* societies; that qualification never concerned them (*see the writings of the time*).
23. The guild masons formed, at London, the third brotherhood, protected, like the others, by a patron whom, later, some writers gave inappropriately the name of G.M. They had their house on Baskingall Street; the number of

members was around 70. The admission was 1pd. 16sh. (45fr.), and the uniform 5pd. (125fr.). They were formed into a body in 1410, under the title of society of *Freemasons*. William *Hankstow* or *Hanktow*, second King at Arms, granted them arms in 1477.

24. One unpardonable mistake for which to reproach the French writers, is that of rendering more obscure for us these old debates, or any other relation, because, writing long after the event, they insist on saying *masonic society*, whereas this qualificative, which did not yet exist, was not created for operative guilds; and to translate the words *freemason*, *freemasonry*, as *francmaçon*, *francmaçonnerie*, instead of saying, according to the truth, *maçon-libre*, *maçonnerie-libre*. The French reader would better know what to think of it, and he would not accord to an era which had but the germ thereof, the philosophical and eminently civilizing spirit which invariably animates French Masonry.
Thory, in the translations that he has given, has not been able to avoid this mistake. We read it in the Epistle (*Address*) that he reproduces by *Laurence Dermotte* (*Acta Latam.*, vol 2, p. 40) and which makes the object of this digression.
25. Thus, the high grades of this supposed Masonry do not even have in common with the symbolic degrees what the *bastards* have in common with the legitimate children.
26. "Well before 1720 and 1721 (25 years), troublesome circumstances had forced Masonry to dwell in obscurity, and the Royal G.L. has long remained engulfed in a deep sleep." (Until around 1785.) - Extract from the letter of October 14, 1786, written by Br. *Murdoch*, Grand Secretary of that G.L., to Br. *Mathéus*, at Rouen.
27. It is in these years, probably in 1741 or 42, and at this occasion, that was established, at Saint-Germain, the lodge *la Bonne-Foi*, remarkable yet today for its well-conducted works.
28. "Up to 1785, Scottish Masonry was composed exclusively of the three symbolic grades. In this period, it instituted itself at Edinburgh as a Masonic authority under the title of *Grand Lodge of the Royal Order of Heredom and Kilwinning*, which conferred one high grade, divided into three points, known under the name of *Rose-Croix of the Tower*. They attributed to this order an ancient origin: they claimed that it had had Robert Bruce as its founder, and as Grand Masters, the majority of the kings of Scotland; but no ostensible document made this assertion. The Royal Order formed establishments in foreign lands and particularly in France, in the lodge of the *Ardente-Amitié* at Rouen, which became its provincial Grand Lodge, and constituted different chapters in the provinces, in the colonies, and in the Kingdom of Italy, in the time of Napoleon I. The G.L. of Saint John of Edinburgh made every effort to oppose the propagation of this Masonry within the extent of its jurisdiction, and it has succeeded, if not in destroying it entirely, at least in circumscribing it into a small number of chapters.
"The *chivalric* grades of England (a) likewise made invasions into Scotland, in 1798. They were brought there by the sergeant-cutter of the military regiment of Nottingham, who, in this period, came to hold garrison at Edinburgh; but they made few proselytes there; and even those who had received them, renounced it soon after.
"It results from what we have just said that the grades and rites which take the

qualification of *Scottish* do not arise from Scotland, where they are absolutely unknown and have never been practiced; and that the charters produced to the support of such origin are fabricated titles. On several occasions, the G.L. of Scotland has solemnly disavowed patents of this type, that are said to have emanated from its authority; and, in order to caution foreign Masons against any assertion which would present it as professing or authorizing so-called Scottish high grades, it has inserted into its regulations, published in 1836, an article conceived thus: *The Grand Lodge of Scotland practices no degrees of Masonry but those of Apprentice, Fellow-Craft, and Master Mason, denominated Saint John's Masonry.*" (*The laws and constitutions of the Grand Lodge of the ancient and honorable fraternity of free and accepted masons of Scotland, c. 1, art. 4.*) - This note confirms what we have said.

a) These are isolated grades, tolerated under the generic name of knighthood (*chivalries*).

29. NOON begins the astronomical day, because with an *octant*, or otherwise, one may always know, with a certain precision, this remarkable hour. Exact MIDNIGHT is never but probable, even with the best chronometers. As to the MORNINGS (save those exceptional ones which draw under the *line*), they are of too great a variability of duration to serve as a constant point for the *fixed* openings of the Masonic works.
30. We read that the Emperor Commodius, fulfilling one day this function, performed it in such a manner that it became tragic. This grade was then given again at Rome in the 2nd century, towards the period of the extinction of the mysteries in Europe.
31. According to this account, may one doubt the ancient origin of the new institution, *Freemasonry*, and its conformity or its analogy with the Egyptian initiation, already demonstrated in the first two degrees?
32. In the ancient initiation, the *villainous companions* were: the *hippopotamus of the Nile*, the Greek *Python* (anagram of Typhon), the *wild boar* which mortally wounded the fair Adonis; the *Giants*, who undertook to dethrone Osiris; the Titans, who attempted to scale Olympus; the *geniuses of darkness and evil*; the *three months of winter*; the Scandinavian wolf; the *Chinese dragon*, which pursues the sun; *Ahriman*. One of these companions is called, in some grades, Abi-Ramah (the one who over-throws the *father*). These monsters, men or animals, are only the natural phenomena, which seem to struggle against the ostensible father of men (the *sun*).

    The four elements play a similar role in the life of man:

    The *water*, *air*, and *fire* are three companions who abandon man (the *master*) to his death. He is restored, at his funeral, by the lustral water, the incense, and the candles. - The fourth element, *earth*, is his point of departure, which resembles the open branch of a compass, which, after its circular revolution, symbol of human life, returns to the same point (the earth) from where he has emerged and into which he will return. - The terrestrial globe will show the same terrible revolutions by the abandon of the three elements: *water*, *air*, and *fire*.
33. The image of this successive and natural law of things, terrible law of life, from death, of the present from the past, law of which they have made such ill use, is ingeniously symbolized in this grade. Indeed, each period or cyclic empire can only be established by the *death* or effacement of that which represented

the empire or the anterior epoch: it is thus that the germ (*son*) kills the grain of wheat (*its father*) in the bosom of the earth (*its mother*); that Uranus *killed* his father Acmon; that Saturn *killed* his father Uranus; that Jupiter, reign of the good, *mutilated*, in order to reign, his *infertile* father Saturn, who, relegated to the darkness of Tartarus, kept the Titans enchained there; that Judas, twelfth apostle, delivered Jesus, his master, to his death; as the twelfth month (December) *kills* the year which ends; as Saturday *kills* the week. Our occident (from *occidere*, to kill), which *kills* the stars, has no other origin; and it is with this mystical language of *imaginary assassinations*, like that of Abel, etc., that the charlatans have added monstrous superfluities to the grade of master.

Ballanche goes further: "Destruction is the great God of this world. According to the immutable and sacred law, the initiate is held to *kill* the initiator; without this, the initiation remains incomplete. Cruel emblem! It is death which produces life." (And the first creature?) (Orpheus, book III.)

34. *Isis* has been the type of a multitude of deities of all lands and all times. The woman, mother, nursing her child, was a sensible image of the earth, nourisher of men. It was therefore under the traits of a *virgin woman* that the initiates of Egypt painted the earth. They called her *Isis*; she became sister and spouse of *Osiris*. The characters of sister and spouse come together in the earth personified: it and the sun are the work of the same author, and the earth is made fertile by the sun. Isis was represented under a thousand various forms; the divinities of the other peoples are but foreign variations of Isis. Nine forms of Isis, nine different costumes, indicated the nine months during which Egypt was freed from the flooding of the Nile. A flute, a trumpet, a mask, or any other symbol, in their hands, designated what games would be celebrated in each of the nine months. Later, they preside, among the Greeks, over the arts and sciences, without them imagining that the *Muses* signify *the months saved from the waters*.

Virgin of the Magi and the Chaldeans. The Chaldean sphere painted, in the heavens, a child being born, called *Christ* and *Jesus*; he was placed in the arms of the celestial virgin. It is to this virgin that *Eratosthenes*, librarian of Alexandria, born 276 years before our era, gave the name of *Isis*, mother of Horus.

Virgin of Buklbaris. An angel (*messenger*) sent from God (*the emanations of the sun*) fertilized the virgin (the *earth*); she conceived (*fertilized by the sun*) and gave birth to the fruits and the harvests, the first-fruits of which dedicated to her.

Ceres, the Greek *Isis*, taken as the *earth*, gives life to *Proserpina*, symbol of the *seeds*, which remain for the six months of winter in the womb of the earth (*infernal places*, *the underworld*, where reigns Pluto who is deemed to have abducted Proserpina). These seeds push up at springtime, to appear and produce during the other six months.

35. These legendries, which have marred this beautiful grade, have confused *Hiram* with *Adonhiram*; neither the one nor the other have been architects. It was Solomon who built the temple and his palace, at least the Bible does not name the executer of his plans. (See Kings, bk. III, chap. VI & VII.) *Hiram*, it says there, chap. VII, verse 14, *worked in bronze, and he was filled with wisdom, intelligence, and knowledge for making all sorts of bronze works*. Verses 15 and 44 give the details of the objects that he founded, of which the principal ones are: the two columns, two seas and twelve oxen, twenty socles and ten vats. The 45th

verse adds: *Hiram made cook-pots, cauldrons*, and *basins: all the vases that Hiram made by order of King Solomon were of the purest bronze*. After this verse, the Bible no longer makes any mention of this founder, who probably returned to Tyre. The *Talmud*, work of the rabbis, conceived in the 2nd century of our era, has *fabulized* his death, which concerns neither the Bible nor Symbolic Masonry.
As regards *Adonhiram*, it is said, ch. V, verses 13 and 14, that, according to the order of Solomon, they took 30,000 workers, 10,000 of which, each month and in rotation, were sent to Lebanon, and that *Adonhiram had the stewardship over all these people*. That is all that concerns this insignificant personage; such is the man who has given his name to *Adonhiramite* Masonry. The Bible does not make any mention of the division, in any stewardship, of the workers into three classes: *apprentices, companions*, and *masters*, nor of the *words of recognition* to receive the *wages*. All were payed then as everywhere, since, and as today (1853) in Paris, where buildings are raised of quite another importance than that of Solomon's Temple: chiefs of the works payed their brigades according to the daily control-registers or sheets.
Thus, all these fables which serve as the basis of the third grade, where the neophyte arrives with all the astonishment that an old tale causes, put into action abruptly without preparation or logic, may be called *coarse*, since one may recognize the falsity thereof in the Bible, whose accounts have, moreover, nothing in common with the initiatic doctrine, whether ancient or modern.
Thus, the veil that they have borrowed makes for an unpleasant incongruity with what precedes in the rite.
Let us rank too in the number of fables the supposed guild of *Master James* and his stone-cutters, and that of the *Father Soubise* and his carpenters, two imaginary colleagues of the founder Hiram, as well as the *duties* or codes that Solomon would have given to their companions. (See their legend.)
Let us leave, then, also the fable, useless to the institution, of the *Sepulchre of Upsala*, which has, in 1777, produced the biblical rite of the *Royal Arch*.
It is not from these dark corners, where the true light has never penetrated, that has come Freemasonry to appear in the world.

36. "Deceived by the Templar doctrine, he claimed that the Masonic order was born in the Terse-Sainte, in the era of the crusades, that knights belonging, for the most part, to the Order of the Temple, had associated themselves then *to rebuild the churches*, destroyed by the Sarrasins; that these latter, in order to make such pious designs fail, had sent emissaries who, under the appearances of Christianity, had confused themselves with the *builders*, and had studied, by these means, to paralyze their works; that having discovered this betrayal, the knights had chosen themselves with the greatest care, and had established signs and words of recognition, in order to be guaranteed of the mixing up of the infidels, etc., etc." - This trickery was not successful.
37. The favorites who accompanied this prince sold, in France, to speculators, *charters for Mother Lodges, bulls for Chapters*, etc. These titles were their property; they did not fail to exploit them for a living. - New anarchy due to the high grades.
38. These last three expressions figure in the declaration of the Duc de *Luxembourg*, on the date of May 1st, 1772 (see G.L. of France) and leads us to believe that this illustrious brother had been, or was in this era, a part of this Sovereign Council.

Later, the *Council of Emperors of the East and West*, believing to stop its decadence, took, on January 22, 1780, and without ceremony, the same title of *Sublime Scottish Mother Lodge of the French Grand Globe, Sovereign G.L. of France* (see its notice).

39. In 1773, appeared the *Art des Gargouillardes*, in-12mo, 26 pages; this writing was directed against the G.L. of France and particularly against the brother Gouillard, professor of law, its Grand Orator. - This brother Bouillard was author of the *Lettres critiques sur la Francmaçonnerie d'Angleterre*, in-8vo of 60 pages.
40. There was one of these at Paris, under the name of *College de Valois*, of which speaks the author of the brochure: *l'Écossais de Saint-André d'Écosse*, (Paris, 1772, in12mo, page 44).
41. Powers given to Stephen Morin, on August 27, 1761.

To the glory of the G.A. of the Universe and under the pleasure of S.A.S. [His Most Serene Highness], the T.M.F. Louis *de Bourbon*, Comte de Clermont, Prince of the blood, G.M. and protector of all the lodges.

"At the Orient of a most enlightened place, where reigns peace, silence, concord, *anno lucis* 5761, and, according to the common style, August 27, 1761.

"*Lux ex tenebris. Unitas, concordia fratrum.*

"We, the undersigned, Substitutes General of the Royal Art, Grand Surveillants and Officers of the Grand and Sovereign Lodge of Saint John of Jerusalem, established at the Orient of Paris; and we, S.G.M. of the Grand Council of the Lodges of France, under the protection of the Grand Sovereign Lodge, under the sacred and mysterious numbers, DECLARE, CERTIFY, and ORDAIN to all the dear brother Knights and Princes spread over the two hemispheres, that, we being assembled, by order of the Substitute General, President of the Grand Council, a request communicated to us by the R.B. *Lacorne*, Substitute of our T.M.G.M., Knight and Prince Mason, was read in session

"Our dear brother Stephen Morin, Knight and Sublime Prince of all the orders of the Masonry of Perfection, member of the Royal Lodge of *la Trinite*, etc., being upon his departure for America, and desiring the ability to work regularly for the advantage and aggrandizement of the Royal Art in all its perfection, may it please the S. Grand Council and G.L. to grant him letters patent for constitutions. Upon the report which has been made to us, and knowing the eminent qualities of the brother Stephen Morin, we have, without hesitation, granted him this small satisfaction, for the services that he has always rendered to the Order, and of which his zeal guarantees us the continuation. "For these causes and for other good reasons, in approving and confirming the T.C.F. [Beloved Brother] Morin in his designs, and wishing to give him testimonies of our recognition, we have, by a general consent, constituted and instituted him, and, by these presents, constitute and institute, and give full and entire power to the said brother Stephen Morin, whose signature is in the margin of the presents, to form and establish a LODGE in order to receive and multiply the Royal Order of Free Masons in all the Perfect and Sublime grades; to take care that the statutes and regulations of the Grand and Sovereign Lodge, general or particular, be kept and observed, and to never admit thereto any but true and legitimate brothers of Sublime Masonry.

"To rule and govern all the members who compose his said lodge, that he may establish it in the four parts of the world where it shall arrive and may remain, under the title of *Lodge of Saint John*, and called *la Parfaite Harmonie*; we give him the power to choose such officers to aid him in governing his lodge as he deems fit, to whom we commande and enjoin to obey and respect him; we order and command all regular Lodge Masters of whatever dignity they may be, spread over the surface of the earth and seas, we pray them and enjoin them, in the name of the Royal Order and in the presence of our Very Illustrious G.M., to recognize in this manner, and as we recognize him, our T.C.F. *Stephen* MORIN as Respectable M. of the Lodge of *la Parfaite-Harmonie*, and we *depute* him, in the quality of our GRAND INSPECTOR into all the parts of the New World, to reform the observance of our laws in general, etc.; and, by these presents, constitute our T.C.F. *Stephen* MORIN our G.M. INSPECTOR, authorizing him and giving him power to establish, in all the parts of the world, the Perfect and Sublime Masonry, etc., etc.

"We pray, consequently, the brothers in general to give, to the said Stephen Morin, the assistance and relief which shall be in their power, requiring of him to do as much with all the brothers who shall be members of his lodge, or that he has admitted and constituted, will admit or constitute, eventually, to the *sublime grade of perfection* that we give him, with full and entire power to create *inspectors* in all places where the SUBLIME GRADES SHALL NOT BE ESTABLISHED, knowing perfectly his great knowledge and capacity.

"In witness of which, we have delivered to him these presents, signed by the Substitute General of the Order, Grand Commander of the Black and White Eagle, *Sovereign Sublime Prince of the Royal Secret*, and chief of the eminent grade of the Royal Art, and by us, Grand Inspectors, Sublime Officers of the Grand Council and Grand Lodge established in this capital, and have sealed them by the great seal of our Illustrious G.M., S.A.S., and by that of our G.L. and S.G.C. At the G.O. of Paris, the year of the light 5761, or, according to the vulgar era, August 27, 1761.

"*Signed*: CHAILLOU DE JOINVILLE, Substitute General of the Order, V.M. of the first lodge in France called *Saint Thomas*, chief of the eminent grades, Commander and Sublime Prince of the Royal Secret. - Prince de ROHAN, M. of the G.L. *l'Intelligence*, S. Prince of Masonry. - LACORNE, Substitute of the G.M., R.D.M. of *la Trinité*, G.E., Perfect Knight and Pr. Mason. – SAVALETTE DE BUCKOLT, G. Guardian of the Seals, G.E. and Pr. Mason. - TAUPIN, etc., Prince Mason. - BREST DE LA CHAUSSÉE, etc., G.E., P.M., Kn., Pr. Mason. - Comte DE CHOI-SEUL, etc., Pr. Mason. - BOUCHER DE LE NONCOURT, etc., P.M. -

By order of the G.L., DAUBANTIN, G.E., P.M., and K.P.M., and R.V.M. of the L. *Saint-Alphonse*, Grand Secretary of the G.L. and of the Sublime Council of Perfect Masons in France, etc."

42. It is only to regret that the excess of *truly abject* means presented by *Gerbier*, in order to add, quite uselessly, to the preponderance of the *Grand Chapter General*, had been accepted, without examination, by the latter, before its union with the G.O. which, most fortunately, was not for nothing, at least ostensibly, in this intrusion. This is true, but, since this shameful misdeed, which is a filthy stain added to others in the institution of the high grades in France, the members of the G.O., charged with drafting circulars on the *Ancient and Accepted* Scottish Rite or statements against the *Supreme Council*, 33rd *degree*,

would have enough decency, unless it be ignorance of the facts (which would be little pardonable), to not cite this false and unfortunate date: 1821, and to make a support thereof. See the circulars of February 25, 1826, of October 19, 1840, and the account of the brother *Lefebvre d'Aumale*, cited in our *Histoire chronologique du G.-O. de France* (Fastes initiatiques).

It is thus that, in a subject where one has reason, one opens oneself to the criticism of his adversaries, and this lacks study and examination.

43. This audacious fanatic, Picard monk, was born in the diocese of Amiens, toward the middle of the 14th century; his true name is *Cucupiètre*. He preached at the council of Clermont, and led, in 1095, the first crusade; then returned to die, in 1115, in a monastery that he had founded at the diocese of Liège.
44. Antoine-Jos. *Pernety*, Benedictine, ascetic writer, alchemist, man of letters, traveler, was born at Roanne in 1716, and died at Valence (*Dauphiné*) in 1801. He was, for a long time, chief of a society of *Hermeticists*, whose nucleus was at Avignon. We have from him: *Dictionnaire hermétique*, *Histoire d'un voyage aux iles Malouines*, with Bougainville, that Pernety accompanied as chaplain.
45. "The name of the philosophy of Plato (*academic* philosophy) is of Asiatic origin. They repeat, for ages, that it came from this that the gardens where it was professed had belonged to a certain *Academus*. The Greeks and the Latins, who studied only their language, are not strong in etymology, they give an account of all with the supposed name of a man, from a river or a mountain: it is in frequent use among them. The fact is that *Cadm*, signifies the *Orient*, and the sciences; to begin with the alphabet, having come successively from Asia into Greece, every scholar was for a long time an *Oriental*, a *Cadmus*, and every place intended for instruction a *Cadmy* or *Academy*."

    (G, DUMAST.)
46. From the Greek *philos*, lover, and *aletheia*, truth.
47. *Alexandre Lenoir*, archeologist, born at Paris in 1762, died in 1839, was never received as a Freemason. Here is at what occasion he became, in 1814, author of the work entitled: *La Franche-Maçonnerie rendue à sa véritable origine*, 1 vol. in 4to, with ten plates.

    The *Histoire générale des religions*, by *de l'Aulnaye* was a colossal undertaking whose publication was forever interrupted, at the approach of the first revolution, from the appearance of the first volume, in 1791.

    The bookseller *Fournier*, owner of the plates of this beautiful work, magnificent plates engraved by *Moreau*, wanted to do something with them; he came to an arrangement with M. Lenoir who had assisted, in 1812, in the sessions of the Masonic convent, to aid it with that strange *indolence* which exists only at Paris. Persuaded that what he had collected at the convent, joined with his archeological knowledge, would supply what only the regularity of initiation gives, he had his *Franche-Maçonnerie* appear which utilized 10 plates from the beautiful work of de l'Aulnaye. This erudite, born at Madrid in 1739, died at Paris in 1830, published, in 1813, although not a Mason, the first good Masonic Tiler. (See the *Cours interprétatif des initiatiques*, p. 159, note 1.) M. Lenoir also had the example of *Thomas Payne* who, foreign to the institution, left a work having for its title: *On the Origin of Freemasonry*, translated from the English by *Bonneville*, in 1812.
48. Masonry makes men free; the *Temple* makes absolute masters and serviles. Its absurd forms render this institution unworthy of respect and esteem. Its

constitution tends to lower the nature of man, whose dignity is raised in Masonry. The ancient Templars were intolerant and persecutors, the ancient initiates recommended tolerance and harmony. The Temple is as far from Masonry as slavery is from liberty; how may there by Templars in masonry!?

49. From the Greek *philos*, lover, and *adelphos*, brother (*who loves his brothers*).
50. *The Luminous Ring or the mysteries of the Orient*, containing the adventures of *Fréderic de Dorna*, translated from the German, Paris, Barba, 1811, in-12mo, with figures, has no relation with these grades.
51. "It would be to despair of the existence of the world," says, at this occasion, the brother *Laurens*, "unless the practice of these essential virtues were to extend beyond the circle of the society of Freemasons."
52. Booklet in-12mo of 278 pages, printed at Liège in 1773, in which the author takes the Masonic quality of *dignitary member of the lodge of True Masons*. In 1773 has appeared the *Vrai Francmaçon*, which give the *origin* and *aim* of Freemasonry, etc., by the brother *Enoch*, Liège, in-12mo. The following year saw published the *Lettres maçonniques*, to serve as a supplement to the *Vrai Francmaçon* of brother *Enoch*; Liège, in-8vo, 81 pages.
    Enoch is obviously a borrowed name.
53. Booklet in-16mo of 16 pages. After the regulation which ends with these words *printed by order*, is found the nomenclature of the officers, that of their functions, their places, the honors to render to them, etc.
54. In one of the rituals that we possess of this grade, they authorize the initiated candidate to leave *his mark* (his jewel) in an urgent need of relief, and they add: "This grade is known at *Algiers*, and, if you happen to be taken there, or if business forces you to go there, by making yourself known, you will receive all the services of which you may reasonably have need."
55. The English Masons possess grades called *knighthoods* that the G.L. tolerates without recognizing them, such as:

Knight of the Star,	Knight of Calatrava,	Knight of the Zodiac,
— of the Temple,	— of the Alcantara,	— of the Annunciation of the Virgin,
— of the Red Cross,	— of the Redemption,	— of St. Michael,
— of Malta,	— of Christ,	— of St. Stephen,
— of the Holy Sepulchre,	— of the Mother of Christ,	— of the Holy Spirit.
— of the Teutonic Order.	— of Saint Lazarus,	

56. The *Misraimites* have renewed this ridiculous belief.
57. *Laurence Dermott* makes mention of the *Royal Arch* in his *Ahiman Rezon*, published in 1756.
    Other authors have often said that the *English Royal Arch* is none other than the *French Royal Arch*, called *Royal Arch of Enoch* or *Knight of the 9th Arch*, from a series called *Scottish*, and which has passed into England.
    The organic regulation of the G.L. of Edinburgh (1736) makes known that there exist in Scotland many guilds which had that denomination as distinctive title, such as the Royal Arch of Glasgow, in 1755, the Royal Arch of Stirling, in 1759, etc., when they addressed themselves to this G.L. to obtain new

constitutions. We read in the *Orient*, p. 366, on the subject of the Masonry of the Royal Arch: "It results from a letter, addressed by a brother to the G.L. of Ireland, that in 1813 this branch of the Masonic tree was scarcely known by name in these countries, and the author of the letter proves it by the following fact:

"In this same year, 1813, the late Duke of *Sussex* had undertaken the noble task of re-establishing a *unity* of rites, ceremonial, and works in all the G.L.'s of the British Empire, To this end, the letters were addressed to the G.L.'s of Scotland and Ireland. The G.L. of Scotland received this important work with the attention that it deserved, and promised that the affair would be taken, later, into serious consideration." - "Incidentally," says the correspondence, "these promises have not been followed by any result; for, still today, if it is only the two G.L.'s of Scotland and Ireland maintaining between themselves, under certain accounts, amicable relations, they continue to differ completely from the G.L. of England, as to the mode of the works." To return to our subject, in 1813, the G.M. of Ireland, who was then the Count of *Donoughmore*, wished to second the vote of his illustrious colleague the G.M. of England, on the subject of the establishment of Masonic uniformity for Great Britain. Consequently, he proposes to declare that Masonry admit only *three degrees*, containing therein the *Royal Arch*. Voices were raised at once on all sides, to request of His Lordship to know what was this Masonic institution of *Royal Arch*, the existence of which was not even suspected in Ireland. Moreover, there was, for a moment, the question of striking the G.M. of Ireland with a vote of censure, for having taken under his patronage, what they considered as an *intrusive degree*.

"The correspondent cites this stroke as a proof of the spirit of ignorance and routine, which, in this era, characterized the Irish Masons, and he adds that, unfortunately, things have changed very little since." All this proves that this rite is a modern creation, and that the *secret* history of its origin is apocryphal; which does not prevent it from being one of the most esteemed in England and the United States; the Masons and men are thus qualified.

58. It is in vain that one would wish to endow *Cologne* with a lodge, from 1716, since the G.L. of England, *the only primitive constituting body*, dates only from 1717. But it is probable that *Hanover*, before *Hamburg*, because of its frequent connections with London, had known Masonry; but without having a regular establishment at first. (See our *Précis historiques d'Autriche, de Bavière, Confédération Germanique, Danemark, duché de Bade, de Brunswick, Hongarie, Prusse, Saxe, Wurtemberg, Westphalie*, etc.)
59. The *Strict Observance* could not, therefore, have begun until 1768, not between 1745 and 1750.
60. These three grades also belong to the *African Architects*.
61. This forced interpretation sufficiently indicates the falsehood of this *history*; let us add that the G.M. having been executed in 1314 and *d'Aumont* not being able to save himself in Scotland, *if the account is accurate*, until 1315, how has he been able to hold a chapter in 1312? There is no dearth of these errors in *Scottish Templar Jesuitism*.
62. The Jesuits call the eagle *épervier* [sparrow-hawk]. The *pelican* is rejected from the system.
63. Such is not the opinion of *Hunter*. See the work of the brother *Th. Juge* on

the ancient rules of the ancient Templars.

64. We see that the Masons of England have even here prevailed in good sense over the Masons of France, who have suffered the non-Masonic establishment of the *Scottish*, that is to say *Jesuitic*, directories.

65. *Ignatius of Loyola* founded at Paris, in 1534, his Order of Jesuits, approved in 1540 by Pope Paul III, under the name of *Clerics of the Company of Jesus*. How could Aumont have reproduced in Scotland, in 1315 or 16, and preserved there a grade that the Jesuits had not yet invented and whose word was formed from his name by anagram: *Notuma*? Moreover, the works of this fourth grade are closed in the name *of the superiors of the united lodges*, and these superiors did not yet exist (*always contradictions*!).

 The candidate, whose name is *Gabaon*, is deemed to have escaped from captivity in order to re-establish the glory of the temple. They put him in the presence of two tableaux representing the interior of the temple of the Jews. Their successive explanation makes up the whole reception. They tell him that the temple of Jerusalem is the great type of Masonry, which, they add very *erroneously*, draws its origin from this very temple, the successive revolutions of which symbolize the persecutions that Masonry (*the Jesuitic order*) underwent. They tell him that the history of the death and assassination of Hiram (of the Burgundian *Molai*) is an *ingenious fiction*, which veils great truths for the Mason. It is with these forced interpretations, these false accounts full of anachronisms, that have been forged nearly all these sorts of systems, whose *supposed history* has been taken to the letter by Masonic writers, who do not even succeed in making a novel of Freemasonry, all while striving to produce the history thereof.

66. See this historical piece in the *Revue maçonnique de Lyon*, 1848, p. 52, 85, 130, and foll., as well as the *Code maçonnique des loges réuniés et rectifiées de France*, such as it has been approved by the deputies of the directories of France, at the national convent of Lyon, in 1778 (1848, p. 244, and 1849, p. 275).

67. "The principal cause which has transmitted," says *Laurens*, "Solomon as the founder of Freemasonry, is the belief held by the lovers of the marvelous that this king possessed the knowledge of the Qabalah and of the *transmutation of metals*, and that the system of Freemasonry is none other than the study of these two sciences. The reason that they give to justify this belief is the profound and nearly supernatural knowledge that they delight to attribute to this celebrated prince, and the immense wealth that he employed toward the construction of the temple of Jerusalem and of his magnificent palace. But the sacred text makes no mention of this extraordinary science, it limits itself to saying that beyond a great wisdom, Solomon *possessed perfectly the knowledge of nature*." - (We see here the occult science very clearly indicated.) "The riches of Solomon, although great, did not originate from an unknown or secret source: the *Chronicles* teach us that his father had left him *100,000 gold talent* and *a billion silver talents*, intended for the construction of the temple of Jerusalem" (Bk. 1, ch. XXII, v. 14). - (*We do not see how David could have procured for himself so considerable a sum. Would this not rather be one of those exaggerations so frequent in the Bible, to make understood the magnificence of the temple and the palace to be built?*)

 "The immense profits brought back to him by the fleet he dispatched, every three years, to Ophir, in the peninsula of Malacca, in the East Indies, or *the gold Chersonèse* of the ancients, in association with King Hiram, was a second source of wealth, according to the *Scripture*. This commerce brought him *450* gold talents, every three years." - (*Well, this would only be 4,500 gold talents, every thirty years.*) (*Essay on Freemasonry*, p. 51 and foll., § II, *on Solomon*. See§ III, p. 62: *on the Philosopher's Stone, on the Qabalah*, etc.)

68. It would be absurd to believe, *says N. Bonneville*, the Templars makers of gold: "The source and origin of their wealth and their vast possessions are due to their courage, to their conquests purchased at the price of their blood, to their intrepidity, to their avidity.
"If they had the secret of making gold, the Templars would be all the more contemptable, for having so often violated their word as knight, engaged for a little gold; for having committed so many cruelties, in order to procure it for themselves. At whatever price it was, they had need thereof. Possessing the secret of making gold, would they have been able to give so many occasions to make themselves hated because of their rapine and their baseness? Let them only recall the complaints of the patriarch of Jerusalem, to whom they refused to pay the tithe; the 1,300 bizantines and the good that they refused to the bishop of Tyberias; let them recall then in cold blood their conduct towards Leo, King of Armenia, and the possessions that they had in his kingdom, estimated at 20,000 bizantines, and again the rights usurped from Henry III, King of England, and all this brigandage that history openly reproaches them and they will see vanish the magic crucible, unless they wish to believe the Templars more culpable than they are," (*les Jésuites chasse de la Maçonnerie* [The Jesuits driven out of Masonry]).

69. We count *three celebrated heads of modern illuminism*: *Saint-Germain*, *Swedenborg, and Schroepffer.*
Saint-Germain is known by his visions and his preaching at Paris, especially in the time of Cagliostro.
Swedenborg acquired a great renown by an adventure related by the journal of Stockholm, the *Monats Schriff*, January 1788; here it is:
"The late Queen of Sweden, *Louise Ulric*, had charged Swedenborg with learning from her brother (father of the King of Prussia then reigning), who died in 1758, the reason for which he had not responded, in his lifetime, to a certain letter that she had written to him. Twenty-four hours later, Swedenborg informed the queen of the contents of her letter, that no one, except her brother and herself, could have known. Astounded, she was forced to recognize, in the great man, a miraculous science (a).
"The King Gustav, being at Paris, confirmed the truth of the anecdote: 'It is true,' he said, 'I was present at the conversation; Swedenborg informed my mother that her letter was related to the revolution occurring in 1756, and which cost the life of *Horn* and *Brahe*.' He added: 'The soul of your brother has appeared to me and has told me that he had not responded because he had disapproved of your conduct; your political imprudence is the cause of the bloodshed. I order you, on his behalf, to no longer mix yourself up with the affairs of the State, and above all to no longer excite troubles of *which sooner or later, you will be the victim*.'"
Schroepffer, the third, was son of a café-keeper. (See his *Notice* hereafter.)

(a) Here is the secret of this mystery: The Comte de H... had intercepted the letter which he remitted confidentially to

Swedenborg, while dictating to him the response to make to the queen (*Essai sur la secte des Illum.*, note VIII, p. 190).

70. We can no longer be surprised at the ideas that the crusaders have been able to accustom themselves of *Jesus*, if, in the 17th century, Swedenborg has such.
71. These symbols have been adopted by the *Carbonari*.
72. We have also from him: *On the White Horse of the Apocalypse*, in-4to, London, 1758; *On the Commerce of the Soul and Body*, in-4to, London, 1769.
73. The author of this book has known them, who appear to enjoy their full reason.
74. Here is the tenor of the *declaration* which destroys this fact:
"Glory be to the thrice great Architect of the whole universe!
"We, the undersigned, G.M. and G.S. of the National G.L. of Sweden, declare, certify, and attest, by these presents, that, as the National G.L. of Sweden has never constituted *operative* lodges of Master, Companion, and Apprentice Knight Mason *outside of the kingdom of Sweden and its dependencies*, neither has it furnished any such constitution to the brother *Zinnendorf* at Berlin, nor constituted any other operative lodge in this place, as being *outside its jurisdiction*.
"Given at the G.O. of Stockholm, this 29th day of July 1777." - Have signed:
"CHARLES, Duc de Sudermanie, National G.M.; A.-N., Comte *de Stenback*, First G.S.; A.-X., Comte *de Lewenhaupt*, Second G.S., and Jean *de Bierken*, G.-Sec."
75. Can a king, or rather a Mason become king, ACCEPT THE Grand Mastership, that is to say can he be head of the nation and head of a particular association? NO: the supreme magistracy that he exercises forbids him and reciprocally forbids the Masons the qualification of *brother*. By ascending the throne, a Mason loses the Masonic character, indelible for all others. He cannot become *the first*, among his equals, *primus inter pares*, since he no longer has any *equals*, unless he abdicates, at the door of the temple, the title of king, which he cannot do. Sovereign organ of the law, and, according to the principles, impassible as it, he could not be bound by the devotion prescribed to the Masons towards one another. Fraternal indulgence is not permitted for him. When the law tells him: *Strike*! it is necessary that he strikes. The faculty of granting pardon is but the fortunate privilege of rectifying the decisions of *justice*, in the sense of *equity*; it would strip that high character of morality, in ceasing to be exercised freely, or in descending unto favor. Masonry itself would lose therein its independence which, alone, may permit it to operate social progress, by following its genius and its inspirations. Placed under the direct influence of the head of State, our institution would be forced to march in his retinue, whereas it ought to march ahead.
History presents only one sole example of a king who was, at the same time, Grand Master of the Order; it is that of *Frederick II*, and they have remarked that this was the period of the establishment of *illuminism*, produced by the need to break the fetters which restrained the social action of the lodges in Germany. Everywhere else the head of State is limited to taking the title of *protector*, the only one which is suitable to the Sovereign, because of the duties of his position, and to the Masons in the interest of their independence. Sweden offers an exception; because Swedish Masonry, whose fifth grade gives civil nobility, actually forms an institution of the State.
76. "It is to the *eclectic philosophers*, according to *Sainte-Croix*, that we owe, in great

part, the knowledge of the doctrine of the initiations into the ancient mysteries. They had themselves admitted in order to speak thereon in their writings."

77. We read in the *Bibliotèque des sociétés secrètes*: "The Freemasons of the English or Eclectic system, forming the *Observantia lata*, cannot, strictly speaking, form a sect; their lodges, save an amicable correspondence, having no relationship between them, cannot form a body.
"Their aim is to re-establish English Masonry, or rather the democratic system of the old Freemasons. They call themselves *eclectic*, because they leave to the lodges the liberty to examine all, to admit only what appears good to them. They were in communication with the Illuminati."
The author of this inexact article could only have been a profane, little educated in the matter that he treated.
78. What figure would *Helvetius*, *Franklin*, *Voltaire*, and other members of this workshop have made, rigged out with the absurd nicknames of *Sovereign Prince Rose-Croix*, *Grand Inspector*, *Grand Inquisitor*, *Grand Commander*? O vanity, you place man at the rank of the beast!
79. "We know from a good source that he has always been the declared enemy of the high grades. Experience had taught him that the high grades are the root of all evil which exists in the Masonic confraternity, and the cause of discord between the lodges and the systems," (*Encyclopædia der Fraumaurerei*, etc., by *Lenning Mossdorf*, v. I).
80. The so-called Sup. Coun. of Charleston. (See hereafter.)
81. In order to make better known the wisdom of this Grand Lodge, we are going to give an extract from a letter, dated at Edinburgh on July 7, 1821, addressed by Alex. *Laurie*, secret. of the G.L., to C. *Morison de Greenfield*, old Jr. Warden of the lodge of *Saint Mary's Chapel*, who had written to him from Lausanne (*Switzerland*), on the subject of the erection of a new lodge:
"We have not printed any instructions; being contrary to the regulations of Scottish Masonry to have something under the form of a catechism.
"The G.L. has never deemed it fitting to engage in much correspondence with the lodges of the continent, by reason that it recognized only the original degrees of *Apprentice*, *Fellowcraft*, and *Master*, comprising the ancient order of the Masonry of *Saint John*; whereas the foreign lodges generally practice and admit other orders into their midst; which the G.L. of Scotland considers as innovations to the primitive institution of Masonry, such as it is recognized by our G.L. in this land."
The Historical Review of Freemasonry, which reproduced this letter, says on this subject and with reason:
"If all the systems and all the isolated grades that they call *Scottish* (there are more than 200), had originated in Scotland, as it appears to result from charters in due form where this origin is recorded, the masons of this land would be, without contradiction, the most fertile of all in mystagogical inventions. But, in reality, such a merit does not belong to them; they have invented nothing, not even the *three grades* that they practice, and *the only ones* recognized by the G.L. of Scotland; and all these charters, all these diplomas, all these regulations dating back to Edinburgh, *Kilwinning*, the imaginary mountain of *Heredom*, are nothing less than apocryphal and fabricated, when they confer the power to practice high grades," (p. 134, Parise, 1832).

82. In 1739, some recalcitrant brothers separated themselves from the G.L. of London, united themselves with the debris of the guilds of *operative masons* and formed a rival (not in philosophy) Grand Lodge, under the constitution of the grand operative guild of York. (See the *Historical brief of Masonry in England.*) These dissidents gave to the G.L. of England the title of Modern Rite and took that of *G.L. of the Ancient Scottish Regime.* Then, having been recognized by the G.L.'s of Scotland and Ireland, they added, to the word Ancient: *and Accepted.* Such is the origin of the title: *Ancient and Accepted Scottish Regime* or *Rite.* But all these G.L.'s practiced only the three symbolic grades. It is therefore an absurd nonsense to give this title to the collection made, long after, of the thirty-three degrees of the Comte de Grasse.
83. 1797. It appears that in this period there existed at Geneva a society of speculative Masons, delivering patents of the 33rd degree. Here is the description of the one that was sold to the brother *Villard-Lespinasse*, become since an officer of the G.O. of France, where he took, with the grade, a new 33° patent, on August 17, 1825:
"His first patent is surmounted by an eagle with its wings deployed, holding a compass in one of its talons, and in the other a key. A ribbon surrounds it with these words: G.-LOGE DE GENEVE. At the foot of one of the columns is a woman holding a balance. it is worded thus:
"In the name and under the auspices of the metropolitan G.L. of Scotland, and under the celestial vault of the zenith, at the 24th *deg.·. long.·. and* 44th *deg.·.* 12m.·. lat.·. (these latitudes and longitudes are as false as the patent). "To our ILL.·. Sov.·. GG.·. Inspectors General, Free Mas.·. of all the ancient and modern gr.·., spread over the surface of the two hemispheres, SALUTATIONS, STRENGTH, UNION.
"We, Sov.·. Gr.·. Inspect.·. Gener.·., comprising the Consistory established at the Or.·. of Geneva, by letters constitutive from the Metropolitan and *Universal* G.L. of Edinburgh in Scotland, on the date of the 10th day of the the first month, 5729." (*Here the fraud is most evident: we know that Freemasonry was not instituted in Scotland until November 30, 1736; and that the fabrication of the high grades, known under the reason of* Royal G.L. of Heredom and Kilwinning, *had functioned long after this date.* See *the institution of Freemasonry in Scotland.*) "After having verified the titles of Knight *Cadosh*, and strictly examining the Very Ill.·. and Kn.·., with regard to instruction and morals, and on all the ancient and modern gr.·., up to the 30th degree inclusive, we have conferred upon him the 31st, 32nd, and 33rd deg.·., final, unique, and sublime of Masonry, in order to enjoy the rights and honors attached to those high and subl.·. gr.·. ...
"Valley of Geneva, under the vault..." (*It is regrettable that the following and especially the signatures are erased.*)
Already, the previous year, the same brother had received the Rose-Croix letter bearing as address: *To the Or.·. of the Univ.·., from a very holy place of the Metropolis L.·. of Scotland, established at Geneva by the numbers 77, S.·. F.·. V.·., the year of the Mas.·. 5796*, etc.
They declare here that he professes the Christian religion, that he is *Mas.·., Kn.·. of the Sword or the East, and to constitute lodge by his presence. Blessed be the one who receives him well!*"
It is without doubt in the same spirit of *regularity* that has been fabricated the so-called Primitive Rite of Namur, in thirty-three degrees. (See this rite.)

84. At the session where the circular was decreed, the brother Frederick *Dalcho*, charged with drawing it up, gave a fabulous account on the existence of the Rite of Perfection, going back to the first crusade, then sleeping from 1658 until 1744, when a Scottish nobleman visited France and *reinstated* the Lodge of *Perfection* at Bordeaux. In 1768, the King of Prussia was *recognized* as Grand Commander by the whole fraternity. CHARLES, crown prince of Sweden, was *continual* Grand Commander and protector in Sweden. LOUIS DE BOURBON, Prince of the blood, Duc de Chartres, and the cardinal DE ROHAN, bishop of Strasbourg, directed its degrees in France. In 1762, the Grand Masonic Constitutions were definitively ratified (*at Bordeaux*? no) at Berlin and proclaimed by the government of all the lodges of the sublime and *perfect* Masonry. There were, moreover, secret constitutions *which existed from time immemorial* and of which it is spoken in this unbelievable fabric of absurd falsehoods, printed at Dublin, in 1808, under the title of *Discourse of the Illustrious Brother Frederick Dalcho.*
There are *illustrations* of every kind.
85. Here is what we read in the ÉTAT DE LA MAÇ DANS L'ANC. ILE SAINT-DOMINGUE, by the brother *Leblanc de Marconnay*, p. 151, Bulletin of the G.O., no. 23: "With regard to a Supr. Coun. of the *Puissant and Sovereign Grand Inspectors General for the French Windward and Leeward Islands of America, 33rd degree of the Ancient and Accepted Scottish Rite*, having its seat at the Cap Français, San Domingo island, and of which the Comte DE GRASSE-TILLY DE ROUVILLE had created himself Grand Commander *ad vitam*, when he brought back to France, in 1804, the *Scottish Rite of Perfection*, which had emerged therefrom, in 1761, by the agency of *Stephen Morin*, this pretended authority has never existed at San Domingo and has never been known there. The brother *de Grasse-Tilly*, after his departure from San Domingo, had been received, in 1802, into the Supr. Coun. of Charleston, and never set foot again on this island."
This citation corroborates perfectly what we have said: What must we think, then, of these fallacious founders, whose materials of construction are guile, fraud, and falsehood to build temples to morals and truth? And what to think of their rite? Are we wrong to call it a trickery?
86. The brother *Thory*, ever disposed to support all that is hostile to the G.O., has taken care, in his *Acta Latomorum*, p. 220 of the 1st vol., to inform his readers that the *M.L. of the Philosophical Scottish Rite* has, for this session, lent its temple and given its support to the lodges of the *Ancient and Accepted Rite*, assembled in order to organize the G.L. of this régime, in rivalry with the G.O.
87. We read, in a brochure entitled: *Essai sur l'institution du rite écossais*:
"The contract of union was read and adopted, save final wording, and, at midnight, the entire fusion of the various degrees of the Ancient and Accepted Scottish Rite, and of its members, took place in the midst of the G.O., and, from this instant, the G.O. observed this rite religiously. However, the brother *Pyron* remained trustee of the act of union, and they were far from presuming that this brother WOULD ABUSE IT ONE DAY."
88. "The Masonic Order has received in France, on April 17 of this year, a Masonico-political organization: one of the brothers of the emperor Napoleon, JOSEPH NAPOLEON, King of Spain, is proclaimed GRAND MASTER of the order. The archchancellor of the Empire, Prince

CAMBACERES, and the King of Naples, JOACHIM MURAT, are named ADJUNCTS OF THE G.M.

"On the 27th of the same month, a deputation of members of the G.O., presided over by the particular representative of the G.O., presented themselves to the Prince Archchancellor, CAMBACERES, to inform him of his election to the dignity of ADJUNCT GRAND MASTER. The prince responded to the deputation that H.M. the Emperor and the King having rendered an account of the object of the Masonic association, and having recognized that its moral aim was worthy of protection, it has been determined to grant it and to give it as head a Prince of the Blood; that it might be, with H.M., the interpreter of the sentiments of fidelity, respect, and attachment of the order for his person; and that, for him, he would go willingly to its works, when H.I.H. the Prince JOSEPH, G.M., *would have made known to him its dispositions*, and that he was of the opinion that an address was presented to him by the G.O., that he desired that the union of the lodges and chapters assured to the Order the brilliance that it had enjoyed in the past, and which is the guarantee of its glory, and that, if there ever existed some point of division, he thought that the general will alone would make every trace of it disappear. The Prince MURAT, likewise, elected ADJUNCT G.M., is, *he added*, in the same disposition.

"This choice, entirely political, does not belong to the French Masons; for the Prince JOSEPH is not at all initiated into the Order and has never appeared at the works of the G.O.," (extract from the *Hist. chron. du G.-O. de France*). "The Prince CAMBACERES was made the GRAND MASTER, and the omnipotence that this title gave him, and the power which resulted therefrom, pleased him much. But this skillful man, greedy for honors, sacrificed, unfortunately, to the vanity of being G.M. of such or such rite, HONORARY VENERABLE of such a preponderant workshop, the UNITÉ, the good of the Order which had been confided to him. His title of Adjunct G.M., his high social position, attached to him all the pretentions of the Masonic parties. Each party wanted to have the G.M., the Prince Archchancellor, as immediate head, in order to maintain itself in the shadow of his name, unless to reclaim, when there would be need thereof, an efficacious power. CAMBACERES, Adjunct G.M. of the Order, head of the G.O., was almost at the same time (July 1, 1806) G.M. and protector of the *Ancient and Accepted Scottish Rite*; honorary G.M. of the *Rite of Heredom* on October 25, 1806; G.M. of the M.L. of the Philosophical Scottish Rite (March 12, 1808);

G.M. of the *Primitive Rite* (1808); G.M. of the *Rite of the Kn. Beneficent of the Holy City* (Rectified Régime), title offered to him by the Directory of Auvergne in 1807; G.M. of the *Regime of the Directory of Septimanie* of Montpellier (1809); finally, honorary Venerable of all the Masonic bodies which had renown and were comprised of titled men: he was the sun which warmed at once the indigenous plants and the exotic plants.

"The unfortunate ease of this celebrated man brought the most fatal blows to the peace and good harmony of the Masonic order, and perpetuated, by authorizing the existence of so many separated sects, divisions that it was especially important to make disappear," (extract from the *Hist. chron. de la Maç en France*).

89. Lieutenant-general of the naval armies, born at Valette (*Provence*), in 1723, died in 1788. He was distinguished by his courage in the American war, but showed little ability there, and was beaten and taken by Rodney into the bloody combat of Dominique in 1782.
90. Have we had reason to protest, in the *Foreword*, against the disastrous effects of ignorance?
91. "At the general assembly of the G.O., April 28, 1799, the brother *Angeboult*, president of the chamber, pronounced a discourse where he said, relating to the archives of the order: 'We have to regret the loss of the *most precious treasures of our archives*; we have even to fear that they have passed into the hands of the profane; for the Masons have taken the oath to re-establish those of which they may be the trustees, and *our losses are not repaired*.' "This unworthy spoliation has continued its ravages, for, a few years after the uniting of the archives of the G.L. of France to those of the G.O., the precious manuscripts, the rare books, the curious charters had disappeared. The collections of circulars, official reports, printed annuals, no longer existed or were incomplete: this is because, for too long, the leaders of the G.O., accustomed to regarding as being their own all the archives, acted like Pashas, taking with hands full and returning nothing. A visit to their libraries or to those of their heirs may see restored more objects than the library of the G.O. possesses," (extract from the *Hist. chron. du G.-O. de France*).
   - It is in some way in order to repair, in part, the deplorable void caused by the unfortunate dispersion of so many useful and precious documents, that we have collected and put in order immense materials, in a manner to present to our brethren: the CHRONOLOGICAL HISTORY of each rite, that of the associations taking the Masonic forms, that of the establishment of the institution in each of the States of the globe, that of the Masonic authority which rules it, and many documents to support it, with our observations which are the fruit of more than fifty years of research, study, and Masonic works. We have begun and traced the path; others will do better.
92. This borrowing has been made from an assembly held towards the end of 1804, at a place on rue Neuve-des-Petits-Champs; and they have there drawn up the regulations of Berlin, May 1, 1786, that they added to the regulation of Bordeaux of 1762 (the one as *authentic* as the other) (Hèrmes, v. I, p. 308).
93. The superabundant titles *in italics* are since the reappearance of the same grades in France.
94. In the new nomenclature, *Provost and Judge is before the Intendant of the Buildings*; but, in seeing, p. 52, the distances of admission, we find that it ought to be thus. *Thory* classifies it the same, p. 125, *Histoire de la fondation du G.-O.*
95. In the 15th and 16th degrees, the King of Portugal, who permitted the Templars to unite into a body (*Order of Christ*), is designated by Cyrus.
96. In this class, the fraud begins to operate; it inverts the order of the grades and adds new ones to arrive at the number 33.
97. See Masonic institution at Haiti (*Saint-Domingue. Fastes initiatiques*).
98. We read on this subject in the *Hermès*: "Never have the Masons who brought Scottish Masonry, divided into thirty-three degrees, been able to say in what consisted of this 33rd degree. Sometimes they said that the password was *Frederick*, sometimes that it was *J. Molay*. They never had the slightest knowledge thereof; and they waited, in order to give it, on papers from

America, which have never arrived."

"This note is given to us by one of the most educated Masons of the Orient of Paris, who asserts to have assisted at the famous session in which the venerable Deputy Inspector *Ph. Toutain*, maintained, in the presence of the brothers *Thory Sr.*, *Bailhache*, *Hacquet*, *Basard*, *La Bailly-Ménager*, and others, that the Masonry of the Ancient and Accepted Rite, in America as in France, contained *only twenty-five degrees divided into seven classes*," (vol. I, p. 310).

99. And yet he knew of it, since in his *Bibliographie historique*, we read, p. 396: "388. Extract from the columns engraved in the Scottish Sov. Chap. of the Ancient and Accepted Rite of the Pere de famille, valley of Angers, in-8vo, 43 pages (1812)."

100. It is in this sense that we have interpreted that vengeance called quite inappropriately *Masonic* in our COURSE *on ancient and modern initiations*. The spirit of this present work must appear different from the one in which the *interpretive course* was written. The remark is fair: this work is the critical examination of the systems which, without being animated by the fundamental spirit of Freemasonry, have taken the form thereof. It has for its aim to lead the true Masons back to the first three grades *with which one cannot dispense*, and with which one *may dispense with all the others*; whereas the COURSE, whose grades were explained after each reception, in solemn and numerous session, could only be apologetic. However, we will demonstrate here that the institution ought to have only three grades; that the French *chapitral rite* is the only one of all the super-Masonic rites which is rational: because it reproduces, in its four orders, the four elements of the beautiful grade of Apprentice. The *Elect* is here only the development of the signification or the allegory of the *Cabainet of Reflection*, and we show, after the interpretation of all the symbols, that there is no more Freemasonry possible after the *Rose-Croix*, which is the last trial by the 4th element, or rather the study of the *fire principle*, which receives so instructive a development in the second part of the grade of Master where the *regeneration* is operated. Moreover, the entirely allegorical facts of these four orders, which make no pretention to history, are easily interpreted by the astronomical aspects of each of the four seasons, of which these four orders are the symbol, and, so to speak, the celestial history. All the other grades of the Scottish system are invalid, foolish, or atrocious. There is only the *Kadosh*, 30th degree; but the Kadosh is the *Elect* (let us leave aside the variants), and the Elect is the *Cabinet of Reflection* and *preparation*:

we begin then a third Masonry, and achieving this latter does not appear to us the least bit possible.

Perfect, then, the *three symbolic grades*, especially the last: Freemasonry is only that.

101. The cross of St. Andrew, in this grade, is but the cross of the *crusades,* masked under this Templar emblem.

102. Saturn has never existed nor reigned but in the *Hermetic work*; and a king that the fable presents to us as devouring his children (*which is true, but alchemically*) does not merit the epithet of good.

103. In all the grades fabricated by the Jesuits in various countries, we noticed a pronounced tendency to make of Masonry a cult and a school of *Catholicism.* In one of their Hermetic grades, the *Écossais vert* or the *Little St. Andrew of*

Scotland, we find this passage: "They have taught you (as a *Blue Master*) to revere the Supreme Being under the emblem of the *Architect of the Universe*, but the *Scottish* Masters ought to revere the Supreme Being in a more perfect manner, that is to say in spirit and truth." Further on, we read: "It is therefore prescribed to you, T.C.F., as *Scottish Master*, to engrave in your heart, for the most holy name of *Jehova* (Jesuit), which is the greatest of those of the divinity, a veneration so profound that it surpasses that of *Adonai* and all those which have been given to the divinity."

104. The lodge of the *Rigide-Écossais* at Paris, having been divided in two parts, through an abuse of confidence of one of them, this latter, in order to avoid every reckoning and every superior jurisdiction, took refuge in the bosom of the Supr. Coun. which admitted it, despite the sharpest objections under the original title of *Rigides-Écossais*.

The wholesome part remained faithful to the G.O. which modified its title to that of Fidèles-Écossais.

*Chemin-Duponte*s, who recounts this fact (4th vol., p. 294), after having vaunted the advantages, for Masonry, of having, in the same land, rival authorities, says here, enlightened by the evidence: "Here is one of the beautiful effects of the plurality, not of the rites (there may be 29 or 30 of them, without the least inconvenience), but of the governing regimes in the same land."

105. We have given the reasons thereof (p.125 and foll.); we pray the reader to be willing to refer thereto, as well as to p. 138, *Comparison of the administration of the G.O. with that of the Supr. Coun.*

106. They are found in the *Tuiler général.*

107. There exists, on the interpretation given to the colors, an interesting work by *Fréd. Portal*, under this title: *Des couleurs symboliques dans le moyen-age, l'antiquité et les temps modernes*, Paris, 1837, in-8vo. It is far from agreeing with this. Thus, to speak only of the rose color, it is said therein that *it borrows its signification from red and white*: red is the symbol of *divine love*, white of *divine wisdom*. We know too that, in the ancient mysteries, the rose was the symbol of *wisdom*, of *discretion*, witnessing the initiation of *Apuleus*.

Let us add that the art of the *selam* [emblematic nosegay, in the East] (*seraglio*) pushed so far into the Orient, also gives numerous contradictions to the too arbitrary interpretations of the *Unknown Philosopher Judges*.

108. We do not think that the history which the initiating brother recommended to the reader was the one that we extract from the Philosophical Dictionary as most approaching the truth:

IGNATIUS OF LOYOLA. "If you wish to acquire a great name, to be a founder, be completely mad, but of a madness which suites your era. Have in your madness a foundation of reason which may serve to direct your extravagances and *be excessively stubborn*. It may happen that you are hung; but if not, you may have altars.

"Honestly, has there ever been a man more worthy of the little houses than *St Ignatius* or *St. Inago* of Biscay, for that is his true name? His head turned to the reading of the Golden Legend, as it turned then to Don Quixote of the English Channel, in order to have read the romance of chivalry. Behold my Biscayenne who first made himself Knight of the Virgin, and who made the vigil of arms to the honor of his lady. The Holy Virgin appeared to him and accepted his services; she returned several times; she led him, her son. The devil, who is on the look-out, and who foresaw all the harm that the Jesuits would do to him one day, came to stir up an imp's uproar in the house, breaking all the windows: the Biscayenne drove him out with a sign of the cross; the devil fled across the wall and left through a large opening, that they showed again to the *curious*, fifty years after the event.

"His family, seeing the derangement of his spirit, wished to have him shut up and put him on a diet: he disencumbered himself of his family as well as of the devil and fled, without knowing where he was going. He encountered a Moor, who took him for what he is, and left him with a quickness. The Biscayenne did not know whether to kill the Moor or to pray God for him; he left the decision to his horse which, wiser than he, returned upon the route to its stable.

"My man, after this adventure, took the part of going on pilgrimage to Bethlehem, while begging for his bread. His madness increased along the way. The Doninicans took pity on him at Manres; they kept him with them for some years and sent him back without having been able to heal him.

"He set out at Barcelona, arriving at Venice. They drove him out of Venice; he returned to Barcelona, ever begging his bread, still having trances, and frequently seeing the Holy Virgin and Jesus Christ.

"Finally, they made him understand that, in order to go to the Holy Land to convert the Turks, the Christians of the Greek Church, the Armenians, and the Jews, it would be necessary to begin by studying a little theology.

Nothing would give my Biscayenne greater pleasure; but, in order to be a theologian, it is necessary to know a little grammar and a little Latin; this did not trouble him at all; he went to college at the age of 33: they mocked him, and he learned nothing.

"He was disheartened, not being able to go convert the infidels: the devil took pity on him this time. He appeared to him and swore to him, Christian's honor, that if he wished to give himself to him, he would make him the most scholarly man of the Church of God. Ignatius did not have it in him to put himself under the discipline of such a master: he returned to his classes.

They gave him the lash sometimes; and he was not the most scholarly.

"Driven from the college of Barcelona, persecuted by the devil, who punished him for his refusal, abandoned by the Virgin Mary, who did not trouble herself at all to relieve her knight, he did not become discouraged. He set himself to traversing the country with the pilgrims of Saint James. He preached in the streets from town to town. They shut him up in the prisons of the inquisition, they put him in prison in Alcala; he fled afterward to Salamanque, and they shut him up there too. Finally, seeing that he was not a prophet in his land, Ignatius resolved to go study at Paris. He made the journey by foot, preceded by an ass which carried his baggage, his books, and his writings. Don Quixote, at least, had a horse and a squire; but elegance had neither the one nor the other.

"He endured at Paris the same insults as in Spain: they made him put on short breeches at the College de Ste-Barbe, and they wanted to flog him ceremonially. His vocation called him, finally, to Rome.

"How has it been possible that such an eccentric has enjoyed, finally, at Rome some consideration, has made some disciples, and has been the founder of a powerful order, in which there have been very estimable men? It is that he was stubborn and enthusiastic. He found enthusiasts like him, with whom he associated. Those, having more reason than him, re-established their own a little: he became more clear-sighted at the end of his life, and he even put some competency into his conduct.

"Perhaps *Mohammed* began by being as mad as *Ignatius* in the first conversations that he had with the angel Gabriel; and perhaps Ignatius, in Mohammed's place, would have done as great things as the prophet; for he was as ignorant, as visionary, and as courageous.

"We commonly say that these things happen but once: however, it was not long ago that an English boor, more ignorant than the Spanish Ignatius, has established the society of those that he calls *quakers*, society quite above the one of Ignatius. The Comte de *Sinzendorf* has, in our day, founded the sect of the *Moravians* [United Brethren]; and the convulsionists of Paris have been on the verge of making a revolution. They have been quite mad, but they have been rather stubborn."

109. This prophecy recalls to us the one that we find in Cicero: Alexander assisting at the execution of an Indian that he had condemned to be burned alive, Calamus, mounted upon the pyre, cried out with enthusiasm: "Oh! The fair departure of my life; my body, destroyed by the flames, is going to let my soul rise freely to the abode of the pure light." - Alexander asked him ironically if he had anything else to say. - "Yes, that I will see you soon." Some days after, Alexander died at Babylon. - Here is another ecstatic deed: Nicocreon, tyrant of Cyprus, had crushed in a mortar the philosopher Néarch; this one, calm and his lips smirking in disdain, cried out to him: "It is not Néarch that you crush, but the vile shell which envelops him."

110. With this tax, it is not astonishing that the order or degree of Unknown Philosopher Judges has never had any celebrity in Masonry.

111. To what?... Is it to death?... We hope not; but the regulation does not say, and to its silence comes to be added Art. 18, which leaves nothing but to give some free field to the conjectures.

112. The explanations given in the 1st grade, on the interpretation of the colors, carries, for *aqua-green*: *active and frank*. The Order demands, then, from its members *activity* and *frankness*.

113. These notions, contrived in 1649, do not exist in the Bible.

114. The words, sign, grip, and steps are found in the *Tuileur général*, as well as the ritual of the KNIGHTS OF CHRIST.

115. You will find in the *Tuileur Général* the words of correspondence and the *characteristics* of this important grade.

116. We could have read likewise *imperial* or *august art*, when, in the 2nd century, *Marcus Aureleus* had himself admitted to initiation.

The origin given by the brother *Dumast* is curious and quite true: "as far as man has begun to reflect on himself, he has seen that, in certain circumstances, knowing and approving of the good, he nevertheless did evil. The *video meliora proboqus, deteriora sequor* has had to prove to him that the power of the desires was stronger than that of reason; he enjoyed only in appearance, and not really, his *free will*. It was necessary, by the use of resistance, to compress the spring of his passions before acquiring the effective liberty to choose and to determine in all the actions of life. Since then, the first idea that has given birth to the countenance of a sage, has been that of a *free* man, *master* of himself; and every institution which tended to make sages has become an art of *liberty* and *royalty*.

"The most beautiful of all the victories is that which one obtains over oneself: the one whose heart is a slave would serve even unto the throne; the one whose heart is free remains free even unto the irons." (See *Hermès*, vol 1, page 169.)

117. We read in the Jesuitico-Hermetic grade *Écossais vert* or the *Little Saint Andrew of Scotland*: "If the adept succeeds in his *projection*, in converting a thousand parts of common metals with only one of his powder, he may say, with reason, that he is *a thousand years old*; while waiting, one can only accord him this age ceremonially."

118. It would be necessary then to modify the oath of the *Apprentice*, which agrees with the greater mysteries, in view of what has been done to him.

119. A Masonic society which would establish in its midst a MAGNETIC ACADEMY, would soon find the reward of his labors in the good that it would produce, and the happiness that it would give. It would be advisable to found there a library composed of choice books, among which would figure the works of the various magnetizers that we cite, the majority of which would be flattered to be among the number of associates. As it is ever and before all necessary to have a good dictionary of the language that one speaks, we recommend, with full confidence, as author in philology, the most satisfying work in this genre, colossal work whose bold conception honors its author, M. MAURICE LA CHATRE, and of which the execution is worthy of its numerous and scholarly collaborators, who carry out this gigantic undertaking, the most vast literary repertoire of human knowledge, containing the analysis of 400,000 volumes. We predict that we will want to speak of the DICTIONNAIRE UNIVERSEL, *Panthéon littéraire et encyclopédie illustrée*, two large, magnificent volumes in-4to with three columns, the first of which is on the verge of appearing.

Its title of *universal* is accurate, for it is the most complete dictionary of the French language, and that of the arts, sciences, and industry, embracing in its development all the special dictionaries.

To the support of the definitions, always well done, the illustrations come to give to the text, as often as interest demands, the drawing of objects, machines, instruments, etc.; the figure of plants and animals, the panorama of certain towns, and the portraits of celebrated men. It is thus that 50,000 subjects, engraved on wood and intercalated into the text, are so many ingenious means by which the attractive instruction obtains by the eyes satisfaction, and completes that offered to the spirit, which fixes it more easily in the memory.

Masons, subscribe! Bring your *stone* to this beautiful national monument. It is a great work of philological and scientific architecture most worthy of your cooperation.

The work appears by issues. Each issue costs 25c. and contains the material from one volume in-8vo. There appear at least 6 per month; around 100 form one volume. - One subscribes, *franco*, rue Notre-Dame-des-Victoires, 32, and at booksellers.

120. We read, in speaking, of two persons who are on *bad terms*, and who cannot endure each other: *they are water and fire*. What slander! Does there exist a mixture which agrees better, and which is more capable of serving as model?

Indeed, when the one is absent, the other is entirely *ice*, and does not become *water* again until the return of the fugitive.

121. The numeral 1 has signified the *living man* (body which stands upright); man is the only one of the living beings which enjoys this faculty. By adding there to a head, we have the sign (P) of the *paternity*, of the creative power; the R signifies *man walking*, going, *Iens*, *Iturus*.

122. Or the binary, is sometimes employed in the sense of *dualism*, *duality*. In Valentinian theology, *Bythos* and *Sige* constitute the primitive *binary* of the beings.
The dyad is also the imperfect state into which a being falls, according to the Pythagorians, when it is detached from the *monad* or God. The spiritual beings, emanated from God, are enveloped in the dyad, and no longer receive but illusory impressions.
This word is said for *couple*; two authors who are working together are called a *literary dyad*.
As formerly the number ONE designated harmony, order, or the good principle, (*one and unique God*, expressed in Latin by *solus*, from where we get *sol*, sun, symbol of God), the number TWO offered the contrary idea. Here, began the deadly knowledge of *good* and *evil*. All that is double, false, opposed to the unique reality, was depicted by the *binary* number. It also expressed the state of contrariety in which is found nature, where all is double: night and day, light and darkness, hot and cold, dry and humid, health and the state of illness, error and truth, the one sex and the other, etc.
We know that the Romans dedicated to Pluto the second month of the year, and that their second day was consecrated to *expiations* in honor of the spirits of their dead. The Catholics have the same consecration: Pope John XIX, in 1003, instituted the feast of the *Trépassé* (those passed to the beyond) by ordering that they celebrate it on November *second*, the *second* month of autumn.

123. The ternary was, for the philosophers, the number *par excellence* and of predilection. We have revealed, in the *Cours interprétatif des initiations* (2nd edition, page 137 and foll.), a large part of the numerous combinations to which they applied this mysterious type, revered in antiquity, and consecrated in the mysteries; thus, are there only three essential grades among the Masons, who venerate, in the *triangle*, the most august mystery, that of the *sacred ternary*, object of their homage and their study. Nature is divided into *three kingdoms*; each of them is triple, from where the *novaire* and the all (*trinity*) make but ONE, represented by the *delta*.
Let us say why the *triangle*, purely geometrical figure, represents God, and how French Masonry facilitates that interpretation.
In geometry, a line cannot represent an absolutely perfect body. Two lines do not constitute a demonstrably perfect figure. But three lines form, by their junction, the *triangle* or the first regularly perfect figure, and that is why it has served and serves still to characterize the *Eternal*, which, infinitely *perfect* by its nature, is, as universal creator, the *first being*, consequently, the first *perfection*.
The *quadrangle* or square, however perfect it appears, being only a *second perfection*, can by no means represent God which is the first. Let us note well that the word for God in Latin and in French, has for its initial the Greek delta or the triangle. Such is the motive, among the ancients and the moderns, for

the consecration of the *triangle* whose sides represent the *three kingdoms* or the nature of God. In the middle is the Hebrew *Yod* (initial of *Jehovah*), animating spirit or the fire, generative principle represented by the letter G, initial of the word *God* in the northern languages and whose philosophical signification is *generation*. - Here, in this subject, is one of the advantages of the French Rite over the incoherent Scottish Rite:

The first side of the triangle, offered to the study of the App., is the *mineral kingdom*, symbolized by Tubalc.·.

The second side that the *Comp.* is to meditate upon, is the *vegetable kingdom*, symbolized by *Schibb.·.* (ear of corn). In this kingdom begins the *generation of the bodies*; that is why the letter G is presented radiant to the eyes of the adept.

The third side, whose study concerns the animal kingdom and completes the instruction of the Master, is symbolized by *Macben.·.* (son of putrefaction). From this triple study or triple science, characteristic of each grade, derives the name of *trinosophe* (who studies or understands *three sciences*, which are the *three grade*s or Masonry).

The Trimurti of Indian theology,

BRAHMA	VISHNU	SHIVA
by: *Creation,*	*Preservation,*	*Destruction,*
by: *Earth,*	*Water,*	*Fire,*
the *Earth,*	the *Water,*	and the *Sun.*

Filial trilogy composed of: personified in the world of ideas and in the world of actions, symbolized by the *lotus* which lives by Such is the primitive, rudimentary symbolic trimurti (*trinity*), summarized in the *lotus* which, for this reason, was the attribute of *Isis*, (nature).

One of the doctrines of *Manes* was the Gnostic trinity: *one* God and *two* principles, the good and the evil. The *father* dwelled in an unknown abode, resplendent with a celestial light; the *son* was the *sun*, and the spirit was the *air*. In his lifetime, Manes had twelve apostles.

The Christian unitrinity is a God in *three persons*, that is to say one God which has a *triple representation*; which is symbolized triunely: as *creator*, *animator*, and *preserver*, for *persona*, person, signifies *perfect representation*; this word is the contraction of *perfecte sonans*, representing perfectly.

The numeral 3 symbolizes the earth; it is a figure of the terrestrial bodies. The 2, upper half of the 3, is the symbol of the vegetable; its lower half is removed from view.

The first *four* German numbers take the names of the four elements.

EIN, *one*, designates the *air*, that element which, always on the move, insinuates itself into all parts of matter, and of which the continual flux and reflux is the universal vehicle of life.

ZWEI, *two*, comes from the Teutonic *sweig* and signifies *germ*, *fecundity*; it designates the *earth*, that fertile mother of all production.

DREI - corresponds to the *trienos* of the Greeks and to our *three*; it designates *water*. That is why the divinities of the sea are called *Tritons*; that the *trident* is the emblem of Neptune, and that the sea or the water, in general,
is called *Amphitrite* (water which surrounds).

VIER, fourth number in the Belgian language, signifies *fire*, and designates, in German, only the number *four*. Moreover, the *fire*, according to *Plutarch*, is the last of the four elements which was discovered.

124. The Gnostics claimed that the whole edifice of their knowledge rested upon a square whose angles were *sighe* (silence), *bathos* (depth), *nous* (intelligence),

and *aletheia* (truth).

125. Thus, matter is represented by the number 9 or 3 times 3, and the immortal spirit having for essential hieroglyph the *quaternary* or the number *four*, the sages have said that man having been deceived and thrown into an inextricable labyrinth, in going from *four* to *nine*, the only path that he had to take in order to come out of these ambiguous routes, from these disastrous detours, and from the abyss of evil into which he had been plunged, *is to retrace his steps and go from* NINE to FOUR.
- The ingenious and mystical idea which has made the *triangle* venerated was applied to the numeral 4 : they have said that it expressed a *living being*, 1, bearer of the triangle , *bearer* △*God*, that is to say man bearing within himself a *divine principle*.

126. The ancients represented the world by the number FIVE. *Diodorus* gives as the cause for this, that this number represents the earth, water, fire, and ether or *spiritus*. From here originates pente which, in Greek, means *five* and *pan* which signifies *all*.

127. Pronounced harshly (*aspere*) *with a gap*. It is only in the dictionary of the Academy and others of the same strength that they teach that they *breathe* while speaking.

128. It is in losing sight of the initiatic sense of things that the majority of characters, so expressive then, have become today nearly insignificant.
It is the same with the characters of writing: the letters were not, like today, reduced to giving the image of an insignificant sound. Their role was more noble. Each of them, by its form, offered a complete meaning which, without counting the signification of the word, had a *double interpretation*, which was adapted to the *double doctrine*. It is thus that the philosophers, when they wished to write in a manner to be understood only by the scholars, confabulated a history, a dream, or any other fictive account with proper names of persons and places which concealed, by the characteristic of the *letters*, the secret of the thoughts of the author. Such were all their religious contextures.
Writing will always be behind the word that it expresses without depicting it, as the word remains behind the thought, which it does not always express completely, because there is in the sound something *unwritable*, as in the thought, something inexpressible.
If we could perfect the ancient writing with depicting the ideas instead of the sounds, there would result therefrom a universal language, intelligible to all peoples; such a book would be English in London, German in Berlin, Chinese in Peking, and French in Paris. It would suffice to know how to read in order to understand all the languages in the manner of the arithmetical characters. It is thus that the Japanese and the Chinese, who have the same graphical signs, understand one another, though speaking a different language; like the sign & for the English and the French; they name it et, we call it and, and its signification is the same. *Delgarme*, *Wilkins*, and *Leibnitz* have occupied themselves with this universal language, called *philosophical*; but *Demaimieux*, in his *Pasigraphie*, has alone proven its possibility.
The characters were thus supplementary to the word, each letter being a figure which represented at once a sound to the ear, and an idea to the intelligence, as, for example, we may cite: F; FE is a sharp sound, similar to the noise of the air traversed with quickness: *foudre* [lightning], *fougue* [ardon], *fureur* [fury].

fusée [spindle], *flèche* [arrow], *fendre* [to cleave], *fuir* [to flee], are expressive words which depict what this signifies. This character renders well what passes with rapidity: *Fortune*, *Fumée*, [smoke, fume], *faveurs* [favors], *fleurs* [flowers], *fetes* [feasts], *flots* [waves], *fleuve* [river]. With what energy the sound of this letter expresses the sharp blow and the swiftness of the *faulx* [scythe], of which its shape is the image! Symbol of destruction, it is the initial of the words: *funèbre* [funeral], funerailles [funeral ceremonies], *famine*, *funeste* [fatal, deadly], *fin* [end].

S (*se*), consonant and *vowel* (since by itself it produces a sound), has had to become the initial of *serpent* (serpens) and of *sifflement* [hiss] (sibilus), depicting at once the reptile and its cry.

T, initial and final of the famous *Thot* to whom is attributed the invention of the Egyptian alphabet, concluded the alphabet of the Hebrews and the Samaritans who called it *Tau*, that is to say *end*, *perfection*. From here comes *terminus*, term, and *terminer* [to bound, limit, terminate, conclude]. The sound that it produces is *striking*; thus, we believe that its shape is that of a *marteau* [hammer], word superior to the *matteus* of the Latins, from where arise the imitative verbs: *taper* [to tap, hit, slap], *tonner* [to thunder], *retentir* [to resound, reverberate]. Its shape also expressed *shelter*, *security*, by the words *toit* [roof], *toiture* [roofing] (tectum), of which this letter is the initial.

It is thus that in reading the name of a mineral or a plant, the initiate perceives at once the nature and quality of the mineral, the usage and particular property of the plant. He penetrated easily into the *essence* of each thing, because that essence had been represented by the characters which rendered it sensible to the eyes of the *literate*.

Let us apply this system to the word ŒIL [EYE], by supposing it composed in this view. A literate person, all while being unaware of the idiom to which the word belongs, could have given an account thereof thus: O, *round body*; E, *spirit*, *soul*, which are adherent to it; I, *bolt* that it hurls (*visual ray*); L, *language* which is proper to it; he will conjecture and translate, in his language, the word *œil*.

Thus, the scholar who had the key of the hieroglyphs was therefore called *literate*. This qualification was just and deserved. Today, since this science is lost, the word has been preserved and they apply it, most improperly, to the persons who have only erudition or literature. They call *belle-lettres*: *grammar*, *eloquence*, and *poetry*. We may say that, among the moderns, *Voltaire* was literate; but among the ancients, he would not merit this title, unless he had joined to his vast knowledge the understanding of *letters*. The literate, in China, form a class of real scholars who understand the value of their numerous characters, and the allegory which serves as veil to the religion of the people. They have the key of the truth which is the sole science.

129. The hieroglyphic *senary* (the *double equilateral triangle*) is the symbol of the commixture of the three *fires* and the three philosophical waters, whence results the procreation of the elements of all things. This is why the ancients had consecrated the number 6 to *Venus*, since the union of the two genres or sexes, and the spagirization of matter by *triads*, are necessary in order to develop that generative force, that prolific virtue, that tendency toward reproduction, innate in all the bodies.

The numeral 6 was the symbol of the terrestrial globe, animated by a divine spirit. The numeral 365 was read from right to left and signified:

the spirit of the animated globe of the earth
5 6 3

130. PAN, which at first signified the *great all*, has ended up degenerating into a rural god. Despite the etymology, they would have scarcely discovered its first meaning, if there had not been preserved his *seven-piped flute*, emblem of the seven planets, the seven notes of music, the seven colors, and the whole *septenary* harmony. In Arcadia, they sometimes represented him without flute, but he had seven stars upon his chest. he wore the *beard*, sign of paternity and generative force, and, furthermore, the *horns*, regarded formerly as sign of nobility and strength.
All the divisions by seven mentioned in the *Apocalypse*, as in all the other sacred books, even of the Indians, prove sufficiently that the *septenary* number, which holds to the *néomique* (lunar) cult, played the greatest role in the mysteries and in the religions.

131. The numeral 7, among the Egyptians, symbolized life; it is why the letter Z of the Greeks, which is but a doubling of the 7, is the initial of *Zao*, I see, and of *Zeus* (Jupiter), father of life.
T, conformed from the character 7, symbolizes *life*, and the letter I, symbol of the earth, expresses the terrestrial beings enjoying life, or the mortals.
The letter of the character I signifies *existence*, Ti signifies *existence of the mortals.*

132. The Gnostic ogdoad had eight *stars*, which took the place of the eight *Cabiri* of Samothrace, the eight Egyptian and Phoenecian *principles*, the eight *gods* of Xenocrates, the eight *angles* of the cubic stone.

133. According to the *Scottish Trinitarian*, 81 is the mysterious number adored by the angels.

134. Ennead signifies assemblage of 9 things or 9 persons. They say the *Enneads of Plotinus*, title under which Porphyry has gathered the 54 treatises of this Neoplatonist in six sections of nine chapters each.
Everybody knows this rather singular peculiarity of 9 which, multiplied by itself or by any number whatsoever, gives a result of which the final sum is always 9, or always exactly divisible by 9.
9, multiplied by each of the ordinary numbers, produces an arithmetical progression of which each member, composed of two characters, presents a remarkable fact, example:

1,	2,	3,	4,	5,	6,	7,	8,	9,	10,
9,	18,	27,	36,	45,	54,	63,	72,	81,	90.

The first line of numerals gives the regular series from 1 to 9.
The second line reproduces that series *doubly*, first in an ascending manner, beginning with the numeral 18, and in an opposite manner by starting from the second numeral of 81.
It follows from this curious remark, that half of the numbers which comprise this progression, here 9, 18, 27, 36, 45 = 135 = 9, represents in an inverse order,
the characters of the second half: 90, 81, 72, 63, 54 = 360 = 90 or 9.
Thus, 45 is opposite 54, 36 to 63, 27 to 72, 18 to 81, and each of these numbers, or all united, always present 9: 99, 99, 99, 99, 99 = 495 = 18 = 9.

135. 10 terminates every interval of number; for, whoever wants to count beyond returns to 1, 2, 3, and counts thus the second group of ten up to 20, the third group of ten likewise up to 30, and thus all the groups often up to 100. After

this number, we begin again, and the interval of 10 thus repeated goes unto infinity. But 10, being only 1 followed by zero, would indicate that outside of the *unity* is naught, and that it is by it alone that all things exist.

On the NUMBER 100. The Emperor Julian, sending 100 figs to Serapion, wrote him a jocular letter in which he speaks praise of the *centenary* number, to which the ancients attached a very great importance, because of its arithmetical properties, appropriating to the aegis of Jupiter 100 pieces of fringe; to Briareus, 100 hands; to Typheus, 100 heads; to Argus, 100 eyes; on the isle of Crete, 100 cities, and at Thebes, 100 gates (100 *palaces*).

136. Or the UNITY, that eminent end toward which all philosophy is directed, that imperious need of the human spirit, that pivot to which he is compelled to attach the cluster of his ideas; the unity, that source, that center of all systematic order, that principle of life, that hearth, unknown in its essence, but manifest in its effects; the unity, that sublime node to which are necessarily rallied the chain of causes, was the august notion toward which converge all the ideas of *Pythagoras.* He refused the title of *sage,* which means *the one who knows*; he created and took the title of *philosopher*, signifying *the one who knows* or *who studies the hidden*, *occult things.* The astronomy that he taught mysteriously was *astrology*; his science of the numbers was based on the Qabalistic principles. We have, under his name, sentences, commonly named *Golden Verses.* Fabre d'Olivet has translated them in *blank* verse; but the majority have not become more *clear.*

137. *Henri-Cornelius* AGRIPPA, philosopher, physician, one of the most scholarly men of his century, speaking eight languages. He was born at Nettesheim, near Cologne, on September 14, 1486, and died in 1536. He professed all the conditions. We have from him: *De incertitudine et vanitate scientiarum*; *De occulta philosophia*; *Declamatio de nobilitate et præcellentia feminei sexus.*

Works often translated and reprinted.

138. *Jérome* CARDAN, philosopher, physician, naturalist, astrologer, and mathematician was born at Paris in 1501. With more instruction than *Paracelsus*, he resembled him by the singular turn of his spirit. He died in 1576. He has left: *De vita propria*; opera, 1663, 10 vol. in-folio.

139. *Aureole-Ph.-Theophrastus* BOMBASTUS VON HOHENHEIM, called PARACELSUS, celebrated physician, alchemist, and thaumaturge, was born at Einsudeln, near Zurich, in 1493. He was initiated into the alchemical and magical operations by the abbé *Tritheim* and by several German bishops from whom came, without doubt, his biblical interpretations. He died at Saltzbourg, on September 24, 1641, at the age of only 48. - *His works* (in Latin) form 3 vol. in-folio, Geneva, 1658.

140. "These *six planets* have been known for all antiquity; the seventh, *Uranus*, was discovered only in 1781, by *Herschell*, creator of *stellar* astronomy. But the occult sciences and the calculations having revealed that the planets had to exist in the number of *seven*, the ancients have been led to have the sun enter into the keyboard of celestial harmonies, and to have it occupy the vacant place. Then, every time they observed an influence which did not depend on any of the six known planets, they attributed it to the sun, thus relating to it all the power of *Uranus*, which they did not know.

"This error appears important, yet it is insignificant in the practice of the results, if in the tables of the ancient astrologers they put *Uranus* in place of the *sun* which is not a planet, but rather a central star, pivoting and relatively immobile, which rules time and measure, and which is not to be turned away from its true functions.

"It follows from this that the nomenclature of the days of the week arising from the Indian planetary system, is faulty, and that the day of the sun (*Sunday*) ought to be the day of Uranus (*Urani dies*, *Uranday*), or any other name that this immense planet would have had.

141. Here is the place to indicate, according to an observer, several *modern discoveries* renewed from antiquity.

The human race seems to proceed from discovery to discovery, whereas, most often, it sees only to regain that which it had lost; for, the majority of modern inventions by which the nations glorify themselves are things that they knew 3 to 4,000 years ago, but that devastation, carnage, and fire have seen forgotten or lost, and that the modern thinkers have only rediscovered. It is thus that:

BUFFON is but a reproduction of *Anaxagoras*, *Empedocles*, and others, who taught, 3 to 4,000 years ago, that everything in the universe is composed of eternal molecules which, stirred by a subtle and active fire, are combined in turn, in thousands and thousands of various manners; that there is, consequently, neither life nor death, but only perpetual transformations.

DESCARTES is but a reproduction of *Leucippeus*, *Democritus*, and others, who taught that the celestial bodies have been formed by a multitude of atoms coming together and turning together, the most heavy moving to the center, the lighter at their circumference, and each of these concretions being included in a fluid matter which receives from their rapid rotation an impulse that it communicates to the weaker concretions.

NEWTON is but a reproduction of *Anaxagoras*, *Democritus*, *Chrysippeus*, *Timeus of Locres*, *Pythagoras*, *Aristotle*, *Lucrecius*, *Marcrobius*, *Plutarch*, who:

Have SAID that the smallest molecule of matter given, can suffice, through division, to fill an infinite space;

Have SPOKEN, the ones of the two forces emanating from the soul of the world and combined in the numerical proportions (the *centripetal* and *centrifugal* forces); the others, of the mutual attraction of the bodies, attraction which makes them *gravitate* and holds them in spheres particular to each of them;

Have INDICATED, finally, the relation between the weight of the bodies with their quantity of matter, and how the gravitation of the planets toward the sun is reciprocal proportion to their distance from this star.

LEIBNITZ, MALEBRANCHE, and so many other moderns, with their *innate ideas*, are only reproductions of the *Chaldeans*, the *Celts*, *Pythagoras*, *Heraclitus*, *Plato*, who have all said that the human soul has emanated from the divine essence; that having *sinned*, it is fallen and condemned to dwell in the body as in a prison, and that philosophy sees only to lead back to the knowledge that it has lost.

FRANKLIN and his LIGHTNING-CONDUCTORS are but reproductions of the *priests of Etruria* who knew how to attract electricity from the clouds.

Our INVENTORS OF STEAM MACHINES are but reproductions of the *Egyptian priests* who made the statues of their gods *move by steam*, and the Egyptian engineer *Hero*, who certainly made locomotives travel on rails, for they have found, in Egypt, grooved routes, and fragments of iron in these grooves.

595 years before our era, the prophet *Ezekiel* had a vision that he described in his first chapter. With some attention, we discover here the description of a LOCOMOTIVE conveyed by the impetus of an interior force and progressing it forth without stopping. (See the *Almanach prophetique* of 1851, p. 49.)

Our MAGNETIZERS are but reproductions of the Egyptian magicians (*magists*), of *Moses*, of *Jesus*, who, scholars(*initiates*) in quite another manner than they, performed many other miracles than theirs.

Our SOMNAMBULISTIC CLAIRVOYANTS are also but reproductions of the *prophets* among the Hebrews, the *Pythias* at Delphi, the *Sibyls* at Cumes, the *Druids*, etc.

How did all these inspired priests of times past acquire this more or less great lucidity, which allowed them to see, more or less clearly, into the *occult world*?

It was by a long and severe regimen of abstinence, by frequent fasts, that they subjugated matter to the spirit. It was by annihilating the body that they gave life to the soul, that they arrived at ecstasy:

Moses isolated himself upon Mount Sinai; *Zoroaster*, upon the Bordjah; *Menou*, on the solitary banks of the Ganges; *Orpheus*, on the mountains of Thrace; the *Druids*, in the depths of the *Celtic* forests.

The possible separation of the material life with the moral life has been undertaken since the most remote antiquity.

Pythagoras said: "When your soul, abandoning this body, radiates freely in the ether, it enjoys there the infinite vision resulting from its incorporeality."

Plato said: "Man, in the beginning, was a spiritual being; it is the spirit which has vested him with a mortal body; so that what we *see of man* is not, properly speaking, man."

Hippocrates said that the soul sees very clearly the inner sickness of the body and can follow its course beforehand.

Philo the Jew, Platonic philosopher, born at Alexandria (Egypt), 30 years before Jesus Christ, of whom he was a contemporary, was well versed in the Qabalah (*Kabbalah*) and the interpretation of the *Sacred Scripture*. Author of several mystical works, where the Fathers of the Christian Church have drawn a great number of sublime inspirations, he wrote:

"When we read in the Bible that God spoke to men, it must not be believed that their ears had been stricken with a material voice, but it is the soul which, being enlightened by the purest light, has radiated toward God across space and has conversed with him." - Indeed, his infinite spirituality cannot make him forge an articulating body of sounds, he can only *speak to our eyes* by the spectacle of the universe; then, *God-Word* is the Eternal manifested in the creatures that he animates.

Philo studied deeply the philosophy of the Greeks. He was, in the year 40, sent to Emperor Caligula, by the Jews, in order to obtain citizenship. He turned to his profit the knowledge that he had of all the Greek systems, in order to represent his national religion as a perfect and divine doctrine, thus opening the way to *Flavius Josephus*, Jewish historian and general, born at Jerusalem, in the year 37, author of the *History of the War of the Jews*, and of *Jewish Antiquities*; who imitated his coreligionist Philo some years later. It is regrettable to find in his *History* passages that a pious fraud has interpolated.

All the accounts of Philo are precious, not only for the knowledge of the

Neoplatonic philosophy, but also for the intelligence of the *Septuagint* and the writers of the *New Testament*, his contemporaries.

There remains from him: *De mundi creatione secundum Mosen*; *De vita Mosis*; *De vita contemplativa*; *De mundo*. The best edition of his works is that of Leipzig, 1828, 8 vol. in-8vo. - They ought to bind some fragments discovered in Armenian versions.

M. DUMAS, in his *Leçons de statistique chimique* of organized beings, has, after a multitude of analyses and innumerable experiments, come to say: "The plants and the animals derive from the air, they are but the air condensed; they come from the air and return thereto."

350 years before our era, *Anaximenes* and some philosophers of the Ionian school, had, through various different processes, discovered the same result.

142. From the Greek *exegeomai*, I explain. Deleuze speaks on this (*Hist. Crit.* v. II, page 295).
143. François-Antoine [Franz Anton] MESMER was born at Weil, Grand Duchy of Bade, in 1734. He went from Paris to England and came to die at Mersbourg in 1815. Celebrated at first, then nearly forgotten, his name reappears today more brilliant and with justice. His writings are: *Mémoire sur la découverte du magnétisme animal; Précis historique des faits relatifs au magnétisme.* Mesmerismus, 2 vol. in-8vo.
144. He is the author of: *Magnétisme animal*, 1807, 1809, in-8vo; *Recherches, expériences et observations physiques sur l'homme dans l'etat du somnambulisme provoqué par l'action magnétique*, 1811, in-8vo.
145. Magnetism, despite the evidence, was treated as imposture and trickery by the Faculty. Then occurred the revolution of 1789, which caused everyone to lose sight entirely of magnetism and somnambulism.
146. See the *Tuileur* of this grade where are found the *characters employed in the theory of the world of Mesmer.*
147. In antiquity, the sacred things were revealed only after serious trials and the initiation into the mysteries of the science. It ought to be with magnetism and somnambulism as with medicine: the *knowledge* and the *practice* ought to be confided only to men *initiated* in a special school having for its aim the art of healing.
148. *Criterium*, mark of the truth. - *Absolute*, independent. - The *absolute* is opposed to the *relative*; it is the essence of things considered in itself, independently of every relation. - The ABSOLUTE is GOD.
149. The augurs, the oracles, the prophetic dreams of the temples, the laying on of hands of the priests, were nothing else.
150. The majority of initiates of the great work had more or less accurate notions thereof: CARDAN spoke mysteriously of it in his 8th book *De mirabilibus.* SWEDENBORG has made mention of it.
151. The fluidic and caloric substance, which emanates from the bodies, penetrates the ground and permits the dog to grasp, by his scent, the trace of its master, and track of the game. The plasticity of this substance allows the seers to follow the *typical* line of a fugitive, as long as the elasticity of his fluid will not have, in the long run, been destroyed by the variable action of the air, to be universalized into the *great all.* And since the elasticity, which is so subtle, of the luminous fluid may be seized and fixed by the daguerreotype, with the greatest reason our *fluido-plastic* emanations ought to be grasped and

recognized by the double sense of odor and sight, always so developed among the seers.

152. "The nervous fluid, formed from our blood, is spiritualized by becoming localized in the brain, from where it escapes to the state of ethereal emanation, in order to be mixed anew into the universal substance," (J.-A. GENTIL).

153. *Mesmer* has substituted, with advantage, the *passes* for the laying on of hands.

154. "Nature, containing the germ of all possibilities, would be *all-powerful*, if it were *intelligent motive force* but as it is but a group of beings, a code of law, a library of knowledge, a store-house of means, we may say that omnipotence does not appertain to it, because it can exist only in the number of properties of a spirit. "If one means by *nature* the unique being of which the universe is the body and God is the conducting genius, then, from this point of view, one may assert that it is all-powerful; but it is necessary to adjoin thereto the title or quality of *creator*, indicating the life and the exercise of a force proper to the acting being. Nature, thus presented, ought necessarily appear animated by an intelligence which is intimately united with it. Then, it has omnipotence, that is to say the force by which it may give being to all the things whose existence is not absurd or does not suppose a contradiction."

Materialism is not atheism.

We have spoken of *materialism*; on this subject, let us combat an error spread in bad faith.

Materialism is very improperly called *atheism*. Atheism is not conceivable: to be *atheist* would be to suppose *effects without cause*, since it is the cause of all that exists that one designates by the word *God* (which is the unknown cause of known effects). Now, such a supposition is absurd, and has never been admitted by anyone, except by ignorance or bad faith. An *atheist* cannot exist, despite the dictionary of *Sylvain Maréchal* and the opinion of other authors who make a great effort to deplore these aberrations of the human spirit (a).

The sole division which exists, among men of good faith, is in the question of knowing whether the cause of all existence is *spiritual* or *material*, that is to say isolated, independent of matter, or rather inherent to matter and making an integral part thereof. But a materialist is not an *atheist*.

(a) "The committee of public instruction has heard the report of a petition addressed to the Chamber of deputies by a Mr. Kœnig, requesting that *atheism* be professed in the name of the State and that a chair be created to this effect." - The Chamber passed the order of the day (*Constitutionnel* of August 8, 1848.)

155. Science counts four types of somnambulism: the *natural*, the *symptomatic*, the *magnetic*, and the *ecstatic*.

Natural somnambulism and *symptomatic* somnambulism are two essentially different states, in that the one takes place only at night; the other, in the day as well as the night, and that the actions of the subject are not the same.

Magnetic somnambulism and *ecstatic* somnambulism differ in that the one is commanded and the other is not; the first is *artificial*, and the other *natural*; in the first, the subject is dependent; in the second, it belongs to him; that is why artificial somnambulism heals the natural when it is substituted for it.

We see that magnetism and somnambulism, in the state where they are found, are two very distinct things.

156. We cite this: "An epileptic said one day, in somnambulism, to the doctor

Londe, that in fifteen days *he would have a duel and that he would be wounded.* This latter took out his notebook and wrote this prediction in it. At the end of the fifteen days, he had an altercation with one of his colleagues.
He fought in a duel and received a sword strike; and while they brought them back in the carriage, he took out his notebook and had his successful adversary read the prediction that had been made," (MALLE, *Exposé des cures opérée par le magnétisme*, v. 1, p. 258).

157. Made from the Greek words: *thauma*, marvel, *ergon*, work: *marvelous science.*
158. Formed from *pro*, previously, for, and from *phemi*, to tell: *prediction of future things*, or speaking for... it is in this last sense that the word of each prophet indicates the object that he treats, or explains the title of his work:
Isaiah signifies *medicine of the philosophers.* (It is he who has said, ch. 46: "You command a worker to make gods for you; you purchase them at the price of gold, and you adore them.")
Jeremiah signifies the *marrow of the sacred emission.*
Daniel, fifth son of Jacob, signifies the *spirit of God.*
They have veiled again what was already veiled in the *Pentateuch.*
159. In the temples of Esculapius, under the vestibules, we find the statues of the *Dreams* and *Sleep* (Pausanias, 1, 2, ch. 10).

On Dreams
"Dreams sometimes indicate in advance
the illnesses of the body." (HIPPOCRATES.)

"*Dreams* being the result, a common affection of the soul and of the body, each, generally speaking, could have dreams; but just as the intelligence (a) is the apanage of humanity, and as certain men with little spirit are better endowed on the side of the body, there were also those whose temperament inclined them to often have dreams, and others who did not.

"The action of *dreaming*, ordinarily having for its cause an illness, chagrin, deep disturbance, or a violent blow to the spirit, and many men being at rest in mind and body, it was impossible to count on a personal dream. This necessitated the consultation of those who had the faculty to see, *in dream*, the affections of others.

"Experience having taught that the dream could be solicited, brought, by friction, touches, preparations, etc., the natural dream was no longer the only one, and all the useful dreams were regarded as a present from the divinity. They went into the temples, at the foot of the altars, asking to dream. Then, finally, for those who could achieve this, there were *dreamer* priests (who entered into magnetic rapport with them). From this comes three types of dreams: 1st *natural* dreams; 2nd, dreams *requested and obtained in the temples*; 3rd, *counsels received from dreamer priests*, called, for this reason, *oracles in dream*," (*Hist. du somnamb.*, by Aubin *Gauthier*).

We know that Socrates had a dream in his prison, *three days before his death* that the Arcadian of Megare was lying with one of his friends when he dreamt of his friend *lying* and *assassinated in an inn*; that *Quinius* was with him, in *Asia*, when he saw, while sleeping, *Cicero who fell into a river*, and that *Cicero* himself was at his home at *Atina*, when he was informed through a dream of what had occurred at Rome on this subject. - Let us add that, even recently, the warriors of South America, would not have dared to engage in a decisive battles without having consulted the dreams of authorized men.

It is necessary to distinguish between the dream that is a vision of the soul during the sleep of the body, and the dream, which is ordinarily, in the brain, but an incoherent recollection of a work done in the state of waking. A true dreamer among the ancients was a venerated man, the other kind was not.

(a) Intelligence means *inner reading*; where the intelligence may read, if it is not in the *memory*, a miraculous, *magical book*, which, in a few sheets, contains the impressions of all our sensations and their innumerable relations.

160. On the Oracles

Oracles date back to the remotest antiquity, as it is true that men have, from all time, been tormented by the need to know the future. They commonly had their temples or places of preaching in sites where they had observed (or established) vapors capable of producing ecstasy (*ekstasis*, delirium of the spirit) among the person seated upon the sacred tripod. This was of magnetic magianism.

The oracle of *Jupiter*, *Ammon*, in Libya, and that of *Dodone* which, according to Macrobius, existed 1400 years before our era, pass for the most ancient. But Plutarch, who lived in the 1st century, puts forth that the oracle of Delphi counted more than 3,000 years of existence.

The *Pythoness of Andora* is celebrated among the Hebrews, by the visit that, according to the first book of Kings (ch. 28, v. 8 and foll.), the King Saul made, in the year of the world 2966.

The sibyl of *Cumes* went to Rome, under Tarquinius, 575 years before our era.

In the prose *Dies iræ* that the Christians of the Latin Rite sing at the funerals:

Solcet seculum in favilla
Teste David cum sibylla,

the witness of the *sibyl*, joined to the *predictions* of David, shows how long the opinion has been maintained that the events relative to Christianity had been predicted by the sibyls.

There have been oracles:

Of *Olympian Jupiter*, at Agesipolis,	of *Serapis* and	in Egypt.
Of *Vulcan*, at Heliopolis,	of *Isis*	
Of *Apollo*, at Claros and Delphi,	of *Trophonius* and	in Greece.
Of *Mars*, in Thrace,	of *Amphiaraus*	
Of *Venus*, at Aphaca,	of *Mopsus*, in *Cicily*, etc.	
Of *Esculapius*, at Epidaure, Aegeus, and Rome,	of *Colophone*, who went into a grotto.	

The nymph *Egeria* went to give her oracles in a consecrated woods, near Rome.

On the Augur (auspice)

The *augur* is a presage, a sign on which they found the divination of the future. This name is also that of the priest charged with observing the celestial omens. he even read the future in the flight, song, and appetite of the birds, from where this name formed from *avis*, bird, and *garrire*, to sing. The Orient is the cradle of the augural science. - The word AUSPICE, made from *avis*, bird, and *aspicere*, to look, also signified *augur* by the flight, song, appetite, etc. of the birds.

On the Aruspex

Aruspex was the name of the priest who consulted, *at the altar*, the movements of the victims and their entrails in order to predict the future. This word is composed of *ara*, altar, and *inspicio*, I observe.

The *augurs* and the *aruspices* formed at Rome a sacerdotal body which, at its origin, was only in the number of three. This number, eventually, increases greatly; which discredited it to the point that *Cato* did not understand how two augurs could look at each other without smirking. Nevertheless, on their decisions depended the great political events. History, moreover, is filled with their bizarre decisions and the marvels operated by their science, with which the politics of the heads of State had more concern than the imagination and credulity of the people.

161. This word comes from *psuche*, soul, and *logos*, treatise: *science of the soul.*
162. From *Phusis*, nature, and *logos*, treatise, science of nature.
163. From the Greek *phusis*, nature, and *gnomon*, indication.
164. In a curious work, entitled *Chirognomonie*, an instructed observer, the captain *d'Arpentigny*, has given the means to recognize the tendencies of intelligence, according to the shapes of the hand that he divides into seven categories.
165. There is, they say, at Berlin, a six-fingered family; the persons who comprise it ought, all things being equal, to have greater sensations that the others.
166. Assemblages of interlaced nerves.
167. The ancients pressed the thumb to the index in sign of approbation and opened it to mark the contrary.
168. According to a custom which goes back to the remostest antiquity, and whose reason was drawn from anatomy: the ancients believed, said *Aulu-Gelle*, that this finger was put into direct correspondence with the heart by means of a special nerve, a circumstance which made it regarded not as the most important of the five fingers, but as the most worthy to wear the *rings*, gained by affection or the marks of some dignity.
169. Word formed from *phren*, mind, and *logos*, treatise.
170. Let us say a word on the two great interpreters, first apostles of this important science:

GALL (J.-Jo.), was born at Triebenbrunn (grand-duchy of Bade) in 1758. After having studied at Bade, Bruchsal, and Strasbourg, he was received as a physician at Vienna, where he practiced for some time. It is in this city that he set forth new views on the structure and functions of the brain.

His doctrine appeared dangerous, and the authorities had his courses shut down. he left the capital of Austria, visited the north of Germany, Sweden, Denmark, coming finally to set himself at Paris in 1807, and opened at the Athenaeum public courses which served to popularize his system. Flattered by the reception that he received in France, Gall had himself naturalized as French, in 1809, and continued his discoveries in phrenology. He had at first proved that the brain was not a simple organ. A deeper examination had caused him to recognize up to twenty-seven encephalic *circumlocutions* to which he attached as many *fundamental faculties*. He assigned to the *animal* or *appetitive* faculties the posterior and lateral parts of the head; to the *intellectual* faculties, the anterior part; to the *moral* qualities, the anterior-superior part. The doctrine of Gall, like all new doctrines, encountered ardent contradictors who accused him of leading to *materialism* (a) and *fatalism* (b); but the celebrated anatomist dedicated an entire volume to these accusations, declaring that he had never confused the soul with the material instruments of which it makes use, nor taught the irresistibility of actions. The Gallican prevailed (c).

We have from him: *Anatomie et physiologie du système nerveux en général et de cerveau en particulier*, 1810-1820, 4 vol. in-folio, and 1822-1825, 6 vol. in-8vo, with a volume of 100 plates in-folio.

Gall died at Montronge, near Paris, at the age of 75, in 1833.

SPURZHEIM (*Gasp.*), celebrated physician, disciple of Gall, born near Trèves (Prussia) in 1766, attached himself to the doctrine of Gall, which he modified slightly. He cooperated in the *anatomie du cerveau*, of Gall. He traveled through France, Germany, England, and the United States, in the aim of popularizing phrenology there.

This doctor died of typhus at Boston in 1833, leaving two works having as titles: *Sur la folie*; *Sur les principes de l'education.*

- A new emulator of Gall, the doctor DEHOULE, already known in the scientific world, saw to make some certain progress in phrenology, of which system he justifies and perfects, that he presents under a new philosophical point of view. He divides the skull into sections and not into *protuberances*, because, according to him, the projections may not exist, whereas the passions and the sentiments always dominate. He draws from his method clear, rational, and positive arguments, which form happy complements to so curious and so useful a science as phrenology.

(a) See note 154 on *materialism.*

(b) Fatalism is, in reality, but a translation of the word *providence.*

(c) *Balzac* has traced well the action of the magnetic fluid in physiognomy and phrenology. (See the *Comédie humaine.*)

171. The old manuscripts present this question: *What do you mean by Masonry*?
Ans. - *I mean the study of the sciences and the practice of virtues.*

172. We cite Nicolas FLAMEL, who labored twenty-five years, from 1357 to 1382, in order to find, on January 17th, the projection in silver, and, on the following April 25th, the transmutation into gold.

173. ORDER OF THE MAGICIANS. This order was instituted at Florence in the 17th century. It was a scission from the BRETHREN OF THE ROSE-CROSS. The initiates wore the costume of the inquisitors.

The magician of François I was named *Gonin*; this fact proves that the King of France believed in magic. The Church of Rome believed in it likewise: we have the evident proof thereof in the *Constitution* of the Pope *Honorius the Great*, where are found the *secret conjurations* that it was necessary to make against the *spirits of darkness*. We give the translation thereof in the *Fastes initiatiques*, with the magical signs.

It even appears, according to the following fact, which is extracted from a manuscript *account of the events of July 1830*, by M.A. Bl..., officer of the State, major of the general Lafayette, that this belief in magic still existed in certain heads at this period. It is the author who speaks:

"The day after the revolution, at the break of day, the general Lafayette ordered me to go identify the position and the forces of the troops which surrounded *Charles X*. They gave me one of the horses that gendarmes of the prefect Mangin had abandoned at the Hotel-de-Ville.

"Near Saint-Cyr, I was accosted by a young seminarian, covered with sweat, who ran on foot towards Rambouillet. This abbé took me, no doubt, for a person attached to the house of the King: he prayed me *gallop off at full speed*, in order to carry as soon as possible to His majesty, the writing hereafter, of which he had several copies:

'To the elder son of the Church, to the King Charles X, King of France and Navarre, by the grace of God, *salutations*!

'SIRE, my good angel has appeared to me, as to *Jeanne* de Vaucouleurs, and has told me: Run to Rambouillet; inform His Majesty that the Duc d'Orleans, his cousin, has renewed the sorcery of his ancestors, that the reverend Martin Delrio (a), priest-doctor of the Company of Jesus, has verified in his *magical controversies*. Tell this good monarch that the Duc d'Orleans, by sacrilege, seeks to replace him on the throne, by the power of the devil, at the example of the old Duc d'Orleans, who gave his sword, his dagger, and his ring to a disavowed monk and to his companions, in order to have them consecrated by fantastic spells, so that he could exercise the sorcery that they foresaw in his spirit, being at the tower of Montigny, near Lagny. He returned them to the Duc d'Orleans; which charm was made so subtlety under the King Charles, his cousin, who scarcely may have perceived it.

'The first charm, made at Beauvais, was so violent, that the King's fingernails fell off; the second, in the city of Mans, had so great a force, that they could not judge whether the King was alive or not: he was spread out lengthwise, without showing any consciousness. But, after he had recovered his spirits and returned to himself, he said: I pray you, remove from me this sword which pierces my body: it is the Duc d'Orleans, my cousin, who procures this evil for me; *evil* that Your Majesty must feel. There is only one remedy: it is to have the Duc d'Orleans and his companions arrested, who are at rue d'Artois.'"

(a)Delrio (Martin-Antoine), Jesuit, erudite commentator, magist author, born at Ancvers in 1551, died in 1608.

174. One understands why we only give the names in Latin and abbreviated; they will be in their entirety in the *Fastes initiatiques*, where will be found the figures of the seven disks and the whole system of magic.

Magianism is a renewed science which has not yet given all its marvels.

In a profound work requiring time and labor that an instructed magist elaborates at this moment, are enumerated and treated the various sciences that comprise magism, according to the seven primitive colors, plus the two outside the line (*black* and *white*) which present the results obtained by the assemblage of the others. This high doctrine will be developed in *Fastes*, with the interpretation of the plates, symbols, hieroglyphs, etc.

175. *Feeling* gives the soul the consciousness of itself through pleasure and pain. They have said of it: Intelligence is its sight, memory its vocabulary, imagination its palette; judgment, reflection, and meditation, are its ministers and its counselors.

176. It is the atmosphereic electricity which, through the intermediary of the lungs, performing the functions of an electric plate, causes the phenomenon of life, because nitrogen, which dominates in the electrical fluids of the atmosphere, and which, with man, is the principal nourishment of his organization, operates the reaction, the transformation of the veinous (*blue*) blood into arterial (*red*) blood.

We know that the lungs always function, and in the same manner in waking as in sleep. The functions of the heart derive from those of the lungs, and these latter are put into play by the atmospheric pressure, whence arises the circulation of the blood.

177. The somnambulists are all the more *lucid* that they are suffering from the organic illness to which is due their lucidity. If this latter is diminished, *have them fast.*

178. We have seen a somnambulist who claimed to be able to recover the remembrance after his awakening. Here is the means that he employed: the magnetizer applied a finger to his forehead and a finger on the solar plexus, *while ordering him to remember.* Was the sleep true (a), or did the will of the magnetizer suffice?

    (a) If the eye convulses, there is sleep; if it is moving, the subject is not asleep.

179. Or rather *Jevo*, of which the Latins made: *Jov*, *Jovis*, *Jovispiter*, whence *Jupiter*, signifying: *I am all that is. Clement* of Alexandria said that in grasping well the pronunciation of this word *Jevo*, one may strike a man dead.

180. The *Schem hamphorasch* were the 72 names of God, drawn Qabalistically from *Exodus*, and corresponding, 8 by 8, to the nine celestial hierarchies. At the same time, the similar 72 attributes of God are drawn from the book of *Psalms* by the same process; from which attributes are composed by the addition of the endings יה or אל (other names of God), the names of the 72 angels which occupy the 72 degrees of Jacob's ladder.
Schem hamphorasch was, among the ancients, the emblem of the plenitude, the omnipotence, the universality of the celestial fire or the uncreated light, which fills, aminates, and fecundates all space.
It is called in Greek: *Ebdomekontadyogrammaton.*

181. *Origin of this name*: the same instruction ends thus:
Q. - *Why are the Knights of the Black Eagle called Rose-Croix?*
A. - A great Hermetic philosopher, celebrated Mason (*Masonry did not exist in the 13th century*), named *Raimond Lulle*, achieved the *celestial marriage of the bridegroom with the six virgins*; there was born therefrom the *messiah* that he awaited. He presented it to a King of England, who had coins manufactured therefrom, where was represented, on one side, a *cross*, and, on the other, a *rose*, and the name of its author abbreviated therefrom. He was created a *Knight*; from here, all the knights of this order, who are few in number, are called *Rose-Croix.*

182. Qabalistic balance of Solomon, commonly called *Qabalistic seal of the philosophers.*

183. A woman of color, a somnambulist, age 48, received one day, for nourishment, during magnetic sleep, a piece of *clay*, that she ate as *cake*, and that she found good. Being awakened, she said that they had made her eat too much, but that she had not experienced any ill effect therefrom.

184. He divined a source, struck at the foot, and water gushed forth.

185. The latest work of this apostle of the science, the *Manuel élémentaire de l'aspirant magnétiseur*, ought to find sympathy among the instructed reader of good faith.

186. Following a very successful effect of table turning, a magnetist conceived the idea to establish dry voltaic batteries, that is to say without acid or material, and which operate perfectly.

187. From the Latin *cardinalis*, formed from *cardo*, hinge, that upon which a thing rolls or turns. These four virtues are: *Fortitude*, *Prudence*, *Temperance*, *and Justice.* The first three are only useful qualities to the one who possesses them, and

not virtues in relation to one's neighbor. Justice alone is a virtue useful to others; but it does not suffice to be just, it is also necessary to be beneficent.

188. From the Greek *sun*, together, and hedra, seat (1st Jewish tribunal).

189. Egypt, 1500 years before Moses, revered, in the mysteries, ONE SUPREME GOD, called the *sole uncreated*. It honored, as subordinates, seven principal gods (from where comes the *semaine* [week], which signifies *sept matins* [seven mornings]).
It is therefore to Hermes, existing 1500 years before Moses, that we attribute the *account* or the *veiling* of the (*Indian*) cult, that Moses *revealed* or *re-veiled*. Moses, according to some authors, would not be the first sacred writer; before being a *revealer*, there was, therefore, a *relater* thereof.
Moses has wished to change in the law of Hermes only the plurality of his *mystical* gods.

190. We give, in the *Fastes initiatiques*, the *seal of Hermes* (universal hieroglyph).

191. After the divinized man (*Hermes*) came the priest-king: Menes was the first legislator and founder of Thebes with one hundred *palaces*. He filled this city with magnificence. From him dates the sacerdotal period of Egypt. The priests ruled, for they made the laws. They say that there were, after him, three hundred twenty-nine who have remained unknown. They chose them from among themselves or among the warriors; but the chosen warrior became a priest on the spot. This crowned priest was only a deified slave that they presented to the administration of the people.
Tired of reigning so servilely, the Kings emancipated themselves. Then appeared Sesostris, founder of Memphis (1643 years, they say, before our era). The sacerdotal election was replaced by the hereditary succession of the warriors upon the throne. From this hero, who carried the name of Egypt everywhere, dates the political epoch of this kingdom. There were several called Sesostris. Cheops, who reigned from 1178 to 1122, had the great pyramid raised which bears his name. He is considered to have persecuted the theocracy and had the temples closed.
Finally, following an Ethiopian invasion and federate government of twelve chiefs, the kingdom fell into the hands of Amasis, man of the people, adventurous and capable soldier, minister of Apries, whom he dethroned and had killed in 570 BC. More thoughtful of the table than of the sacerdotal traditions, he annihilated the power of the priests. he submitted to Cyrus, but he revolted against his successor Cambryse II, who invaded Egypt, Amasis died before the conquest of his kingdom, around 525, three years before his vanquisher. Thus perished this ancient theocracy which, for so many centuries, showed with pride its priests crowned in Egypt to the world.

192. What often renders troublesome the interpretation of the old fables, and what causes the variety of the genealogies among the various mythographers, is this multiplicity of manners to consider the same object. Everything, in nature, is reduced to one sole cause, to one sole principle; but this principle is susceptible to so many forms, so many modifications, and so many diverse and successive states, that, if one does not apply oneself to grasping them by means of the magnetic art or of astronomy, one may never unravel the chaos of the ancient mythologies.

193. *Isis* was sometimes represented under the form of a *ship* with seven pilots, emblem of the seven days of the week. It is under this form that the *Swedes*, a

northern nation, worshipped her. The Manichaeans honored *Osiris* and *Isis* under the form of two *ships*. - Paris was called *Lucototia* or *Lutetia*; in Hebrew, *lukotaim* means *boats*. *Leukothoe* was a goddess of the sea. Isis was the goddess of the *Parisii* (Parisians), and the arms of the capital are still an *ancient ship* (a). Clovis, founder of the ancient church *Sainte-Geneviève* (who engendered life), gave it the property of the priests of Isis, that is to say the territory situated between Paris and the village of Isis, presently *Issy*. We see again, in 1514, the figure of the universal Isis in the abbey of Saint-Germain-des-Prés. The cardinal *Briconnet* had this figure broken, which was venerated by the people.

(a) L, sacred letter, has been the initial given to the great centers of initiation, because of *Larissa* (in Turkish *Jeni-Sher*), ancient, rich, and celebrated city of Greece, containing a *great Pythagorean philosophical school*, from which was *Anaxillas*, a Pythagorean who was accused of magic and exiled from Rome under Augustus. From here, according to the initiates, comes *Latuim*, *Lutetia*, *London*.

194. *Typhon* signifies, like *Eve*, serpent and life: by its form, the serpent symbolizes the life which circulates throughout all nature. When, at the end of autumn, the woman of the constellations seems (on the Chaldean sphere) to crush with her heel the head of the serpent, this figure prognosticates the season of winter, during which life appears to be withdrawn from all beings and to no longer *circulate* in nature. That is why *Typhon*, (anagram of *Python*) also signifies *serpent*, hibernal symbol which, in the Catholic temples, is represented surrounding the terrestrial globe, that the celestial cross surmounts, emblem of redemption. - If the word *Typhon* derives from *Tupoul*, it signifies a *tree which produces apples* (*mala*, the *evils*), Judaic origin of the fall of man.
Typhon also means *who supplants* and signifies the human passions which drive out from our heart the lessons of wisdom. In the Egyptian fable *Isis* writes the sacred word for the instruction of men, and *Typhon* erases it in proportion.
In morals, he signifies *pride*, *ignorance*, *falsehood*.

195. From the Greek *tris*, thrice, and *megas*, great.

196. Democritus has found at Memphis a curious Jewess called *Mary* (Mary the Egyptian): she had been instructed by the Egyptians, 470 BC. His treatise on the *Hermetic Philosophy* is printed in the collections. Thus, *Mary*, who, according to some authors, told the Hebrew people that *she spoke to the Eternal like Moses*, was not the sister of this legislator, as some editions have it (see the *Red Book*, p. 58), and the Hebrew calendars, the 10th of the month of *Nisan*.

197. This celebrated English monk, born at Ilchester in 1214, studied at Oxford and Paris where he acquired an instruction superior to his era, especially in the occult sciences and in the study of magianism, which earned him the nickname of *admirable doctor*. Accused of sorcery, he was put in prison and remained there until the advent of Clement IV. Persecuted anew to the death by this pope, he was confined for ten years in the convent of the Franciscans of Paris. Set free, he died a short time later in 1294. They attribute to him the invention of the *magnifying glass*, the *air pump*, a *combustible* substance analogous to phosphorus, and above all the *experimental method* that he practiced, etc. He has left, which concerns us, *Epistola de secretis operibus naturæ et artis*, and DE NULLITATE MAGIÆ, Paris, 1542; this latter apostatic title did not preserve him from a second imprisonment.

198. We see that, in order to achieve the execution of the work, it is necessary to understand well what the hermetic philosophers meant by this philosophical or Hermetic fire.

The scholar *Pernety* expresses himself thus: "Our philosophical fire is a labyrinth, in the detours of which the msot capable can lose himself; for it is occult and secret. The fire of the sun cannot be this secret fire; it is interrupted and unequal. It cannot provide a heat ever the same in intensity and duration. Its heat cannot penetrate the depths of the mountains, nor animate the coldness of the rocks and the marble which receive the mineral vapors by which are formed the gold and silver.

"The vulgar fire of our cooking prevents the amalgam of substances susceptible to being mixed. It consumes or makes evaporate the delicate bonds of the constituent molecules: it is in fact a *tyrant.*

"The central and innate fire of matter has the property of mixing the substances and giving them new forms. But this fire, so renowned, cannot be the ordinary fire, which produces the decomposition of the metallic seeds; for *what is of itself a principle of corruption cannot be a principle of regeneration*, unless it is accidentally."

Pontanus, propagator of the doctrines of *Artephius* (a), says on this subject: "Our fire is mineral and perpetual, it does not evaporate unless it is excited beyond measure. It partakes of the sulphur; it does not proceed from matter.

It destroys, dissolves, congeals, and calcinates all things. A great ability is necessary to discover it and prepare it. It costs nothing, or almost nothing. Moreover, it is humid, charged with vapors, penetrating, subtle, gentle, ethereal. It analyzes, transforms, does not enflame, does not consume, surrounds all, contains all. Finally, it is alone of its kind. It is also the fountain of vital water in which the king and queen of nature bathe continually. This humid fire is necessary in all the operations of alchemy at the beginning, in the middle, and at the end, for the *whole science is in* this fire. It is at once a natural, supernatural, and anti-natural fire; a fire at once warm, dry, humid, and cold, which neither burns nor destroys."

The *sages* of antiquity and the philosophers of the Middle Ages have expressed themselves with the same reserve and the same mystery on the nature and properties of this magnetic, that is to say *electric*, fire.

(a) Celebrated Hermetic philosopher who lived in 1130. He left several works on alchemy, and a treatise *De Vita propaganda*, where he claims to be 1025 years old.

199. *Jean d'Espagnet*, president at Bordeaux, in 1620, is considered to be the author of the Arcanum hermeticæ philosophiæ; others attribute this treatise to the *imperial knight*, that they believe to be a foreigner.

200. *Lux* comes from *luke*, light, whence comes *lukos*, wolf, jackal, which was the emblem of the sun, the rising of which it announces, ·like the cock, by its cries. "At Thebes," says Macrobius, "the sun was depicted under the form of a wolf or jackal." There is no depiction of the wolf in Egypt.

201. The sacred letters used by the priests were named after Ammon.

202. In Egypt they could not kill an ibis or a sparrow-hawk, even involuntarily, without losing their life. In antiquity, the veneration of some peoples for the birds was such that *Zoroaster*, in his precepts, forbade their murder as a crime.

203. The *evangelical* animals are one of the thousand emblems imagined to express

the four elements or the four principles of the bodies, and yet they correspond materially to four constellations, which form the retinue of the sun-god, and occupy, at the winter solstice, the four cardinal points of the sphere.

The hierophants so combined the dogmas and symbols of their religion, that these symbols may be explained accurately enough by three different systems (*allegorical*, *historical*, and *astronomical*), without understanding the only true interpretation, the only one that they had in sight in the formation of their theogony, that is to say the *physical interpretation* that they veiled with an extreme care, in order to ever preserve the exclusive knowledge thereof. Their aim was that, if some perspicacious spirit came to suspect that the Egyptian religion was emblematic, and that it made, in order to grasp the meaning thereof, efforts all the more difficult as the sacred writing was known only by the priests, he could be easily deviated from his research by one of the three routes which were offered to him from the very first, and that they seem to have traced under his steps in order to better mislead him. The fourth strewn with thorny brambles, forming at each step inextricable detours, was nearly impossible to discover. If, however, despite all the precautions of the hierophants, some indiscreet initiate, or some profane endowed with a penetrating sense, had attempted to lift the veil, initiation or death had them promptly delivered from a dangerous enemy. Such, finally, was the vigilant care of the *priests*, that a long series of centuries did not see their secret betrayed.

204. This is also a natural alkali salt that is found dissolved in the waters of several lakes in Egypt and Africa and crystalized on the shores.

205. This is why Jeremiah said: "When you wash yourselves with *nitre* and you (*Jerusalem*) purify yourselves with much borith herb, you remain soiled before me in your iniquity, says the Lord," (chap. 2, vers. 22).

206. *Nitrous acid*, which eats away and dissolves metals, except gold.

207. *Nitro-muriatic acid*, which is the solvent of gold.

208. We read in the feuilleton from the *Presse* of 4 October 1851: "A specimen of a new metal, *donarium*, having been sent to the *Brittanie Association for the Advancement of the Sciences*, M. Faraday has taken this occasion to note that the chemists have seen with regret the rapid increase of the number of metallic bodies. But he has added, it is probable that we will soon owe to some of these supposed elements the honor of arriving, by new modes of research, at the COMPLETE DECOMPOSITION OF THE METALS.

"In the same session, M. Duman, *presenting considerations on the probability that certain bodies considered as elementary may be decomposed*, confirmed and completed the foresights of the English physicist.

"Applying this ideal to the metals, he shows indeed that those which are substituted for one another, in certain compounds, may be *transmuted* into one another; and this consequence led him to recall the opinion of the *alchemists* on the TRANSMUTATION OF METALS."

209. The director of the Sèvres porcelain factory makes, as we know, rare and precious stones, and particularly rubies, that the most capable jeweler could not distinguish from those that nature has furnished.

210. A physicist, under the name of *Eteilla*, established at Paris, on July 1st, 1795 (year II), a school of *magic*, where he lectured publicly, and whose courses were posted on the walls of the capital.

Already *Schroeder*, called the *Cagliostro of Germany*, had, in 1779, opened in a lodge of Saarburg his school of *magic*, *theosophy*, and *alchemy*, in four grades, to which he gave the name of *Rectified Rose-Croix*. (See page 115.)

211. In 1243, the Pope Gregory IX pronounced anathema against the Emperor Fredrick II, saying that he drew against him the *medicinal sword* of Saint Peter, and published, *in the spirit of gentleness*, the sentence of excommunication. This spirit of gentleness unbound the subjects of the emperor from their oath of fidelity, deposed him, and gave his crown to another prince.

    A good curé of Paris having received the order to publish this excommunication, said before the congregation: "I have order to denounce the emperor as excommunicated. I am unaware why; I have only learned that there is a great difference between him and the pope. I cannot say which side is right; consequently, as far as I am able, I excommunicate the one of the two who is wrong."

212. While awaiting a monument worthy of him and his admirers, his ashes rest modestly in the Montmartre cemetery, at Paris.

213. M. Toussenel, inspired by Fourier, has, in his *Zoologie passionnelle* (the spirit of the beasts), and with the picturesque style which distinguishes the keen and scholarly writer, writes some curious things on the sidereal origin of many plants, fruits, animals, and metals.

www.ingramcontent.com/pod-product-compliance
Lightning Source LLC
Chambersburg PA
CBHW051727260326
41914CB00031B/1775/J
* 9 7 8 1 9 4 6 8 1 4 0 5 0 *